T0305573

Marx's *Capital*, Capitalism and Limits to the State

Marx's Capital, *Capitalism and Limits to the State* examines the capitalist state in the abstract, and as it exists in advanced capitalism and peripheral capitalism, illustrating the ideas with evidence from the North and the South.

The volume unpacks the capitalist state's functions in relation to commodity relations, private property, and the crisis-ridden production of (surplus) value as a part of the capital circuit (M-C-M'). It also examines state's political and geographical forms. It argues that no matter how autonomous it is, the state cannot meet the pressing needs of the masses significantly and sustainably. This is not because of so-called capitalist constraints but because the state is inherently capitalist. Each chapter begins with *Capital volume 1*. And each chapter ends with theoretical/practical implications of the ideas which taken together counter existing state theory's focus on state autonomy and reforms and point to the necessity for the masses to establish a new transitional democratic state. But the book goes 'beyond' Marx too, as it deploys the combined Marxism of 19th and 20th centuries.

Marx's Capital, *Capitalism and Limits* will interest scholars researching state-society/economy relations. It is suitable for university students as well as established scholars in sociology, political science, heterodox economics, human geography, and international development.

Raju J Das is Professor at York University, Toronto. His teaching and research interests are in political economy, class theory, the capitalist state, and international development. His recent books include *Marxist Class Theory for a Skeptical World*. He is associated with a number of scholarly journals: *Dialectical Anthropology*; *Race, Class and Corporate Power*; *Critical Sociology*; *Human Geography*; and *Science and Society: A Journal of Marxist Thought and Analysis*.

Routledge Frontiers of Political Economy

Economic Ideas, Policy and National Culture
A Comparison of Three Market Economies
Edited by Eelke de Jong

Political Economy of Contemporary Italy
The Economic Crisis and State Intervention
Nicolò Giangrande

Reconfiguring the China–Pakistan Economic Corridor
Geo-Economic Pipe Dreams Versus Geopolitical Realities
Jeremy Garlick

The Political Economy of Transnational Governance
China and Southeast Asia in the 21st Century
Hong Liu

Economics, Science and Capitalism
Richard Westra

Production, Value and Income Distribution
A Classical-Keynesian Approach
Enrico Bellino

The Failure of Markets
Energy, Housing and Health
Craig Allan Medlen

Marx's *Capital*, Capitalism and Limits to the State
Theoretical Considerations
Raju J Das

For more information about this series, please visit: www.routledge.com/Routledge-Frontiers-of-Political-Economy/book-series/SE0345

Marx's *Capital*, Capitalism and Limits to the State

Theoretical Considerations

Raju J Das

Routledge
Taylor & Francis Group

LONDON AND NEW YORK

First published 2022
by Routledge
4 Park Square, Milton Park, Abingdon, Oxon OX14 4RN

and by Routledge
605 Third Avenue, New York, NY 10158

Routledge is an imprint of the Taylor & Francis Group, an informa business

© 2022 Raju J Das

British Library Cataloguing-in-Publication Data
A catalogue record for this book is available from the British Library

Library of Congress Cataloging-in-Publication Data
A catalog record for this book has been requested

ISBN: 978-0-815-34795-8 (hbk)
ISBN: 978-1-032-24881-3 (pbk)
ISBN: 978-1-351-16800-7 (ebk)

DOI: 10.4324/9781351168007

Typeset in Bembo
by Apex CoVantage, LLC

This book is dedicated to all those workers and small-scale producers of the world and their organic intellectuals and political organizers, who fight against the state's defence of capitalism and who are passionate to establish a transitional socialist state, a state that will ensure that the majority – that is, the poor, the common men and women, and children – meet their economic needs in an ecological sustainable and equitable manner and that they enjoy genuine democratic rights.

Contents

List of figures   x
Acknowledgements   xi

1   Introduction   1

   1   Waning and waxing of intellectual interest in the state 1
   2   Existing state theorizing 3
   3   The state, Capital volume 1, *and the Lenin legacy 6*
   4   What is to be done theoretically? A need for
   a dialectical approach 8
   5   An overview of the argument 14

2   A critical review of Marxist state theory *post* **Marx**   22

   1   The capitalist class agency perspective 22
   2   The capitalist class structure perspective – the political moment   23
   3   The capitalist class structure perspective – the economic
   moment 24
   4   The state actors agency perspective 28
   5   The working-class agency perspective 34
   6   Structural-strategic approach 36
   7   Existing state theory: a critique of its intellectual context and
   political implications 38
   8   Conclusion 50

3   The state and class relations   57

   1   The state and economic relations 58
   2   From economic relations to class relations (and their gender and
   spatial nature) 61
   3   The state and class struggle 65
   4   The state and the dominant class as two arms of the class
   structure 69
   5   Class society and state functions 71

6 *Forms of class relation and forms of class-state: some historical examples 73*

7 *Multiple state forms* within *given class forms 78*

8 *Summary, and theoretical and political implications 80*

**4 The state's internal relation with capitalism
   and capitalists**   88

1 *An internal relation between the state and the capitalist class 91*

2 *Limits on the state's functioning 94*

3 *Summary, and theoretical and political implications 96*

**5 The state, capitalist commodity relations, and
   labour power**   99

1 *Use-value, exchange value, and the state 99*

2 *Value relations and the state 105*

3 *The state, the 'peculiar commodity', and the labour circuit 107*

4 *The state and commodity fetishism 110*

5 *The state and counter-tendencies to equality and freedom
   in commodity relations 111*

6 *Summary, and theoretical and political implications 116*

6 The state and capitalist property relations   125

1 *Forms of private property 125*

2 *State-mediated class differentiation as a basis for capitalist private
   property 126*

3 *State-assisted extra-economic 'production' of capitalist private
   property 128*

4 *Capitalism, theft, and anti-theft laws 132*

5 *Summary, and theoretical and political implications 133*

**7 The state, and capitalist production, exploitation,
   accumulation, and crisis**   139

1 *The state and the 'M-C(MP+. . .' phase of the capital circuit (the
   sphere of money and means of production) 141*

2 *The state and the 'C (. . . + LP)' phase of capital circuit (the
   sphere of labour power) 144*

3 *The state and the 'P' phase of capital circuit (the sphere of
   commodity production) 145*

4 *The state and the 'C'-M' phase of capital circuit (the sphere of
   realization) 151*

5 *The state and capitalist accumulation 153*

6 *The state and tendencies/counter-tendencies towards the crisis of
   accumulation 156*

7 *Summary, and theoretical and political implications 160*

Appendix: Studying the state-crisis relation 167

8 The state and the agency of capitalists and state actors 173

1 Structure and agency 174

2 Capitalists' agency 175

3 State actors' agency 181

4 Limits to state function in support of capitalist interests 185

5 Summary, and theoretical and political implications 188

9 The state and the agency of the working class 195

*1 State's pro-worker interventions and the labour
circuit (C-M-C'-R-C) 195*

*2 Driving forces behind state action in favour of workers
(and small-scale producers) 198*

3 Limits to state's pro-worker interventions, and why? 203

*4 Bringing it all together: broader theoretical reflections on the state
and forms of working-class struggle 215*

5 Summary, and theoretical and political implications 225

10 State forms: Geographic and bureaucratic 239

1 Geographical forms of the state and capitalist accumulation 240

2 Bureaucratic state form and political domination by the state 247

3 Summary, and theoretical and political implications 251

**11 Capitalism, imperialism, and the state in the global
periphery** 256

*1 Disarticulated development of productive forces in the
periphery 257*

*2 Peripheral social formation dominated by 'backward'
capitalism 259*

*3 Imperialism retarding development of productive forces in the
periphery 263*

*4 Class basis of the peripheral state, and peripheral state functions
and form 267*

*5 The state, exploited classes, and class struggle from below in the
periphery 276*

6 Coercive nature of the peripheral state's democratic form 281

*7 Class contradictions of development and threat to peripheral state's
legitimacy 286*

8 Summary, and theoretical and political implications 290

Bibliography 300

Index 317

Figures

6.1   Forms of private property   126
7.1   The capital circuit and the state   141
7.2   How does the state make available means of production
      to capital?   144
7.3   Marxist crisis theory   157
8.1   Capitalists and state employees   175
9.1   The Hartley Act, and class struggle from above   209
9.2   Marx's general theory of accumulation, class struggle,
      and the state   212
9.3   The state and value   223
11.1 Theorizing peripheral capitalism   268
11.2 State elites and the peripheral state   285

Acknowledgements

I began my intellectual career with state theory and with a publication on the topic in *Science and Society* (in 1996) when I was still a doctoral student at the Ohio State University. In response to the publication of the article, Professor Bertell Ollman of New York University wrote a nice letter to me. He also made a criticism: that it is not enough to see state action as a response to class struggle. He said that it was necessary to see the state action *itself* as a form of class struggle from above. I have taken this point to heart. I owe much to him over the years, whether it comes to class or the state or indeed the dialectical method itself.

I have also benefitted from my interaction with various other scholars, including Sabah Alnasseri, Greg Albo, Tom Brass, Joseph Choonara, Kevin Cox, Sheila Delany, David Fasenfest, Barbara Foley, Jamie Gough, Robert Latham, David Laibman, Stavros Mavreadeus, David McNally, the late Leo Panitch, Dick Peet, Murray Smith, Tarique Niazi, and Michael Roberts. I am grateful to them all.

I made rough drafts of the diagrams used in the book. Ashley Chen, a former graduate student of mine and now a school teacher, kindly converted these into their publishable form. She has also saved me from many typographical and bibliographical errors. I am ever grateful to her.

This book has its origin in an invitation, in 2015, to me from Andy Humphries, the senior Economics Editor at Routledge, London, to write a book on political economy. I offered to write a book that updates Marx's *Capital volume 1*, from specific vantage points that have been neglected. There was supposed to be one chapter on the state, which, over time, became this book on state theory. Andy ensured that I had the freedom to imagine and re-imagine the original book on *Capital 1*. I have unfortunately missed many deadlines, but he has been extremely patient with me. I am grateful for his useful editorial comments and constant encouragement.

1 Introduction

This is a book on state theory. It builds on Marx's (1887) *Capital volume 1.*[1] It is partly a response to the fact that the full potential of that foundational text of Marx and of Marxism for the development of state theory has not been fully realized. But this book on the state goes 'beyond' the Marx of *Capital* and indeed Marx as such. The vantage point of the book, unlike that of much of the existing discussion on the state, is the entire classical Marxism that Marx (with Engels) initiated and that was developed by the revolutionary Marxists of the 20th century.

Much state theorizing has been excessively concerned with the so-called autonomy of the state. It also under-emphasizes the common attributes of the capitalist and pre-capitalist forms of the state, so it *under*-conceptualizes the *class* content of the (capitalist) state itself. It lacks an international orientation too: it is, more or less, focused on the state in (Western) advanced capitalist countries, thus ignoring the similarities and differences between the state in advanced capitalism and the state in the periphery (i.e. the less developed world). Besides, state theory has tended to have reformist implications. For all these reasons, and given the recent intellectual criticisms and political struggles against the neoliberal form of the state, there is a need for a fresh discussion on the state, with an alternative Marxist theoretical orientation.

1 Waning and waxing of intellectual interest in the state

The intellectual interest in the capitalist state has waned and waxed. It appears to have gone through several phases of rising and declining interest since the first two decades of the 20th century. The waning and waxing of the interest in the capitalist state have closely, if not entirely, followed those in Marxism. Following a gap since 1918 when Lenin's *The state and revolution* was published that closely followed Engels' (1884) *Origin of the family, private property, and the state*, and Marx's (1871a) *Civil war in France*, the Marxist theoretical interest in the state began in the early 1960s and picked up towards the late 1960s and continued till the late 1970s.

Since the early 1980s, there has been a drastic decline in grand theorizing of the state. This decline is partly due to the influence of post-modernism which

DOI: 10.4324/9781351168007-1

rejects 'metanarratives'.[2] Certain interpretations of globalization and what is known as neoliberalism ('de-regulation' of businesses by the state)[3] have also contributed to the decline in the interest in state theory:

> Marxist state theory and, increasingly, the state as an analytical object have been the victims of an improper burial. They have been buried by a conservative shift inside and outside of the academy. They have been buried by an assumed decline of the state in the face of globalizing and localizing forces.
>
> (Aronowitz and Bratsis, 2002: xi)

In more recent times, there are signs of a slowly rising theoretical interest in the state, as partly indicated by a symposium titled 'Marxist state theory today', published in the Marxist journal, *Science & Society* (2021). There are also many other recent interventions (Ellner, 2017; Lasslett, 2015; McNally, 2019; O'Kane, 2020). This new intellectual interest reflects a new, or a newish, conjuncture. As Alami (2021: 163) notes in an article in the *Science & Society* symposium on state theory, 'a number of social phenomena . . . have conjointly rendered the role of the state *more visible* in the economy'. The phenomena include 'a "return" to various forms of state-led development across the global South since the early 2000s' as well as 'extensive state intervention following the 2008 global financial crisis in the global North (including the massive bailouts of systemic financial institutions and quantitative easing)'. To these social phenomena, one could add the immensely increasing control over income and wealth in the hands of the capitalist class (especially, its multibillionaires section) as well as the Covid-19 pandemic, which has prompted massive, if geographically uneven and politically contested, state interventions. All these phenomena have indeed produced an opportunity to rethink the existing ideas about the state, including in its neoliberal form. In fact, some commentators (e.g. Elliott, 2021; Plender, 2008, Saad-Filho, 2020) are already debating the end of neoliberalism and beginning of progressive (i.e. welfare-oriented) state policies. The titles such as *The return of the state* have begun appearing (Allen et al., 2015).[4] The theoretical interest in the state is likely to increase, with a rising interest in Marxism and growing radicalization among sections of the population, especially the younger men and women, in part prompted by the global economic crisis of 2008 compounded by the pandemic and worldwide mass immiseration (Jeffries, 2012; Niemuth, 2017). Vast sections of the population are critical of the big business and pro-corporate state policies and demanding anti-corporate actions from the state (Das, 2022a). According to a poll conducted in 28 countries, including the United States, France, China, and Russia, 56% agree that 'capitalism as it exists today does more harm than good in the world' (John, 2020).

There is, of course, something ironical about the alleged 'eclipse' and assumed 'return' of the state. It is true that 'by the early 1990s, globalization theory was being juxtaposed [by some] against state theory, with the latter allegedly in rapid retreat' (Barrow, 2021: 171). However, insofar as state policies have been 'critical to stabilizing the [global] financial crisis' (ibid.) and dealing with the 'effects' of globalization (to which the state policies had also contributed), it is ironically globalization itself that is at least partly responsible for a new interest in understanding the state.

2 Existing state theorizing

In any case, in the post-1960s state theory, a large number of books and articles have been written on the state (these are extensively and critically reviewed in Chapter 2). In this literature, the nature of state power has been addressed from multiple vantage points. The latter could be stated broadly as the following: capitalist class agency, state actors agency, working-class agency, the structure of capitalist economy, and the structure of the capitalist state.

The existing literature has advanced our understanding of the state in many ways. According to some, pursuing its own interests, the capitalist class uses the state as an instrument, with the state lacking autonomy; this idea correctly implies that the state is not as neutral as liberals think. According to others, separated from the means of production, workers do not have to be extra-economically forced to work for a wage. So the very structure of capitalist relations allows the state an autonomous space, so the state is not an instrument. Yet, given that the state is institutionally separate from the capitalist economy and that therefore it depends on taxes and loans from capitalists, the state must promote capitalist production and exchange without which its own material basis will be at risk. The state uses its structurally given relative autonomy to support capitalists whose interests are often mutually conflicting. With globalization of production and exchange, however, some argue, the autonomy of the state has been somewhat reduced. In another school of thought, what the state does reflects the balance of class struggle outside the state as well as inside the state within which opposed classes are present. There are still others according to whom state actors (high-level politicians and bureaucrats) have their own autonomous interests, but ultimately their relation with capitalists is like that between two partners who pursue their common interests as well as the interests of their own.

These ideas do reveal important aspects of the state. Some of these ideas are also, more or less, shared by Marx in *Capital volume 1* (I will also often use *Capital 1*) or are consistent with Marx's ideas about the state in that text. Yet these ideas in existing state theory *taken together* are problematic in many ways.

It is said that the state acts in the interests of capitalists *because* it is directly influenced by capitalists and/or by non-capitalist groups with capitalist ideology who occupy important positions within the state. But what is it about the state that allows capitalists to control the state as an instrument? And why does the same state not allow socialists, or workers interested in a cooperative society practising popular democracy, to control the state? It is often said that the capitalist state cannot do this or that because the capitalist class constrains state's actions (for example, the state depends on taxes). To me, constraints on the state exist, but these constraints have a derivative existence. They do not define the essential nature of the state.

The state has to be seen as inherently having a class character. Just as humanity has taken a long period of time to get underneath the production of surplus value until Marx, a similar situation exists with respect to the class character of the state. How important it is to examine the class character of the state can be gazed from the following lines from Engels, whose contribution to state theory matches Marx's contribution to theory of surplus value and who is Marx's true intellectual heir in terms of state theory:

> Just as the movement of the industrial market is, in the main . . . reflected in the money market and, of course, in *inverted* form, so the struggle between the classes . . . is reflected in the struggle [within the state] between *government and opposition*, but also in inverted form, no longer directly but indirectly, not as a class struggle but as a fight for political principles, and so distorted that it has taken us thousands of years to get behind it again.
>
> (Engels in Marx and Engels, 1975: 399; italics added)

Existing theory does recognize the class–state relation. However, to the extent that the state *is* seen as an organ of class rule, it is often seen as maintaining a reconciliatory balance between the opposed classes. Such an approach *under*-conceptualizes the class character of the state – the state as a means of oppression of the exploited classes which are always in a relation of struggle with the exploiting classes. Such an approach also forgets that to be a Marxist proper requires more than recognizing the influence of class relations and class struggle on the state (and on other aspects of society). It therefore forgets that recognizing the *existence* of the class character of the state must include recognizing the imperative of the *abolition* of class relations and of the *establishment* of a transitional proletarian state as a necessary stage for the abolition of class relations. Consequently, in spite of its class vocabulary, much existing state theory, implicitly or otherwise, has an objective effect: it is the revisionist idea that democratic rights dilute the inherently class character of the state.[5] There is an under-emphasis on the limits to not only the democratic character of the capitalist state (i.e. whether and how it is democratic) but also to the extent to which the state can provide economic concessions to the masses.

This problem of the *under*-conceptualization of the class character of the state exists in part because much of the empirical context for theorizing has been the liberal-democratic state, especially in advanced capitalist countries, and that too when their capitalism was at a rising stage ('Golden Age' of capitalism). Indeed, much theoretical thinking about the capitalist state – like that in social sciences as such – has been made on the basis of what happens in a few advanced capitalist countries of the world and at a rather concrete level at that. But such thinking cannot be taken to represent statements that need to be made on the basis of the *general* tendencies of capitalism. Nor can such thinking represent the statements about the state to be made from the standpoint of the capitalist system as a *global* system (the world market), which 'imperiously dominates the national markets' (Trotsky, 1931a) and which contains significant political-economic divisions between richer and poorer countries. The state in existing state theory is then, more or less, a form of the state whose ability to provide limited concessions and maintain a modicum of democratic rights is partly due to its imperialist position in the world market. It is the latter position that allows surplus transfer from the periphery which has its own specificities while bearing fundamental similarities, at the level of class relations, with the advanced countries. Concomitantly, even if Marxist discussion on state theory might be said to have begun with the peasantry,[6] there is very little in existing theory about the modern-day small-scale producers (non-exploiting independent producers with various degrees of integration into markets), which, in the context of the periphery, includes its vast peasantry; there are millions of small-scale producers in the advanced countries too. Small-scale producers suffer immensely because of the capitalist market which they are inserted into and which the state defends.

So what have been relatively neglected are the ways in which the nature of the state is shaped by the class relation as such and by capitalism-in-general as one form of class relation (of which advanced capitalism is, in turn, a specific form). What has been under-emphasized, therefore, is the possibility of a class theory of the state, or a theory of the state for class society, that is, a general trans-historical theory of the state, which must form the basis for a theory of the capitalist form of the state.[7] In the process, the focus has been on the extent to which the liberal democratic capitalist state has an independence relative to the capitalist class and/or its hegemonic fractions. There is just *too* much emphasis *not* on *why* the capitalist state works the way it does but on *how* the capitalist state works (its so-called specificity): that it has a degree of autonomy.

A fetishism of autonomy − a kind of 'autonomism' − has indeed received a disproportionate amount of emphasis in state theory. Scholars have been concerned with the *specificity* of the capitalist state relative to 'the pre-capitalist state', often indicating that only the capitalist state is the real state. As a result, the fact that *all* forms of the state must keep the masses in subjugation on the basis of actual/potential coercive action (along with non-coercive mechanisms) in order to reproduce the exploitative property relations, has been under-emphasized, and consequently, the democratic and concession-giving character of the bourgeois state valorized. Another corollary of autonomy fetishism is the surprisingly insufficient attention to the political economy − materiality − of the state. Indeed, much theoretical discussion on the state explains the state and the political in terms of the political, thus resorting to politicism (Das, 1999).[8] To me, the 'sociology' of the state is no substitute for the political economy of the state. This is why the full potential of Marx's *Capital 1* for the development of state theory must be fully realized.

The question of the class character of the state and the question of how exactly it functions (e.g. how autonomous it is) belong to different levels of analysis. The two questions do not have the same causal importance in explaining what the state does. The first has primacy. And the degree of autonomy is much less than often assumed. Very little autonomy is needed to subjugate the masses and to reproduce capitalist property relations. The separation of the state from capitalist economy is more a matter of the surface reality of capitalism. The fact that commodities, including labour power, are exchanged freely and that no one can force a worker to work for *a* certain capitalist explains *how* the state works (i.e. its so-called independence). It does not, and cannot, explain the fact that in capitalism there is, and there will be, a state to subjugate the masses and be used as a means of exploitation. That there is a state in capitalism is explained by the same fact that there is a state in pre-capitalism, and this is where Marx's and Engels' general statements about the state, well-articulated by Lenin, are useful.

An excessive emphasis on the structural aspects of the state has been corrected in some of the writings in the 1980s and 1990s. Yet the relation between the state and class struggle has remained under-examined because class struggle itself has remained under-examined: class struggle is viewed simply and automatically as the struggle for some concessions. Much of existing state theory is therefore reform-oriented. In fact, ideas about the state have become ideological justification for a theoretical and political escape from revolutionary action. State theory tends to ignore the following fact: if classical Marxism encourages common people to go beyond the rule of capitalists, that implies that the capitalist state cannot meet the fundamental needs of the masses significantly and durably, no matter how *autonomous* the state as a structure is, no matter how progressive and autonomous the state actors are, and no matter how intense the struggle of the masses merely for concessions is. The question is, why can the state not meet the fundamental needs of the masses significantly and durably?

3 The state, *Capital volume 1*, and the Lenin legacy

While there are problems within contemporary state theorizing, there are some 'problems' within classical Marxism too. Engels had interesting things to say about the state and, especially the state in pre-capitalist societies, which shaped Lenin's views. But what about Marx and, especially the Marx of *Capital 1*, which is truly Marx's most important theoretical work?

There is a difference of opinion, sometimes subtle, concerning the status of the state in *Capital volume 1*. In his book *33 Lessons on Capital*, Harry Cleaver says, 'Marx doesn't analyze the state in the abstract but rather shows us concretely in that text where the state appears in the form of its specific apparatuses' (Cleaver, 2019: 51). Like Cleaver, Jacques Bidet (2009: 68) says that in *Capital volume 1*, Marx does not offer 'a theoretical elaboration' on the state. He says that '[t]here is something missing in the discourse of *Capital*, the absence of an articulation between bourgeoisie and the state' (ibid.). Similarly, Mike Lebowitz (2009: 328–9) thinks that a concept of the state *does not exist* in *Capital*, but it is implicit and that 'it is possible to reconstruct Marx's concept of the capitalist state as the object and result of class struggle', as the 'latent state' of wage workers. For some (e.g. David Harvey), however, it is not just that the state is missing theoretically. Marx could not have dealt with the state theoretically: 'Conscious class strategies and state interventions are not admissible in the theoretical framework Marx has established' (Harvey, 2010a: 165).

Many decades ago, Bertell Ollman (1976: 220) had said that 'a systematic exposition of the Marxist theory of the state is more essential now than ever'. Marx's 'analysis of the relations between the state and the capitalist economy from the vantage point of such economic Relations as commodity, capital, labor and value (as found in *Capital*) was only mildly distorting of [the] real complexity' that existed 'when the state exercised minimal control over the economy' (ibid.) as during Marx's time. However, 'with the state's role so enlarged' as in the 20th century and in the 21st, 'an understanding of the state-economy relationship (and therefore of capitalism) within these limited dimensions is seriously deficient' (ibid.). That is why, according to Ollman, 'Marx's political economy must be not only brought up to date but supplemented by what might be called a Marxist "economic polity"' (ibid.). A few decades after, Ollman said, '*Capital* contains a theory of the state that, unlike Marx's related economic theories, is never fully worked out' (Ollman, 2003: 136).

I agree that Marx does not write *extensively* about the state either theoretically or empirically in *Capital*. There is little explicit discussion on the state in his analysis of commodity relations, labour process, methods of exploitation, and general theory of accumulation. But his political economy does point to an implicit theory of the state that has to be made more explicit. This task has to be conducted more adequately than has generally been done, including even in state derivation-ism discussions.

Elements of state theory do exist to a *much larger extent* in Marx's *Capital* than often realized.[9] That text strongly suggests how 'the state appears as government, as legislation. . . , as police and armies' as well as the parliament (Cleaver, 2019: 51). Indeed, as Marx himself emphasizes, the state appears as factory inspectors and medical doctors who act on behalf of workers when it comes to the regulation of the working day and the protection of children and women in the workplace. *Capital 1* also suggests how it is that the economic laws of capitalism are modified by the laws and actions of state and how the political force, power of the state, is itself economic in character. *Capital 1* indicates that the capitalist state, the sphere of the extra-economic, actually reveals something about commodity exchange and commodity production in capitalism.

The capitalist society is one where the wealth produced by the direct producers takes the form of commodity, so our 'investigation must therefore begin with the analysis of a commodity' (Marx, 1887: 27). If this is the case, then what sort of theoretical analysis of the state does this necessarily point to? This is especially important to ask because under the neoliberal form of capitalism, which began in the 1970s in many advanced countries and in the late 1980s and early 1990s in many parts of the periphery, there has been a tendency towards commodification of everything. If capitalism is a society where, as Marx says, production and exchange are ruled by the law of value, where workers are without any control over property and production and are exploited by capitalists, and where laws of capitalist accumulation limit the extent to which the conditions of the majority can be improved, then what sort of state theory is presupposed by Marx's analysis in *Capital 1*?

Marx says that political processes are, more or less, based in economic processes. If this is the case, then what could possibly show better the character of the capitalist state than the nature of capitalist commodity relations and relations of exploitation and accumulation (which he focused on in *Capital 1*)? If the 'spontaneous' development of capitalism and the competitive logic act as an economic force, and if capitalism develops and exploits and dispossesses people '*not merely by the force of economic relations, but by the help of the State*' (Marx, 1887: 181; italics in original), then what can we say about the state at a *theoretical* level? If Marx begins *Capital 1* with the concept of associated producers (and the idea that there is commodity fetishism because workers do not have *control* over production) and ends *Capital 1* with a clarion call for expropriating capitalists,[10] then what general implications for our understanding of the capitalist state and its limits do such claims by Marx indicate? The answers to these sorts of questions *prompted by* Marx's thinking in *Capital 1* should form an important part of state theory.

Marx did write about the state outside of *Capital*. But, as widely known, his writings were too scattered to produce a coherent theory. As also widely known, Marx wanted to write an entire book on the state, but he was not able to.[11] To some extent, among the classical Marxists, Lenin's work on the state – this includes, especially his well-known *The state and revolution*, written in 1917, and his relatively-neglected lecture on the state at Sverdlov University in 1919 – fills this gap.[12] Lenin, like Marx and Engels, rightly emphasizes the need for workers' conquest of state power. Yet, Lenin's near-exclusive focus is on the repressive character of the state in support of the propertied classes, so his work contains little analysis of the capitalist state's *economic* role, which, interestingly, also parallels his 'neglect' of the relation between imperialism and the state.[13] The analysis of the state's economic role – what it can do and what it cannot – is necessary in order to remove the illusions about the state's ability to serve the masses. In any case, and more generally, Lenin's 'relative neglect' of the relation between *economy* and the state has a somewhat negative implication for his conceptualization of the transitional state, as Leon Trotsky points out.

4 What is to be done theoretically? A need for a dialectical approach

I will answer this question briefly, and at a general level, by providing some guidelines here. The actual chapters will put these into practice, in part by critically building on existing ideas, with the intention to respond to the existing weaknesses in state theory as I see them.[14]

State theory should be more than about state-*economy* relation. State theory must encompass statements about social relations and attendant mechanisms in a class *society*, the statements that explain: what necessarily happens to the state, what the state is driven to do, how it impacts different classes and class fractions, and what can be done about the failure of the state to solve the problems of humanity. Because the state has many (often mutually contradictory) dimensions, it demands a dialectical approach. This approach 'allows for the kind of multiple one-sidedness that is the necessary result of studying a subject within the different perspectives associated with its different aspects' (Ollman, 1976: 219).

The dialectical approach to the state that I advocate in this book must see the state as a *relation* in the sense that its nature is shaped by its relation with things and processes that are not state institutions. There is a constant interaction and connection (and inter-penetration) between the state and civil society (an aspect of the state stressed by Weberians such as Migdal, 1988). In addition, the state itself is a structure of relations among various parts of the state, a structure that is in turn a part of a wider structure of social relations. These structures of relations set up certain mechanisms which produce certain effects on people's material and subjective experience, which in turn impacts the state.

The dialectical approach must see the state as a *thing* too: after all, the state includes the police, prisons, army, courts, bureaucracy, and so on. This 'thing' aspect of the state, its formidable material solidity, cannot be obscured by saying the state is a relationship. The state is a thing, and it is not a thing. The state is a relationship. Like capital, the state is a relationship/process expressed as things.

In the dialectical approach, relations are both harmonious and conflict-ridden. The state is constituted by relations of harmony as well as tensions between and among different parts (institutions/organs) of the state. But relations are more contradictory than harmonious because the state is the political form of the content of social relation which is fundamentally antagonistic (more on this later). The state represents an inter-penetration of opposites. Among other things, this means that the state is important both in terms of (a) what it actually does, and (b) what it decides not to do (or the fact that it fails to do what it promises to do). State action and state *inaction* are two aspects of the same coin, in a context that is shot through contradictions, which are, above all, contradictions between the basic classes.[15]

In the dialectical approach, there is a need 'to examine every question from the standpoint of how the given phenomenon arose in history and what were the principal stages in its development' (Lenin, 1919a). This principle applies to the state. The state has temporality. It is not static: like all things, it undergoes changes, both gradual and sudden. It undergoes changes in part because of its conflict-ridden character. Dialectics not only points to temporality. Given its stress on relationality, dialectics also invites us to examine the spatiality of things, which refers to relations between places and scales, and between things and their spatial/scalar organization. The state is spatially constituted and organized, and its effects are spatial (geographically specific).[16]

In the dialectical approach, objective conditions constantly shape and are shaped by subjective ideas, even if the objective conditions have the ultimate primacy. There are ideas about the state on the part of people as they exist as bearers of class and class fractional relations. These relations shape how the state works. Yet the state is dominantly an objective material reality at any given point in time. If the state has material conditions of existence (including the fact that people need to produce things to meet their needs), if the material conditions exist under certain social relations, then one must examine the state in relation to these social relationships. These relations, above all, are relations between classes (and also relations of cooperation that may exist in any society).

The dialectical approach helps us guard against eclecticism. Lenin (1949: 23) says in *The state and revolution*, eclecticism 'seems to take into account all sides of the process, all trends of development, all the conflicting influences, and so forth' but 'in reality it provides no integral and revolutionary conception of the process of social development at all' (ibid.). One way in which to avoid eclecticism is to see the state from multiple vantage points which may be mutually opposed, and at multiple levels of generality, keeping the economy, and the interests of different classes, at the centre of thinking.

The dialectical materialist approach indeed demands that the mechanisms by which the state works be analysed from multiple *vantage points*: state's economic versus extra-economic dimensions; state's *functions*[17] versus its social-political and geographical *forms*; and the state as influenced by, and influencing, capitalist *structures* and *agencies* of classes. The state also must be seen from the opposed vantage points of the working-class and capitalist class interest: the capitalist class and the working class are internally connected, so the ways in which the state helps the capitalist class can only be separated analytically, and not in reality, from what the state does to help the working class. Going beyond the two-class model, the state must also be seen in relation to *non-capitalist* commodity producers who constitute an important part of the capitalist market economy.

In the dialectical framework, the state must be theoretically analysed at multiple historical levels of generality. These include: class society, capitalist form of class society, and the historically and geographically specific forms of capitalist society. The state analysis must also cover the state during the transition from class society to a classless society.[18] The distinction between the form and content is crucial to the dialectical approach to the state (as indeed to everything else).

The dialectical view must produce a *causal* analysis of the state at a theoretical level, without which any empirical analysis of the state would be impossible. That is, it must examine the state in terms of its necessary class *roots/conditioning* and necessary class *effects* (effects on different classes and class fractions) by asking and addressing a series of inter-connected questions.[19] For example, how is the state shaped by the need to hold a society together? How do economic conditions – including class relations and accumulation – shape, and are shaped by, the state? Which (class) agents try to seek control over the state, and why and how? How does the state shape the struggle between classes and struggles of classes over state power, and how is it shaped by these struggles? To what extent and how is it that those who manage the affairs of the state come to possess a degree of autonomy, and how is that autonomy used? What connection is there between their self-interested pursuit of power and the interests of different classes? What combination of coercive and non-coercive mechanisms does the state employ to maintain class order and general public order? How exactly is state power exercised in different instances (e.g. different policy interventions)?[20]

Further, while the state represents itself as an entity for everyone in society, why does it fail to meet the needs of the majority and why does it prioritize meeting the needs of the ruling class? Or why is it that people can only obtain what Marx calls in *Capital 1* 'meagre concession wrung from capital'? Why does the state fail to meet the needs of the masses (e.g. provision of high-quality education and healthcare, and a living wage) even while doing so might serve some long-term interests of capital? And while the state fails to meet the needs of the masses, why do the masses continue to hope that the state – or this or that institution of the state – will meet their needs? What is the relation between the state, and capitalist production and production relations? This question is a part of a larger question: what is the relation between the state and society, including its different classes, and class struggle?[21] What obstacles are produced by the state towards anti-capitalist and socialist revolution?

To answer these and similar questions and to explore the complexity of the state, state theory must really stand on the shoulder of the giants. There has been an under-emphasis within state theory on the full spectrum of Marxism. By this I refer to the ideas not only of Marx and Engels but also of Lenin, Luxemburg, and Trotsky, and the ideas of those who take these thinkers seriously (among all the classical Marxists, the excellent ideas of Trotsky on the state remain under-utilized).[22] Unlike much of 'post-Marx' state theorizing, or indeed theorizing of society as such, this book takes a broad view of classical Marxism: the Marxism of the combined 19th and 20th centuries (Das, 2020a).

There are thus important theoretical rationales for this book. There is also a practical reason, as indicated earlier. Much criticism of the state and of capitalism, even within Marxism including Marxist state theory, is from a standpoint according to which progressive state policies can significantly improve the conditions of the masses. Such a standpoint is indicative of what Lenin (1917) calls 'unreasoning trust in the government of capitalists, those worst enemies of peace and socialism'. The objective political implication of much state theorizing is reformism which reflects the belief of wide layers of the population according to whom the state can durably and significantly resolve their problems.[23]

A dialectically opposed standpoint is necessary. Irrespective of whether the state is neoliberal or not, the intractable problems of the masses (workers and non-exploiting small-scale producers) such as poverty, unemployment, inequality, and ecological degradation cannot be significantly and durably resolved by the state if the state is what it is (the state's main duty is to defend the exploitative structure of social relations which cause the problems in the first place). In other words, an adequate Marxist state theory must provide *theoretical reason* for a ruthless criticism of that *unreasoning* trust in the state, the trust that legitimizes the state even when it fails to meet the needs of common people and even when it indeed hurts and kills common people when they fight for their legitimate rights that reflect their genuine needs. Accordingly, state theory must provide a theoretical rationale for the revolutionary conquest of state power by the masses and the establishment of a new type of state (i.e. a *transitional* state that is democratically controlled by the masses) which can play a constructive role in helping the masses begin building socialism and creating conditions for its own abolition (i.e. abolition of the state). More precisely, if the conquest of state power by the masses is in order as classical Marxists have correctly emphasized, then what kind of state theory is implied? To answer this question at a theoretical level is a goal of this book.[24]

The practical implication of the theoretical stance of the book should be repeated. The reason why it is not enough to prioritize class and class struggle in the analysis of society must be taken as the reason why it is not enough to prioritize class and class struggle in the analysis of the state too. Mere (economic) class struggle (i.e. the trade union–type struggle) will not solve the problems of the masses until they control state power. That means that the capitalist state must be partly seen as an obstacle to that project. A proper Marxist state theory does not merely relate the state to class struggle; it must point to the inherent lack of the control of the masses over the state and to state's fundamental character as a coercive organization to maintain the class order by oppressing the masses. Therefore, a proper Marxist state theory must point to the inevitable and unavoidable need for the conquest of state power and establishment of a new transitional state, as Lenin, following Marx, had emphasized. *This* lesson of Marxism is, however, not an essential part of the thinking of most state theorists. In fact, the story of Marxist state theory – as of Marxism as such – is, in many ways, the story of running away from Lenin and his theoretical-political legacy (revolutionary Marxism), just as the story of mainstream (conservative-cum-liberal) thinking as such is the story of running away from Marx. Thomas (2002: 74), a Gramscian scholar, echoes many state theorists when he says: 'Lenin's legacy had, not to mince words, outlived whatever usefulness it may once have had, closer to the turn of the twentieth century.'[25]

So, in this book, in offering an outline of Marxist state theory, I integrate some of the existing ideas from post-Marx (not post-Marxist) academic state theory with the insights from *Capital 1*. In fact, each of the chapters after Chapter 2 (which is a critical review of existing ideas), that constitutes my outline of Marxist state theory, starts from a point that Marx makes in *Capital 1* or a question he asks there. Further, while the Leninist legacy (revolutionary Marxism of the 20th century) is ignored and diluted in existing state theory, I critically use *that* legacy in thinking about the state. This allows me to respond to some of the major theoretical weaknesses in existing state theory as I see them. Each of the chapters after Chapter 2 ends, as well, with a discussion not only on theoretical implications but also on *practical* implications of the ideas presented: understanding the state is guided by, and must guide, the question of what is to be done with/to the state.

The outline of the Marxist *state* theory I present here is broadly in line with the Marxist *class* theory I have presented earlier in the sense that the state is conceptualized at the level of class, capitalism in general, and capitalism as it exists in more or less advanced countries (Das, 2017a). I deal more specifically with the state at the level of class relation as such and in relation to the dialectical totality of capitalism as a form of class relation. I view the relation between the state and class to be much closer than indicated in existing theory. In terms of the analysis of the state from the standpoint of the interests of the exploited classes, my main emphasis is on the working class, but I also pay some attention to small-scale producers who are connected to capitalists, albeit in different ways than workers are. While my focus is on the class-state and on the capitalist state in the abstract with an eye towards the advanced countries (where the more general mechanisms discussed fully play out), I also pay attention to the specificity of the peripheral state, in the context of imperialism, a topic that Marx did not pay much attention to (in part given the time in which he lived) but Lenin and his legacy did. In fact, I take an international approach to capitalism and the state, with the theoretical mechanisms illustrated through empirical examples from the North and the South.

I examine the capitalist form of the state in relation to how it intervenes in support of capitalist economic interests in terms of its defence of capitalist property and commodity exchange and in terms of its support for the production of value. In examining the economic role of the state, I employ Marx's capital circuit. I then argue that the ways in which the state performs pro-capitalist functions are shaped by: 'instrumentalist' ties between the (members of the) capitalist class and the state; inter-capitalist competition; and the autonomy of officials of the capitalist state who within limits can pursue their own interests. I examine the limits to state's pro-capitalist economic intervention that exist because of the crisis-ridden nature of capitalism itself which the state cannot resolve; of course, such limits adversely impact the masses. The state can introduce measures on behalf of the masses in response to their struggle and in the longer-term interest of the capitalist class as a whole (or of its dominant factions). But the state is limited in terms of what it can do for the masses too, given that their interests and those of the propertied classes (capitalists and large landowners) are fundamentally antagonistic. The state is also limited because of the crisis-ridden nature of capitalism which puts a brake on economic development and therefore on significant redistribution of income and wealth, and which may dry up state's resources. What is important in society is not just what the state does (i.e. its functions) but also its form which impacts state's functions. State forms include its geographical form and bureaucratic form. All the different aspects of state functions and state forms have one major thing in common: the state represents the lack of control over state power by the masses, and this means that until they establish a transitional state under their own popular-democratic control, they cannot begin to resolve their economic-ecological problems (e.g. economic miseries, ecological crisis) and political-cultural problems (e.g. attack on their democratic rights, oppression of women and racialized and religious minorities).

5 An overview of the argument

Any attempted re-articulation and reconstruction of Marxist state theory must be based on a critical recuperative review of the existing ideas about the state that are more or less inspired by Marx. So in Chapter 2, I lay out the various vantage points to the state and then present a series of inter-connected criticisms.

Nearly all of the Marxist state theory has been about capitalist society only (and this partly reflects Euro-centricism in existing theory). But capitalism is only one form of class society. So there is a need to 'scale up' the analysis of the state – that is, to analyse the state at the level of class relations as such 'before' examining the state at the level of capitalist class relation. In *Capital 1*, Marx says that unequal distribution of property leads to the appropriation of surplus product from the direct producers, by those who have the monopoly over private property. But without the active assistance of the state, would these types of property owner be able to maintain their monopoly over property and appropriate surplus labour from direct producers? The answer is no. There is an internal relation between the state and class relations. So I begin my own outline of the theory of the state by examining the state at the level of class relation (Chapter 3), which sets the context for the discussion on the different dimensions of the relation between the state and capitalist form of class society (in Chapters 4–11).

In examining the state's internal relation with class relations, I begin with the claim that the state is influenced by economic relations/conditions. The scope of 'economic relations' is expanded to include the structure of class relations, and the state is related to class relations. I focus then on the state and class *struggle*. To say that the state exists because of class relations and because of class struggle does not explain why it is that the state does not support *the exploited class* in its struggle against the exploiter class. So I explore the idea that the state and the exploiting class are two arms of the totality of the body of class relations. As forms of class relation change, so do the nature and forms of the class-state. Here I also make some remarks on the state in pre-capitalist societies. I argue against those Marxist scholars who seek to dilute the importance of the relation between the state and property relation. I also make remarks on some under-stressed aspects of the state that have an implication for understanding the state in the transitional post-revolution society, where there can be elements of the capitalist state without the capitalists. In the process, and in part by building on Leon Trotsky, this discussion brings to light a potential source of weakness in Lenin's theory of the state.

Having explained the nature of the state at the level of class relations, I explore the different dimensions of the *capitalist* state in Chapter 4 and the remainder of the book. Marx clearly thought that the capitalist state could not eliminate the problems created by capitalist production and exchange based on capitalist private property. Why? One explanation is that the state itself depends on accumulation. This idea *appears* to be in some of the writings of Marx himself. In more recent times, some scholars have indeed argued that the capitalist state cannot do this or that for the ordinary people because the capitalist class constrains state's actions. The idea that the state depends on capitalists for taxes, loans, and so on and that capitalist structure, or capitalists as individuals, constrains the state is somewhat true from the standpoint of relatively concrete aspects of capitalist class society. But overall, this is an inadequate view informed by the ontology of external relation according to which the state and the capitalist class (including individual capitalists) exist as separate things, and then they interact.

Another idea is that there are no *inherent* obstacles to the state being able to make capitalists serve the majority and that therefore the obstacles can be removed by, say, adequate pressure from below. This idea presupposes an external relation between the state and the working class. In other words, the relation between the state and working class is an empirical relation, the strength of which varies across regions/countries and historical periods. The approaches to the state based on the external relation between class and the state must be contested. To contest these ideas requires that we see their relation as an internal one rather than an external one.

So, in Chapter 4, I discuss the relation between the structure of the state and capitalism as an internal relation. I discuss then how the structure of the state operates within a series of limits, some of which are more stringent than others. I conclude by reflecting on the idea of the separation of economic power from political power: I assert that economic power and political power are two sides of the same coin. This chapter contains an overview of the entire theoretical framework for understanding the capitalist state in the book.

In my view, if the state supports capitalist accumulation, it is not fundamentally because it depends on capitalists and on capitalist economy for its survival (that it needs taxes and loans, and so on). The fact that it needs taxes and loans must be explained first in terms of state's class character. Its so-called economic dependence on capitalists and capitalists-controlled economy is a concrete expression of the fact that it is inherently a class institution, which means that in the capitalist form of class society, the state is fundamentally – it is already – a *capitalist* institution. So it must not only support capitalist property rights but also seek to promote the expansion of wealth in its capitalist form. There can be no capitalist class relation without capitalists having capitalist property rights and right to exploit direct producers, and this exploitative and contested class relation cannot exist for a moment without the state (especially its coercive powers against the masses). In this *concrete* sense, the state is 'constitutive' of, although not a cause of, the capitalist class relation: it codifies the class relations (exploitative production relations) into juridical relations and reproduces them politically against the resistance of the working class (and it seeks to mitigate the destructive effects of intra-capitalist class competition).[26] Given class relations, there is a need for the state (special public power). In this sense class relations are prior to the state. Once the state exists, it needs taxes and loans in a society. So it is the classness of society which explains the classness of the state that is behind state's so-called reliance on private accumulation. Consider this: the state does have all the power in the world to dispossess capitalists, take over their property and be self-reliant. Or, indeed, the state has the coercive power to take the property from a tiny minority and give it to the vast majority and help them use it collectively in order to meet their needs, and the majority can set aside some resources for the management of their common affairs (i.e. to do things that are necessary for the society as a whole). If the capitalist state does not do this, and therefore, if it is reliant on capitalists financially, it is because the state is, above all, a class – capitalist – institution. The state is the capitalist state *not* because it relies on the capitalist class. The state *relies* on the capitalist class *because* it is the capitalist state.

The state power is necessarily a form of class power. That is, the relation between the two forms of power is an internal one and not an external one. The state power is the power of the exploiting classes in all pre-socialist class societies. The capitalist class controls the means of production and the surplus value, and it commands far more exchange value than the working-class people (and small-scale producers) do, and it is the class that 'controls' political power as well. The obverse side of this is the fact that proletarians (and small-scale producers) lack control over exploitative property, surplus value, and indeed over labour process, and it is also the class that lacks control over state power (and must therefore achieve state power for it to gain control over the economic aspects of class structure of society). It is not for nothing that Lenin, whose thinking is ignored or under-emphasized in much state theory, claims in *The state and revolution* that Marx 'developed his theory of the class struggle consistently, down to the theory of political power, of the state' (Lenin, 1949: 27). Fundamental aspects of state theory must be a part of class theory.

State power – both in terms of what the state does and what it does not – is very much implicit in Marx's analysis of the commodity character of capitalism. I build on these insights to explore the relation between the state and commodity relations in Chapter 5. I relate the state to the three attributes of the commodity in capitalism (use-value, exchange value, and value). I discuss the state in relation to the nature of the peculiar commodity (labour power). I outline some implications of Marx's ideas about the state and value relations for a future world beyond value relations. I thus briefly connect Marx's *Capital* to the 20th century (and more recent) discussion on the ability of the post-capitalist state to construct 'socialism in one country'.

The sphere of the exchange of commodities, including labour power, is one where not only freedom, equality, and Bentham rule but also where property rules (Marx, 1887: 123). Why property? 'Property, because each disposes only of what is his own' (ibid.). There is therefore a need for state intervention to make sure this rule is protected. In Chapter 6, I discuss the relation between the state and capitalist property rights. I begin with a typology of private property and then discuss the role of the state in relation to the production of private property in capitalism, including in relation to the ongoing dispossession of small-scale producers. I conclude with a discussion on how it is that many contemporary Marxists under-emphasize the importance of private property in the analysis of the state. I also discuss the Marxist proposal for the abolition of private property, as a part of the process that includes abolition of the state.

Capital is value in motion. It is not enough for the state to merely defend capitalist property rights and commodity relations. Therefore, the state must take steps to promote capitalist accumulation in the long-term interests of the capitalist class and especially its economically and politically hegemonic fraction(s). Following the completion of the sale and purchase of commodities, including labour power, and on the basis of capitalist property rights, all of which the state supports, the process of capitalist production (labour process) begins. The workplace (the space of labour process or the hidden abode of production) is a space of certain rights of the exploiting class. These rights are defended by the state. Therefore, the sphere of production, including the workplace, reveals important attributes of the state. As in the last two chapters, I partly rely on *Capital 1* to show, in Chapter 7, how the logic of capitalist social relations and production produce an imperative for the state to act. In society, fresh wealth (new wealth) cannot be produced *merely* on the basis of primitive accumulation (Marx) or even of class differentiation by commodity circulation (Lenin). On the basis of commodity circulation and creation of capitalist property from pre-capitalist or non-capitalist (small-scale owners') property (discussed in Chapters 5 and 6), fresh wealth (capitalist value) is ultimately produced inside the hidden abode of production, and it is here that the state plays an important role.

The capital circuit (M–C–M′) in its expanded form can serve as a method of systematic presentation as well as a method of analysis of the role of the state in relation to the totality of capitalist relations, including production relations. I discuss how the state is connected to the successive phases of the capital circuit: purchase of means of production and the labour power, commodity production in value form, and realization. I then discuss the state's role in relation to accumulation; here I closely follow Marx's discussion in chapter 25 of his *Capital 1*. I then turn to the state's role in relation to the tendencies *and* counter-tendencies towards crisis relying on *Capital volume 3* as well as Henryk Grossman and some recent authors. Finally, I reflect on the implications of my discussion for the concepts of socialism and state capitalism, including by returning to Leon Trotsky on this topic.

The state must protect capitalist private property, support commodity relations and the exploitation of labour, and create general and specific conditions for accumulation. But the ways in which the state performs these actions in support of the capitalist class are not automatic/spontaneous. They are shaped by the agency of the capitalist class, especially its ties with state actors (decision-making politicians and officials). They are also shaped by the agency of state actors. This is discussed in Chapter 8. I also discuss the limits to what state actors can do for capitalists.

In Chapter 9, my focus turns to what the state does to 'help' the working class in part as a response to the working-class agency. I begin by partly building on the detailed arguments about state's role concerning commodity and property relations in Chapters 4–5, and I then discuss the state's pro-worker interventions. I do this in relation to what I call 'the labour circuit'. I turn to the driving forces behind the state's pro-worker measures and argue that there is an objective pressure on the state (e.g. general and long-term interests of capital) to intervene on behalf of the masses but that this objective pressure is 'subjectively' mediated by the struggle of the masses. I then discuss the limits to what the state can do for workers under capitalism, the limits that exist because of the capitalist control over property and production, nature of capitalist accumulation and its crisis-proneness, and the capitalist state's bureaucratic functioning and its anti-worker politics. Finally, I offer general theoretical reflections on the ways in which the state is connected to working-class interests and struggle.

Having focused on *state functions* (actions) in relation to the different classes in Chapters 4–9, I turn to the other aspect of the capitalist state: *state form*. In particular, I discuss geographical and bureaucratic forms of the capitalist state and their political implications. The geographical form includes such issues as the (uneven) territorial reach (organization) of the state and the scale division of labour within the state between more local and more central branches of the state, which are partly behind the uneven geographical impacts of state action. The geographical form of the state also includes the multiplicity of national states under global capitalism. The bureaucratic state form is one of the major vehicles through which the state functions and exercises domination over common people mainly in the interest of the ruling class(es). The class-state, and especially in its capitalist form, cannot exist except in its bureaucratic form, which reproduces the relation of separation of the state from common people.

In Chapters 4–10, I examine the state in relation to capitalism at a general level and in the context of advanced capitalism, so I turn to the state function and state form in the periphery in the final chapter (Chapter 11). Much of the analysis of the state in the abstract and in the context of advanced countries does apply to the state in the periphery, because both are characterized by the dominance of capitalist class relations. Yet the state in the periphery has certain specificities. As in all the other chapters, here as well, I build on *Capital 1* for some of the necessary insights. By using Marx's concept of the subsumption of wage labour, I conceptualize class relations in the periphery and relate them to the state. I also explore the implication for the peripheral state of the many specificities of the peripheral social formation that are related to its class character and to the level and the nature of its economic development. I discuss then the state action and state form in the periphery in relation to the state's social basis in the bloc of proprietary classes as well as to lower-class struggles. I speculate on the potential threat to the legitimacy of the peripheral state. Finally, I briefly discuss what the approach of the masses should be to the state in the periphery as well as the core.

Notes

1　The present book on state theory originally began as a single chapter in a 14-chapter book on Marx's political economy as based in *Capital volume 1*. This book has now become a part of a series of three books on the state (two of which remain to be completed), and this is in addition to a book on the 'more economic aspects' of *Capital volume 1*. So the original book on *Capital volume 1* has become four books, including the present book on the state.

2　There has been 'a shift of emphasis, within the left, away from the study of "political power" to a more disaggregated vision of power as a dispersed and undifferentiated phenomenon (from Foucault and Habermas to Deleuze and Guattari)' (Aronowitz and Bratsis, 2002: xi).

　　In the Foucauldian literature, '[t]he state loses all its past privileges and becomes one contingent site of power among so many others' and 'the state is reduced to a mere effect of power relations' (Kalyvas, 2002: 111).

3　'[A] central principle of neoliberal thinking posits that the regulation of the market should be insulated as far as possible from any popular-democratic pressures [and state intervention], which will only distort its operations' (Watkins, 2021: 6).

4　Skidelsky (2021), in a chapter of a new book, *The Return of the State*, sketched out some ideas for what the UK government should do: taking responsibility for all procurement affecting the health of the nation; a public sector job guarantee for the unemployed; ensuring sufficient demand through redistribution rather than relying on personal debt; and capital controls to reduce government dependence on international credit markets. In the current climate, none sounds nearly as unfeasible as they would have done 5 years ago.

5　According to revisionism, '[p]olitical freedom, democracy and universal suffrage remove the ground for the class struggle' (Lenin, 1908).

6　At a very early stage of his writing career, Marx (1842), in writing about the 'theft' of wood, said that the state should defend the customary law against the greed of the rich. In the *Eighteenth Brumaire*, Marx (1852a: 62) said, '[T]he state power . . . represent[s] a class, and the most numerous class of French society at that, the small-holding peasants.'

7　Jessop (2016: 1, 5) says that there can be no 'general and transhistorical theory of the state'. Similarly, according to Barrow (2021: 172) '[t]here is no general theory of the state' although there can be 'theoretically informed analyses of states in capitalist (and other) societies'. However, I affirm the possibility, and indeed the necessity, of a general, and indeed, a 'transhistorical' (transhistorical at the level of class society) theory of the state.

8　'State theorists often (not invariably) ignore political economy, focusing instead on a different "problematic" – the nature and extent of the relative autonomy of state managers' (Kotz and McDonough, 2010: 121).

9　See O'Kane, 2014. See also the discussion on state derivationism in Holloway and Picciotto (1978).

10 Harvey (2010a: 301) wrongly thinks that this call is only 'the *rhetoric* of the *Communist Manifesto*'. I disagree (see Das, 2022a for a detailed discussion of Marx's revolutionary theory of class and the state, in that text).

11 'An outline of his overall project gives the state a much more important role in his explanation of capitalism than would appear to be the case from a glance at what he completed' (Ollman, 2003: 137).

12 Colletti says that *The state and revolution* is 'by far and away the greatest his greatest contribution to political theory' (in Hay, 1999: 162).

13 Of course, 'the outcome of Lenin's analysis [of capitalism and imperialism] is not the same as the analysis itself' (Lewis and Malone, 1996: xv). Lenin's method, which puts the accent on class relations and political economy, does encourage and help one to analyse the economic role of the state.

14 Given that this book is on *theory*, I take seriously Erik Wright's (1985: 292–294) remark that theoretical reconstruction is stimulated by, among other things, 'discoveries of conceptual inconsistencies and dealing with the ramifications of earlier conceptual transformations'. Wright says that there are four general strategies that 'underlie many successful productions of new concepts: drawing new lines of demarcation; respecifying existing lines of demarcation; reaggregating categories under more general criteria; and decoding the conceptual dimensionality of a descriptive taxonomy'.

15 For example, actively protecting the interests of capitalist private property owners when there is a challenge to these rights, and not going against private property when doing so would be in the interests of the majority – these are two sides of the same coin.

16 It is true that 'case studies of certain state policies in specific policy areas are necessary to gain both theoretical understanding and political perspectives which cannot be gained either through deductive reasoning or immediate experience' (Offe and Ronge, 1982: 249). While I strongly believe in this principle, for lack of space, I do not engage in case studies *in this book*, although I illustrate the general arguments by giving examples of specific policy interventions from the North and the South.

17 These include state's specific actions/policies, including those that support general conditions for accumulation.

18 The nature of the state also varies in terms of the degree of its concreteness: the capitalist state, neoliberal or interventionist capitalist state, or democratic or fascistic capitalist state.

19 In pursuing causal analysis of the state, one must avoid extreme determinism. A fruitful way to conduct causal analysis of X is to see the act of causing as the act of setting limits within which Y has a degree of autonomy. Class relations can set limits within which the state as a structure and as a collective of people can act with a degree of autonomy. 'There is clearly a difference between a process of setting limits and exerting pressures . . . and that other process in which a subsequent content is essentially prefigured, predicted and controlled by a pre-existing external force' (Williams, 1976: 32, 34).

20 This paragraph is partly informed by Ollman (2003: 138).

21 The underlying assumption here is that capitalist production and its relations, even if they are the basis of society, do not exhaust what is covered under the term 'society'.

22 I have included selected ideas from Lukacs and Sartre in some of my discussion, without implying that I agree with everything these writers have said or indeed with their politics.

23 This is indicative of a general trend: much academic analysis reflects uncritical and common sensical views of the lay public which are packaged in a language which sounds sophisticated and is often difficult to understand.

24 Similarly, my book *Marxist class theory for the skeptical world* asked: if the conquest of state power by the masses is in order, what kind of class theory can provide the theoretical justification for it? (Das, 2017a).

25 The relative or absolute neglect of the Lenin legacy (i.e. the legacy of revolutionary Marxism) is both direct via critique of Lenin and indirect via critique of a larger body of

work that includes Lenin. For example: what Panitch means by 'the new theory of the state', the stuff that was built on the basis of Miliband, Poulantzas, O'Connor, and so on in the 1960s and afterwards, was new because it 'was concerned to displace the narrowly ideological official Marxism of the Communist parties' (Panitch, 2002: 90). The 'new theory of the state', more or less, excludes Lenin.

26 The separation between the mode of production and class relation on the one hand and the state (which constitutes their political form) on the other is more for analytical convenience than anything else.

2 A critical review of Marxist state theory *post* Marx

Capital volume 1 contains important insights about the state in relation to capitalist exchange and production. But Marx never wrote a theoretical treatise on the state. This gap has been sought to be filled by others, especially since the 1960s. In state theory, nature of state power, including the question of why the capitalist state fails to meet the needs of the masses, has been addressed from multiple vantage points. These could be stated broadly as the following: capitalist class agency, state actors agency, working-class agency, and the structure of capitalist economy (and of the capitalist state).

This chapter presents a review of the ideas about the state more or less inspired by Marx and Engels.[1] It allows us to see how Marx's own ideas about the state in *Capital volume 1* and elsewhere relate to contemporary state theory and vice versa. It first lays out the various vantage points to the state (in Sections 1–6).[2] It then mounts a series of inter-connected criticisms (in the penultimate section), which constitute the points of departure for my theoretical analysis of the state beginning in Chapter 3.

1 The capitalist class agency perspective

The dominant class[3] and its individual members use the state as an instrument to maximize their long-term and common interests and also to meet the special interests of specific groups of capitalists (Meckstroth, 2000: 56, 60). This perspective is called instrumentalist, the origin of which can be traced to Marx and Engels: they characterize the state in *the Communist Manifesto* as a committee for managing the common affairs of the whole bourgeoisie and in *German ideology* as 'the form in which the individuals of a ruling class assert their common interests' (Marx and Engels, 1845).

There are several mechanisms through which the state works as an instrument of capital, as emphasized in the British and the American literature.[4] There are close ties between capitalists and politicians/bureaucrats. For example, individual members of the dominant class and/or those educated middle-class people who share the ideology of the capitalist class and support its interests occupy top unelected bureaucratic positions or gain seats in the parliament and thus directly influence the state. Members of the capitalist class influence the state by

DOI: 10.4324/9781351168007-2

funding pro-capitalist political representatives as well as think tanks, media, and even academia.[5] Conscious of their common class interests, acting with a high degree of cohesion and solidarity and transcending many of their differences (Miliband, 1969: 48), capitalists directly, or through their lobbyists and associations, advocate for and against certain policies. They try to make sure that the state performs its basic role which is to defend capitalist class interests and that the state policies do not deviate too much from that goal. Marx himself referred to the lobbyist efforts of capitalists. The fact that the capitalist class and its individual members use the various institutions and personnel of the state as an instrument in order to meet their own needs explains why the state fails to meet the needs of the masses. In the period of neoliberal capitalism, the top layers of the state are more closely allied with capitalists than during the earlier times. This has led to the neoliberalization of the structure of the state itself, where state actors themselves (e.g. former World Bank employees) believe in, and implement, neoliberal policies (Patnaik, 2010).

2 The capitalist class structure perspective – the political moment

The idea of the state as an instrument is based on the idea of capitalist class agency. This idea has been criticized for assuming that the capitalist class acts with an ideological cohesion which may not exist. The instrumentalism idea has also been criticized for ignoring structural constraints which force the state to serve capitalists irrespective of who controls the state. Instrumentalism also ignores the autonomy of the state structure that is enabled by the structure of capitalism. That is, the instrumentalist idea does not recognize that to act in the general interest of capital, the state must be able to act against the interests of particular capitalists. This means that, it has been argued, the state should have more autonomy from *direct* capitalist control than the instrumentalist theory allows (Block, 1987).

According to Poulantzas,[6] who was influenced by the French Marxist literature (Althusser), irrespective of who controls the state, the goal of the state is to maintain the unity of a social formation divided into classes and thus to reproduce the political hegemony of the exploiting class (Poulantzas, 1968: 54).[7] 'The state has the particular function of constituting the factor of cohesion between the levels of a social formation. This is precisely the meaning of the Marxist conception of the state as a factor of "order"' (Poulantzas, 1968: 44). This role conditions state's other functions including its economic functions (Poulantzas, 1968: 54, 187, 1978: 44).

Poulantzas says that the state functions differently for different classes. With regard to the dominant class, the state tries to organize its different competing fractions into a power bloc under the leadership of the hegemonic fractions (Poulantzas, 1968: 137, 190, 239). To the dominated classes, the state presents itself as representing the general interests of all members of society (by converting them into juridically created citizens, not into members of a class)

(Poulantzas, 1968: 133). This notion of the general interest is not trickery but a real fact: the state gives to the economic interest of certain dominated classes guarantees which may even be contrary to the short-term economic interests of dominant classes but which are compatible with their political interests and their hegemonic domination (Poulantzas, 1968: 191). By doing this, the state aims precisely at the political disorganization of the dominated classes, in that the economic concessions help prevent the dominated classes from attacking the political basis of exploitation by the dominant class, that is, state power itself (Poulantzas, 1968: 188, 1978: 127).

The state is not a toy, or an instrument, in the hands of the capitalist class. It has a degree of autonomy. This autonomy is possible and necessary. The autonomy is possible because of the capitalist class structure. Capitalism generally requires that all barriers to free and equal exchange be, more or less, destroyed. This is especially so with respect to labour power as a commodity. The separation of direct producers from the means of production in capitalism means that direct political power does not have to be exercised in order to appropriate surplus labour from them (Poulantzas, 1968: 129), a point originally made by Marx (1887: 523). This fact produces the specific autonomy of the political and the economic (Poulantzas, 1968: 129). In other words, it is possible for an outside authority (the state), separated from the sphere of capitalist production and exchange, with a monopoly on the use of force, to exist (Hirsch, 1978: 61).

Not only is state autonomy possible. It is also necessary. To perform the two different roles (to organize the warring groups of the dominant class and to disorganize the working class), the state has to be relatively autonomous from, and must not be controlled directly by, dominant classes and factions. Relative autonomy allows the state to not only arrange compromises (with workers), but also intervene against the long-term economic interest of (one or other fraction of) the dominant class. Such compromises and sacrifices are sometimes necessary for the realization of their political class interests (Poulantzas, 1968: 284–328). According to Poulantzas, such interventions can be useful for the long-term economic interest of the dominant class as well (e.g. absorption of 'the surplus' of monopoly production). The autonomy of the state is only relative, however. The capitalist state, in the long run, can only correspond to the political interest of the dominant class(es). This is the negative limit to state autonomy. But within this limit, the degree and the form of relative autonomy (i.e. how relative, how it is relative) depend on the precise conjuncture of class struggle (e.g. configuration of the power bloc, degree of hegemony of the power bloc, relation between capital and labour) (Poulantzas, 1968: 289, 1976: 10).

3 The capitalist class structure perspective – the economic moment

While from one angle, there are political constraints on the state (the fact that political hegemony of the exploiting class needs to be maintained), from another angle there are economic constraints on the state as well. But Poulant-zas' approach under-stresses the economic interventions of the state. Therefore, ideas from Marx's *Capital* have been used to show how the laws of motion of capitalism shape the state's economic interventions (Holloway and Picciotto, 1978: 19). It is necessary for the state to intervene, and it is possible for it to intervene, especially in relation to the economic interests of capitalists. This perspective has been called state derivationism that originated in Germany.

A common ground between the political-structural approach (as discussed in the previous section) and the economic structural approach (as discussed in this section) is that the capitalist structure is a reason for state's relative autonomy. Since the state is outside the sphere of productive activity, it is forced to depend on the bourgeoisie for its survival. State revenue is needed not only to pay salaries to state employees. An important part of state's rev-enue is also needed to give concessions to the masses to keep them in check. It is capitalist accumulation that governs the state's ability to give material concessions to the dominated classes, without which liberal democracy will be difficult to maintain. So the state has a structurally mandated need not to disrupt capitalist accumulation (Hirsch, 1978). Conditions for accumulation have to be created within

> the boundaries of its state – on the one hand to make sure that resistance to exploitation by the mass of the population is kept to a minimum, on the other to enhance the competitiveness of nationally based capital as opposed to capital that is based abroad.
>
> (Harman, 1991)

The state is capitalist because it must rely on capitalist accumulation. The concept of institutional self-interest of the state captures the structural con-straints on it: the state's institutional self-interest is in capitalist accumulation because of the fact that the state lacks the power to control the flow of those resources which are nevertheless indispensable for the control of state powers (Offe, 1984: 120). The fact that the state depends on the capitalist economy for its own revenue limits its autonomy. However, this dependence 'is often concealed by the way in which it raises its revenues – by taxation of incomes and expenditure, by government borrowing or by "printing money"', all of which appear to be 'quite different from capitalist exploitation at the point of production', which is why the state 'seems like an independent entity which can raise the resources it needs by levying funds from any class in society' (Harman, 1991).

The room for manoeuvre for a party managing the affairs of the state does exist, but it depends on financial possibilities which depend on taxes and welfare expenses. When capitalist accumulation is successful, then the state's tax income-level is high. 'The material foundation of the state is thus directly connected to the accumulation of capital; no government can get past this dependency' (Heinrich, 2004: 212). Bob Brenner, David Harvey, Bob Jessop, and others concur.[8]

What exactly does the state, with its varying levels of autonomy, do economically? Broadly speaking, there are five functions. Firstly, competing with each other in pursuit of surplus value, individual capitalists will not produce certain things that are necessary for capitalist accumulation because such production is not profitable (e.g. labour power with a certain level of education and health, a built environment for an efficient circulation of commodities) (Altvater, 1978).[9] So the state must socialize the production of these things if accumulation is to take place.

Secondly, driven by competition for maximum value, capitalist production might threaten the existence of society, for example, by destroying natural resources or the reserve army of labour. What is needed is not just restriction on individual employers/investors but a society-wide force against capitalists in the form of legislations. In this way, the state creates general, long-term conditions for capitalist accumulation. Thirdly, a most fundamental tendency of capitalism is the falling rate of profit, which manifests the contradictory character of capitalism. The state is expected to mobilize counter-measures (Hirsch, 1978: 97).

Fourthly, capitalism suffers from a tendency towards the paralysis of the commodity form of value (Offe, 1984). Labour itself is a fictitious commodity. This means that what Marx calls dull economic compulsions are not enough to transform labour power into wage labour. Labour power has to be actively commodified. Capital, in certain situations, also fails to be involved in exchange relations. The state has to recommodify capital and labour (i.e. it has to ensure conditions for accumulation and sale of labour power). The state thus produces the conditions of production in the general interest of the capitalist society as a whole, not just of capital or labour, to ensure that individuals of both classes can enter into exchange relations. Fifthly, of still greater importance, in terms of the commodity form, is the role of the state as a guarantor of the stability of exchanges and therefore of the form of value (Callinicos, 1987: 100); the state serves as a lender of last resort thus preventing the collapse of the monetary order and banking systems. Sixthly, the state must regulate capital-labour relations, if necessary, by repression.

Finally, the state has to protect capitalist operating under its jurisdiction. This is an explicitly geographical function that entails various strategies, three of which seem very important (Callinicos, 1987: 99–102). Firstly, 'Every capitalist state requires a military establishment in order to maintain control over its territory and enforce its interests vis-à-vis other states' (Callinicos, 1987: 100). Here military expenditure is crucial in that 'a substantial portion of every national economy is regulated by direct (and often very cosy) relations between the state concerned, and either local defence contractors or other states' (ibid.: 100). Secondly, military expenditure by the state (defence contracts to the military-industrial capitalists) plays a crucial role in the recovery of national economies and in economic restructuring (cf. Grossman, 1929). Thirdly, the state protects its national markets (protectionism). This often involves imperialist intervention on the part of some states.

There are thus three aspects of the capitalist structure that drive state action: the realm of the market and inter-capitalist competition, state's institutional separation from the economy, and the nature of capitalist exploitation (free wage-labour). And to the extent that state interventions succeed in promoting capitalist accumulation, however temporarily, workers might benefit from an increase in investment, within limits. But various interventions on behalf of capital are directly anti-worker.

There are many reasons why state policies may not work for capitalism as well as intended. Firstly, the interests of capital are not wholly given and that they must be articulated in and through what Jessop (1990) calls 'accumulation strategies'. These must advance the immediate interests of the different frac-tions of capital (located in different territories) and must secure the long-term interests of the class (and especially, of its hegemonic fraction) which must, in turn, sacrifice some of its short-term economic interests. It is not easy for the state to figure out what these interests will be in a context where different fractions of capital have different interests and where capitalists' and workers' interests are antagonistically related.

Secondly, more intense demands on the state threaten to overburden it (Offe, 1984). To counter this, the state resorts to corporatism. But corporat-ism fails because including groups with veto power in decision-making, and parcelling out state functions, can undermine the state's steering capacity, while what is needed is autonomy for the state in the face of the greater demands placed upon it. As mentioned, no capitalist faction knows exactly what policies (or accumulation strategies) are necessary, and yet a state is expected to invent decisions and production rules to maintain accumulation. But given the state's bureaucratic form, the state is unable to do this: state's bureaucracy is not struc-turally equipped to invent such rules, as bureaucracy is designed to follow fixed legal structures in processing certain inputs and cannot be creative enough. In addition, state policies pose a threat to the dominance of the capitalist in exchange relations and create disincentive on the part of capital and labour. When market success depends less on taking risks in the market and more on state policies, commodification of labour and capital is seen as an artefact of politics. This weakens normative and moral fibres of capitalism and threatens to produce a crisis of legitimacy (Offe, 1984). Thus, capitalism needs an inter-ventionist welfare state to create conditions for accumulation, but the welfare state (or an interventionist state) undermines the capacity of the state to create these conditions. This leads to what Jessop (2002: 275) calls 'Offe's paradox'. As Offe himself puts it, 'while capitalism cannot coexist with, neither can it exist without, the welfare state' (Offe, 1984: 153). The Offe's paradox partly explains why there are limits to why the state cannot meet the needs of the masses.

Ideas about the relation between the structure of social relations of pro-duction and the state have been applied to the global periphery. So, from a more structural perspective, Hamza Alavi (1972, 1982) says that unlike the Western state which is based in Western class societies, the superstructure in the colony is over-developed in relation to the structure of society in colony, where the state needs to mediate within a more complex class structure than in Western societies. In the colony, the state has to look after the interests of landlords, native capitalists, and metropolitan capitalists. This legacy continues. The state fails to override the interests of any of these classes to pursue *national* developmental objectives. Similarly, the analytical Marxism of Pranab Bardhan (1998) argues that the state, as in India, works basically on behalf of a coalition of dominant proprietary classes: rural capitalists, urban capitalists, and top state actors.

Connected to these ideas about the state in the less developed world is the idea of the peripheral capitalist state; this idea stresses imperialism's effects on class interests which the state serves (Ougaard, 1982). In the periphery, national bourgeoisie is weak, and foreign bourgeoisie has much influence. The state works in the interest of foreign capital seeking cheap labour and resources, and tries to maintain the level of business confidence to attract MNCs (multinational companies) investment upon which the health of the domestic economy depends. As long as the dependent state knows its place within the world system and pursues dependent development in cooperation with centre capital, it can draw support from international capitalist organizations and the centre state. The dependent state is created by the world system and is sustained by it (via training, aid, and so on). No matter how strong the state is, it cannot transcend the structural requirement of the world system (it must pay interest to the banks of metropolitan countries; it must repress labour to hold wages down for MNCs). In certain conditions, the peripheral state has played (a limited) developmental role (I will return to this in Chapter 11).

4 The state actors agency perspective

While the capitalist structure sets constraints on how the state works, the agency of state actors is also important. There are several ideas concerning state autonomy within the Marxist literature: non-correspondence; partnership; territorial versus capital logics; institutional–conjunctural mechanisms; over-developed nature and developmentalism; militarism and public order.

Non-correspondence approach

This is the state autonomy approach 'proper', whose rise coincided with that of neoliberalism.[10] A major representative of this approach is Skocpol (1979) who draws on both Marx and Weber and who is also influenced by Fred Block. This approach is post–Marxist. Its main feature is the belief in the non-correspondence between the economic and the political. This means that there is no necessary relation between the class character of society and the nature of the state (Wood, 1996: 52).

For Skocpol (1979: 31) states are organizations controlling (or attempting to control) territories and people. State organizations work within a national and international context. They must operate within the context of class-based socio-economic relations which condition/influence these organizations and the activities of state rulers (Skocpol, 1979: 29–30). Geopolitical conditions also create tasks and opportunities for states and place limits on their ability to cope with external and internal tasks. The state, in short, is fundamentally Janus-faced, with an intrinsically dual anchorage in class-divided socio-economic structures and an international system of states (Skocpol, 1979: 32). All states are potentially autonomous, in the sense that they may formulate and pursue goals that are not simply reflective of the demand or interest of social groups, classes, or society (Skocpol, 1985: 9). However, the degree to which they actually are autonomous, and to what effect, varies from case to case (Skocpol, 1979: 29–30). The state has interests of its own, which are not necessarily equivalent to, or fused with, the interests of the dominant class (Skocpol, 1979: 27); indeed, fundamental conflicts of interest might arise between the existing dominant class and the state rulers (Skocpol, 1979: 27, 30). They may compete over appropriating resources from the economic reproduction process. For example, society's resources may indeed be used by the state to enhance its autonomy. This may potentially threaten the dominant class(es). Similarly, Harris (2018) argues that the relation between capital and the state is contingent, for example, when it comes to immigration control and free mobility of capital allowed by the state.

In contrast to classical Marxism, Skocpol's approach is that state power is not inevitably used for dominant class interests, short term or long term. Instead, the two basic tasks of the state are to maintain order and to compete with other actual or potential states. True, states usually function to preserve the existing class relations. But that is because doing so is normally the smoothest way to enforce orders (Skocpol, 1979: 30). It is this task of maintaining order that defines its autonomous relation with subordinate classes. Although both the state and dominant class(es) share a broad interest in keeping the subordinate classes in place in society and at work in the existing economy, the state's own fundamental interest in maintaining sheer physical order and political peace may lead it to enforce concessions to the subordinate classes (Skocpol, 1979: 30). These concessions may come at the expense of the interest of the dominant class(es), but they are not contrary to the state's interest in maintaining order.

Partnership approach

This refers to the idea of partnership between state bureaucracy and capitalists. In line with Marx's (1852a) ideas about the autonomous Bonapartist state (for example, in his *18th Brumaire*), Miliband (1983) says that there are two sets of impulses to state action: external (interests of classes) and internal (interests of state actors). Internal impulses are of two types: the self-interest of state managers, and their conception of the national interest. Since the capitalist state is itself a source of power, prestige, and high salaries, it can serve the self-interest of state managers. Further, those who seek state power persuade themselves that achieving it and holding on to it are synonymous with the national inter-est, whose service is their paramount interest. Internal and external impulses to state action are related, of course. This is in the sense that state managers have been imbued with the belief that the national interest is bound up with the well-being of the capitalist enterprise. So: state actors' interest = capitalists' interest = national interest. Hence, state actors have been attentive to capital-ist interests (Miliband, 1983: 70). Or, as Harman (1991) writes: 'Any state bureaucracy which fails to' help capitalists with accumulation 'is going to see the resources it needs for its own privileges and its own functioning dry up'.[11] That is why decision-making state actors as a group is 'compelled to act as an agent of capital accumulation and to identify *its own interests as national capitalist interests* in opposition both to the interests of foreign capital and the working class' (italics added).

Consequently, the relation between state managers and capitalists is one of partnership between two different, separate forces, linked to each other by many threads, yet each having its separate spheres of actions (Miliband, 1983: 72). The state is never a junior partner, however; the contradictions of capitalism, and class pressures and social tensions, necessitate a more pro-nounced role for the state. But it has to act in the class context – so long as a government works within it (i.e. the capitalist limit), so long does the partnership hold (Miliband, 1983: 73). Like all actors, state actors exercise human agency but within structural constraints, but the dependence of state actors on capitalist accumulation is not passivity: 'Servants may anticipate the orders of their master, or try to stay on the masters' good side while doing as little as possible, or try to play one master off against another' (Roberts, 2017: 218).

Against post-Marxist state autonomists, according to whom the state is completely independent of capitalist class or any other class interest, Miliband (1983: 74) argues that there cannot be a state for itself, a state which is not a partner of anyone. It is difficult to see, he says, how there can be a state whose interests conflict with all classes or groups in society, as Skocpol (1979, 1985) and Meckstroth (2000) claim. The partnership does not mean a merger of the agency of state actors and the agency of the dominant class but it does mean that the state is able to act with considerable independence in regulating class conflict and maintaining and defending the social order of which the ruling class is the main beneficiary.

Alex Callinicos (2017) pursues the partnership idea when he says that 'the mutual alignment of the state and capital in any case doesn't simply represent the former's servile adaptation to the latter'. He says that there is a 'partnership between state managers and capitalists, in which each side pursues their inter-ests, while remaining interdependent'. A policy might finally be 'favourable to the interests of capital' but such an outcome 'may result from a protracted suc-cession of interactions in which the equilibrium position is discovered through a process of trial and error', which suggests that 'the higgling among capital-ists and state managers may serve to redefine the equilibrium position at a very different point, in terms of institutions and policy mix, from where they started'.

> This is one way of conceiving major changes in economic policy regime – say the shift from *laissez faire* to Keynesianism in the 1930s and 1940s, or the adoption of neoliberalism in the 1970s and 1980s . . . as a partially blind, partially ideologically directed discovery process that, in seeking to restore favourable conditions for capital accumulation, may significantly redefine the character of the accumulation process.

This process is complicated and protracted partly because 'neither capital nor the state is homogeneous'.[12]

Like Miliband, Block (1987b) also recognizes that state actors have their independent interests and powers. But Block claims that the exercise of state power takes place in class contexts. State managers are collectively interested in maximizing their power, prestige, and wealth but within political rules of the game given by a set of political institutions. For example, in a democracy, if state managers maximize their self-interest too much, that may jeopardize their chances of returning to power. On the other hand, the bourgeoisie or any other propertied class cannot survive without the state, so they have to seek a modus vivendi with state managers. This modus vivendi has been favourable to capital: state managers have been restrained from attacking private property and have implemented pro-capital policies.

Territorial and capitalist logics approach

This is a structural approach to state autonomy, one that treats the state as a structure of relations. Following Giovanni Arrighi, David Harvey (2010b: 204) says:

> A distinction . . . arises between a logic of power, driven by territorial imperatives and political interests . . . and a capitalistic logic of power that arises from the accumulation of money power in private and corporate hands searching for endless growth through profit-making.

'By territorial logic' Harvey means 'the political, diplomatic, economic and military strategies deployed by the state apparatus *in its own interest*' (p. 204–5; italics added). In contrast, '[t]he capitalist logic . . . focuses on the way in which money power flows across and through space and over borders in the search for endless accumulation. This logic is more processual and molecular than territorial' (ibid.). "The logic that attaches to the territoriality of state power *is very different from* the logic of capital' (p. 156; italics added). The capitalists wish to place their money 'wherever profits are to be had' so they need open spaces in which to move – and state borders can get in the way of that' (p. 205). The two logics are not reducible to each other; however 'they are closely inter-twined' (ibid.). They come together to create fusion which is manifested in 'the state-finance nexus (now represented by the world's central banks)' which means 'a confluence of state and financial power' (Harvey, 2010b: 48).[13]

Institutional-conjunctural approach

This approach to state autonomy is evident in Leo Panitch's work. According to him, the study of the capitalist state must delineate the state institutions in terms of their 'structural selectivity' vis-à-vis the field of political struggle; it must 'maintain a constant stream of empirical research on the specific linkages between state institutions and class actors in terms of ideology, personnel, relations of dependence and influence, and so on', and it must 'situate the first two in relation to the state's functions of promoting capital accumulation and the legitimating capitalist domination of the social order' (Panitch, 2002: 100). More recently, Panitch says:

> [T]he state is neither merely a class instrument nor just composed of class actors but a set of distinctive public institutions which are dependent on, but have *autonomous capacities* to act on behalf of, the capitalist system.
> (Panitch and Gindin, 2015: 18; italics added)

Extending and supporting the political Marxist claim about the separation of the economic from the political (extra-economic), Panitch says that 'state institutions [are] more or less relatively autonomous from class representation and pressures' (ibid.: 10). This implies that the various activities of the state institutions 'cannot be directly traced from some abstract "logic of capital", nor should every state action be attributed to furthering the interests of some or all capitalists' (ibid.). In making this claim, Panitch presupposes that maintaining law and order through 'specialised institutional forms and capacities' and thus reproducing an unequal society are somewhat *independent of* the state's actions that aim to 'facilitate capital accumulation and contain economic contradictions and crises' (ibid.). And, like Alavi, Jessop, Callinicos, and many others, Panitch argues that '[i]t is mainly through processes of trial and error in coping with specific problems in any conjuncture that state actors learn the possibilities and limits of state action in capitalist societies' (ibid.).

State autonomy is expressed in the fact that 'states have actually done that the capitalist classes themselves could not do in promoting and sustaining capital accumulation and social relations' and understanding this 'is in fact crucial to answering the question of why capitalism has survived into the twenty-first century' (p. 11). Panitch says that, therefore,

> the key strategic point we draw from this . . . is that the transformation of the state in the context of a fundamental shift in the balance of class forces must centrally involve transforming public institutional forms, purposes and capacities. (p. 18)

Over-developed and developmentalist approaches

Unlike the Western state, the superstructure in the colony is over-developed in relation to the structure of society in colony. This legacy continues in the post-colonial condition. The post-colonial over-developed state appropriates a very large part of the economic surplus and deploys it in bureaucratically directed economic activity in the name of promoting economic development. Its power has been extended through a range of developmental agencies and para-statal authorities. At the core of this state is a bureaucratic-military apparatus which controls and subordinates indigenous classes. This state is not an instrument of the single class. It works on behalf of landlords, native capitalist class, and neo-colonial capitalist class. The need to mediate among all these classes gives the state a lot of autonomy. Alavi says that there is a structural imperative, which means that the state is not a puppet, that it can take independent actions, and that it can make 'errors' (for example, it can go against the interests of dominant classes), but it can do so only within limits, and must correct its errors sooner or later.

The state is autonomous of narrowly bourgeois interests. Such a state is nonetheless constrained by capitalism whose general interests it must satisfy. From a development perspective, this relatively autonomous state can, under some conditions, be a modernizing state, a disciplining state, an active state, and a pervasive state in the promotion of capitalist development under its national-territorial jurisdiction. Using its autonomous powers, the state removes barriers to capitalism that landlords' power typically creates, makes available cheap finance, creates social and physical infrastructures, protects national enterprises against foreign competition, keeps labour in check, and forces individual capitalists to operate within a national developmental agenda of the state.[14]

Military public order approach

Carter develops a theory which has more in common with the anarchist Bakunin than with Marx. In this theory, which rightly sees the state in its geo-political context, a state (as in post-Revolution Russia) selects economic relations which promote technological development because it is functional for the state to do so. It helps increase the surplus that is needed for developing its defensive capacity. This is important not just because it helps the state compete militarily with other states but also because it enables the state to protect the economic relations which it has chosen to preserve. Given that states compete militarily with one another, and that each state is interested in having as productive an economy as possible in order to remain militarily competitive, state elites will tend to support economic class relations which they regard as most appropriate for furthering technological development (Carter, 1998: 173–5).

5 The working-class agency perspective

In this perspective, the changing balance of class forces determines the role of the state over space and time. State functions reflect a complex parallelo-gram of economic, political, and ideological forces rather than the immediate economic interests of the dominant class (Poulantzas, 1968: 190). The state is always divided by class contradictions. This means two things. On the one hand, different branches of the state 'are often the preeminent representatives of the diverging interests of one or several fractions of the power bloc' although subject to the unity of the state power of the hegemonic fractions (Poulantzas, 1978: 133, 142), so that state policy emerges out of the collision of many micro-policies representing the different fractions. On the other hand, state policy also depends on the relation between the state and the dominated classes because state power is founded on an unstable equilibrium of compromises. Compromise means that state power can take into account the economic inter-ests of some dominated classes; equilibrium means that while economic sacri-fices are real and provide the ground for an equilibrium they do not challenge the political power which sets precise limits to that equilibrium; unstable means that the limits of the equilibrium are set by the political conjuncture, including class struggle (Poulantzas, 1968: 192; see Gramsci, 1971: 182). And the state itself is a terrain of class struggle in that dominated classes are present in the state 'in the form of centers of opposition to the power of the dominant classes', as in later Poulantzas (1978: 142). The state is therefore neither an instrument nor a subject, but a relation. More precisely, the state embodies a power relation-ship between classes and among class factions (Poulantzas, 1976: 12–3, 1978: 128–9).

Esping-Anderson et al. (1976) say that the object of working-class struggle is not policies that are either pro-worker or anti-worker; rather, the policies that the working-class struggles over have varying degrees of classness. For exam-ple, while both minimum-wage law and adequate guaranteed income for all workers are commodified circulationist policies, the former causes minimum disturbance to commodity relations, but the latter poses a greater threat to the interests of capital since it threatens labour's separation from the means of subsistence.

Erik Wright makes a similar argument. Within a given system of production, certain property rights can be socialized and others remain private (Wright, 1993: 24). A firm can therefore have a mixed ownership character. Capitalists may own machines and can use them to generate profit in any way they like. But in reality, they may not have absolute rights on the machines: 'They can only set them in motion, for example, if the machines satisfy certain safety and pollution regulations imposed by the state' (Wright, 2005: 13). Thus, through such mechanisms as state regulations (and union restrictions), 'some dimensions of the property rights in the machines have been transferred from the capitalist to a collective agency', that is, to the state (ibid.). Such redistribution of rights and powers constitutes a form of variation in class relations, that is, in *classness*.

Just as the concept of the capitalist state is rooted in capital's drive for surplus value, the concept of 'the wage-labour's latent state begins with a focus upon the impulse of workers to satisfy their needs'(Lebowitz, 2009: 329). Wage workers, like other commodity sellers, have the need for contract enforcement and other such things needed in a commodity-exchanging system. Workers make the state legalize unions while capital is against unions. Since unemployment weakens workers, 'the state latent in the needs of wage-labourers is one which will foster conditions of full employment' (p. 330). A state acting in their interest can provide 'that which is needed for common satisfaction of needs, such as schools, health services, etc.' (p. 330). In all this respect, 'the state latent in the concept of wage-labour functions much like trade unions' (p. 331). Thus, the state binds not only different fractions of capital but also does it bind individual wage workers, who compel the passing of state legislation in their common interests. But like trade unions, 'the state latent in the concept of wage-labour does not go beyond the capital/wage-labour relation' (p. 332).

Lebowitz (2009) says that 'the capitalist state remains within the bounds of the capitalist relation and supports its continued existence' neither because 'the state *must* support the reproduction of capital' nor because 'the gains workers can make through the state create illusions and sap their otherwise revolutionary spirit'. 'Rather, capital *itself* spontaneously produces illusions – illusions which tend to dissuade a challenge to capitalism as such'. 'It is precisely insofar as workers look upon the requirements of capitalism 'as self-evident natural laws'', as a part of their common sense, 'that makes the capitalist state the guarantor of the reproduction of capital' (p. 335–6). The fact that workers take capitalism for granted and do not challenge it makes the capitalist state the guarantor of the reproduction of capital (p. 335).

From the analytical Marxist standpoint (like that of Erik Wright), Przeworski and Wallerstein say that a government can increase the workers' share of national income by taxing capitalist income and transferring these revenues to the working class. By coordinating wage demands with taxation policy, the state can achieve virtually any income distribution desired – including driving capitalist consumption to near zero – without reducing the rate of investment (Mayer, 1994: 191). Przeworski and Wallerstein conclude that the state in a capitalist society is not structurally dependent upon capital in any static sense. A government sympathetic to the working class is not powerless in the face of capital. There exist policies by which it can redistribute income without wrecking the capitalist economy (p. 192). This refutation of structural dependence theory vindicates the claim of social democrats and Keynesian liberals that a pro-worker government can manage a capitalist economy to give workers as much as they would get under socialism. Hence, socialism becomes ethically unnecessary and politically unlikely in democratic capitalist societies (Mayer, 1994: 192).

From a Polanyian-Marxist perspective, Block (2019), extending his approach to state autonomy in capitalist societies, points to 'the variability in the power exercised by owners in such societies' that can only be explained by factors that 'lie outside of the system of property and production' (ibid.; italics added). It is 'the legal and political system' that 'determines which profit-making strategy', whether productive/efficient or predatory, 'will dominate in a particular society' (ibid.). He says, '[M]ultiple forms of dependence of business groups . . . on state action provides a critical resource or lever for *those seeking political change*' (Block, 2003: 300; italics added). He also says that the economic rules of the game that 'often serve to reinforce the power of business interests . . . can also be changed . . . to make resistance, at least within developed countries, to egalitarian reforms more difficult', so he concludes that therefore 'there are no inherent obstacles to restructuring market societies along democratic and egalitarian lines'(Block, 2003: 300–1).

Using Weber, and echoing Erik Wright, Block (2019: 1171) argues that 'the power exercised by an ownership class is a variable, not a constant as is suggested by property-based essentialism' and the actual amount of power exercised depends on, and is limited by, deep economic and non-economic divisions within that class and by the organization of its opponents (e.g. workers) who can have 'considerable influence over the state'. These views are echoed by Bittle (2015: 147): laws of the state are 'a site for struggling against the dominant ideology of corporate capitalism' and that 'the state is the only countervailing force capable of holding corporations to account', so 'efforts should continue for the state to enact and adequately enforce laws that hold corporations to account for their harmful acts'.

The state autonomy approach of post-modernist Marxists also imputes much power to the ability of the state to improve the conditions of the common people. They argue against 'the etatism that pervaded Marxian politics in the twentieth century' which 'had been dominated by the figure of the state as the ultimate instrument in the hands of the ruling class' (Bhattacharya and Seda-Irizarry, 2015: 676). In place of the Marxist view of the state, the post-modernist Marxist view is that 'the state is pulled and pushed in different contradictory directions', so 'intervening in individual social processes cumulatively could have as *much, if not more, of a transformative effect on the state as any political practice targeted at the state*' (ibid.; italics added). This sort of ideas is a part of broader approach according to which the popular pressure on the state, including through elections, will produce some kind of socialism through the so-called democratic road. This echoes Kautsky (1892) when he says that 'the working class must strive to influence the state authorities, to bend them to its purposes . . . Great capitalists can influence rulers and legislators directly, but the workers can do so only through parliamentary activity'.

6 Structural-strategic approach

Jessop has been a major state theorist over the last three decades or so. He calls himself a plain or non-dogmatic Marxist (Jessop, 2016: 97–8). He has been seeking to build a theory of the state by finding a common ground between the approaches that are more structural and those that are more agency-oriented, where agency is seen in terms of strategies. To quote from a recent writing of Jessop:

> [S]tructure consists in differential constraints and opportunities that vary by agent; agency in turn depends on strategic capacities that vary by structure as well as according to the actors involved. . . . [The] biased composition of constraints and opportunities can only be understood in relation to specific strategies pursued by specific forces in order to advance specific interests over a given time horizon in terms of a specific set of other forces, each advancing its interests through specific strategies.

Structures are constraining but not absolutely so, nor are agents unitary or aware of their conditions:

> Because structures are only strategically selective rather than absolutely constraining, scope exists for actions to overwhelm, circumvent, or subvert structural constraints. Likewise, because subjects are never unitary, never fully aware of the conditions that affect (their) strategic action, never fully equipped to engage in strategic reflection and learning, there are no guarantees that they will largely realize their strategic goals.
>
> (Jessop, 2016: 55)[15]

This ontological view of structure and agency is applied by Jessop to the state. His 'strategic-relational' state theory, which is to be contrasted to capital- and class-theoretical theories, has the following main components (Jessop, 2008: 35–9).

Firstly, the state is

> [a] system of strategic selectivity, i.e. as a system whose structure and *modus operandi* are more open to some types of political strategy than others. Thus a given type of state . . . will be more accessible to some forces than others according to the strategies they adopt to gain state power; and it will be more suited to the pursuit of some types of economic or political strategy than others because of the modes of intervention and resources which characterize that system.[16]

Secondly, the state has no essential institutional and/or class unity. It is the state managers' different strategies that impose a measure of coherence on the activities of the state, so the state becomes 'a site where strategies are elaborated'. The state is indeed 'the site, the generator, and the product of strategies' (Jessop, 2008: 35).

Thirdly,

> the current *strategic selectivity* of the state is in part the emergent effect of the interaction between its past patterns of *strategic selectivity* and the strategies

adopted for its transformation. . . . In turn the calculating subjects that operate on the strategic terrain constituted by the state are in part constituted by the *strategic selectivity* of the state system and its past interventions.

(ibid.: 37)

I will return to Jessop in the following.

7 Existing state theory: a critique of its intellectual context and political implications

The existing literature does unpack multiple aspects of the state. Yet, taken together, it has some serious problems. There are four in particular.

The focus is more on the how, less on the why: or obsession with 'autonomism'

The instrumentalist idea ignores/under-emphasizes the constraints imposed on the state structure or on the state actors by the structure of capitalism itself. The structure of capitalism is to be differentiated from the constraining action of individual capitalists or groups of capitalists as bearers of the capitalist structural relations: even if there are no ties between the state actors and capitalists, the state will, more or less, create conditions for accumulation. In fact, empirically, there are cases where that is the case.[17] For there to be instrumental (agentic) ties, there has to be the state as a structure of relations in the first place. The focus on agentic ties fails to answer the question of why there is the state. The theory, like much state theory as such, does not also consider the coercive power of the state as signifying the fundamental class character of the state. The state can and does, of course, favour specific capitalists in part based on their ties with specific actors/institutions of the state, but that is *not* an essential aspect of the state. It is said that the state acts in the interests of capitalists because it is directly influenced by capitalists, but what is it about the state that allows capitalists to control the state? Why does it not allow socialists to control it?

The political structuralist view as advanced by Poulantzas and the like has problems. If the instrumental control by members of the ruling class is ruled out, then it is not clear what actual mechanisms shape – constrain – state actions. Why is it that a state that is relatively autonomous must meet the dominant class interests, that is, organizing the dominant classes/class fractions and disorganizing the dominated classes. And if the state is as autonomous as the theory says it is, then what stops it from meeting the needs of the masses in significant ways: if the state can give concessions to win their consent in the political interest of the capitalist class, why do masses suffer so much? And what stops state actors themselves, many of whom are from the non-bourgeois background, from making use of their positions within the state to meet their own needs? And, once again, what about the coercive functions of the state? If it is the case that 'the state is not a class instrument, but rather the state of a society divided into classes' (Poulantzas, 1968: 285), then is there inherently nothing capitalist about the state? Is the state merely an entity that maintains cohesion of society which then benefits capitalists?

There is just too much emphasis on *how* the capitalist state works: lacking autonomy, it is used as a tool in the hands of capitalists, or it has a degree of autonomy because of its structural specificity, which is used to benefit capitalists.

> The specificity of the modern State . . . refers precisely to the relative separation of the political from the economic, and to the entire reorganization of its respective spaces and fields implied by the total dispossession of the direct producer in capitalist relations of production.
>
> (Poulantzas, 1978: 54)

The argument is that the separation of the political from the economic allows the state to act autonomously of the personal ties between state actors and capitalists. This is not incorrect, but what is really the theoretical significance of this aspect of the state – that is, its specificity, and its separation from society? The *form* of the state intervention – *how* the state acts (that it acts with a degree of autonomy) – becomes a more important question than the question of the very content of the state, that is, *why* it is that the state must act on behalf of the capitalist class.[18]

State autonomy is especially emphasized in two areas of state theory: the developmental state and welfare state literatures. In the discussions of the welfare state in the West, autonomy of the state is emphasized while ignoring the international dimensions: the threat of communism from the post-revolution societies, apart from the fact that advanced capitalism was experiencing a relatively high (even if declining) rate of profit after the World Wars, unlike in the period since the late 1970s. In the developmental state thinking, state elites in the relatively less developed countries (LDCs) can promote economic development if they can solve the collective action problem of competing capitalists and stop being captured by individual capitalists or by groups of capitalists, and they can even promote the welfare of the masses, if they are progressive. In fact, in no poor capitalist nation that is geographically and demographically large (e.g. India) has there been a successful autonomous developmental state. Besides, even if the autonomous state can promote economic development (as it did in East Asia), it is capitalist development that is not only exploitative; it also politically suppresses workers' rights (Burkett and Hart-Landsberg, 2003). And it subordinates developing nations to imperialism.

There is something nationalistic about existing theory's claim about state power. As we have seen, the autonomy of Western welfare state is emphasized often in abstraction from its international condition. The 'failure' of '1917', or the failure of the transitional state, to help workers construct socialism is used as empirical evidence to dismiss Lenin's theory of the state and revolution, but this is done in a way that *ignores* the global historical-geography of that 'failure', including such factors as: major capitalist states' antagonism towards, and encirclement of, the former USSR; the international law of value; the failure of revolution in advanced countries in part thanks to the (coercive) actions of the Western states; emergence of Stalinism as a combined result of these factors, and so on. Similarly, autonomy of the state is emphasized in the context of some less developed nations without mentioning its global dimension: the political-military mentorship and financial support that the developmental state received during the imperialist nations' fight with communism in the 1960s and 1970s. I refer to the fact that the US provided all kinds of support to East Asian states in order to stop the spread of what it saw as a communist threat.

Dilution of the class character of the state

Given its fetishization of state autonomy, the existing state theory relatively neglects the question of what is common between the capitalist form of the state and its pre-capitalist form. Much state theory under-stresses the necessarily class character of the state. The idea that the state's goal is to unite different fractions of capital, which is partly why the state needs to be autonomous, puts the emphasis on particular capitals. This approach neglects capital as a whole in relation to labour. Clarke (1978: 46) indeed complains that Poulantzas has 'no concept of capital-in-general independent of the state'. That is, capital as a whole exists only politically, only through the state which organizes different fractions of capital into a bloc. Jessop (1982: 221) says that the state is capitalist to the extent that its effects are conducive to the reproduction of the conditions of capital relations of production and capital accumulation. Here the state's inherently capitalist character, which is a mechanism, is reduced to the *effects* of the state's action. Similarly, because the state reproduces commodity relations as such in which *all* classes of capitalist society are involved, it does not safeguard any specific class, according to Offe and Ronge (1982). They say that 'the most abstract and inclusive common denominator of state activities . . . is to guard the commodity form of individual economic actors' in advanced capitalism, and this means that the state does not guard 'the general interests of a particular class'. Much rather, it guards 'the general interest of *all classes* on the basis of capitalist exchange relationships' (ibid.: 252; italics added).[19]

The class character of the state is also diluted when one argues, as does Block, that non-class axes of power (e.g. political power that flows from the control over a party or over access to state power) can be more important than class relations. So the Marxist emphasis on the primacy of property relations is considered inferior to Polanyi's 'primacy of politics': in the latter concept, democratic states and societies subordinate markets to achieve socially progressive goals (Block, 2011: 6). For some, the relation between capitalists and the state is a matter of contingency rather than necessity and is indicative of a high level of state autonomy. This is mistaken. Harris (2018: 218) says: '[A]llowing capital mobility in essence broke – or profoundly weakened – the link between capital and the State, or at least made it, from the viewpoint of corporations, one of contingent calculation rather than unquestioned predetermination.' Harris also thinks that the example of immigration controls is an evidence of the 'autonomy' of state policy-making from capital and class structure. Creaven says:

> This [argument] is remarkably weak. As Callinicos rightly points out, capital does indeed have an interest in the existence and persistence of these state measures, irrespective of whether or not the working class is 'united and threatening'; after all, only by keeping the workers divided can their unified resistance to capitalist rule be forestalled.
>
> (Creaven, 2000: 261)

As we have seen, Carter, Skocpol, and others say that the state's geopolitical military activities are independent of class processes. But war-making can be a class process (for example, military competition can be a mechanism of feudal accumulation) and, in contemporary times, war-making is an important part of military-industrial capitalism (Callinicos, 1987: 160–71). Besides, why is the state interested in maintaining order, who benefits from it, who is a threat to order, and why? What is it about class relations that make the state maintaining order coincide with the state keeping the class relations intact coincide? What is problematic in the post-Marxist 'autonomist' theories is the idea that maintaining order and military competition have no necessary connection to class antagonisms.

A form of the relative neglect of the class character of the state occurs when theorists ignore, or under-emphasize, any distinction between the state and class structure. Harman (1991) says that 'state revenues are comparable to the other revenues that accrue to different sections of capital – to the rents accruing to landowners, the interest going to money capital, the profits from trade going to commodity capital' or from 'capitalist exploitation at the point of production' (ibid.). So there is no distinction between the state actors and the members of the capitalist class. Just as there is continual conflict between these different types of capitalists over the sizes of the different revenues, 'so there is continual conflict between the state bureaucracy and the rest of the capitalist class over the size of its cut from the total surplus value' (ibid).

> The state bureaucracy will, on occasions, use its own special position, with its monopoly of armed force, to make gains for itself at the expense of others. In response to this, *the other sections of capital* will use their own special position – industrial capital its ability to postpone investment, money capital its ability to move overseas – to fight back. Yet in all this the different sections of capital cannot forget their mutual interdependence.
>
> (ibid.; italics added)

Harman's terms, 'the rest of the capitalist class' and 'the other sections of capital', suggest that state bureaucracy, necessarily, is one of the many segments of the capitalist class itself. Such an approach would make it difficult to explain the state in terms of capitalist class relations.

In terms of the dilution of class character of the state, consider the influential work of Jessop. Jessop rightly refuses 'a radical distinction between state power and class power' (2008: 31), but he does not do this from the standpoint of the primacy of class relations. For him, class as a structure of relations is not as powerful as many Marxists have thought. Arguing in a semi-pluralist style, Jessop, echoing Brock, says that 'class power and domination are inevitably limited', and this is 'because of the contradictions and antagonisms inherent in the capital relation'[20] or because of 'the existence of other forms of domination and of competing principles of societal organization' than class relations (Jessop, 2016: 98).

Jessop emphasizes the differential impact of the state on the capacity of 'class-relevant' forces to pursue their interests. Although the state may be more open to some policies and less to others, it does not display this selectiv- ity *irrespective of* the ways class forces pursue their policy preferences – the state does not display its selectivity *irrespective of* the strategies that class forces deploy. This implies that there is nothing prior to the ways in which the state impacts classes: that is, irrespective of how classes actually politically behave, the state cannot be said to have any structural bias in favour of, or against, certain classes. What indeed is a *structural* relation between the state and classes becomes a matter of *strategic action* of classes, that is, action mediated by the strategies of classes.

It is easy to agree with Jessop that the state system will have differential impact on the capacity of class and class-relevant forces. But Jessop says that this is not because of the class nature of the state as such but because of 'the relation between state structures and the strategies which different forces adopt towards it' (Jessop, 2008: 36). The state 'comprises an ensemble of centres that offer unequal chances to different forces, internal and external, to act for dif- ferent political purposes' (2016: 247). 'State power is a complex social relation that reflects the changing balance of social forces in a determinate *conjuncture*' (ibid.; italics added). So the *inherently* class nature of the state is under-stressed. To the extent that the class nature is discussed, it is more a matter of quantity rather than essential quality. Consider the following statement, for example: the state 'does *differentially* advance the ideal or the material interests of capital (or both) by comparison to the exercise of powers by other classes and social forces' (Jessop, 2016: 97; italics added). The state is just more pro-capitalist and less pro-workers.

The vocabulary of Jessop's work is dominated by such class-neutral terms as 'the state as a complex institutional ensemble', 'a site of political practices', 'various institutions', 'capacities', 'ensemble', 'agency', 'projects', 'subjects', 'strategies', 'selectivity', 'subsystem', 'ecological dominance', 'structuration of social relations', 'social power', and so on (Jessop, 2016: 246–8). He does not mention class, socialism/communism, Lenin, and the like, even once in the section 'Whither state theory' in a recent book of his (Jessop, 2016: 246–9).

Consider Jessop's general definition/characterization of the state:

> [T]he state can be defined as a relatively unified ensemble of socially embedded, socially regularized, and strategically selective, institutions, organizations, social forces and activities organized around (or at least involved in) making collectively binding decisions for an imaginary political community.
>
> (Jessop, 2002: 40)

There is nothing about class here. This neglect of class is also clear when he says that the state is a 'distinct ensemble of institutions and organizations whose socially accepted function is to define and enforce collectively binding decisions on the members of a society in the name of their common interest or general will' (Jessop, 1990: 341) in a context of class domination. So the state has no essential class character. It just happens to operate in a class context. This is consistent with his claim that state theorizing is just a specific instance of examination of the relation between structure and strategic action (Jessop, 2016: 249).

Under-conceptualization of class struggle

While there is some existing discussion on how class struggle affects state policies, this relation is under-conceptualized. It does not adequately appreciate the fact that economic and political concessions from the state – especially those that are significant and are, more or less, durable – are less because of the struggle for these concessions as such and more because they are the by-products of revolutionary struggle, and that this revolutionary struggle – struggle against the capitalist rules of the game – is exactly something that the state necessarily suppresses.

Over-emphasis on capitalist class fractions in the work of such writers as Poulantzas leads to an under-emphasis on class struggle between capital and labour at the level of the state. Indeed, Poulantzas writes,

> The contradictions . . . reflected within the state are those among the dominant classes and fractions and between these and their supporting clsses, far more than the contradictions between the power bloc and the working class. The latter are basically expressed in the bourgeois state at a distance. (in Clarke, 1978: 47–8)

Also, Poulantzas' structuralism colours his view of class struggle, in the sense that class struggle is seen as constrained by, and confined within, the structure. As a result there is little indication that class struggle can also influence the structure that constrains it (Holloway, 1991: 97; Wright, 1978: 21).

For Poulantzas and those who follow him (e.g. Jessop, Thomas, and many others), state power is to be understood as the condensation of, or form taken by, class struggles that vary historically and spatially. The state is the factor of cohesion and equilibrium of a social formation. This view is very close to the view that the state really is able to reconcile the opposed classes, even if in a contradictory manner. This is fundamentally anti-Marxist because in Marxism, the state arises precisely because reconciliation between the basic classes is *not* possible (see more on this in the following).

Unlike Poulantzas and other structuralists, Clarke does not think that class and state as structures are permanent. Rather they are subject to, and reproduced through, class struggle. While Clarke stresses class struggle, the emphasis on political economy of capitalist production – what he calls the abstract analysis of capitalist – suffers from a relative neglect, however. The class struggle approach from Clarke and others tends to under-stress the role of the state in ensuring accumulation.

Lebowitz (2009: 335–6) says that as workers accept capitalism as natural, this fact allows the state to guarantee the reproduction of capital. In other words, the balance of power – class politics, and not the class character of the state itself – is a reason why the state works on behalf of capital. Lebowitz argues that the struggle to make the state an agency of workers must be continuous. This process will change the workers into a political agency and will change their conditions. 'We cannot be indifferent to the form of the state *as an agency of workers*' (p. 336: italics added).[21]

Many theorists fruitfully emphasize the influence of class struggle on the state. But it is not enough that Marxist state theorists recognize the relation between the state and class struggle. (Some non-Marxists do that as well.) As Lenin (1949: 11) says in *The state and revolution*, 'the bourgeois, and particularly the petty-bourgeois, ideologists, [are] compelled under the weight of indisputable historical facts to admit that the state only exists where there are class antagonisms and a class struggle'. But then they dilute the class character of the state which prompts Lenin to assert: 'From what the petty-bourgeois and philistine professors and publicists say, with quite frequent and benevolent references to Marx, it appears that the state does *reconcile* classes' (ibid.; italics added). Much state theory, sadly, reflects Lenin's (1949) characterization of the thinking about the state on the part of 'the petty-bourgeois and philistine professors and publicists'.

The fact that the state is an organ of class rule is sought to be more explicitly refuted by many. For example, Bratsis (2002: 252) says that the Leninist approach is guilty of viewing the state as a unified subject because of its assumption that 'the individuals who "control" the state share a class consciousness without explaining how this may happen and what conditions are necessary for this process to be successful'. So the objective class character of the state is mistakenly assumed to depend on the nature of consciousness of those who manage the affairs of the state.

Reformism

In terms of political implications, the existing state theories appear to be different but they have much common ground: taken as a totality, they are more reformist – or reform-oriented – than not. Intellectual *over*-emphasis on the autonomy of the state is associated with an *under*-emphasis on the revolutionary approach to the state, that is, with political reformism. There is a mistaken attempt on the part of some to treat existing theories as being (consistent with) the revolutionary Marxism of Lenin and Luxemburg.[22]

According to Poulantzas, because the state has a degree of autonomy and is not an instrument of the capitalist class, as Ellner (2017) notes, it can be used for the working class on the basis of its *tactical* (not *necessarily strategic*) alliance with other elements (e.g. 'socialistic' elements that are inclined towards the reform of the system but not its elimination, including even parties such as the US Democratic party). This view is far from Marx's call to overthrow capitalism. As Ellner argues, if, as per the later writings of Poulantzas, the relatively autonomous state is not a tool in the hands of the capitalists and if it is a terrain of struggle, then this means that it is possible to have not only tactical alliance but also strategic alliance between the proletarians and the reformist elements (better-paid educated workers and even sections of the capitalist class). Such a view also rejects the big day – ruptural revolutionary idea – scenario where the working class seizes power.

Thomas (2002: 76) notes, Poulantzas' *State, Power, Socialism* is much more Gramscian than orthodox Leninist. In it 'Poulantzas tells us that class struggle should aim not at capturing the state apparatus from without, but rather at transforming it from within', a stance for which Thomas praises Poulantzas. Thomas (2002: 77) adds that according to Poulantzas, who settled accounts with some of his past Leninist views, 'a successful democratic transition to socialism . . . would have to be more flexible than the axiomatic and legendary Leninist coup d'état'. In other words, '[i]t would instead have to involve at one and the same time coordination of action within the state, action to transform the state, and action at a distance from the state'. Poulantzas has stressed 'the need to preserve and extend the institutions and values of representative democracy alongside, though not at the expense of, direct rank-and-file democracy in the transition to socialism' (Thomas, 2002: 77).[23]

According to Thomas (2002: 78), 'Poulantzas was stimulated . . . to complete his trajectory from Leninist vanguardism to a distinctively left-Eurocommunist position under the impulse and impetus provided by his very own analyses of contemporary authoritarian regimes'. Thomas (2002: 74) praises what he calls Poulantzas' 'principled denial of the continuing validity of the Leninist "dual power" strategy of building up a counterstate outside the capitalist state', and he also praises Poulantzas' logic of the denial: that strategy 'had done nobody any good in Greece or Portugal, and that, in any case, the capitalist state had, by the late 1960s or early 1970s, undergone significant, and presumably irreversible, changes since Lenin's time'.

The upshot of all this is that institutions of the state, including those that claim to be representative, do not have a necessary class character, and these can be modified to suit the interests of the masses. It is true that the instrumentalist theory can have a politically progressive implication: to the extent that the state functions the way that instrumentalism describes, such a view helps demystify the liberal view of a class-neutral state (Ollman, 1982). Instrumentalists, with a revolutionary tendency, believe that state policies in the real interest of the majority can happen only after revolution, so they rule out the possibility of workers' organizations being in an alliance with others (e.g. moderate social democratic parties) managing the state (Ellner, 2017: 34). Since the state does not have much autonomy, leftist governments might not be able to do much for the masses. However, if the capitalist character of the state is because of the nature of state actors (personnel) and that the state is capitalist in the sense that state actors share capitalist views and are linked to (or are themselves) capitalists, then it follows that if the personnel are working-class people, the state can serve working-class interests. This is the objective implication of the instrumentalist irrespective of the specific subjective intentions of writers such as Miliband.

Indeed, Miliband was not opposed to the strategy of working within the state, and he thought that at the local scale, middle-class elected officials of the left can do much for the working class (Ellner, 2017). According to Heinrich (2004: 202), '[the] instrumentalist conception of the state usually leads to the demand for an *alternative* use of the state'. In this conception, the idea that the state can contribute to welfare of everyone 'should finally be taken seriously and the interests of other classes more strongly taken into consideration' (ibid.). Some instrumentalists (e.g. those with reformist tendencies) 'believe that under capitalist relations a different politics . . . is possible' and that ' "better" policies are expected from the participation of leftists parties in government' (Heinrich, 2004: 202). When such a government disappoints the workers, instrumentalists believe that that is an unnecessary cost of compromise or because of the betrayal of the leaders of leftist parties (Ellner, 2017). Over time, Miliband's and Poulantzas' ideas about the state showed convergence in terms of instrumentalism and structuralism or in relation to the topic of state autonomy. And Miliband, like Poulantzas, was critical of Lenin's state theory, including his idea about the need for smashing the bourgeois state and establishment of a proletarian state under the democratic control of the proletarians.

Panitch (2002: 103–4) rightly believes that '[t]he point of radical theory . . . is to effect real political change' and that the state theory which was developed since the late 1960s has had a specific political implication. But the question is, what *kind* of implication? Panitch argues for

> fundamentally changing the old social-democratic or Communist parties, or, more likely, building new ones concerned with and capable of not just entering the state, but transforming its structures, linkages with civil society, and relations with other states.

In these lines, Panitch describes his own approach towards what is to be done – an approach which, in terms of its objective effects on politics, is, at best, a 'left-social-democratic' approach.

Indeed, Panitch, who is rightly critical of the state autonomist theory for its reformism,[24] says that '[w]e need to reappropriate the concept of structural reforms from the IMF's agenda. . . [and we need to see these as the] reforms which do not just ameliorate capitalist conditions but build cumulatively towards overcoming those conditions' (Panitch and Gindin, 2015: 19). As the quantity of reform obtained by common people through their struggles increases, a time will come when the state will be qualitatively changed, so there is no need for any revolutionary approach. Gradualism will do. It is as if there is nothing about the capitalist state that will stop this from happening. Panitch believes that it is possible, under capitalism, to build public institutions 'to allow for the diverse capacities and expressions of humanity to be nurtured. This must become a central strategic concern of socialists, which the old notion of "dual power" *and* the new one of "changing the world without taking power" both completely avoid' (ibid.). Panitch stresses 'the importance of making the public goods and services required to meet workers' collective needs the central objective of class struggle' (p. 17). Panitch continues:

> Indeed we must be mindful of whether even national let alone local or sectoral campaigns for higher incomes translate effectively into *class* struggles, insofar as such campaigns may emphasise *competition among workers for greater access to individualised consumption.*
>
> (p. 21; italics added)[25]

Such a view has two implications. One is that workers' economic daily struggle against capitalists is under-emphasized. Another is that it can directly negate Lenin's and Marx's *theory of the state*: 'The worn-out concepts of the smashing of the state and the withering away of the state do not begin to capture this' (i.e. his approach) (p. 19). This approach is miles away from Lenin's and Marx's view on the state. This is the kind of approach that belonged to the 'indifferentists' whom Marx (1873) mocked at using their voice:

> [I]f the workers replace the dictatorship of the bourgeois class with their own revolutionary dictatorship, then they are guilty of the terrible crime of *lèse-principe.* . . . Workers must not even form single unions for every trade, for by so doing they perpetuate the social division of labour as they find it in bourgeois society; this division, which fragments the working class, is the true basis of their present enslavement.

One can agree with Panitch that the working class does need its own institutions. But these are not the type that the Lenin legacy argues for (e.g. councils of workers as proto-state organizations; democratically organized disciplined parties with a high level of theoretical, political, and historical consciousness).

> The types of parties that can transform working classes into leading agents of social transformation have yet to be invented. Recognising this will

finally free us from the moorings of either 1917 or 1945 that have so badly
tethered previous attempts at party-building or renewal.

(Panitch and Gindin, 2015: 20)

Panitch seems to want to go beyond both revolutionary Marxism of Lenin and
commonly prevalent social democratic ideas. For him, '[t]he goal is not to turn
the state into a working-class instrument but to transform public institutions
so that they are oriented to acting on behalf of all humanity in a democratic
socialist system' (p. 18–9).[26]

Consider a former student of Leo Panitch, Stephen Maher, a supporter of
democratic socialism. Writing for a recent symposium on state theory in a
Marxist journal, he says: 'The contemporary democratic socialist revival should
be understood as an opportunity for *transforming* the state' through 'electoral
campaigns and extra-institutional workplace struggles and social movements'
(Maher and Khachaturian, 2021: 192). Like many others', Maher's approach to
Lenin implies the following: what happened *empirically*, that is, in a given *historical* context and within the *geographical* boundary of Russia (i.e. the failure of
1917 revolution to establish socialism), can be employed to critique Lenin's *theory* as such. This is clear when Maher says: 'This history [Russia's post-1917 his-
tory] is often blurred by [Leninists'] calls for smashing the state today' (p. 194).

Scholars like Maher, of course, recognize that '[t]he state is inherently structured to reproduce capitalism' (so class relations impact the state), but, that is
only a half-truth to them, for the state 'also presents opportunities for democratic movements to counter-organize within and across its institutions' and, as
Poulantzas had argued, 'it provides a terrain on which working-class demands
can be formed, contested, and possibly implemented' (p. 194). The state can
be democratized 'so that it governs differently' (p. 196), and this will open up
opportunities for a democratically run economy: 'The struggle to transform
the state is indispensable for democratizing the economy' (p. 197). Without
overthrowing capitalism, the capitalist state and the capitalist economy can be
slowly democratized through socialist strategies. These strategies include things
like the new green deal (state investment in new green technologies, and the
like) and nationalization of banks, development of 'public, participatory institutions for the democratic planning of investment', and so on. In part influenced by his mentor (Panitch), Maher argues:

> Waging a struggle within and against the state would require building new
> forms of participation and working-class organization, all aiming for even-
> tually breaking with capitalist social relations. Yet if the latter is to take
> place, it will be neither through a single rupture with the existing order,
> nor a smooth evolution.

(p. 197)

It is recognized that there are limits to what can be done by the state, but
'[w]ithin certain limits', the capitalist state, given its contradictions, can 'serve

as a terrain of struggle' (p. 195). It is one thing to say that the state can be a terrain of struggle for reforms. But this claim cannot be conflated with the claim
that the *capitalist* state will wither away and be transformed into a socialist state,
through the struggle for reforms. Scholars like Maher do not ask: how can
the limits be breached, and what happens when the limits are (close to being)
breached? That there are limits to what the state can do is recognized, and the
need to break with capitalism is broached, by democratic-socialist state theorists, but such discursive intervention is more rhetorical than real: they go on
as if there are no limits.

Consider David Harvey (2019), who has recently said that capitalism is too
big to fail (more on this later), which means that the state can be used to significantly improve the conditions of the masses by putting pressure on capitalists.
About the state, Harvey (2008a: 20) further says:

> Merchant capital went outside of the constraints of feudal power in its
> explorations and exploitation of the world market. In effect this was a
> geographical strategy that gained power from outside of the bastions of
> feudalism and then, having surrounded the latter, forced them to surrender
> to bourgeois power. The state that protected feudal interests was captured
> and transformed and put to bourgeois uses (is the US state as currently
> constituted anything other than an executive committee for the protection
> of corporate interests?).

Harvey draws a political lesson from the aforementioned discussion that the
capitalist class can be captured and transformed by the working class (gradually)
in its own economic interest, even at the local scales:

> While socialism in one country (let alone city) may be impossible, this
> does not mean that the territoriali-sation of political struggle, the occu-
> pation of this or that city, region or nation state as a staging ground for
> broader assaults upon the political power of capitalist elites, is irrelevant.
>
> (ibid.)

In other words, if, in capitalism, the bourgeoisie uses the state, why not the
working class? Or if, in a feudal society, capitalists gradually gained state power,
then in capitalist society, why can the working class not gradually gain economic power? That the bourgeois revolution and socialist revolution are different in their fundamental class content is blurred. That the working class must,
unlike the bourgeoisie, achieve state power first is, more or less, thrown to the
wind. Underlying this mistaken view of social change is a mistaken theory of
the state. The practical implication of the state autonomy approach, including
the developmental state thinking, is also reformist. It imputes far too much
power to the state apparatuses to promote development in the global periphery.

In short, the objective effect of the ideas of the stalwarts of state theory –
Miliband, Poulantzas, and many others and those who have been influenced

by them – is reformism. Miliband's left social democracy (left of labour) and Poulantzas's euro-communism[27] are not dissimilar to the ideas that are 'popular among the proponents of the pink tide in Latin America in the 2000s, or among leading thinkers and supporters of Syriza in Greece' and elsewhere (Barker, 2019). And their ideas were very similar to those of more recent academic Marxists such as Harvey, Wright, Panitch, Block, and so on, who have written about the state. Direct proletarian assault on the state to replace it is not on their agenda. Broadly, their ideas are Kautsky-ite: the state should not be smashed but changed from within through constant struggle for permanent, or uninterrupted, reforms.

One reason why I have discussed the reformist character of much state theory is that the reformist views are a window to the nature of the explanatory views about the state. Of course, one could say that a theorist's explanatory analysis of the state is correct, but their views on what is to be done about the state may be reformist. This may be true within limits. I am more inclined to think that if the views of a theorist about what is to be done with the state are reformist, then their underlying views about how to explain the state are likely to be inadequate:

> If it is possible to place a given person's general type of thought on the basis of his relation to concrete practical problems, it is also possible to predict approximately, knowing his general type of thought, how a given individual will approach one or another practical question. That is the incomparable educational value of the dialectical method of thought.
>
> (Trotsky, 1973: 431–2)

Therefore, a necessary task of Marxist state theory should be to expose the futility of the philosophical and theoretical ideas behind the advocacy for 'permanent' reforms, including on the part of some who call themselves Marxists. I cannot help thinking that their wrong explanatory views of the state and society are behind their reformist political prescription concerning the state and society.

8 Conclusion

Existing theoretical ideas have contributed to our understanding of the state in many ways. According to some, the state works on behalf of capitalists because capitalists and educated middle-class men and women, who share their ideology and support the particular or general interests of capitalists, occupy top unelected bureaucratic positions or gain seats in the parliament or otherwise influence the state. In other words, the capitalist class uses the state as an instrument, with the state lacking autonomy. Alternatively, because workers, separated from the means of production, do not have to be physically forced to work for a wage, a separate sphere of extra-economic coercion exists, which is the state, but the state uses its relative autonomy to defend political hegemony of capitalists, and to create general conditions for capitalist accumulation which the competing self-interested capitalists will not ensure or which they might indeed undermine. The state keeps working masses disorganized by giving concessions, and it keeps the different fractions of the capitalist class united. A part of this argument is institutional separation-ism: the idea that state is institutionally *separate* from capitalist economy and the state depends on taxes, so the state must do things to promote capitalist production and exchange without which its own material basis will be at risk.

In another school of thought, what the state does reflects the balance of power between the basic classes outside the state and inside the state, within which opposed classes are present. For some, class struggle ultimately reproduces the state, and for others, class struggle for economic concessions can undermine the boundary between the economic and the political and therefore threaten state power itself (struggle against high rent becomes the struggle against the courts that protect the rent system itself).

The state's benefits for the masses are limited because of various general mechanisms. The state is controlled by the dominant class and used by it as an instrument, making it serve its own interests. This limits what the state can do for the masses. Alternatively, if the capitalist structure is such that the state is institutionally 'separate' from the sphere of capitalist accumulation (as mentioned earlier), the state, at least, in part, for its own survival, must promote capitalist accumulation. This in turn means that the state can only do limited things for the masses, except that by promoting capitalist accumulation, the state can indirectly benefit the masses by helping create jobs and suchlike. State actors have their own autonomous interests too, and to the extent that their interests coincide with the capitalists interests, the state does not fundamentally benefit the masses.

These ideas *do* reveal important aspects of the state and are therefore useful. Some of these ideas are also more or less shared by Marx in *Capital volume 1* or are consistent with Marx's ideas about the state in that text. These ideas are, however, problematic in many ways. It is said that the state acts in the interests of capitalists because it is directly influenced by capitalists, but what is it about the state that allows capitalists to control the state? And why does it not allow socialists – or workers interested in a cooperative society – to control it? It is often said that the capitalist state cannot do this or that because the capitalist class constrains state's actions as the state depends on taxes (for example, it is said that the state cannot tax capitalists because they will move elsewhere or will go on an investment strike). The constraints on the state do exist; it is true that the state is indebted or the state depends on taxes. But, to me, these constraints have a *derivative* existence – they do not define the essential nature of the state. The separation of the state from capitalist economy is more a matter of the surface reality of capitalism. The major problem is the fact that, and this might be hard to believe, the inherently class character of the capitalist state is under-emphasized in much existing theory, and that means that the limits to the extent to which state can provide concessions are under-conceptualized. This reproduces what Lenin calls 'unreasoning trust' in the capitalist state.

The class character of the state and how exactly it functions (e.g. how autonomous it is) belong to different levels of analysis. They do not have the same causal importance in explaining what the state does. The first has primacy. And the degree of state's autonomy is much less than assumed. The fact that commodities, including labour power, are exchanged freely and that no one can force a worker to work for a certain capitalist explains *how* the state works, but it does not, and cannot, explain the fact that in capitalism there is, and there will be, a state. That there is a state in capitalism is explained by the same fact that there is a state in pre-capitalism, and this is where the theoretical ideas from Marx/Engels and from the Lenin legacy about the state are useful.

Finally, a word about the style of state theorizing. I accept that Marxist language needs to be different from the language used by others, to some extent. Marx (1887: 20) says:

> It is . . . self-evident that a theory which views modern capitalist production as a mere passing stage in the economic history of mankind, must make use of terms different from those habitual to writers who look upon that form of production as imperishable and final.

And it can be at times a little difficult to understand in part because the content of analysis refers to fundamental, often-hidden, structures of relations. Yet a large amount of state theorizing suffers from avoidable abstractionism and verbosity.[28] The 'ratio' of substantive content to the number of words used is often rather low. This means that statements that are super-abstract and verbose explain little about the state and can hardly be a guide to class struggle against it.

Yet, there is much in existing state theory that *is* useful. In the next nine chapters, I combine some of the existing ideas from the post-1960s state theory with the insights from Marx and Engels as well as the ideas from Lenin (and his intellectual legacy, especially Trotsky) to offer an outline of a Marxist state theory that is broadly in line with *Capital volume 1*. Given the centrality of that text to my perspective, in *every* chapter, I begin with a question (or a comment) from that text.

Notes

1 It is conventional to organize reviews of state theory around the Poulantzas–Miliband debate. The current chapter refrains from this discursive strategy, although it discusses the ideas of the duo. The debate 'erupted within a paradoxical historical context defined by the political rebellions of 1968 and the dominance of a social science preoccupied with "pluralism" and "system equilibrium"' (Barrow, 2002: 5). That debate *has* remained an important part of the landscape of state theory.

2 Parts of this discussion draw on Das (1996, 2006).

3 By this, I refer here to mainly capitalists. I use the term 'capitalists' to include large-scale landowners too: the surplus value that they appropriate includes mainly profit, but it may also include ground rent.

4 According to Miliband, whose early work popularized the instrumentalist theory, personnel at the height of the state system (including the government, legislature, bureaucracy, army, and judiciary) have tended to belong to the economically dominant classes (1977: 69). In other words, the bourgeoisie directly controls the state: they have legislative seats, advise the government, sit on commissions and regulatory boards, make decisions on behalf of the state, present (even write) actual bills for legislative consideration, fund political parties, and so on.

5 The state has many institutions which have differences among them, but they act, more or less, coherently as parts of the same system because of their common ideology: most state elites, including those who are not members of the capitalist class, 'accept as beyond question the capitalist context in which they operate' (Miliband, 1969: 72–75).

High-level state actors, including those who are bourgeois by class origin and those who become bourgeois by virtue of their education, connections, and way of life (Miliband, 1977: 69), share bourgeois ideology. That is, they share a commitment to the rationality of capitalism and a belief that the national interest is inextricably bound up with the wealth and strength of capitalist enterprises. It is natural, therefore, that they seek to help businesses and businesspersons (Miliband, 1969: 76–77). Creaven (2000: 264–265) writes:

> [T]he state elites of contemporary capitalist societies are recruited almost entirely from the ranks of the propertied 'upper class', share common patterns of socialisation and education with those who are destined to become 'captains of industry', maintain close social networks (including ties of marriage) with fellow members of this class (and with no others), and often maintain business interests and connections even during their tenure as state officials. This can hardly be seen as demonstrating a merely contingent relationship between state and capital, as is claimed by opponents of the 'instrumentalist' view of the state.

Hay (1999: 166) says, instrumentalist mechanisms that explain the nature of *the state in capitalist society* include '[s]ocialisation, interpersonal connections'.

6 See Ducange et al. (2019) for a recent discussion on his work; see also Thomas (2002).

7 As Poulantzas (1969: 73) famously said,

> if the function of the State in a determinate social formation and the interests of the dominant class in this formation coincide, it is by reason of the system itself: the direct participation of members of the ruling class in the State apparatus is not the cause but the effect, and moreover a chance and contingent one, of this objective coincidence.

8

> Because all elements of society depend on private investment for economic growth, for employment, and for tax revenue to finance state expenditures, governments are obliged to make the profitability of 'their' capitalists a priority, at least given that capitalist property relations are unchallenged.
>
> (Brenner, 2006: 23)

> Politicians and state bureaucrats typically seek to enhance the wealth and power of their state both internally and in external relations. To do so . . . requires that they facilitate accumulation within their borders to find ways to extract wealth from elsewhere.
>
> (Harvey, 2010b: 205–206)

The state is 'interested in the accumulation of wealth and power on a territorial basis', so it promotes capitalist accumulation (Harvey, 2014: 157).

'[T]he reproduction of the state relies heavily on the fortunes of capital, because state revenue depends on the profitability of enterprise and the level of employment' (Saad-Filho, 2019: 195). If the state implements unacceptable policies, then capital will refuse to invest and pay taxes and if necessary will resort to violence (p. 196).

Jessop (2012: 335) says that 'the modern state's activities depend on a healthy, growing economy – which ties political programmes to economic imperatives'.

9 'The state performs various non-class processes that secure conditions of existence for private industrial capitalists. These include guaranteeing private property, limiting trade union challenges, . . . , [etc.]' (Wolff and Resnick, 2012: 233).

10

> The state autonomy perspective that emerged in the 1980s involved the theoretical assertion of the institutional autonomy of the state at the very time when the structural power of capital and the strategic and ideological reach of capitalist classes has become perhaps never more nakedly visible, with the arrival of neoliberalism.
>
> (Panitch (2002: 92, 103).

11 Just as the individual capitalist can choose to enter in one line of business rather than another, but cannot avoid the compulsion to exploit and accumulate in whatever line he goes into, so the state bureaucracy [and politicians] can move in one direction or another, but cannot ignore the needs of national capital accumulation without risking its own longer term future.

> (ibid.)

12 While Trump banned Muslim immigrants into the US, most of the big IT companies, which operate globally and employ cosmopolitan workforces, objected to the ban.

13 In this nexus,

> the state management of capital creation and monetary flows becomes integral to . . . the circulation of capital . . . The reverse relation also holds as taxes or borrowings flow into the coffers of the state and as state functions also become monetized, commodified and ultimately privatised.
>
> (ibid.)

14 There is a large amount of literature on this topic (see Chapter 11).

15 This view is contrasted to the view 'that regards structure as equally constraining or facilitating for all agents' (Jessop, 2016: 55).

16 In other words, as Bratsis (2002: 259–260) says representing Jessop's view,

> strategic selectivity radicalizes the contingency of the ways by which the form of the state participates in the production of class domination; . . . states are not neutral sites with reference to political strategies of social forces, but are more open to some political strategies than others.

17 The social backgrounds of state personnel vary widely. The bourgeoisie may not occupy important positions in the state. For example, throughout most of the 19th century, in capitalist Britain the whole business of government remained the guaranteed domain of the landed aristocracy, not the bourgeoisie.

18 'Marxist state theory has a tendency to treat the modern state as a distinctly political organ disaggregated, relatively speaking, from the economic structure of society', that is, from the class structure and political economy of society (Lasslett, 2015: 641).

19

> It is the acknowledged result of a discussion conducted internationally among Marxists in the 1960s and 70s about the social form of capitalist state power, that the 'class

character' of this does not consist – or at least, not principally – in the use of state force against (protesting) workers, in overt class justice and other direct forms of oppression and disadvantage, but rather in the neutrality of state power vis-à-vis any kind of private property.

(Gerstenberger, 2009: 669)

'In this way, the characterization of bourgeois state power as the 'executive of the bourgeois class as a whole', as Marx and Engels wrote in the *Communist Manifesto*, while very enlightening historically, was theoretically criticized as insufficient' (ibid.; see Das, 2022a for a defence of the idea of the state in that seminal text).

20 This is also Fred Block's argument, as we have seen.

21 Given this view, Lebowitz's (2009: 337) comment that the capitalist state cannot be used to go beyond capital loses its force.

22

[W]hat is Miliband's 'instrumentalist' claim that the state has been captured by the capitalist class by way of its political organization other than a repetition of Lenin's argument that the state is an instrument of the capitalist class and, necessarily, his defense of organization and the role of the revolutionary party (a result of the instrumentalist concept of power common to both)?

(Aronowitz and Bratsis, 2002: xiii)

What is Poulantzas's 'structuralist' claim that the state is capitalist by virtue of its functions and acts to disorganize the working class other than a repetition of Luxemburg's argument that the state apparatuses are by function bourgeois and, necessarily, her defense of self-organized and autonomous working-class movements (that is, outside the formal and legal logic of 'the state' and hierarchical organization)?

(ibid.)

23

Without a parliamentary, representative forum within which issues could be raised, ventilated, discussed, and decided upon, there would and could be no guarantee that the emergent organs of direct, rank-and-file democracy would not be crushed by a self-appointed vanguard party . . . It follows that the liberties of a plural party system are not, and should not be regarded as being, anything but a Lenin-defined smoke screen concealing the maneuverings of a predatory bourgeoisie seen as the personification of capital (even if in practice they can become little more than this).

(ibid.)

24 Panitch (2002: 96) refers to state autonomy theory as 'sheer liberal/social-democratic voluntarism that most clearly defines what I have called the impoverishment of state theory'.

25 Panitch also says, '[W]e must be mindful of whether . . . campaigns for higher incomes translate effectively into *class* struggles, insofar as . . . they ignore the ecological consequences of production oriented to greater individualised consumption' (ibid.; italics added). And underlying idea here is that if workers' need for a higher living standards is met, there will be more ecological damage, so the burden of ecological sustainability is on the shoulders of workers.

26 'The weight of finance in allocating capital and in disciplining states, business and ultimately workers, makes converting banks and other financial institutions into public utilities especially important in terms of accessing and allocating resources for any progressive policy' (pp. 18–19).

27 See Carrillo (1977) on euro-communism.

28 Here is an example:

[W]hat is conventionally called 'power' is a complex, overdetermined phenomenon and can serve at best to identify the production of significant effects (i.e., significant or pertinent at the level of abstraction and degree of complexity in terms of which the explanandum is defined) through the interaction of specific social forces within the limits implied in the prevailing set of structural constraints.

(Jessop, 2008: 29)

[T]he state is neither a unified subject nor a neutral instrument but an asymmetrical institutional terrain on which various political forces (including state managers) contest control over the state apparatus and its distinctive capacities; and . . . class power depends less on the class background of those nominally in charge of the state or their subjective class identities and projects than on the differential class relevance of the effects of the exercise of state capacities in a complex and changing conjuncture.

(Jessop, 2008: 31)

3 The state and class relations

In *Capital volume 1*, Marx (1887: 164) begins to develop his class theory by saying this:

> Wherever a part of society possesses the monopoly of the means of production, the labourer, free or not free, must add to the working-time necessary for his own maintenance an extra working-time in order to produce the means of subsistence for the owners of the means of production.

This is the case whether the property owner in question is 'the Athenian . . . well-to-do man. . . , Etruscan theocrat, . . . Roman citizen. . . , Norman baron, American slave-owner, Wallachian Boyard, modern landlord or capitalist' (ibid.).

But would these types of property owner be able to maintain their monopoly over property and appropriate surplus labour from direct producers, without the assistance of the state? After all, and as Leon Trotsky (2008: 145) rightly says, '[p]roperty is a relation among people. It represents an enormous power *so long as* it is universally recognised and supported by that system of compulsion called Law and the State' (italics added).

But could the author of *Capital* really have forgotten about the state's relation to class? As we will see in this chapter (and in the remainder of the book), Marx certainly did not. In fact, one can say that he almost began *Capital volume 1* with a statement about the state, although hidden in a long footnote (as discussed later), where he talks about the state at the level of class – that is, about the class-state.

Much of the Marxist state theory has been about capitalist society, which is only one form of class society. There is a need to 'scale up' the analysis of the state – that is, to analyse the state at the level of class relations and then at the level of, say, capitalist class relation. In this chapter, I examine the state at the level of class relations, abstracting from the nature of the state under capitalism.

I begin with the claim that the state is influenced by economic relations. This claim is discussed in Section 1. The scope of 'economic relations' (or, economic conditions) as a concept is expanded to emphasize the structure of class relations. The state is related to class relations in Section 2. In Section 3,

DOI: 10.4324/9781351168007-3

I focus on the state and class *struggle* on the assumption that the relation of the state to class relations is not the same as its relation to class struggle. To say that the state exists because of class struggles does not explain why the state does not support the exploited class in class struggle. So, in Section 4, I explore the idea that the state and the exploiting class are two arms of the totality of class relations. I thus argue for an internal relation between the state and class relations. In Section 5, state's two main functions – basic and non-basic functions – are dealt with. The state functions on behalf of the exploiting class but not entirely so. Section 6 deals with the idea that as forms of class relation change, so do the nature and forms of the class-state. Here I also make some remarks on the state in pre-capitalist societies. Section 7 discusses how political forms of the state vary even within a given form of class society. The final section criticizes those scholars who seek to dilute the importance of the relation between property relation (which is an important aspect of class relation) and the state. It then makes remarks on some under-stressed aspects of the state in a way which has an implication for understanding the state in the post-revolution transitional society, where there are elements of the capitalist state without the capitalists. In the process, it brings to light a potential source of weakness in Lenin's theory of the state which is that it under-emphasizes the economic conditioning of the state.

1 The state and economic relations

The state is a 'special apparatus for the systematic application of force and the subjugation of people by force' in a class society (Lenin, 1919a). The state represents a 'special, public power', which 'consists not merely of armed men' in a standing army and police but 'also of material adjuncts, prisons, and institutions of coercion' (Lenin, 1949: 12).[1] Of course, the state does not rule by coercion alone: '[T]he State is the entire complex of practical activities with which the ruling class not only justifies and maintains its dominance, but manages to win the active consent of those over whom it rules' (Gramsci, 1971: 244).

The question is, why does such a violent (territorial) apparatus exist? And when it exists, against whom is it violent, and on behalf of whom, and why? One possible explanation is that the state is a part of the wider division of labour in society. Engels says: 'Society gives rise to certain public functions which it cannot dispense with. The persons appointed for this purpose [that is, state actors] form a new branch of the division of labor *within society.*' (Engels in Marx and Engels, 1975: 398). Now, the fact that the state actors perform the special functions gives 'them particular interests, distinct, too, from the interests of their mandators'. The state actors 'make themselves independent of the latter and – the state is in being' (ibid.). Not just independent. Their own interests can contradict the interests of society as a whole. And, out of the 'contradiction between the interest of the individual and that of the community the latter takes an independent *form as the State*', thus indicating that the state is the form of social relations, or rather contradictory relations indicative of individuals' alienation – separation – from the community (ibid.; italics added).

This form – that is, the state – is 'divorced from the real interests of individual and community', and yet it is

> at the same time as an illusory communal life, always based, however, on the real ties existing in every family and tribal conglomeration – such as flesh and blood, language, division of labour on a larger scale, and other interests-and especially, . . . on the classes.
>
> (ibid.)

To the extent that the state is separate from society, this leads some to hold a view that the state came to exist because of 'the growing complexity of social life, the differentiation of functions' (Lenin, 1949: 13). This is a false view: the fact of growing complexity in society in itself does not explain the state's separation from society and its particular nature: it does not explain why it is that state functions – protection and reproduction of social relations of production – need to be performed by a body that is separate from the ordinary members of society, and indeed it does not explain why it needs to be violent. Complexity may explain the need for a government (an entity to conduct some tasks in the interest of society as a whole such as protection from a pandemic) but not the need for the state as such.[2] If the state represents alienation of all the people and the contradiction between individual interests and common interests of people, then why does it act on behalf of one part of society (the dominant class or the exploiting class)?

Political processes cannot be explained primarily in terms of the political. As the fundamental realm of the extra-economic, the state is rooted in, and shaped by, objective *economic* conditions/relations which are in turn shaped by the state. The economic relations have the ultimate primacy in such interaction. Marx and Engels (1845) say: '[T]he social organisation evolving directly out of production and commerce . . . in all ages *forms the basis of the State*' (italics added). And the state shapes production and commerce too.[3] As they emphasize in *German ideology*, the state continually evolves 'out of the life-process of definite individuals', but the individuals, not in terms of how 'they may appear in their own or other people's imagination' but 'as they operate, produce materially'. So it is the objectively existing 'material life of individuals', that is, 'their mode of production and form of intercourse', that forms 'the real basis of the state and remains so at all the stages at which division of labour and private property are still necessary, quite independently of the *will* of individuals' (Marx and Engels, 1845). Marx (1987) says in *Poverty of philosophy*: 'Legislation, whether political or civil, never does more than proclaim, express in words, the will of economic relations.'

In *Capital volume 1*, Marx makes a significant point about the political (and the political includes the state) in a rather trans-historical sense. He does this, interestingly, in a famous footnote right in the very first chapter 1 of the book (in the section on the fetishism of the commodity). He begins with the idea that in certain time periods (e.g. the middle ages and ancient times), politics and religion, and not 'material interests', are said to reign supreme. But then, he says, '[T]he middle ages could not live on Catholicism, nor the ancient world on politics. On the contrary, it is the mode in which' people living in these societies 'gained a livelihood that explains why here politics, and there Catholicism, played *the chief part*' (Marx, 1887: 59; italics added).

Recently, India's (Gurcharan) Das (2003), a former CEO reincarnated as a neoliberal-capitalist ideologue, says, 'Whereas economics is at the centre of China's agenda, politics continues to dominate our debate in India's Parliament, in the newspapers and on the street.' For the Hindu Right, for which Das has sympathy, of course, Hindu culture is central to India with its 5,000 years of history. According to Hedgewar, the founder of India's Hindu-fascistic organization, 'The Hindu culture is the life-breath of Hindusthan [Indian society]. It is therefore clear that if Hindusthan is to be protected, we should first nourish the Hindu culture' (quoted in Roy, 2021).

Marx might have summarized these views like this: the idea that the mode of production generally determines the social, political, and intellectual life is very true for modern-day materialistic China, but not for India in which Hindu religion and politics reign supreme. Marx would then present his own alternative approach by saying, Indians during ancient period under Hindu kings could not live on Hinduism nor can they do so now under those who militantly engage in the authoritarian defence of Hinduism vis-à-vis other religions. Nor can they live on politics now, including religious politics. It is the (crisis-prone) mode in which Indians gain a livelihood that governs (a) their political and cultural life and (b) the appearance that they reign supreme vis-à-vis their economic life. For Marx, indeed, 'the economic structure of society . . . is the real basis on which the juridical and political superstructure is raised and to which definite social forms of thought correspond' and for him, 'the mode of production determines the character of the social, political, and intellectual life generally' (Marx, 1887: 58).

The state is fundamentally shaped by economic conditions/relations. Engels explains what 'economic relations' means and how it is connected to the state. 'By economic relations' (or economic conditions), 'we understand the manner in which men in a given society produce their means of subsistence and exchange the products', so economic relations/conditions comprise 'the entire technique of production and transport'.

> According to our conception this technique also determines the mode of exchange and, furthermore, of the distribution of products and hence also . . . the division [of society] into classes, and *consequently the relations of lordship and servitude and* consequently the state, politics, law, etc.
>
> (in Marx and Engels, 1975: 441; italics added)

The state (or more generally, the political moment of society), of course, reacts back on the economic relations/conditions. In a letter, Engels clarifies the 'materialist conception of history' that he and Marx had developed, according to which 'the *ultimately* determining element in history is the production and reproduction of real life. Neither Marx nor I have ever asserted more than this' (Engels, in Marx and Engels, 1975: 394). More specifically:

> The economic situation is the basis, but the various elements of the superstructure – *political forms* of the class struggle and its results such as *constitutions* established by the victorious class after a successful battle, etc., *juridical forms*, and even the reflexes of all these actual struggles in the brains of the participants, political, juristic, philosophical theories, religious views and their further development into systems of dogmas – also exercise their influence upon the course of the historical struggles and in many cases preponderate in determining their *form*.
>
> (ibid.: 394–5; italics added)

Althusser (2001: 106) makes a claim that bears some affinity to Engels' point: 'Class contradictions between capital and labour (as between other basic classes) are always "overdetermined" by the state, religion, political movements, national past, local customs, world context, etc.' One can agree with this on the condition that certain processes – class relations and economic development – are more important than other processes.

To understand the state, one must ask: what is it about the economic conditions/relations that makes the state do what it does? The state is not merely rooted in relations and conditions that are economic. The state is rooted in the *class* form of economic relations/conditions. To understand the state, one must begin with the economic aspects (e.g. economic development) and with the class relations of society.[4]

2 From economic relations to class relations (and their gender and spatial nature)

In the earliest form of human society, where there was no systematic class exploitation, there was no state (a specialized coercive mechanism) as there was no need for it. Class relations and antagonisms beget, and reproduce, the state. How/why is the question. This is important to answer given the fact that the state is widely seen as a class-neutral entity.

We began this chapter with Marx's famous formulation about class in *Capital 1*. Monopolization over the means of production in the hands of a few creates a necessary condition for the appropriation by them of surplus product from direct producers, as Marx says. Indeed, surplus product/labour is central to class societies:

> Surplus-product must have been produced by the slave, or the slave-owner would not have kept any slaves. Surplus-product must have been produced by the serf, or serfdom would have been of no use to the landed gentry.

Surplus-product, only to a considerably greater extent, is likewise produced by the wage worker, or the capitalist would have no need to buy
labour power.

(Trotsky, 1939)

Class relations develop when the development of productive forces beyond the
original classless society reaches a stage where the production of surplus is possible and when that surplus is taken away and controlled by a minority class
from a majority class. A small group begins to control property (that is, property
in the means of production) and the surplus, and others do not, and therefore
the latter have to perform surplus labour. So 'unequal' relations of property and
surplus give rise to exploitation which happens when a class – the majority
class – surrenders a large part of what it produces (the surplus is that large part)
to the class that controls property. And these relations are supported by the state.

Classes are characterized by their position in the social system of economy,
and primarily by their relation to the means of production. In [devel-
oped] . . . societies, *property relations are validated by laws* [of the state].

(Trotsky, 1991: 210; italics added)

Or, as Lenin (1919b) famously says in his *A great beginning*:

Classes are large groups of people differing from each other by the place
they occupy in a historically determined system of social production, by
their relation (*in most cases fixed and formulated in law*) to the means of
production, by their role in the social organisation of labour, and, consequently, by the dimensions of the share of social wealth of which they
dispose and the mode of acquiring it.

(italics added)

The exploiting classes include slave-owners and feudal landowners in pre-capitalist societies, and capitalists in modern societies. Exploited classes are slaves
and serfs in pre-capitalist societies. Wage-workers are the main exploited class
under capitalism. Capitalists and workers (the proletariat) are not the only
classes, however.

in every capitalist country, side by side with the proletariat, there are always
broad strata of the petty bourgeoisie, small proprietors. Capitalism arose
and is constantly arising out of small production. A number of new 'middle strata' are inevitably brought into existence again and again by capitalism (appendages to the factory, work at home, small workshops scattered
all over the country to meet the requirements of big industries, such as the
bicycle and automobile industries, etc.). These new small producers are
just as inevitably being cast again into the ranks of the proletariat.

(Lenin 1908)

To the extent that the state has to be theorized from the standpoint of exploited classes, the latter, for me, include, apart from wage workers, non-exploiting strata from Lenin's 'broad strata of the petty bourgeoisie, small proprietors'. For convenience, I call them small-scale producers: they are small-scale property owners who do not exploit anyone and who are mainly exploited in the markets for input, output, credit and insurance. They are also exploited when they work as part-time wage-labourers. In rural areas, small-scale producers are often peasants: self-sufficient peasants (or middle peasants) and poor peasants (semi-proletarians). Note that many indigenous groups are small-scale producers who may own some or all of the property collectively and whose dependence on markets may be limited and therefore they continue to hold some communitarian ('primitive communistic') values. I exclude what are called rich peasants ('well-to-do peasantry', in Lenin's language) who are proto-capitalists, from the category of peasants and therefore from small-scale producers. I use 'common people' (sometimes, 'people'), 'the majority class', 'the exploited', 'masses' and 'lower classes', to refer to workers *and* small-scale producers together.

The relations among classes in the social economy – property relations and performance-appropriation of unpaid labour – shape, and are shaped by, the state. As Marx (1894: 576) explains in *Capital volume 3*: 'The specific economic form, in which unpaid surplus-labour is pumped out of direct producers, determines the relationship of rulers and ruled', as that relation 'grows directly out of production itself and, in turn, reacts upon it as a determinant'. Marx adds that it is 'the direct relationship of the owners of the conditions of production to the immediate producers', that is, the class relationship, 'in which we find the innermost secret, the hidden basis of the entire social edifice'; the 'upper layer' of this edifice is the state (ibid.). In sum, economic development and class relations, which mutually influence one another and constitute the economic moment of society, together shape the state (and the state shapes the economic moment, in turn, as we will see).

One cannot understand the state without understanding its causal relation to class relations across class societies. Marx (1844) says:

> [T]he *slavery of civil society* is the natural foundation of the *modern* state, just as the civil society of slavery was the natural foundation of the state in antiquity. The existence of the state is inseparable from the existence of slavery. The state and slavery in antiquity – frank and open *classical* antitheses – were not more closely *welded* together than the modern state and the cut-throat world of modern business.

There are two additional points that need to be made about the relation between class relations and the state. One is that in class society, it is not only the case that surplus is appropriated from the majority class and concentrated in the hands of a minority class, thus forming the basis of the state. It is also the case that surplus is taken away from certain kinds of areas (e.g. rural areas or indeed less developed regions) and geographically concentrated in other kinds of areas (e.g. urban areas or more developed areas). There is an urbanization of class relations and class exploitation. Emergence of class society coincides with a geographical form of social antagonism. In ancient society, with its 'class relation between citizens and slaves':

> We already find the antagonism of town and country; later the antagonism between those states which represent town interests and those which represent country interests, and inside the towns themselves the antagonism between industry and maritime commerce.
>
> (Marx and Engels, 1845)

Marx (1973: 483) says in *Grundrisse*: '[W]here the individual family chiefs settled in the forests', as among the Germanic tribes, 'long distances apart, the commune exists . . . only in the periodic gathering-together of the commune members, although their unity-*in-itself* is posited in their ancestry, language, common past and history, etc.' Marx concludes: 'The *commune* thus appears as a *coming-together*, not as a *being-together*, as a unification made up of independent subjects, landed proprietors, and not as a unity'. Therefore '[t]he commune . . . does not in fact exist as a *state* or *political body*, as in classical antiquity, because it does not exist as a *city*' (ibid.). Marx says that '[w]ith its coming-together in the city, the commune possesses an economic existence as such; the city's mere *presence*, as such, distinguishes it from a mere multiplicity of independent houses' (ibid.).

There arises not only town-country dichotomy in a class society. With 'unequal' class relations also rise unequal gender relations whereby a disproportionate amount of reproductive work in the sphere of the family falls on women and where men come to control property more than women do (Das, 2022b). People not only produce and reproduce the means of subsistence (e.g. food and shelter) and the material means to produce them. They also need to produce the animate and conscious tools without which such production will not occur: human beings. Marx and Engels (1845) say that men and women, 'who daily remake their own life, begin to make other' men and women, 'to propagate their kind'. This means that 'the relation between man and woman, parents and children, the family' comes to constitute an important aspect of 'historical development' of humanity. '[The] family. . . [is] where wife and children are the slaves of the husband. This latent slavery in the family . . . is the first property' (ibid.). If the state is the institution that defends and codifies the rules of private property (in inanimate objects), this imperative contributes to the state defending and codifying the unequal relations between adult men on the one hand and adult women and children on the other, although the state's role in defending private property has primacy.

Thus, as a class society arises, four kinds of unequal relation come into being. These are unequal relations: between classes, between rural and urban areas, between men and women, and between the state and dominated/exploited classes.

3 The state and class struggle

The objective existence of class relations is one thing. Class struggle is a different matter, even if the two are closely connected. Class struggle is the proximate factor that drives the (changes in the) relations between the state on the one hand and relations of property and surplus labour (i.e. class relations) on the other.

In all societies, with or without classes, human beings have certain needs – need for food and shelter, and so on, as well as need for culture – which must be met to ensure their continued existence (reproduction). In class societies these needs are not met for a vast majority. This is because of the structure of class relations (i.e. lack of control over property and surplus, and so on) and because of the concrete effects of class relations on people (i.e. unequal distribution of income, leisure time, and the like). Because of the operation of class relations, there is not only (increasing) concentration of control over productive resources in the hands of a few but also appropriation of surplus from direct producers. An artificial social scarcity is created: scarcity both in the access to the means of production and means of consumption. The fact that common people have needs that have to be satisfied goes against the interest of the exploiting class and of those who are primarily responsible for managing the state. To the extent that people's needs are not met, there is bound to be a struggle on their part, sometimes covert, sometimes overt, sometimes violent, and sometimes peaceful. Potential and actual class struggle from below, therefore, in turn, necessitates a set of institutions to keep the majority suppressed by the use of, or the threat of the use of, violence, and by less violent means. In other words, a political mechanism must exist which keeps the people subjugated/suppressed and to meet the needs of the property owners, on the basis of the use of violent and non-violent methods, with the threat of violence *always* being there.

When class struggle happens, this cannot be suppressed directly by people themselves based on persuasion or by localized coercion exercised by people themselves. The conflict over the unequal control over property and surplus labour is far too fundamental – it is unresolvable within the sphere of society where people pursue their individual interests. A separate body is needed to maintain order, order in a class society: the need to maintain order takes a class colour. A separate social sphere is necessary to ensure that the classes with conflicting economic interests do not consume themselves and the society as a whole in fruitless antagonistic struggle. So in a class society, 'it became necessary to have a power, seemingly standing above society, that would alleviate the conflict and keep it within the bounds of 'order' (Engels, 1884: chapter 9). And, 'this power, arisen out of society but placing itself above it, and alienating itself more and more from it, is the state' (ibid.). By keeping class struggle in check, the state makes it possible for the monopolistic control over property in the hands of a few as well as class exploitation (appropriation of surplus labour from direct producers by property owners) to continue. The fact that 'the state arose from the need to keep class antagonisms in check, but also arose in the thick of the fight between the classes', as Engels says, implies that the state 'is normally the state of the most powerful, economically ruling class, which by its means becomes also the politically ruling class, and so acquires new means of holding down and exploiting the oppressed class' (ibid.).

Lenin connects Marx's theory of class exploitation (the idea, as mentioned before, that 'Wherever a part of society possesses the monopoly of the means of production', there will be exploitation of direct producers by the minority class) to the state, when he says:

> History shows that the state as a special apparatus for coercing people arose wherever and whenever there appeared a division of society into classes, that is, a division into groups of people some of which were permanently in a position to appropriate the labour of others, where some people exploited others.
>
> (Lenin, 1919a)

Every economically dominant class, or a class in the process of becoming economically dominant, seeks mastery over the state which, to use Marx's words, is the *'concentrated and organised force of society'* (Marx, 1887: 534; italics added). Engels (1884) says that the state is 'the official representative of society as a whole', but it is the official representative of *class* society. The state is 'the state of that class which itself [represents], for its own time, society as a whole: in ancient times, the state of slaveowning citizens; in the Middle Age, of the feudal nobility; in our own time, of the bourgeoisie' (ibid.).

> The ancient state was, above all, the state of the slave-owners for holding down the slaves, just as the feudal state was the organ of the nobility for holding down the peasant serfs and bondsmen, and the modern representative state is the instrument for exploiting wage-labor by capital.
>
> (ibid.)

The state consists 'of a group of people engaged solely, or almost solely, or mainly, in ruling' (Lenin, 1919a). As soon as the society is divided into the exploiter (the minority) and the exploited classes (majority), '[p]eople are [also] divided into the ruled, and into specialists in ruling, those who rise above society and are called rulers, statesmen' (Lenin, 1919a). Indeed, '[the] exploiters inevitably transform the state . . . into an instrument of the rule of their class, the exploiters, over the exploited' (Lenin, 1918).

As we have seen, appropriation of surplus product is central to how class societies operate. Surplus product is produced by slaves, serfs, wage workers, and the like, which is why these classes exist, and because they exist there is class struggle over surplus product as appropriation of their surplus adversely impacts their interests:

> The class struggle is nothing else than the struggle for surplus-product. He who owns surplus-product is master of the situation – owns wealth, *owns the state*, has the key to the church, to the courts, to the sciences and to the arts.
>
> (Trotsky, 1939; italics added)

Indeed, '[h]istory is full of the constant attempts of the oppressed classes to throw off oppression. The history of slavery contains records of wars of emancipation from slavery which lasted for decades' (Lenin, 1919a). The class struggle from below, the struggle of the masses, has to be negated. This is no laughing matter, however: to achieve the task of negation, the state must be, ultimately, a violent institution. 'Neither under slavery nor under the feudal system could a small minority of people dominate over the vast majority without coercion' (Lenin, 1919a). Because the state represents the exploiting class, it therefore represents a minority, because the exploiting class is always a minority.

To represent the interests of a minority against those of a majority, systemic use of, or the threat of the use of, force is necessary in order to make it possible for class exploitation to exist and continue and to ensure that the low-class struggle does not threaten dominant-class property rights. That force is the state. Its 'bureaucratic military state machine' oppresses, crushes, the masses (Lenin, 1949: 40). A violent public power with an enormous means of physical coercion is indeed necessary because 'a self-acting armed organization of the population has become impossible since the split into classes' (Lenin, 1949: 12). 'The state is a special organization . . . of violence for the suppression of some class' in the interest of other classes (Lenin, 1949: 26).[5]

> [The state is] a special category of people set apart to rule others and who, for the sake and purpose of rule, systematically and permanently have at their disposal a certain apparatus of coercion, an apparatus of violence, such as is represented at the present time . . . by armed contingents of troops, prisons and other means of subjugating the will of others by force – *all that which constitutes the essence of the state.*
>
> (Lenin, 1919a: italics added)

It is inadequate to say that the state exists merely for the defence of society. 'It is not the tasks of defense which create a military and state bureaucracy, but the class structure of society carried over into the organization of defense. The army is only a copy of the social relations' (Trotsky, 1991: 44).

The use of violence is a part of a wider set of processes embodied in the state:

> The State is not an end in itself. It is only a machine [an instrument] in the hands of the dominating social forces. Like every machine it has its

motor, transmitting and executive mechanism. The driving force of the State is class interest; its motor mechanism is agitation, the press, church and school propaganda, parties, street meetings, petitions and revolts. The transmitting mechanism is the legislative organization of caste, dynastic, estate or class interests represented as the will of God (absolutism) or the will of the nation (parliamentarism). Finally, the executive mechanism is the administration, with its police, the courts, with their prisons, and the army.

(Trotsky, 1931b)

The state exists not only because of the *structure* class *relations*: in fact, it exists both because of the mechanisms of class relations and because of the *effects* of class relations (e.g. inequality in income and access to consumption items). The second reason, one that Lenin tends to miss, needs some emphasis (I return to this in the Conclusion section). As long as there is not enough for everyone to meet their needs and therefore access to resources has to be regulated, there has to be a regulatory mechanism backed by the use of force. That mechanism is the state.

In societies where the level of development of the productive forces is low, where everyone is in a constant struggle with everyone else to get enough to live on for himself out of a national income too small to go around, a *large supervisory apparatus becomes necessary*.

(Mandel, 1969)

Therefore,

[a]ll who exercise state functions, who are part of the state apparatus, are – in one way or another – watchdogs. Special police and regular police are watchdogs, but so are tax collectors, judges, paper pushers in government offices, fare-collectors on buses, etc. In sum, all functions of the state apparatus are reduced to this: surveillance and control of the life of the society in the interests of the ruling class.

(Mandel, 1969)

Indeed, the state is necessary to 'regulate inequalities in the sphere of consumption' (Trotsky, 1991: 47), which is an effect of a combination of (a) the low level of the development of productive forces (which can be fettered by existing class relations) and (b) the lack of control of the masses over production.

In a series of interesting but relatively neglected lines on the state, Sartre (1960) makes some insightful comments that reinforce what has been said earlier:

The State. . . *exists* for the sake of the dominant class, but as a practical suppression of class conflicts within the national totalization.

(p. 639)

If classes exist. . . , then, in effect, the State institutes itself in their struggle as the organ of the exploiting class (or classes) and sustains, by constraint, the statute of the oppressed classes.

(p. 637)

[T]he State cannot take on its functions without positing itself as a mediator between the exploiting and the exploited classes. The State is a determination of the dominant class, and this determination is conditioned by class struggle. But it affirms itself as a deep negation of the class struggle.

(p. 639)

To sum up, the state must ensure the extraction of social surplus from direct producers. Exploitation is possible only when monopolistic control over property exists. So, in all societies, the state defends the exploitative relations of private property in the means of production. The state has to be thus seen within the context of the relation between those who control society's productive resources and those who do not, which shapes the class character of the state, which in turn shapes its relation with those who are ruled. Indeed, property 'represents an enormous power *so long as* it is . . . supported by that system of compulsion called Law and the State' (Trotsky, 2008: 145; italics added). The state must also defend the conditions of inequality in consumption.

Finally, and to reinforce a point made earlier, 'it appears that the state does reconcile classes', while in reality, and 'according to Marx, the state is an organ of class rule' (Lenin, 1949: 11). Most people believe that the state creates and maintains order. But for Marxists, as Lenin says, this order means, above all, *not* 'the reconciliation of classes' *but* 'the oppression of one class by another'. People say that the state alleviates class conflicts, but to alleviate class conflicts means, once again, *not* reconciling classes *but* 'depriving the oppressed classes of definite means and methods of struggle to overthrow the oppressors' (Lenin, 1949: 11).

4 The state and the dominant class as two arms of the class structure

The idea that the state as a structure of relations originates in the structure of class relations does not fully resolve an important question concerning the nature of the state. For me, quite precisely, the question is as follows. If the state has to ensure that the antagonistic classes might not consume themselves and society in sterile struggle (Engels, 1884), then why does the state not work on behalf of the majority class, those who produce surplus? Would maintaining order and keeping class conflicts within limits not be easier if the state is in the hands of the majority class? If it is the case that elements in the dominant class control the public authority whose main task is to serve the *common* interests of society, what is it about the state that allows such control, and why does the majority class (the exploited) not control the state? If the state is the state of the economically dominant class, then it cannot be because: there is the state, there is the economically dominant class, and they just come together in a mutual alliance.

Since the beginning of class society, the people who perform the role of the state, and the people who, with their monopolistic control over society's productive resources, are the exploiting class, are two parts of the same totality. This is the totality of class relations. The nature of the overlap in terms of 'personnel' or agency – the extent to which state managers themselves appropriate surplus product or those who appropriate surplus product are also state managers – is a contingent matter. The structure of class relations thus has a necessarily political character: the state and the exploiting class are two arms of the body of class relationship. One arm signifies economic exploitation and exclusion, and another arm signifies political oppression (and also exploitation via taxation, forced labour, and the like). Of course, the nature of the economically dominant class changes (slave owners to nobility, and so on). Whichever class is the rising class economically is the class that seeks to control political power; the political power belongs to the economically dominant class. As Marx and Engels (1845) say in *German ideology*, 'every class which is struggling for mastery . . . must first conquer for itself political power in order to represent its interest in turn as the general interest'.

Then this means that in every class society, there is a class that lacks political power and that therefore it struggles for political mastery. Power and powerlessness in terms of the control over the state are hallmarks of 'classness'. The class that controls means of production and its use is the class that generally controls political power, including its coercive and ideological apparatuses. The class that lacks the control over property and its surplus is the class that lacks control over state power and must therefore achieve it for it to gain – or reinforce/sustain – control over the economic aspects of class structure of society (i.e. property, production, surplus, and so on). The economically exploited men and women are the people who are the governed/ruled. The economically exploiting men and women are the ruling class.

The structure of the state (i.e. political power as it is concentrated in the state) and the structure of class relations are internally (i.e. necessarily) connected. One cannot exist without another. If the class relation is 'the direct relationship of the owners of the conditions of production to the immediate producers' (Marx, 1894: 576), then the state must be seen as the direct political relationship between the two basic classes. Indeed, as Marx says in *Jewish question*, 'From a *political* point of view, the *state* and the *organization of society* are not two different things. The state is the organization of [class] society' (Marx, 1844). And, as Engels says:

> The possessing classes – the landed aristocracy and the bourgeoisie – keep the working people in servitude not only by the power of their wealth, by the simple exploitation of labour by capital, but *also by the power of the state – by the army, the bureaucracy, the courts.*
>
> (in Marx and Engels, 1975: 244; italics added)

So, the servitude of the majority class (workers and small-scale producers) consists of two inter-connected mechanisms: economic exploitation by the possessing classes (mainly capitalists) and political subjugation through the power of the state. The power of the state, ultimately, is the political power of the exploited class, more or less, is 'the most concentrated strength of the ruling class' (Trotsky, 1977: 122):

> [The state's] nature is political. . . , because the state, the instrument of power, is the political superstructure *par excellence* upon the economic foundation. But this political power serves not only to 'regulate' political matters, in the narrow, technical sense of the word, (that is, internal matters of the state apparatus itself), but also and above all economic, cultural, ecclesiastical and other matters.
>
> (ibid.)

The state power is necessarily a form of class power, even if the exercise of state power is mediated by the internal structure of the state and by the interests of self-seeking politicians and officials. That is, the relation between the two forms of power is an internal one and not an external one. The state power is, ultimately, the power of the exploiting classes in all pre-socialist class societies. So, how class relationships influence the state and how the relatively autonomous state elites react to the pressures of class and act in their own interests as well belong to what is called state theory.

5 Class society and state functions

The state has basic (primary) functions and non-basic (secondary) functions. In terms of economic function, the state tries to make sure that the property-owning class is able to augment its property by appropriating surplus labour and in other ways (e.g. war, colonization, and so on). Marx (1887: 534) wrote of 'the power of the state' as an economic power in that it seeks to 'hasten . . . the process of transformation of the feudal mode of production into the capitalist mode'. In terms of the political function, which ultimately is the main function, the state's role is to keep the masses in check, as already indicated.

However, the state also performs many secondary tasks, so its tasks are not exclusively on behalf of the economically dominant class. There are the functions which any government must perform in order to keep the society going, whether or not they are of any direct special advantage to the ruling class. These include: measures against a pandemic; city sanitation; protection against natural disasters; and promotion of education, culture, and health. A given state, with its own geographical boundary, exists as a member of the family of states. As a 'national' state, it manages the common affairs of the ruling-class people with their different interests under its jurisdiction as against the rival ruling classes operating under the jurisdictions of other states. It helps its own ruling class remain competitive vis-à-vis its rivals. Military spending is partly about this.

Besides, the ruling class itself is shot through with intra-class economic and other conflicts, so the state has to resolve conflicts within the ruling class. The state also has to resolve conflicts within the class of direct producers. And the state might pursue tasks that serve the interests of those who manage its affairs, even if it has to act against the dominant class once in a while:

> The task of the political state is not just to serve the immediate interests of the governing class. It must also act to preserve social cohesion; and though these two goals are ultimately at one, there can be acute conflict between them in the short or middle term.
>
> (Eagleton, 2011: 205)

The state's main task is the reason why the state exists (i.e. keeping the exploited masses in check and reproduce existing class relations).[6] The non-basic tasks are more governmental rather than 'statal' or state-related: the governmental tasks would continue even without class divisions. So every action of the state is not to be seen as being 'necessarily in the direct collective interest of the ruling class' (Creaven, 2000: 192). But when there is a conflict between the basic and non-basic tasks, the latter will be subordinated to the basic task. Whenever there is a serious danger to property rights of the ruling class, various fractions of the ruling class (and their political representatives) tend to be united. The state helps them unite. It acts as their greatest chamber of commerce or trade union organization. As Sartre says, '*the State* constitutes itself as a mediation between conflicts within the dominant class, in so far as these conflicts run the risk of weakening it in the face of the dominated classes'.

> [The state] embodies and realises the general interest of the dominant class over and above the antagonisms and conflicts of particular interests. This amounts to saying that the ruling class *produces its State*.
>
> (Sartre, 1960: 638)

Even when the state performs its general tasks, these are performed in ways that are shaped by its class character as the state of the economically dominant class.[7] Precisely because of this, that is, because the state is dominantly the state of the exploiting class, which is a small minority in all class societies, there is a need to maintain its class neutrality. The state must appear to be above society, to be above the conflicts between and within classes.

> The real contradiction of the State is that it is a class apparatus pursuing class objectives and, at the same time, positing itself for itself as the sovereign unity of all, that is, in the absolute Other-Being which is the nation.
>
> (Sartre, 1960: 642)

Apart from the distinction between the main and secondary tasks, there is another distinction to be made: a dialectical distinction between what the state does and what it decides not to do. In a society with class divisions (and class fractional divisions), what the state does for one class (or class fraction) amounts to it not doing anything for the opposed class (or opposed class fraction). If the property owners are thrashing the masses for opposing exploitation and if the state does not do anything to stop the property owners, then from one angle, this means that the state is not doing anything for the masses and that it is doing something for the ruling class. From another angle, this also means that the state *is* doing something for the exploited: it is ensuring a condition for them to continue to be exploited and subjugated.

6 Forms of class relation and forms of class–state: some historical examples

The state and class relations are internally related. As the form of class relation changes, there is also a change in the form of the class–state, including the degree of the structural overlap between state personnel and the ruling-class people.

While it is true that class societies are *different* one from another on the basis of 'the mode in which . . . surplus-labour is in each case extracted from the actual producer, the labourer' (Marx, 1887: 153), what is *common* to all forms of class society is that surplus labour is extracted. A presupposition of surplus extraction is that effective control over property is in the hands of a minority in the face of potential and actual opposition from the exploited. And this is not possible without the state.

As mentioned, the state exists wherever there are class divisions. And, as the form of class society – that is, as the form of exploitation (slavery, feudalism, capitalism) – changes, so does the form of the relation between the ruler and the ruled. In other words, while the state's basic role is to reproduce a class society and to serve its ruling class, the actual ways in which it executes its functions and relates to classes and class fractions are different in different class contexts. This difference is determined by the forms in which surplus is actually extracted,[8] along with various empirical (i.e. time- and place-specific) conditions such as race, religion, caste, gender, environmental factors, the historical 'survivals' of a place, and geopolitics of a country, all of which are contingently, if not un-importantly, connected to the class context. Sometimes, the relation between the state and class will be a little more autonomous than in other societies (or contexts).

In capitalist class society, the state does not ordinarily force members of the working class to work for this or that capitalist. It does not have to. Dispossessed of property, workers will be forced to work for a capitalist for a wage. This fact does not mean, however, what Eagleton thinks: '[T]he state under capitalism has more independence of class relations than it does under, say, feudalism' (Eagleton, 2011: 205).[9] To me, the state under capitalism is no more independent of *class relations* than it is in pre-capitalist societies. What *is* true is that 'the state under capitalism has more independence' vis-à-vis *individuals/groups* belonging to the capitalist class (or, occasionally, vis-à-vis short-term economic interests of the capitalist class as such). Indeed, one's employer (or rentier or pawnshop owner) does not have to be a prime minister or an army general. But in pre-capitalist societies, where direct producers have control over their means of production, economic exploitation is more directly effected through political power (via decentralized form of state power), so the people who economically exploit tend to be those who have direct access to state power – they directly possess state's coercive power.

In *Capital volume 3*, Marx (1894) says that, in all societies, where 'the direct labourer remains the "possessor" of the means of production and labour conditions necessary for the production of his own means of subsistence, the property relationship must simultaneously appear as a *direct* relation of lordship and servitude'. This means that 'the direct producer is not free; a lack of freedom which may be reduced from serfdom with enforced labour to a mere tributary relationship' (ibid.). According to Amin (2009: 222), developed precapitalist class societies took the form of tributary society. Feudalism is a specific type of tributary society, and slavery being an exception that existed in the interstices:

> In the tributary stage, productive forces are developed beyond primitive communism, surplus labour extraction is controlled by the dominance of the superstructure within the context of an economy governed by use-value, but there are market exchanges internally and externally (between localities and regions).[10]

In these societies, 'the surplus product is . . . like a tribute paid to the exploiting class', hence the name tributary mode (p. 227). The surplus is extracted on the basis of violence and religious ideologies (p. 229).

In pre-capitalist societies, the personnel that manage the affairs of the state on behalf of what is the economically dominant class can overlap with those who are the exploiters: the state as such appears to be, and is, the appropriating class (in the tributary mode of production).

> Should the direct producers not be confronted by a private landowner, but rather, as in Asia, under direct subordination to a state which stands over them as their landlord and simultaneously as sovereign, then rent and taxes coincide, or rather, there exists no tax which differs from this form of ground-rent.
>
> (Marx, 1894: 576).

'Under such circumstances', then, Marx continues:

> there need exist no stronger political or economic pressure than that common to all subjection to that state. The state is then the supreme lord. Sovereignty here consists in the ownership of land concentrated on a national

scale. But, on the other hand, no private ownership of land exists, although there is both private and common possession and use of land.

(Marx, 1894: 576)[11]

The class process and the state process collapse then into one single process in a rather direct manner. What is effectively the economically dominant (exploiting) class is the collective of the people who manage the state. The rather direct relation, *at the level of the structure*, between the state and class relations, can be found in various regions of the pre-capitalist world *at the level of the bearers of the structures*.

In ancient Greece, for example,

> the state was the direct appropriator of surplus-labour; this was indeed its essential function. . . . [T]he state was not simply a 'third power' designed to bring order to the class-struggle between appropriating and producing classes; nor was it even, as in a fully developed class-state, an instrument acting on behalf of an appropriating class but entering only indirectly into the process of class-exploitation. It was in effect the appropriating 'class', the direct master of a huge dependent labour-force.
>
> (Wood, 2012: 99)

This meant that being a subject of state was also about being a dependent labourer, a servant, a serf (p. 100). So 'public power, instituted to undertake socially necessary functions . . . has often been the original basis of the claim to and capacity for surplus appropriation' (p. 294–5).[12]

A similar process appeared to be evident in ancient China.

> The Chinese imperial state reproduced, on a large scale, a pattern of state-formation that was probably more the rule than the exception in 'high' civilizations of the non-capitalist world: a bureaucratic hierarchy descending from a monarch to administrative districts governed by royal functionaries and fiscal officials, who extracted surplus-labour from subject villages of peasant producers for redistribution up the hierarchical chain.
>
> (Wood, 2012: 62–3)

This was the case too in, for example, New kingdom of Egypt (the Egyptian empire), and the vast empire of Incas (ibid.).

The close relationship between the state process and the class process existed in Europe, however unevenly. For example, in France, unlike England, 'the centralized state appears to have developed (at least in large part) as *a class-like phenomenon* – that is, as an independent extractor of the surplus, in particular on the basis of its arbitrary power to tax the land' (Brenner, 1985a/2005a: 55; italics added). Further:

> The state could develop . . . as a competitor with the lords, largely to the extent to which it could establish rights to extract the surplus of peasant

production. It therefore had an interest in limiting the landlords' rents so as to enable the peasants to pay more in taxes – and thus in intervening against the landlords to end peasant unfreedom and to establish and secure peasant property.

(ibid.)

The state machine then incorporated many landlords.

The state as an independent class-like surplus extractor: this terminology is used by Brenner to stress 'the novelty of the new form of centralized surplus extraction (tax/office) associated with the development of French absolutism and its *conflict* with the established decentralized form' (i.e. serfdom or lordship) (ibid.: 59). Yet Brenner says that one should not over-emphasize 'the points of separation and conflict between the systems of surplus extraction and between the monarchy and the aristocracy, and that it is important not to pass over the points of interconnection and inter-penetration' and how 'the rise of the one helped compensate for the decline of the other' (Brenner, 1985b/2005b: 262–3, 288–9).

In pre-capitalist India, there was also a very close and direct relation between the state process and class process. The Indus valley civilization, which existed about 5,000 years ago, had a well-developed class society. It comprised peasants, pastoral nomads, slaves, urban poor, artisans, merchants, priests, and rulers, along with their dependents such as warriors, scribes, and servants (Habib, 2016: 59). There was private property on a large scale in the Indus valley civilization (ibid.), especially in the cities. In fact, the Indus valley civilization *was* a city-based civilization. The existence of cities implied the existence of the state. Some people produced food (in rural areas), and others took it away. The state controlled the peasants whose surplus was extracted in the form of tax or tribute, without which the towns could not have existed.

The Indus state was involved in war-making: it subjugated surrounding areas (Habib, 2016: 60). The state possessed armed means to subjugate other areas and to keep the subjugated population in check. It also used religion to legitimize authority. The Indus valley state kept the society together. It had a lot of administrative control over society as evident not only from the fact that it planned the layout of the towns with straight roads which were maintained well but also from the way in which it stopped building encroachment on the roads (Habib, 2016: 60). There was much institutional uniformity which would not be possible without centralized control. Such uniformity is evident from the standard system of weights, the use of administrative seals, standard size of bricks, and so on (Habib, 2016: 60).

The state and class relations were closely inter-related in ancient India post the Indus valley civilization too. In what is known as early Vedic age (1500–1000 BC), large herds of cattle were a kind of 'capital' from which the cultivators drew their animal power (Habib and Thakur, 2016: 12). 'Those herds could also serve as a means by which surplus extracted out of agriculture was stored.' Those who possessed the surplus were the rulers and priests, who later became Kshatriyas and Brahmans castes/*varnas*, who were the upper castes (Habib and Thakur, 2016: 12).

In the late Vedic age, the increasing power of the king was reflected in the growth of a conventional assemblage of officials serving him, including army commander, tax collector, chamberlain, charioteer, paymaster, courier, and many others (Habib and Thakur, 2016: 44). The internal structure of the state was deeply hierarchical. For example, in terms of salary, the prime minister would be paid 48,000 *panas* (coins) per annum, and the staff of accountants and writers were paid 500 *panas*, thus giving the ratio of 96:1 (Thapar, 2000: 57). Such stratification was probably reflective of the stratification in the wider society.

In the later period in ancient India (200 BC to 300 AD), there was property in land as well as in cattle (needed to draw water for irrigation and for ploughing). Property in land and cattle and whether labour was free or forced were the basis of class distinctions (Habib, 2013: 99). Major classes were 'plough owners' (the gentry) who lived 'in houses' and who got people to farm their land, and there were others such as peasants and unfree men and women serving as hired labourers who lived in huts and not houses (Habib, 2013: 99–100). Lower classes surrendered a large part of their surplus in the form of tax to the state and rent to the gentry.

Talking about the state in ancient India as such, one of the most prominent historians of ancient India, Romila Thapar, says that 'its purpose was to protect the people as well as the institutions of family and private property and to maintain law and order' and that 'this was the justification, in the main, for paying taxes to the state or to the king who symbolized the state' (Thapar, 2000: 55). The state's tax from the cultivators was 1/4th to 1/6th of the gross product, in addition to often-unpaid forced labour for collective purposes (ibid.: 57).

The state 'assigned different parts of its possessions to individual officials [e.g. commanders] and left it to them to collect whatever they could to maintain themselves and their retainers, while presumably delivering a contracted amount to the royal treasury' (Habib, 2013: 102). A commander could hold a province in service tenure (i.e. to provide him with his own income and resources for maintaining his troops), and he could then sub-assign a village to one of his captains. This has been described as feudalism from above (Habib, 2013: 102). The rulers imposed a tribute on ordinary people in the form of agricultural produce and horses, cattle, and gold (Habib and Thakur, 2016: 15). The ruling and the warrior class enriched itself through tribute which was supplemented by booty (raids or fights for cattle from common people of alien groups or tribes) (Habib and Thakur, 2016: 15).

In post-Vedic times, in Mughul India (early 1500s to mid-1800s),

> The land revenue . . . for particular territories was assigned by the Mughul emperor, by way of . . . temporary transferrable assignments . . . in lieu

of salary to his military commanders and bureaucrats. The latter and the emperor comprised the ruling class.

(Habib, 1995: 238)

In this sense, tax and rent were one. 'Every revenue-collection operation was a minor military expedition even in the usual routine of Mughal administration; at any time the countryside might seethe with discontent and rebellion as the pressure of demand became too heavy' (Habib, 1995: 257). Zamindar's (tax collector's) formal share of the total surplus, including the allowance for collecting the revenue, was about 18%. It could be as high as 25% of the total revenue collected.

7 Multiple state forms *within* given class forms

As the form of class society changes, the nature of the state changes. If appropriation of surplus requires immediate coercion, there tends to be a greater degree of overlap between those who appropriate surplus and those who are in charge of coercion (state actors). In addition, each form of class society itself – slave-owning, feudal, capitalist society – presents 'a mass of political forms' (as well as 'a variety of political doctrines, opinions and revolutions'), and 'this extreme diversity and immense variety . . . can be understood only by firmly holding, as to a guiding thread, to this division of society into classes, this change in the forms of class rule' (Lenin, 1919a). As the nature of class relation changes, the methods of violence also change: the weapons of violence correspond 'to the technical level of the given epoch' (ibid.).

Consider the different forms of the pre-capitalist state, with respect to slavery:

A monarchy is the power of a single person, a republic is the absence of any non-elected authority; an aristocracy is the power of a relatively small minority, a democracy is the power of the people. All these differences arose in the epoch of slavery.

(Lenin, 1919a)

And, with respect to feudalism:

The change in the form of exploitation transformed the slave-owning state into the feudal state. This was of immense importance. . . . And here too the forms of state varied, here too we find both the monarchy and the republic, although the latter was much more weakly expressed. But always the feudal lord was regarded as the only ruler. The peasant serfs were deprived of absolutely all political rights.

(ibid.)

And the capitalist state forms can also be different. It can be, more or less, liberal democratic. Or it can be the fascistic state form which emerges due to the failure of the liberal democratic state form to defend the democratic rights of people and the failure of the capitalist system to meet the economic needs of the common people who suffer because of the crisis-ridden capitalist system that is supported by *all* forms of the capitalist state. Yet, in spite of different forms of the state not only across class societies but also within a class society, there is something common to them all. It is the class content of the state, as we have already seen. As Lenin (1919a) explains:

> The state is a machine for the oppression of one class by another, a machine for holding in obedience to one class other, subordinated classes. There are various forms of this machine. The slave-owning state could be a monarchy, an aristocratic republic or even a democratic republic. In fact the forms of government varied extremely, but their essence was always the same.

Strictly speaking, class relations have the dominant, but not exclusive, influence on the state. Underlying the enormous difference in terms of state forms and functions, there is, of course, the difference in the form of class society in terms of say, the level of economic development with which class relations are closely related. The ways in which the appropriation of surplus product from direct producers occurs, i.e. class relations, can act as a fetter on the development of productive forces. At a more concrete level, the development of productive forces may be retarded by factors such as the lack of appropriate technology; ecologically sustainable interaction with, and control over, nature; and the availability of enough able-bodied people. The state is shaped by the relative economic backwardness – that is, relative to both what is needed to meet everyone's needs, and relative to what is possible if class relations and other obstacles did not exist. So one must assess 'the character of the state from the economic backwardness' of a country (Trotsky, 1991: 49).

In addition, while the state is heavily and fundamentally influenced by class relations, those who manage the affairs of the state can have a powerful and independent role. This is especially the case when there is a periodic equilibrium between classes: As Engels (1884: chapter 9) says, 'By way of exception, . . . periods occur in which the warring classes balance each other so nearly that the state power as ostensible mediator acquires, for the moment, a certain degree of independence of both.'[13]

In certain historical conjunctures, once the state exists because of the antagonistic class relations, it can shape the evolution of the property-owning classes and strata and change the form of a class society: it can help create a new (proto) property-owning class (e.g. urban capitalists) from an old one (e.g. rural landlords). This process in which a state rooted in *non*-capitalist class relations promotes capitalism gives the false impression that the state is independent of *class relations as such*.

The state – in terms of its existence as a structure of relations and in terms of actions of those who manage the state – is fundamentally shaped by class relations and economic conditions associated with class relations. Even while the state appears to act like the dominant class or appears to have created class relations, the fact of the matter is the following, and it bears repeating this point:

> The material life of individuals . . . is the real basis of the state and remained so at all the stages at which *division of labor and private property* [which are component aspects of class society] are still necessary. . . . *These actual relations are in no way created by the state power; on the contrary they are the power creating it.*
>
> The individuals who rule in these conditions – leaving aside the fact that their power must assume the form of the *state* – have to give their will, which is determined by these definite conditions, a universal expression as the will of the state, as law, an expression whose content is always determined by the relations of this class, as the civil and criminal law demonstrates in the clearest possible way.
>
> (Marx and Engels, 1845; italics added)

No matter how important the state is, the fundamental cause of society's problems is not in the state, because the state itself is rooted in class relations. Marx (1875) in his *Critique of the Gotha programme* is critical of anyone who

> instead of treating existing society (and this holds good for any future one) as the *basis* of the existing state (or of the future state in the case of future society), . . . treats the state rather as an independent entity that possesses its own intellectual, ethical, and libertarian bases.

8 Summary, and theoretical and political implications

The existence of the state is rooted in the economic basis of society, including, especially in its class relations. In the materialist-dialectical approach to the class-state outlined earlier, there are multiple inversions which indicate that certain approaches have primacy over other approaches. (a) A *process* view of the state must have primacy over a view of the state that treats it merely as a thing (e.g. apparatuses). The state (as a set of apparatuses) is a process of the masses being kept in check in the interest of the exploited class. (b) The state must be seen above all as an *objective* reality: its objective aspects must have primacy over the subjective aspects (how it is perceived). Once again, the state continually evolves 'out of the life-process of definite individuals, but of individuals, not as they may appear in their own or other people's imagination, but as they . . . produce materially' (Marx and Engels, 1845). (c) Among the objective aspects, it is the *economic* factors (production and exchange) that are more important than non-economic (e.g. political) factors. But it is not enough to say that the state is shaped by the economic sphere (or civil society or the sphere where people pursue their own interests). (d) The economic sphere must be immediately seen as a site of class relations involving private property and exploitation over other relations (including individual actions), and the class relations have a determining role, and this means that the state is basically the state of the economically dominant class and not of the exploited classes. The state must be seen at the level of private property and appropriation of surplus labour/product, that is, at the level of class relations.

The relation between the state and class relations has different elements: the political oppression of the masses as an element of their class experience is shaped by the class-exploitation element of class experience.[14] The latter is not possible without the property relations element.[15] The exploitation aspect of class and its oppression (political subjugation) aspect prompt, and are mediated by, class struggle. A basic problem of production in a class society is how to extract surplus product: the exploited tends to resist not only the fact that they do not control property but also the fact that they have to perform surplus labour which does not benefit them but which benefits another class.[16] Economic exploitation is a coercive affair, and means of coercion are ultimately in the hands of the state. Exploitation (along with the separation of workers from means of production and subsistence) compels the exploited class to resist and revolt against the exploiter class, so political oppression is simultaneously necessary. It is not an epiphenomenon. Political power is an essential aspect of class relation. Indeed, the state is a product, and an expression, of the irreconcilability of class antagonisms. The state arises where, when, and insofar as class antagonism objectively cannot be reconciled. The existence of the state proves that the class antagonisms are irreconcilable.

If the state just existed and impacted class relations and all classes, without it having to necessarily *protect* the fundamental interests of the exploiting class as against that of other classes, then people could fight against class exploitation and significantly reduce the problems caused by class relations. If class relations were merely about economic exploitation of the majority by a tiny minority with its control over property, then people's economic struggle against the property-owning class could diminish, durably and significantly, the adverse effects of class relations. And such a struggle, with some difficulty perhaps, could even remove the structure of class relations. In fact, the belief that such a thing is possible is at the heart of much of the Marxist and 'progressive' thinking about class and the state. Such a view is mistaken. Against this, the approach to the state that I defend here is that in the history of class society, a time comes when to remove the structure of class relations, one must remove the state, without which class structure – including private property relations – cannot exist and cannot be reproduced. It is therefore worth reiterating that the direct producers are not just economically exploited and excluded from control over private property; they are also simultaneously politically oppressed or subjugated. They lack control over state power, which is mainly its coercive power. They are powerless in two senses therefore: economic and political.

The property question is then absolutely crucial to the state question. Marx (1847) says:

> The question of property, depending on the different levels of development of industry, has always been the vital question for a particular class. In the 17th and 18th centuries, when the point at issue was the abolition of *feudal* property relations, the question of property was the vital question for the *bourgeois* class. In the 19th century, when it is a matter of abolishing *bourgeois* property relations, the question of property is a vital question for the *working class*.

The state's major task *is* to defend exploitative property rights. So the following statement from Resnick and Wolff, two post-modernist Marxists, does not make sense:

> To own property in a particular society need not empower the owner to employ another human being or to participate in state decisions; that would depend, for example, on ideological and political conditions in that society. To be propertyless need not require a person to sell labor power; that would depend, for example, on whether propertyless persons had socially recognized access to income from other sources [such as the state].
>
> (Resnick and Wolff, 2006: 119)

Therefore, the authors argue, 'To wield state powers of all sorts need not require ownership of property; that would depend on the social rules whereby power is granted to individuals' (ibid.). It is true that whether a given propertyless person must sell labour power would depend on whether he/she has socially recognized access to income from sources such as state, but if the state provided adequate means of subsistence to *all* propertyless, would there be class relations of any sort? And if the state does not and cannot do so, then the question is, why not?

The class nature of the state is attested not by the fact that every act is exclusively in the direct interest of the ruling class only, but by the fact that all other interests are, more or less regularly, subordinated to the interests of the ruling class, that the acts of the state are decisively shaped by what the ruling class and its political representatives take its interests to be. Acts of the state take place only within the framework of the interests of the ruling class.

It is important to recognize the similarities between the capitalist state and pre-capitalist-type states in order to understand the relatively autonomous role of the capitalist state and its actors. Without doing that how would one understand the independent role of the czarist state in Russia or the state in Japan where the *samurai*, the hereditary military nobility and officer caste, and warriors of medieval and early modern Japan 'had to *create* capitalism and a capitalist class of which they could be part' (Ollman, 2003: 200; italics added)? If they were independent of class relations as such, why did they not create a socialist state?

The state is affected by numerous processes in a class society. It is affected by the changing balance of power of the basic classes, that is, by class struggle, which often coexists with other kinds of struggles such as ecological and anti-oppression struggles. The state is affected by the need to sustain class exploitation and wealth accumulation in the hands of property owners, by external threats to a society, by the autonomous interests of state officials/politicians, by the need to intervene on behalf of society as a whole (clearing forests, making roads, providing for people during a pandemic or natural calamity, or checking excessive environmental damage), and by the contradiction between productive forces and relations leading to the crisis of production – all within the limits of the class logic of the state, that is, the need to suppress the direct producers and reproduce exploitative private property rights. Engels (1886) says that 'the will of the state is, on the whole, determined . . . in the last resort, by the development of the productive forces and relations of exchange'.

The emphasis on the class character of the state means that the state actually has a dual function. It defends the structure of class relations and the effects of class relations. That is, it defends private property and exploitation, and it also defends the inequality in consumption and income, which is dominantly caused by private property and exploitation. This under-stressed aspect of the state (i.e. the relation between the state and inequality), along with the fact that, as Engels says, the state is affected by the level of the development of productive forces, has an implication for understanding the post-capitalist transitional state, revealing a potential limitation in Lenin's thinking. Trotsky (1991: 45–6) wrote in *Revolution betrayed*:

> A socialist state even in America, on the basis of the most advanced capitalism, could not immediately provide everyone with as much as he needs, and would therefore be compelled to spur everyone to produce as much as possible. The duty of the stimulator in these circumstances naturally falls to the state, which in its turn cannot but resort, with various changes and mitigations, to the method of labor payment worked out by capitalism. It was in this sense that Marx wrote in 1875:
>
> > 'Bourgeois law . . . is inevitable in the first phase of the communist society, in that form in which it issues after long labor pains from capitalist society. Law can never be higher than the economic structure and the cultural development of society conditioned by that structure.'

Trotsky continues, now referring to Lenin:

> In explaining these remarkable lines [from Marx], Lenin adds:
>
> > 'Bourgeois law in relation to the distribution of the objects of consumption assumes, of course, inevitably a bourgeois state, for law is nothing

without an apparatus capable of compelling observance of its norms. It follows (we are still quoting Lenin) that under Communism not only will bourgeois law survive for a certain time, but also even a bourgeois state without the bourgeoisie!'

To the extent that the state has important economic functions in all societies, it will, more or less, have those functions in the transitional society too. Trotsky (1991: 46–7) explains in *Revolution betrayed*:

> Insofar as the state which assumes the task of socialist transformation is compelled to defend inequality – that is, the material privileges of a minority – by methods of compulsion, insofar does it also remain a 'bourgeois' state, even though without a bourgeoisie. These words contain neither praise nor blame; they name things with their real name. . .
>
> It is because Lenin, in accord with his whole intellectual temper, gave an extremely sharpened expression to the conception of Marx, that he revealed the source of the future difficulties, his own among them, although he did not himself succeed in carrying his analysis through to the end. 'A bourgeois state without a bourgeoisie' proved inconsistent with [the principle of] genuine Soviet democracy.

The relation between the state and inequality in consumption *is* an important matter. 'The dual function of the state', that is, the protection of specific property relations and regulation of inequalities, 'could not but affect its structure', as revealed by the experience of 1917, which 'theory was unable clearly to foresee'.

> If for the defence of socialized property against bourgeois counterrevolution a 'state of armed workers' was fully adequate, it was a very different matter to regulate inequalities in the sphere of consumption. Those deprived of property are not inclined to create and defend it. The majority cannot concern itself with the privileges of the minority. For the defence of 'bourgeois law' the workers' state was compelled to create a 'bourgeois' type of instrument – that is, the same old gendarme, although in a new uniform.
> (Trotsky, 1991: 47)

Then, apart from the matter of consumption inequality, there is the matter concerning the low level of the development of productive forces as such. The state must promote the development of productive forces (either for 'society as a whole' or in the interest of the economically dominant class). What happens if the private property is overthrown, but the low level of the development of productive forces exists in part because of isolatedness of the revolutionary transition and attendant bureaucratism within the post-revolution society, constituting a form of 'combined development' where advanced social relations (that is, relations indicating transition to socialism) coexist with relatively backward level of economic development and common people not enjoying an adequate amount of means of subsistence?

It is not just private property relations that explain the nature of the state. Relative economic backwardness can also contribute to the state's continued reproduction. This is a theme that has been relatively neglected, including by Lenin.

> Basing himself wholly upon the Marxian theory of the dictatorship of the proletariat, Lenin did not succeed . . . in drawing all the necessary conclusions as to the character of the state from the *economic backwardness and isolatedness* of the country. Explaining the revival of bureaucratism by the unfamiliarity of the masses with administration and by the special difficulties resulting from the war, the program [i.e. Lenin's socialist programme) prescribes merely political measures for the overcoming of 'bureaucratic distortions': elections and recall at any time of all plenipotentiaries, abolition of material privileges, active control by the masses, etc. It was assumed that along this road the bureaucrat, from being a boss, would turn into a simple and moreover temporary technical agent, and the state would gradually and imperceptibly disappear from the scene.
>
> (Trotsky, 1991: 49–0; italics added)

There are some practical implications of the class theory of the state. One is that as long as class relations exists, the state, the main task of which is the political subjugation of the masses, will exist. So the overthrow of class relations, including property relations, and the overthrow of the *existing* state are a necessary condition for a classless and stateless society. There is another implication which is connected to the last one. If the state arose with class divisions and if therefore there was no state in the original ('primitive') classless society, that means that people *can* manage their affairs without the state in a future society which is classless and which is economically much more developed than any form of society in the present or in the past.

> For Engels, the possibility revealed by the gentile constitution was a major guarantee that the Marxist vision of the withering away of the State in a future communist society was not a recipe for chaos, as was argued by his opponents.
>
> (Bloch, 1983: 82)

Yet historical experience has shown that in the post-1917 societies, the state remained a very powerful agent vis-à-vis ordinary people. As we have seen, this can be explained on the basis of the class theory of the state.[17]

Notes

1 The reader may recall that the references to Lenin (1919a) are from a lecture that Lenin gave on the topic of the state at the Sverdlov University. The references to Lenin (1949) are to Lenin's famous work on the state, *The state and revolution*, written in 1917.
2 As Hoffman (1995) has argued, it is important to maintain the distinction between government and the state. Miliband (1969: 49–50) says: '[T]he fact that the government

does speak in the name of the state and is formally invested with state power, does not mean that it effectively controls that power'; so it is mistaken to think that 'the assumption of governmental power is equivalent to the acquisition of state power'.

3

> The economic structure does not *exclusively explain* 'the character of the state, but it assigns these other influences a minor role. . . . The state normally sustains accumulation and this is largely explained by the nature of the economic structure'.
>
> (Wetherly, 2002: 204–205)

'And that emphasis on economics is fundamental to an understanding both of the working of the state and the ways in which these workings are legitimised, both nationally and globally' (McLennan, 2007: 428).

4   Althusser's (2001: 251) much-discussed formulation, which bears the stamp of Marx's long footnote in chapter 1 of *Capital 1* that I referred to earlier was that 'the economy is determinant in that it determines which of the instances of the social structure occupies the determinant place'.

5   Commenting on Lenin's position, Shandro (2014: 277) rightly says that the state cannot establish order by reconciling the antagonistic classes and that it must hold their irreconcilable antagonism in check by oppressing the exploited classes.

6   This claim will be modified when we discuss the state in the capitalist society.

7   Even when the state does something to fight a pandemic or to mitigate environmental damage, its actions make sure that the property-owning class makes money at the expense of the masses.

8   And these are different not only between pre-capitalist and capitalist forms of class society (as discussed in this chapter) but also *within* the capitalist form of class society.

9   Poulantzas (2008: 289) says that 'the very meaning of the state under capitalism is different from the meanings it can take on in other – pre-capitalist – modes of production'.

10 According to Banaji, the tributary mode of production is 'a mode of production where the state controls both the means of production and the ruling class, and has "unlimited disposal over the total surplus labour of the population"' (Banaji, 2011: 23). Banaji adds:

> Formulations like Miliband's 'partnership of state and capital' will simply not work for tributary régimes, where, as Trotsky understood in his brilliant pages on the peculiarities of Russia's historical development, the Muscovite state shaped the evolution of the possessing classes in a fundamental way and quite unlike anything seen in the West. (ibid.)

11 Although Marx emphasizes land, cattle are also an important means of production.

12 However, Wood (2012: 295) then says (which is problematic to me) that 'the state – in the broad sense – has not emerged from class divisions, but has, on the contrary, *produced* class-divisions and has produced the state in the narrow sense'. To me, for the state to produce class divisions, it has to first exist. So one must ask, 'Why does it exist in the first place?'

13 Engels' adds: 'Such were the absolute monarchies of the 17th and 18th centuries, the Bonapartism of the First and Second Empires in France, and the Bismarck regime in Germany.'

> The absolute monarchies of the seventeenth and eighteenth centuries were strong because the power of the nobility and the bourgeoisie was evenly balanced, though even in this case the state cannot be said to have been independent of the relations of production. (Creaven, 2000: 267)

14 Exploitation happens inside national boundaries. It also happens across national boundaries (exploitation of workers in imperialized countries by imperialist capital – more on this in the last chapter).

15 In the capitalist class society, an additional element is added: exchange relations. It is through these relations that means of production are bought and sold, and without this happening, exploitation in the sphere of production cannot occur. Unless workers can access means of subsistence only through the market, their status as exploited workers cannot continue.

16 This shows that coercion and persuasion do not always work.

17 It should be added that for the post-revolution state to wither away, it is not enough that private property relations are abolished, although that is necessary. There has to be a change in the realm of consciousness in the public sphere and in the 'private sphere': a communist consciousness is necessary.

4   The state's internal relation with capitalism and capitalists

Having explained the nature of the state at the level of class relations, I will now explore the different dimensions of the *capitalist* state in this chapter and the next eight chapters. Let us begin with where Marx ended in *Capital volume 1*. Marx (1887: 542) ended his book with a clarion call for 'the expropriation of a few usurpers by the mass of the people', that is, expropriation of the capitalists. Why did he do so? Why did he not think that the state could eliminate the problems created by capitalist production and exchange based on capitalist private property?

Given that humanity suffers from a large number of intractable problems such as poverty, inequality, precarity, unemployment, ill health, environmental degradation, and so on, we must ask, 'Why can the capitalist state, which is supposed to meet the common needs of society, not make the capitalists address these problems?' One explanation is that the state itself depends on capitalist accumulation. This idea *appears* to be in some of the writings of Marx[1]:

> To this modern [i.e. capitalist] private property corresponds the modern State, which, purchased gradually by the owners of property by means of taxation, has fallen entirely into their hands, and its existence has become wholly dependent on the commercial credit which the owners of property, the bourgeois, extend to it, as reflected in the rise and fall of State funds on the stock exchange.
>
> (Marx and Engels, 1845)

Further:

> With the development and accumulation of bourgeois property, i.e., with the development of commerce and industry, individuals grew richer and richer while the state fell ever more deeply into debt. It is therefore obvious that as soon as the bourgeoisie has accumulated money, the state has to beg from the bourgeoisie and in the end it is actually bought up by the latter. . . . Even after the state has been bought up, it still needs money and, therefore, continues to be dependent on the bourgeoisie.
>
> (ibid.)

DOI: 10.4324/9781351168007-4

In more recent times, some scholars have argued that the capitalist state cannot do this or that for the ordinary people because the capitalist class constrains state's actions, as discussed in Chapter 2. For example, it is argued that the state, which depends on the capitalist class for its own survival, cannot subject the capitalists to much regulation (including taxation) because, if this happens, then the capitalists will geographically move their investment or will go on an investment strike. David Harvey (2010b: 197) says:

> The 'success' of a particular state (national or local) is often measured by the degree to which it captures flows of capital, builds the conditions favourable to further capital accumulation within its borders and achieves a high quality of daily life for its inhabitants.

The implication of this is that the ability of the state to achieve a high quality of life for the people depends on its ability to capture flows of capital which is mobile and which is much more mobile than it was during Marx's times. Similarly, Chris Harman (1991) says:

> The state has to adjust to the needs of particular capitals because it depends on them for the resources – particularly the revenues from taxation . . .: if it goes against their interests, they can move their liquid assets abroad.

It is also said that the capitalists, or the people who share their ideology, occupy important positions within the state apparatuses and use the state in their own interests, so the state is helpless.

The idea that the state depends on capitalists for taxes, loans, and so on, and that capitalist structure, or capitalists as individuals, constrains the state is true from the standpoint of the relatively concrete aspects of capitalist class society. But overall, this is an inadequate view underlying which is the ontology of external relation according to which the state and the capitalist class (including individual capitalists) exist as separate things, and they then interact.

Another idea is that there are no *inherent* obstacles to – there are no inherent constraints on – the state being able to make capitalists serve the majority, that is, to implement reforms in the interests of the majority, and that therefore the obstacles can be removed by, say, adequate pressure from below (see Block, 2003). In other words, if the state does not meet people's needs, it is because of the lack of adequate political pressure from below. This idea also presupposes an external relation – this time, an external relation between the state and, not the capitalist class, but the working class. The assumption here is that the state and the working class exist separately, and then the working class interacts with the state through its political pressure on it and that there is no inherent 'bias' of the capitalist state against the working class. The relation between the state and working class is an empirical relation, the strength of which varies across regions/countries and historical periods. All these approaches to the state based on the ontology of external relation between class and the state must be thoroughly contested.

One must ask, 'What is it that prohibits the state from forcing the capitalists, a tiny minority of people who monopolize over the means of production and subsistence, to do things that serve the majority?' After all, the state possesses the monopoly over the coercive power of society (in the form of police, prisons, and the army, and so on), and it can easily use it against a tiny group of men and women in the interest of the vast majority. Or, at the minimum, and for the sake of an argument, what is it that bars the state from making capitalists produce things that people actually need and can afford and from making them provide secure employment with a living wage that is inflation-adjusted and ensure that capitalists' rate of profit is no more than a given percentage? What stops the state from dispossessing this minority, which dispossesses and/ or exploits the majority, and from taking over the enterprises of the minority and running them, initially, at least, on behalf of common people and thereby eliminating state's dependence on capitalist accumulation? What prevents the state from curtailing the capitalists' ability for investment strike or their geographical mobility simply in order to accumulate more and more wealth? It is said that a law that increases tax on capitalists or that makes them pay higher wages will lead to capitalists moving their investment abroad or hiding their money outside of the boundary of the state. Here the assumption is that the state, for example, the state in the US, cannot do much about this. But then when states in the periphery take a small step to provide subsidized food to workers and small-scale producers or subsidized inputs and credit to farmers or to socialize some enterprises, how is it that international financial institutions (IMF and the like) are mobilized by the powerful states to discipline the peripheral states? And how is it that the combined military power of advanced states concentrated in, say, NATO, is deployed against individuals or groups of individuals or certain states that are said to be doing things against the interest of advanced states? Why can all states not take action against capitalists moving their money from, say, high tax areas or high minimum wages areas? Why can state power not be mobilized to ensure that capital cannot make use of geographical difference across countries to play off one country against another?

These and related questions are not ordinarily posed, but they need to be. To pose these questions requires that we use a different ontology of the relation between capitalists and the state. And to pose these questions and address them also, concomitantly, requires that we recognize that the matters of economics are deeply political and the matters of politics are deeply economic.

In Section 1, I discuss the relation between the structure of the state and capitalism as an internal relation, including the idea that the state and capitalists are two arms of the same thing (= the totality of capitalist social relations). In Section 2, I discuss how the structure of the state operates within a series of limits, some of which are more stringent than others. In the concluding section, I critically reflect on the idea of the so-called separation of economic power from political power, arguing that economic power and political power are two sides of the same coin. In a sense, this chapter provides an overview of the entire theoretical discussion on the capitalist state in the book.

1 An internal relation between the state and the capitalist class

If the state cannot abolish capitalist private property or if it cannot regulate capitalists to make them serve the majority, it is not *because* capitalists as a class itself (barely top 1–10% of the population of a country) are so powerful politically vis-à-vis the state. The ultimate and fuller reason is somewhere else. Unpacking this reason requires a different ontological approach to the relation between the state and the capitalist class relation, that is, that we see their relation as an internal one rather than an external one.

How the capitalist class and the proletariat class function is partly given by their respective political relation to the state, and not just by their mutual economic relation with one another (i.e. the fact that one class exploits another class). As mentioned before, the capitalist class controls the means of production and the surplus value, and it commands far more exchange value than the working class, and it is the class that 'controls' political power as well.[2] Private property owners' control over property is a political act and not just an economic act. Capitalists control the market and the workplace. And capitalists' control is at the level of society *as a* whole. This means, among other things, that goods and services are produced for the sake of profit-making and that the quality of life of common people depends on that profit logic and on the decisions made by capitalists, while the needs of common people do not determine what gets produced and how they are produced (whether people can afford to consume what is produced and whether the method of production is healthy and ecologically sustainable). The various aspects of capitalists' control are codified, protected, and defended by a coercive state.

The obverse side of the capitalist class control over economy and the state is the fact that the class of proletarians lacks control over property, surplus value, and indeed labour process itself. And the class that lacks economic control lacks control over state power: it experiences powerlessness or the relative lack of power. The proletariat is not just a class which is economically exploited and lives a precarious life. It is also a class which is politically oppressed/dominated. And this political oppression/domination is not just in the sphere of exchange relations (e.g. labour market) and in the sphere of work relation, but also at the level of society as a whole.

The state is to be seen as being 'constitutive' of the totality of the class relation between capitalists and workers in a specific (relatively concrete) sense, while *it is the case that* class relations explain the state more than the state explaining the class relations. The capitalist class relation and the state have a 'symmetrical' internal relation: one cannot exist without the other. This means that the nature of the basic classes, or how they function, depends partly on their relation to the state and that the state is what it is because of its relation to each of these classes and to the relation between these classes. In other words, the state is internally related to the relation between capitalists and workers as the two basic classes of capitalist society.[3] In the capitalist class society, as in other class societies, the relation between classes is (a) the sum of the relation between the state and all classes in a society and (b) the relation between each of the classes and the state. The class relation is a totality. It is the whole system of economic and political (and discursive) relationship between the entire capitalist class, and the entire working class (and other classes such as small-scale producers), a system that is supported by the capitalist state.

The internal relation between the capitalist state and the capitalist class means that they are two arms of the social relationship called capitalist class relation. One arm signifies the exploitation of the majority and its (near) separation from property, and wealth-accumulation in the hands of the capitalists. Another arm signifies the political oppression/subjugation of the majority by the state. In other words, one arm signifies the capitalist class as a whole, and another arm signifies the state which is, above all, the coercive instrument to reproduce the capitalist class relations. To think about the state as an internal relation of capitalism is to examine the state at a definite level of analysis (the level of appropriators of surplus value as such), and then the various types of such appropriators (the diverse capitalist fractions).

The state is, more or less, the political affairs department of the rule of the capitalist class (surplus value appropriators) in the modern society. The bourgeois state is the capitalist class which is organized as the ruling class: '[P]olitical power is precisely the official expression of [class] antagonism in civil society' (Marx, 1987: 149). The capitalist state is a specific form – political form – of the very existence of the capitalist class. It is true that relative to pre-capitalist property owners, the capitalist property owners are less constrained by the state, and this means that '[t]hrough the emancipation of private property from the community, the State has become a separate entity, beside and outside civil society' (Marx and Engels, 1845). Yet the state 'is nothing more than the form of organisation which the bourgeois necessarily adopt both for internal and external purposes, for the mutual guarantee of their property and interests' (ibid.). With the gradual progress of modern industry, 'the class antagonism between capital and labor' intensifies, and with this, the state power, more and more, assumes 'the character of the national power of capital over labor, of a public force organized for social enslavement, of an engine of class despotism', as Marx (1871a: 23) says in his *Civil War in France*.

The *content* of social power (class power) of capitalists is expressed in the *form* of state power. To the extent that political power is the official/public expression of class antagonism, political oppression of the working class as a class is an *inherent* part of the nature and experience of that class. Separated from the mechanisms of control over the means of production, the working class is exploited by the capitalist class which monopolistically controls the means of production: *this* is a large part of the very essence of the capitalist class relation. But that is not all, because there can be no monopoly over the instruments of production, nor can there be any exploitation (i.e. monopoly over surplus labour/product), *without* the instrument of exploitation. More than anything else, the capitalist state *is that* instrument of exploitation. It is a *weapon* of the capitalist class against the masses. This is not *necessarily* in the sense of the state being used by capitalist class people on the basis of ties between them and state actors.

The association between the capitalist class and the state has been indeed close historically and not just logically. In fact, '[e]ach step in the development of the bourgeoisie was accompanied by a corresponding political advance of that class' (Marx and Engels, 1848: 15). Itself an 'oppressed class under the sway of the feudal nobility', 'the bourgeoisie has at last, since the establishment of Modern Industry and of the world market, conquered for itself, in the modern representative State, exclusive political sway' (ibid.), without which its economic exploitation of the common people would not be possible. Yet, while the capitalist class has political sway over the state, it denies the working class the right to fight for the status of the first class (the dominant class) in society.

In many societies, at a given point in time, this or that political party (or this or that coalition of parties) of the capitalist class manages the common affairs of the state and of the capitalist class as a whole (led by a dominant capitalist fraction). But this does not mean that the state is *not* under the control of the capitalist class, any more than individual members of the working class being able to change their capitalist employers on a regular basis means that they, as a class, are not subjugated to, and exploited by, the capitalist class as a whole. The different political parties are, more or less, the slightly different mechanisms through which the economic interests of the different fractions of the capitalist class and of the whole class are politically represented. America's Republican Party and the Democratic Party, or India's Congress party and the BJP, are *both* parties of the bourgeoisie, with trivial differences between them in terms of the economic policies they pursue on behalf of the capitalist class. This is the case even if one party favours certain capitalists over other capitalists or can be slightly more conciliatory to the masses than another party.

Once the capitalist class is the dominant political class, it is more or less the case that '[t]he executive of the modern state is but a committee for managing the common affairs of the whole bourgeoisie' (Marx and Engels, 1848: 15). The management of common affairs includes the defence of bourgeoisie's property ownership against the potential/actual political resistance from the masses and ensuring general conditions for accumulation of capital even if that means a massive economic cost to the masses. The interests of the masses are fundamentally incompatible with the interests of the capitalists, and therefore the state must always threaten violence, or use violence, when necessary, in order to protect the interests of the capitalists. The imperative of the management of common affairs of the capitalist class also means that the state can go against the interests of specific capitalists if their individual interests appear to go against the long-term interests of the capitalist class and/or against the political interests of the party in power.

The processes of wealth accumulation in the hands of capitalists that the state must support go right against the interest of people, the direct producers (wage workers and non-exploiting small-scale producers). This is responsible for class

struggle on their part (actual and potential), which in turn prompts class struggle from above – class struggle from above by the state on behalf of the exploiting class or the class struggle of the exploiting class implemented through the
state. Often, the class struggle from above necessitates state violence. Thus, the
ways in which the state defends capitalist property rights and contributes to
capitalist accumulation create conditions for, and require, violence. Not surprisingly, Lenin (1949) describes the state as a special coercive force, a force that
belongs to the exploiting classes and is used against the exploited classes. In fact,
the essence of the state is that it defends capitalist property rights, including the
right to exploit, and subjugates the people by the use, or threat of use, of violence: '[T]he bourgeois pay their state well . . . so that without risk they should
be able to pay poorly; by good payment they ensure that the state servants are a
force available for their protection – the police' (Marx and Engels, 1845).

The essence of the state is *not merely political* though, that is, the fact that it
resorts to violence. The essence of the state is that it resorts to violence *in the
interest of the exploiting class*, that is, to ensure class exploitation. As Engels (1884:
chapter 9) says, 'the modern representative state is the instrument for exploiting
wage-labor by capital', under normal conditions.[4] The capitalist class that the
state supports is a small minority class. To sustain the rule of a tiny minority
over the vast majority, state power is essential, and state power takes the form
of violence, actual or potential.

2 Limits on the state's functioning

It is in the very nature of capitalist state power that it will fundamentally protect
the interests of the capitalist class. This fact – the fundamental class character
of the state – sets limits on the state functioning. There are three limits. In the
outermost (maximum) limit, by using its coercive powers (and/or by the threat
of use of these powers), the state must ensure commodity relations and the
right of the capitalist class to own property in its specifically capitalist form: to
buy and sell for profit, to appropriate surplus (whether in production or outside), to dispossess the small-scale producers, and so on. Then come two inner
limits. One is that the state must create consent to its rule and bourgeois class
rule in the minds of the masses by giving material concessions and by ideological conditions (education, propaganda, identity politics, and the like), for the
continued existence of capitalism. And note that repeated use of violence and
repeated threat of the use of violence tend to produce consent to the system
out of fear. Within limits, the state can allow for the diversity of ideas that people learn, including some criticisms of capitalism and the state (and of capitalist
parties), but the state cannot tolerate a situation, or promote a situation, where
the majority become anti-capitalist in their ideology from the standpoint of
abolishing capitalism. Similarly, within limits the state can provide some material concessions but not to the extent that the reliance of common people on
the capitalist class is significantly reduced, allowing them to stop being wage
labourers.

The other inner limit concerns the economic interventions of the state (discussed in detail in Chapter 7): this exists because of the fact that it is not enough that the state defends capitalist private property rights or creates conditions where people believe in the sanctity of capitalist property rights and of commodity relations. The state must ensure conditions for accumulation within the framework of capitalist property relation and subordinate the needs of the masses to the logic of profit-making. Marx (1894: 573) says in *Capital volume 3* that 'the development of the interests of capital and of the capitalist class, of capitalist production, forms the foundation of national power and national ascendancy in modern society' and that 'the interests of the capitalist class and the amassing of riches in general' are pronounced 'to be the ultimate aim of the state'.

While both capitalists and misers seek to enrich themselves, there is a difference between them: the capitalist class, unlike the miser, is subjected by the coercive economic mechanism of competition to a 'boundless drive for enrichment' and a 'passionate chase after value'. It must therefore constantly invest money to expand money. In fact, when the system seems to come to a halt (as in a crisis), the state starts making sure that, for example, the rate of exploitation of the working class, including by imperialist oppression, is heightened in order to create fresh ground for raising the rate of profit. Although each state carries out its capitalist functions generally within its geographical area of jurisdiction, the more powerful states – imperialist states – exercise their powers more globally (more on this in Chapter 11).

The degree of stringency of the limits increases as one moves from the innermost to the outermost limit and especially when class struggle intensifies. No matter what, and even if the state is unable to adequately help the capitalist class to accumulate wealth (or indeed to feed the common people), it must protect its capitalists' right to control property and to exploit the men and the women it employs. The capitalist state is not in the business of getting rid of property rights of owners of (big) business as a whole. The limits are inter-related: ensuring conditions of accumulation resulting in some economic growth and employment not only helps capitalists economically. State-enabled economic growth produces finances (through taxes, for example) to fund such things as poverty alleviation and employment generation.[5] The latter measures in turn help the state minimize the threat to capitalist property rights and thus legitimize itself.

Given the internal relation between the dominant class and the state by virtue of which the state must promote capitalist accumulation and respond to class struggle, its actual concrete interventions may vary from time to time and may not always have the intended effect. So the actual policy interventions are driven by mechanisms that are more concrete than the internal relation discussed earlier: there are different concrete ways, to be explored in concrete research, in which the state meets the needs of the capitalist class. Different capitalist fractions have different conceptions of what accumulation strategy is, and in part because of this, personal and institutional relation between state actors and capitalists or their organizations is important. So are institutional relations (e.g. relations between the chambers of commerce and the state actors). In other words, the actual ways in which the state serves the capitalists are mediated by the agency of individual capitalists or groups of capitalists as well as state actors action (discussed in Chapter 8). State functions are also impacted by the state's forms, both geographical form, and state form in terms of whether it is, for example, democratic or fascistic. Finally, as explained in Chapter 11, the relation between the state and capitalism is impacted by capitalist class relation at the scale of the world market (that is, by imperialism) and therefore has a degree of specificity in the context of the LDCs.

3 Summary, and theoretical and political implications

The argument made in this chapter that there is an internal relation between the state and the capitalist class goes against the excessive emphasis placed within Marxism on the separation of the political from the economic. The separation is more apparent than real. The idea of the separation means that individual capitalists generally do not need to exercise extra-economic coercion against other capitalists or against their workers in economic transactions. Creaven (2000; see also Wood, 2012) says that 'the structural configuration of capitalist relations of production', that is, the separation of the direct producers from access to the means of production, 'enables their routine reproduction by economic mechanisms without the continual intervention or threat of intervention of politico-military force in the class struggle' (ibid.). This approach, in my view, while it captures a part of the reality, is deficient: it sees capitalism and its state not only from the standpoint of *individual* capitalists rather than as a class, but also from the standpoint of pre-capitalist societies. In pre-capitalist societies, *individual* owners of property (e.g. feudal lords) have political power by virtue of having control over property, a situation that is different from capitalism, where individual capitalists *as* capitalist property-owners do not possess public political power merely by virtue of being capitalists. But the capitalist class *as a whole, by virtue of their control over property,* does exercise political, cultural, and juridical functions in the lives of the masses (Eagleton, 1991: 113) in the sense that these functions are collectively performed by the collective capitalist, the state. Note that at the level of the capitalist class as a whole, the working class has no choice not to work for a wage, and it cannot choose between capitalist and non-capitalist employers. The implication for the state of this unfreedom of the working class vis-à-vis the capitalist class is under-emphasized.

The internal relation between the state (political power) and those who control property has important theoretical and political implications. Firstly, the internal relation thesis does not mean that capitalists and those who manage their common affairs within the state (politicians and bureaucrats) are one class (this is discussed in some details in Chapter 8). Secondly, to say that the state is the dominant part would be like saying that security officers that guard capitalists' property are the real owners of the property which the capitalists enjoy for a fee (to paraphrase a point Marx made, to which I will return later). In fact, 'the bourgeois do not allow the state to interfere in their private interests beyond a point and give it only as much power as is necessary for their own safety and the maintenance of competition' (ibid.).

Thirdly, and related to the last point, the internal relation thesis raises the matter of the distinction between economic and political power. Those people who talk about merely economic power of capitalists do so in order 'to sidestep the question of how to transform society without the conquest of state power' (Trotsky, 1977: 121). In fact, 'the distinction between political and economic power . . . [is a] terminological trap':

> 'Economic power', as such, does not exist. There is *property*, different forms of property. State power provides the opportunity to retain, or on the contrary, to abolish capitalist property, depending on whether state power belongs to the bourgeoisie or to the proletariat.
>
> (ibid.)

The capitalist class relation is intimately a political relation between the state and the totality of class relations and between the state and capitalist class interests. If political power is really 'the most concentrated strength of the ruling class' and serves the economic interests of the capitalist class and big landowners, then what is on the agenda is the seizure of political power through revolution against the state and not a never-ending pursuit of mere democratization and humanization of the state. The nature of state power is political, and political power is important. Indeed, '[w]hy do we fight for the political dictatorship of the proletariat if political power is economically impotent? Force (that is, state power) is also an economic power' (Engels, in Marx and Engels, 1975: 402).

The class rule is based on, and supported by, the state that uses its claimed monopoly of means of violence in support of the class that monopolizes the means of production. Because the interests of this class and the interests of the masses are irreconcilable (which is why the state exists), so replacing the rule of capitalist class cannot be a peaceful method:

> *The class theory of society* and historical experience equally testify to the impossibility of the victory of the proletariat through peaceful methods, that is, without grandiose class battles, weapons in hand.
>
> (Trotsky, 1933; italics added)

Therefore, one must reject reformism as well as 'the perspective of a peaceful transformation of capitalism into socialism' (ibid.):

> In the last analysis, the theories of reformism, insofar as reformism generally has attained to theory, are always based upon the inability to understand that class antagonisms are profound and irreconcilable.
>
> (ibid.)

Notes

1 I say 'appears to be' because Marx's view is not fully captured in these quotes, as we will see later.
2 '[R]eal power today lies with the banks, corporations and financial institutions, whose directors had never been elected by anyone, and whose decisions can affect the lives of millions' (Eagleton, 2011: 202).
3 In this sense, to use Ollman's terminology, the state is the name of a relation (r) (i.e. the relation between the basic antagonistic classes, above all), so it is *itself* a relation (R), just as capital which is the name of the relation between capital and labour is *itself* a relation.
4 'Exceptional periods . . . occur when the warring classes are so nearly equal in forces that the state power, as apparent mediator, acquires for the moment a certain independence in relation to both' (ibid.).
5 'If economic growth was no longer the goal, unemployment would increase and there would be less funding for projects such as child poverty, and people would be *un*happier' (Davidson, 2016: 215). Amy Bridges (1974) suggests that the state's legitimacy is dependent on the economy doing well, and this makes the state necessarily serve the interests of the capitalist class.

5 The state, capitalist commodity relations, and labour power

Karl Marx memorably begins *Capital volume 1*, his magnum opus, with the following words:

> The wealth of those societies in which the capitalist mode of production prevails, presents itself as 'an immense accumulation of commodities,' its unit being a single commodity. Our investigation must therefore begin with the analysis of a commodity.
>
> (Marx, 1887: 27)

Could such an analysis of the commodity in the capitalist society point to an analysis of the capitalist state? The answer is yes.

If capitalism is based on a world of commodities, including common people's ability to work, for that very reason, it also presupposes state power without which commodity relations cannot exist on a scale that they do in capitalism. State power – both in terms of what the state does and what it does not – is very much implicit in Marx's analysis of the commodity character of capitalism. I will build on his insights to explore the relation between the state and commodity relations. I also illustrate some of the ideas from *Capital 1*, by using empirical facts from different parts of the world, including from the Global South.

In the first two sections, I relate the state to the three attributes of the commodity in capitalism (use-value, exchange value, and value). In Section 3, I discuss the state in relation to the nature of the peculiar commodity (labour power) in part by using the concept of what I call labour circuit. In the final section, I outline some implications of Marx's ideas about the state and value relations for a future world beyond value and thus briefly connect Marx's *Capital 1* to the 20th-century (and more recent) discussion on the ability of the post-capitalist state to construct 'socialism in one country'.

1 Use-value, exchange value, and the state

Capitalism is characterized by the more or less free purchase and sale of commodities. A commodity has three attributes: use-value, exchange value, and

DOI: 10.4324/9781351168007-5

(labour) value. Use-value – the utility of a commodity – inheres in it. Exchange value is 'the proportion in which values in use of one sort are exchanged for those of another sort, a relation constantly changing with time and place' (Marx, 1887: 27). One commodity can be exchanged for many. Value (or labour value) is the fact that every commodity represents a certain amount of socially necessary abstract labour time (explained later). I argue later that the state is related to each of the three aspects of the commodity.

To the extent that the wealth of societies dominated by the capitalist mode of production appears as an 'immense collection of commodities' (Marx, 1887: 60), then the capitalist state – that 'official representative of society as a whole' (Engels, 1877) – must maintain the commodity form/status of things (of use-values). As inanimate objects, '[c]ommodities cannot go to market and make exchanges of their own account' (Marx, 1887: 60). There must be 'their guardians' – that is, 'their owners . . . who must place themselves in relation to one another, as persons whose will resides in those objects' (ibid.). The state must ensure that commodity owners relate to one another on the basis of freedom and equality.

In fact, the sphere of purchase and sale of commodities is 'a very Eden of the innate rights of [human beings]', and in this sphere 'alone rule Freedom, Equality, Property and Bentham' (Marx, 1887: 123). There is freedom 'because both buyer and seller of a commodity . . . contract as free agents, and the agreement they come to, is but the form in which they give *legal expression* to their common will' (ibid.; italics added). The state represents – embodies – this legal expression. There is equality because each guardian of commodity 'enters into relation with the other, as with a simple owner of commodities, and they exchange equivalent for equivalent' (ibid.). The state is supposed to make sure that there is no cheating and fraud. There is respect for property because each guardian of the commodity 'disposes only of what is his own' (ibid.). There is no scope for grabbing what belongs to someone else. In other words, the state makes sure that there is respect for property. And, of course, there is 'Bentham, because each looks only to himself' (ibid.). The only force that brings the guardians of commodities 'together and puts them in relation with each other, is the selfishness, the gain and the private interests of each' (ibid.). The state, more or less, reproduces and supports these values. All in all, the rule of 'Freedom, Equality, Property and Bentham' (ibid.) creates opportunities for, and presupposes, state action, in the sense that the state is supposed to ensure this rule.

The state is presupposed by commodity relations because of a positive (coordinative) and a negative (punitive) reason that Marx does not explicitly discuss. Firstly, in a society with a massive and expanding division of labour, concrete labours in different places throughout the world need to be inter-connected through exchange on the basis of abstract labour, so the state action is necessary to coordinate the myriad commodity relations. Commodity exchange implies a division of labour in society where different producers produce different commodities. This social division of labour (which is also a spatial division of labour) in turn requires 'a division of labour' between society and the state. The large-scale commodity exchange that is characteristic of capitalism and the fact that a commodity's exchange values are 'constantly changing with time and place' (Marx, 1887: 27) require a society-level coordination in time-space. This task falls on the shoulders of the collective agency of the state.

It is the state indeed which introduces various rules to support and sustain commodity relations in the overall interest of the 'community' of commodity owners and to resolve any conflict among them. It makes sure that the guardians – the commodity owners – 'must behave in such a way that each does not appropriate the commodity of the other, and part with his own, except by means of an act done by mutual consent' and that 'they must, therefore, mutually recognise in each other the right of private proprietors' (Marx, 1887: 60). The relation between commodity owners as mediated by, and within, the state is a *juridical* relation: 'This juridical relation . . . expresses itself in a contract, whether such contract be part of a developed legal system or not' (ibid.). It is 'a relation between two wills' (ibid.). Although, the state is 'the reflex of the real economical relation between the two' (ibid.), state's coordinative activities are crucial to the reproduction of commodity relations, including those that involve both capital and labour. There is also need to create a geographical built environment to connect different commodity producers located in different geographical sites of concrete labour. The state seeks to fulfil this communal or society-wide need.

Secondly, there is a punitive reason why the state is presupposed by – necessary for – the existence of commodity relations. The rules of commodity exchange can be violated by the guardians of commodities whose self-interest ('Benthamism') lies in expanding their command over commodities (and over money, the most abstract 'form' of commodities), so punitive actions by the state may be necessary. Commodity owners are all equal in that they all have the same trait (they own commodities) and that they relate to one another on the basis of equality. Yet commodity relations can be unequal because some commodity owners, prior to any commodity exchange, may have more exchange value (e.g. more quantity of a given commodity or of its monetary value) than others, and in order to expand their command over commodities and to improve their status *as commodity owners*, some may inflict *extra-commodity* relations or unequal exchange on others and defraud them. To the extent that the defrauding happens with the help of extra-economic means (i.e. actual use, or threat of use, of coercion), commodity relations are political (extra-economic) matters and not just economic matters. There is therefore a need to 'guard the guardians' to make sure that a given guardian of the commodity does not force another to sell their commodity below the market price or part with their commodity against the wish of the owner. There is a need for a (political) guardian of the guardians (of economic commodities). The state is that guardian. Dominantly a site of *extra*-economic relations, the state must ensure that commodities are exchanged on the basis of *economic* relations, that is, without extra-economic coercion or without a significant quantity of extra-economic coercion.

Commodity relations are not necessarily a peaceful matter. The state's defence of existing commodity relations on the basis of *freedom and equality* contribute to *un*freedom and *in*equality. There is unfreedom, including the fact that workers are not free not to sell their labour power to the capitalist class. There is inequality, including in the form of class differentiation among commodity producers, and inequality between the big business and small-scale owners.[1]

It is not just that state's functions aim to codify/sustain/reproduce commodity relations. To some extent, the very existence of the capitalist state, that is, its separation from society, has something to do with the commodity form of use-values. In a world where everything is being turned into a commodity, it is useful to recall Pashukanis' (1924) fundamental question about the nature of capitalist state:

> [W]hy does the dominance of a class not become that which it is, i.e. the actual subordination of one part of the population to another, but instead assumes the form of official state authority? Or, . . . why is the apparatus of state coercion created not as a private apparatus of the ruling class, but distinct from the latter in the form of an impersonal apparatus of public power distinct from society?

The capitalist state form exists because of the generalized commodity character of society where commodity owners are free and equal and who are supervised by an abstract collective subject, the state.

However, contrary to Pashukanis' idea that commodity relations are associated with non-coercive action of the state,[2] 'disputation and contestation is intrinsic to the commodity, in the fact that its private ownership implies the exclusion of others' (Mieville, 2005: 126), so 'violence – coercion – is at the heart of the commodity form'. The reason is that

> [f]or a commodity meaningfully to be 'mine-not-yours' – which is, after all, central to the fact that it is a commodity to be exchanged – some forceful capabilities are implied. If there were nothing to defend its 'mine-ness', there would be nothing to stop it becoming 'yours', and then it would no longer be a commodity, as I would not be exchanging it.
>
> (Mieville, 2005: 126)

Taking the analysis from the individual to the societal level, one can see that force must be a general condition for the maintenance of commodity relations. 'In commodity production, "need" and "right" stand opposed' in the sense that '[e]xisting property relations', which are not yet productive relations, 'systematically separate producers from the objects of their need, on an everyday and continuous basis'. So society is organized in such a way that it 'constantly impels individuals, groups, classes and other collectivities' to invade 'the rights of others'. In other words, '[t]he motive to trespass, steal, invade, oppress, rob and generally transgress property right is continually recreated through the pressure of material need' (Mieville, 2005: 127).

> Hence this system of social production relations generates a permanent and general requirement for means of 'defence', i.e. for means of violence and its organization. Without a constant threat and/or application of force, commodity production would stand in danger of rapid subversion and breakdown.
>
> (ibid.)

Commodity exchange requires a medium of exchange, so the state 'puts in circulation bits of paper on which their various denominations . . . are printed' (Marx, 1887: 83). 'Capital is nothing more . . . than money put back into production and circulation to yield more money. If money is to represent real values the same kind of State regulation of money supply and credit is called for' (Harvey, 2012: 274). While necessary it might even take out of circulation certain currencies in circulation (de-monetization). Such a policy can have massive effect on common people.[3] The state has to make sure that insofar as currencies 'take the place of gold to the same amount, their movement is subject to the laws that regulate the currency of money itself' (Marx, 1887: 83). It has to make sure that the money in circulation 'must have an objective social validity of its own': 'This compulsory action of the State can take effect only within that inner sphere of circulation which is coterminous with the territories of the community' (ibid.: 84). The state is also a guarantor of the stability of exchanges and therefore of the form of value (Callinicos, 1987a: 100). The state acts as the lender of last resort which prevents the collapse of the monetary order and banking systems.

Commodity relations have a spatial – scalar – form, and this fact has implications for the state. The commodity relations happen at multiple spatial scales. The global scale is very important for capitalism: 'The production of commodities, their circulation, and that more developed form of their circulation' which is called world-embracing commerce, or trade, 'these form the historical ground-work from' which capitalism rises (Marx, 1887: 85). Incidentally, this global character of capitalism means that the proletariat, essentially, has a global existence:

> The proletariat can . . . only exist world-historically, just as communism, its activity, can only have a 'world-historical' existence. World-historical existence of individuals means existence of individuals which is directly linked up with world history.
>
> (Marx and Engels, 1845)

The world geography of trade indicates that capitalism is a global phenomenon from its very origin. Commodity owners engage in transactions with one another on a global space which is politically divided into multiple territories governed by their states, some of which are more powerful than others. The state shapes commodity exchange not only at the national scale. It also shapes commodity exchange at the global scale, including on the basis of imposition of customs duties.[4] For a nation to sell its wares in another (distant) nation, the extra-economic state intervention is necessary. The national states of powerful merchants have contributed to commerce by helping merchants, by giving them charters and security.[5] The sale of commodities from South Asia in England was heavily restricted by the British state in the 18th century in order to protect British industry. Thanks to the pressure of the British manufacturers on their government,

> By 1720, laws had been passed forbidding the wear or use of printed or dyed cotton cloth. In 1760 a lady had to pay a fine of £200 for possessing an imported handkerchief! Moreover, heavy duties were imposed on the import of plain cloth.
>
> (Chandra, 2009: 92)

The British colonial state also forced people in the colonies to engage in commodity exchange (for example, to produce indigo) where it did not exist and resisted any effort to preserve modes of production and subsistence not based on large-scale commodity exchange.

Indeed, when powerful states perform the task of the guardian of commodity relations at the global level (to guard the other states guarding commodity rules in their territories) and when they impose commodity relations and/or impose unequal commodity exchange on 'weaker' countries, those powerful states become *imperialist* states (I will return to this topic in Chapter 11). Given the massive expansion of global trade and enormous movement of currencies, the need for guarding commodity relations becomes that much important, hence laws to promote 'free trade' (against, for example, state interference in economy). There are also laws against money-laundering.[6]

In capitalism, almost all the things produced are commodities (this is Marx's assumption) or are subjected to commodification. But in reality, this is not true: not everything is a commodity, a few things are a commodity only partially, and the process of commodification is not a linear process. It is important to note that the commodity status of things is contested in part under pressure from common people who lack the means of exchange to buy the use-values that they need, so the state is partly involved in the determination of what is and what is not a commodity. Use-values (e.g. a vaccine) may be enjoyed in non-commodity or a semi-commodity form when the state supplies them for free or at a subsidized rate. Child care, for example, is a commodity here, and it is not a commodity there. As Martha Friendly (2019) notes, the commodity status of childcare exists to a much greater extent in North America and Australia than in Nordic countries. This geographical unevenness partly reflects the variation in the degree to which the commodity character of capitalism is contested, rather than taken for granted, by wage earners and small-scale producers, who lack an adequate command over exchange value and are there-fore adversely affected if they have to pay for everything.[7]

The dominant aim of capitalist production is *not* to directly meet the needs of people. 'Use-values are only produced by capitalists, because, and in so far as, they are the material substratum, the depositories of exchange-value' (Marx, 1887: 131). The capitalist's aim is 'to produce a use-value that has a value in exchange, that is to say, an article destined to be sold, a commodity'. Not just that. Their aim is 'to produce a commodity whose value shall be greater than the sum of the values of the commodities used in its production' (ibid.), that is, a commodity which will give the capitalist a profit. Thus, capitalism abstracts from the nature of use-values. It is indiffer-ent to whether a commodity is smelly or flavourful. It is even indifferent to whether a commodity is harmful to the body (if it is, say, cancerous) or to nature (increased toxicity in water or air). Whichever product can be sold more profitably, not necessarily what people need for a healthy life, will be produced and sold. This means that if a commodity c_1 is more profitable than a commodity c_2 but people's needs are met better by c_2, then large-scale commodity producers resort to a curious commodity (i.e. advertising) to make people believe that they actually need to consume and buy c_1. Often advertising spreads misinformation about commodities and creates unhealthy needs (e.g. tobacco) (Williams, 1980). This may prompt state intervention against such action, but there are limits to what the state can do (I return to this in the following).

The fact that the motive of capitalist production is the production for exchange and not for meeting human need has another implication for the state: it imposes constraint on what the state can do for common people. The state, which claims to represent, and is often seen by many as representing, the general interests of society, fails to make sure that there are enough of the things that people actually need (e.g. nutritious food, shelter, protective equip-ment during a pandemic). The state has little control over the ways in which society's total labour is allocated to the production of different things. As a result, whatever is available in the market is usually assumed to have some use.

2 Value relations and the state

A commodity has many exchange values (e.g. a laptop can be exchanged for 100 pens or 10 shirts). Exchange values 'are only the mode of expression, the phenomenal form, of something contained in it, yet distinguishable from it' (Marx, 1887: 27). Value is the 'common substance that manifests itself in the exchange value of commodities' (ibid.: 28). To say that commodities have value is to say, above all, that they are products of human labour, albeit human labour of a specific kind. A given thing/service 'consists of the same unsubstantial real-ity' (ibid.), a certain amount of labour power which exists irrespective of the concrete forms it takes (e.g. laptop-making labour or cane-making labour), that is, abstract labour, which is the stuff of value.

The magnitude of value of an article is measured by 'the quantity of the value-creating substance, the labour', contained in that article (p. 29). The quantity of value-creating labour 'is measured by its duration' (e.g. weeks, days, and hours of labour) (ibid.). This does not mean that 'the more idle and unskilful the labourer, the more valuable would [their] commodity be, because more time would be required in its production' (ibid.). In fact, '[t]he labour time socially necessary is that required to produce an article under the normal conditions of production, and with the average degree of skill and intensity prevalent at the time' (ibid.) in a given territory (e.g. a country under the jurisdiction of a state).[8]

What determines the proportion in which one commodity is exchanged for many other commodities within a country or across countries is the social value (or simply, value) of the commodities: a socially necessary amount of abstract or homogenous labour performed under average conditions.[9]

The labour that defines value is socially necessary labour. 'In general, the greater the productiveness of labour, the less is the labour time required for the production of an article, the less is the amount of labour crystallised in that article, and the less is its value' (Marx, 1887: 29–30). So the value of a commodity (v) 'varies directly as the quantity (q), and inversely as the productiveness (p), of the labour incorporated in it' (ibid.: 30). This productiveness is a function of the average amount of skill of the working men and women, the state of science and technology as well as the social organization of production and quality of the means of production (ibid.: 29). This productiveness is also a function of physical/natural conditions.[10]

The state is potentially related to each of these circumstances, a fact Marx abstracts from. Anything that the state can do to reduce the costs of discovery of, for example, minerals (e.g. oil drilling) will affect their value. The state can change the state of development of science and technology via its investment in education and research. The state invests resources in transforming the physical/natural environment as well (e.g. irrigating a dry area or increasing an area's geographical accessibility).

A commodity must be produced at its value, within a given geographical territory defined by the commodity circulation. It could be the area under the jurisdiction of the nation-state, and it could be the world market, which is where the law of value ultimately operates. If an enterprise spends x minutes to produce a laptop, while the average amount of time taken to produce a laptop is $x/2$ minutes, that enterprise runs the risk of going out of business, unless it is subsidized by the state bridging the gap between the individual and social value. By supporting capitalist commodity relations, the state supports some capitals better than other capitals. By investing in science and technology and through other measures, the state can create a situation where the value of commodities produced by capital under its territorial jurisdiction is reduced below the global average and where a country's global competitiveness is thus enhanced.

3 The state, the 'peculiar commodity', and the labour circuit

Commodities (e.g. corn, computer, genetically engineered seeds, Artificial Intelligence, education in private schools) are all products of human labour. In capitalism, the labour that produces commodities is itself a commodity (we are abstracting from the labour of a small-scale producer working on own account). 'It is only from this moment that the produce of labour universally becomes a commodity' (Marx, 1887: 124). In capitalist enterprises, wage-workers do not sell to the owner the products that they produce. They sell labour power. Labour power or the 'capacity for labour' is 'the aggregate of those mental and physical capabilities existing in a human being', which they exercise whenever they produce a use-value (ibid.: 119). Labour power is a peculiar commodity unlike other animate and inanimate commodities. The state has to maintain this peculiarity, which has many aspects.

So an important form of commodity exchange in capitalism is the one between the seller of labour power (worker) and the buyer of labour power (capitalist) who function 'as free persons, as independent owners of commodities; the one possessing money and means of production, the other labour-power' (Marx, 1887: 272). The sale and purchase of labour power requires a certain condition which has to be produced: double freedom of labour. The first aspect of this freedom is that people are economically forced to sell their labour power because they possess no means of production.[11] This is a negative freedom which is discussed in the next chapter. The second aspect of the double freedom is that the person must be free from any obstacle to them, freely selling their labour power. This freedom, a positive freedom, exists only when the seller is the sole owner of the commodity, who does not sell himself/herself but only their ability to work for a certain number of hours every day and week. Unlike a slave labourer, the wage labourer 'must constantly look upon his labour-power as his own *property*, his own commodity . . . by placing it at the disposal of the buyer temporarily, for a definite period of time' (Marx, 1887: 119).

Capitalism is indeed characterized by the fact that 'labour-power can appear upon the market as a commodity only if, and so far as its possessor . . . offers it for sale, or sells it, as a commodity' (Marx, 1887: 119). For this to happen, they 'must be the *untrammelled owner* of' their capacity for labour, that is, of his or her person (ibid.; italics added). The owner of labour power and 'the owner of money meet in the market', and there is only one difference between them: 'one is buyer, the other seller; both, therefore, *equal in the eyes of the law*' (ibid.; italics added). The state has to make sure that the labour power is a commodity and continues to remain so, that is, a person is not extra-economically forced to sell their labour power to a given buyer/employer and that a person must have the freedom to withdraw selling their labour power when they wish to.

Labour freedom, labour's commodity status, that the state generally seeks to protect, is beneficial to labour and to capital. It is better to work and live as a free labourer than an unfree/slave labourer. Because workers own their commodity labour power, they can sell it to whoever they want to and wherever they want to: if they receive lower wages from buyer b_1 in one place than what the buyer b_2 in another place offers, then they are free to sell it to b_2. To the extent that the buyer, b_1, pays lower-than-average wages and can benefit from the unfreedom and immobility of particular sellers of labour power, then he/she (b_1) can have a competitive advantage over another buyer (b_2). So the state makes sure that no such unfair advantage occurs in the labour market.

Individual commodity owners need rules that govern commodity *exchange* but such rules and mechanisms of maintaining those rules constitute *a use-value* which cannot be bought and sold for a profit and which cannot therefore be supplied by capitalists because of their self-interested character. This applies to the peculiar commodity (labour power). The capitalist and the worker cannot maintain the labour power in its commodity status: they cannot ensure that the labourer is able to treat 'his labour-power as his own *property*' and he and the owner of money deal with each other 'on the basis of *equal rights*' (italics added) (Marx, 1887: 119). Only the state, characterized by a semblance of the separation from the private interests of workers and capitalists, can do so in the interests of the 'community' of workers and capitalists. 'Wherever free labour is the rule, the laws regulate the mode of terminating this contract' (Marx, 1887: 123). The fact of a free labourer is codified in state laws: '[O]nly the independent labourer, and therefore only the labourer *legally qualified* to act for himself, enters as a vendor of a commodity into a contract with the capitalist' (italics added) (ibid.: 194).

There is a sense in which different types of labour are the same: leather work, scavenging, computer-typing are all equal in that they represent the expenditure of a certain amount of mental and manual energy.[12] This fact contributes to the notion of equality in society which is then reflected in state's laws about equality: all the people are equal before law. So not only does the state maintain the commodity status of the products of labour and of labour power, but also does it maintain the equal status of people involved in different kinds of labour.

Like any other commodity, labour power has value. Value of labour power is the average value of the necessary commodified means of subsistence which people need to live. The value of this commodity has some peculiarity, with implications for the state. The value of labour power includes the cost of satisfying different needs (a definite quantity of muscle, brain, and the like is expended, which has to be replaced; shelter, healthcare, education, and so on) and the cost of replacing the people who die. (Wage is the monetary form of this value.)

The state plays a role in meeting some of the needs and in regulating how these needs are met. Needs are shaped by the physical environment, which is in turn changed partly by state action (e.g. policies concerning the environment). Habits and expectations and the level of civilization also shape human needs, adding a cultural element to human need. Here also the state plays a role as it partly serves as a repository of human history and memories and subjected to pressure from workers (to expand their needs).

If the state is involved in the determination of the value of labour power, it is then involved in production of labour power itself. Some of the state-aided technical change can reduce the value of labour power by shortening the time taken to produce the means of subsistence or to produce the means of production that produce the wage goods. It can affect the cost of the maintenance of labour through policies of taxation of subsistence of items and through its import policies where cheap articles produced abroad enter a national market thus lowering the cost of reproduction. By contributing to the value of labour power in non-commodified forms (e.g. state-funded schools), the state can also lower the value of the bundle of necessaries (i.e. wages that private capital pays), other things constant. A general point to be made here is that the state, to enforce equal exchange involving the sale of labour power and indeed sale of all other commodities, has to be involved in an activity which is not based on equal exchange: for example, the tax that the state receives is a tribute.

The commodity relations are characterized by the principle of not only freedom but also equality: commodity owners 'exchange equivalent for equivalent'. This general principle applies to buyers and sellers of labour power. Not only should sellers of labour power be free to sell their commodity (and that the state seeks to make sure that this happens) but also the price of their commodity, labour power (i.e. wage), should be equal to the cost of its production. Marx generally assumes in *Capital vol. 1* that this is the case, but he is also aware that in the real world, this is not.[13] Millions of people receive a wage that is below the cost of production of their labour power, including the cost of food and shelter, education for children, and so on. This is indicated partly by the population below the 'poverty line' in every country of the world.[14] This happens even in advanced countries such as the US.[15]

The state intervenes on behalf of workers in the realm of exchange (e.g. labour market). This can be understood by using Marx's formula for simple commodity circulation (C-M-C). C-M-C has to be modified into C-M-C'-R-C. The state connects to each phase of the labour circuit, especially given the fact that '[i]n contradistinction . . . to the case of other commodities, there enters into the determination of the value of labour-power a historical and moral element' (Marx, 1887: 121), which, in turn, is a product of the interaction between class struggle for improvement in living conditions, and state policy.

Let us begin with C. The state shapes the determination of the value of the commodity labour power (C): it influences what sorts of commodities are to be included in the value of labour power. The state, within limits, shapes the rate of employment – that is, whether, and to what extent, men and women can indeed sell their labour power for a given wage (M). Often wages fall below the value of labour power, so the state is involved in the determination of the wage (M) through, for example, its wage policy. It may also supplement the private wage with a social wage in the form of various anti-poverty and welfare measures. Through its monetary policy and other policies (including those that put a lot of money in the hands of the super-rich), the state can shape the price of wage goods (that is, it can cause inflation) and therefore the actual size of the basket of wage goods common people can access (C').

The consumption of these commodities, mediated by un-commodified labour including especially of women at home (R), where all kinds of cost-cutting, thrifty conduct, and financial planning happen, in turn reproduces the commodity labour power (C). The state also intervenes in the sphere of reproduction, where, among other things, the commodities bought with the money wage are processed and consumed, often by women. The state has laws that regulate marriage and parental rights and control over family's property. The state has a degree of oversight over parents' role in children's education and healthcare. On the basis of all these successive phases (C, M, C', and R), the original C (that is used in the workplace) is reproduced anew as C. The cycle continues.[16] In terms of a theoretical tendency, the cycle operates at the global scale. And empirically, the cycle increasingly operates at the scale of the world market with the gradual emergence of a global labour market.

4 The state and commodity fetishism

Commodity fetishism is an important trait of capitalist society. It refers to the fact that commodities 'behave' as if being sold and bought is in an inherent part of being a useful thing, even if it is the case that '[s]o far no chemist has ever discovered exchange value either in a pearl or a diamond' (Marx, 1887: 53). Commodity fetishism means that life in capitalism is objectively based on the fact that if I have a need for a laptop or a lollypop, these must be bought (I cannot have direct access to these), which means that these must be produced and sold for a profit. Commodity fetishism means that, for example, for every potato one has, one wishes to have as many eggplants as possible from the other person one is in an exchange relation with, so these commodities effectively start relating to one another replacing the direct relation between the two people in question. One does not care about the conditions under which the other person is living and working.[17]

The veil of commodity fetishism is not and cannot be removed 'until it is treated as production by freely associated people, and is consciously regulated by them in accordance with a settled plan' where 'the labour power of all the different individuals is consciously applied as the combined labour power of the community' (Marx, 1887: 51–2). But the state is the biggest obstacle to this possibility because it maintains the commodity status of things that people need: it protects the private character of production and the commodity status of the products of labour. The state reproduces a system where the production for sale for profit subordinates the production for directly meeting human needs. The state cannot ensure that society produces things that meet people's needs, whether 'they spring from the stomach or from fancy' (i.e. physical and cultural needs). The state is bound by the law of commodity fetishism. The state is also responsible for keeping the veil of the geographical form of commodity fetishism: because the state, in its national-geographical form, does not allow the rational mobilization of world's resources across existing national boundaries, without which 'world-historical existence of individuals', of the proletariat, mentioned earlier, is not possible.

The fetishism of the commodity applies to labour power as a commodity in ways that Marx does not reflect on. This is the fact that the commodity labour power, which exists in the labour market, as meat does in the meat market, 'behaves' as if it inherently has an exchange value. This means that people must sell themselves (sell their labour power) for a wage (some money) for them to meet their needs which they inherently possess. Anyone who challenges this fetishism and aspires to a society where everyone contributes to society depending on their abilities and finds opportunities for productive work, and where everyone's needs are met, will be disciplined by the state. Even the limited amount of welfare some workers might get is made dependent on performing wage work. People accept – and have been taught from childhood to accept – the limits to the state action by accepting the fetishism of labour power as a commodity. The state cannot do anything significant to weaken the commodity status of the only possession that common people have: their ability to work. The only way to live under the capitalist state is to live as wage slaves.

5 The state and counter-tendencies to equality and freedom in commodity relations

The sphere of purchase and sale of commodities, including labour power, is 'a very Eden of the innate rights' of people, and in this sphere 'Freedom, Equality, Property and Bentham' alone rule (Marx, 1887: 123). In actual practice, however, this rule is violated, and here as well the state is involved. While the state seeks to, is expected to, ensure labour freedom, it often is the case that labour is not free. In pre-capitalist societies, direct producers could not sell their labour power freely, thanks to various feudal rules. In capitalism, there is also unfree labour in many cases. Child labour itself is unfree labour (Das and Chen, 2019).[18] There are at least 150 million child labourers, including at least 60 million girls, in the world now (ILO, 2017). They are not legally qualified to act as sellers of labour power. Many adult labourers – at least 25 million – are also unfree (ibid.). Many of them are under debt bondage, a situation that used to exist in Marx's time as well.

The existence of unfreedom of the sellers of labour power is not an accident. While the general tendency in capitalism is that people have the freedom in the labour market, it is the case that whenever and wherever there is a need on the part of capital to discipline labour in order to extract more surplus value, capital seeks to impose unfreedom on labour (or, convert free labour into unfree labour), suggesting that capital dispossesses labour of its freedom to freely enter and/or exit the labour market (Brass, 2011; Das, 2013). Unfree labour violates an important principle of commodity exchange. The extent of unfree labour depends on the imperative of competition between buyers of labour power as a commodity and their need to competitively cut labour cost, and on the extent of class struggle and resistance against unfree labour. Therefore, there has been a need for the state to take action (as we will see in the next chapter). The state's non-doing is this: it has not done enough to eliminate unfree labour.[19]

Labour freedom includes freedom of geographical movement. It is a fundamental right inside (many) countries.[20] Correspondingly, capital's control over labour as a class includes control in its *geographical* form, and this shapes state's own action. While the state is generally committed to promoting free labour, it is also involved in restricting the freedom of labour, in the interest of (sections of) capital in a specific country/region and time. It restricts the movement (out-migration and in-migration) of labour. This means that people cannot sell their commodity (labour power) *wherever* they like to.[21] There are also no compete agreements, sustained by the state, whereby workers are stopped from leaving their current employers.[22]

There is restriction on labour mobility at the level of the world market. In a world of more than 7 billion people, there are only 164 million migrant workers, the majority being men (ILO, 2018). Capital is much more free to move across countries than labour is. Such restriction is imposed by the state of advanced capitalist countries on labour from the LDCs, while they put pressure on the states of LDCs to allow free movement of capital to exploit labour there. Of course, some states (e.g. the Canadian state) are more friendly towards foreign labour than other states.

Marx assumes that wages cover the cost of reproduction of labour power, as mentioned earlier. In reality, this is the not the case: wages fall below the value of labour power. And, the state is complicit in this gap. The reason for this is that other things constant, the lower the wages, the higher the surplus value, and it is the role of the state to make sure that a higher rate of surplus value is appropriated by the ruling class. So the state acts to keep wages within limits, in favour of the buyers of labour power. It is the case that 'during the historic genesis of capitalist production, the bourgeoisie, at its rise, wants and uses the power of the state . . . to force them within the limits suitable for surplus-value making' (Marx, 1887: 523). During the historical genesis, increasing wages beyond a limit or receiving wages beyond a level invited state penalty. The state makes sure that wages remain within limits so that the capitalist class has a reasonable rate of profit. This situation characterized not only the early stage of capitalism in Europe but also capitalism during the current times, especially in the periphery. In addition, promoting economic globalization (free trade), the states of advanced countries trigger a race to the bottom in terms of wages. This tendency was there during Marx's time as well to some extent. In 1870s, a British politician remarked: '"If China . . . should become a great manufacturing country, I do not see how the manufacturing population of Europe could sustain the contest without descending to the level of their competitors" (*Times*, Sept. 3, 1873, p. 8.)' (Marx, 1887: 430). Marx goes on to say something which is so contemporary: 'The wished-for goal of English capital is no longer Continental wages but Chinese' (ibid.).

Wages have remained within limits broadly favourable to capital, thanks partly to the state. This is indicated by the decreasing ratio of wages to the value of the product (national income) that workers make.[23] When wages rise beyond a point, the state takes step to reduce wages by, for example, raising the interest rate and creating unemployment. Similarly, even if daily or weekly wages increase, the price of labour power per hour (hourly wage) may be reduced because of capitalists prolonging the working day for a given daily wage. In addition, when the per-hour wage during the normal part of the working day is low, this 'compels the labourer to work during the better paid over-time, if he wishes to obtain a sufficient wage at all' (Marx, 1887: 386). The state engages in a case of non-doing: it does little to prevent a drop in wages.

The level of wages is partly a function of the relative power of capital and labour, as mediated by the state. So complementing the state interventions aimed at regulating wages in favour of capital is the fact that workers' trade union activity is often restricted or even prevented by the state. This has happened historically, as during Marx's time.[24] This happens in our time.[25] It is often criminalized.[26] Coercive powers – those of police and army – are used against workers, and these powers are supplemented by capitalists' own coercive agents, legal or illegal.[27] Even when real wages fall, and this happened, for example, in England in the 16th century, causing 'the condition of the labourers. . . [to] become much worse' (Marx, 1887: 524), 'the laws for keeping them down remained in force, together with the ear-clipping and branding of those "whom no one was willing to take into service"' (p. 524). Whether or not the ruling classes needed any regulation of wages, it 'was unwilling in case of necessity to be without the weapons of the old arsenal' (p. 524). It was only in 1813 that 'the laws for the regulation of wages were repealed' in England (p. 525).

The state acts against workers not just in terms of wages and working day. As we have seen, workers and capitalists, as commodity owners, are nominally equal in eyes of the law. 'The rule of law forbids the dispossessed sellers of labor power and the owners of the means of production equally from stealing bread' (Bonefeld, 2021: 179). However, in case of a contract-breaking, the state often punishes individual workers more severely than it does individual capitalists.[28]

A peculiar character of labour power as a commodity is its 'perishability'. If a sweet potato is not sold for a couple of days, or if a machine is not sold for a few weeks, their use-value will not be affected. This is not true about the labour power. If a person cannot find wage work, that is, 'If his [or her] capacity for labour remains unsold, the labourer derives no benefit from it', but there is 'a cruel nature-imposed necessity that this capacity has cost for its production a definite amount of the means of subsistence' (Marx, 1887: 122). This commodity (labour power) cannot be separated from its owner and kept in a fridge. Labour power has a bodily location: it inheres in the bearer of the commodity. If it is not reproduced through regular consumption of food, clothing, medicine, and so on, its possessor, a human being, will simply die The body is the bearer of labour power.[29] Note also that bearers of commodity labour power have feelings. Loss of work – not being hired by anyone (rejection) – hurts men and women emotionally, which is why there is a strong association between depression and unemployment (Dooley et al., 2000). The state is directly or otherwise responsible for the immense emotional suffering of the working class.

The body has to be reproduced for the continued mental and physical existence of labour power. This is possible only when the buyers (capitalists) buy labour power, and the buyers will buy it only when they can make a profit off it. The state does not guarantee that people can sell the only commodity they possess, with a decent price for the commodity (i.e. a good compensation). This is state's *non-doing*. This non-doing has enormous consequence for people. The state is directly or otherwise responsible for immense economic and emotional suffering of the working class. And to the extent that being unemployed/under-employed and earning a very low income weakens workers' bargaining power (and to the extent that, one may add, the state fails to ensure a remunerative price for small-scale producers), state's non-doing has adverse *political* impact on the masses, as far as their relation to the state and capitalists is concerned.

Consider a wage strike in response to the fact that workers are not paid a wage to cover the cost of maintenance. What happens to the two types of commodity owners who are considered equal in the eyes of state laws? Capitalists do not make money during a strike, but they do not die because of the lack of food and shelter. If workers do not work and do not have food and other necessaries, for a few weeks, they will simply die. The question is this: what happens if the state feeds the workers every time they go on a strike. This would help the workers keep the use-value of their commodity intact; they would remain 'the guardian' of their commodity. This would therefore break the intransigence of the buyers of labour power. The state *not* feeding the workers during a strike or when they are locked out by employers, this act of not-doing, is also an act of *doing*: it *is* an intervention on behalf of the buyers of commodity labour power and against the sellers of that commodity. For there to be equal exchange, there has to be an exchange, and for there to be an exchange, there have to be owners of commodities, but the state fails to make sure that workers remain commodity owners and that they indeed remain bodily alive. Capital and labour – or the capitalist as the personification of the imperative to accumulate capital, and the labourer as the personification of labour time – cannot be equal in reality, no matter how equal they might seem as commodity owners/sellers and in the eyes of the state.

Consider small-scale producers. Many of them produce commodities for large-scale companies. If they go on a strike, refusing to deliver their products unless a better price is paid, and if the strike continues for several weeks, not only do they not have much saving to live on but also do their products may lose their use-value (they may go rotten, for example). What would happen if the state supplied large-scale refrigeration facilities to these farmers and an income support during the strike? This would allow these commodity producers to engage in a transaction based on 'the equivalent for the equivalent' with the large-scale buyers of their commodity. The state does not do this. No wonder, hundreds of thousands of farmers commit suicide every year in the world, including in India and in African countries.

The very process of commodity exchange, which is supposed to be equal and voluntary and is supposed to benefit all, kills many people who are involved in that process. This fact goes against the most fundamental presupposition of commodity exchange: commodity owners must live to exchange commodities. The much-discussed right to life – which the state supports at a general level – in bourgeois discourse is vacuous therefore. Often there is more concern for the right to life of animals (e.g. holy cows for Hindus, other animals that animal rights activists care much about) and of unborn babies (for sections of the Christian community) than for human beings who die because they cannot sell the only possession they have (usually their ability to work) (or some crop, as in the case of small-scale producers). Every day 25,000 people – including 10,000 children – die because of hunger: that is, more than 40 people – including 15 children – every second (Holmes, n.d.). Some 854 million people worldwide are estimated to be undernourished, and they experience slow death every day.

Marx (1887: 122) decides 'to assume provisionally, that the possessor of labour-power, on the occasion of each sale, immediately receives the price stipulated to be paid for it'. In reality, workers are paid several weeks after they perform their work. In this sense, the use-value of the labour power – labour – is given as a loan to the capitalist. There are many potential consequences of workers' loan to the capitalist. Note that independent small-scale producers also receive the payment for their goods weeks and sometimes months after they deliver the products to the state, merchants, ago-industrial capitalists, or many others.

Indicated here is the fact that there are different temporalities of life for different classes, even if both are commodity sellers. While the worker receives wages weeks after performing their work (i.e. weeks after selling its commodity – labour power), and the small-scale producers receive money for their product weeks after they sell it, they have to pay the property-owning class for the things that they need (e.g. food, medicine, and so on) at the time of buying them and even *before* they begin to consume a thing (people have to pay rent *in advance*). Thus, propertied class people, who control the means of production and subsistence, receive a credit from the masses who are always short of money. The state does little.

Workers and small-scale producers are sometimes forced to buy things on credit from mercantile capitalists, often at a higher-than-normal price, and the state generally sustains these usurious relations (including those involving payday loans scheme). People may buy inferior goods (adulterated food) which have adverse health implications, and they do this because they do not have enough money to buy better quality food. The state does little, at least partly, for 'fear' of too much interference in the capitalist market.

There is another aspect of commodity fetishism: when some have more exchange value (more money) than others, commodity exchange is still seen as being free and equal (because all have one trait: commodity ownership). So the problem of inequality is seen as a matter of individual failure. And the state defends and sustains this idea and this practice.

Thus, the state sustains commodity relations in various ways. These include the codification of the rules that support the existence of the classes that depend on the sale/purchase of commodities and conditions for generalized commodity production; coercive enforcement of relations among commodity owners based on the idea of free and equal exchange; stopping the violation of the law of commodity exchange when it happens; and enforcing unequal exchange when necessary.

6 Summary, and theoretical and political implications

In some form or another, the state is a necessary precondition for the continued existence of values. It is clear that in relations to commodity relations, the state is involved in different kinds of roles. Firstly, the state, the sphere of extra-economic coercion, makes sure that commodity exchange can freely happen, that is, that one parts with what truly belongs to one, that there is therefore no cheating or extra-economic coercion in the sphere of economic exchange. It also affects the ways in which commodity exchange happens (e.g. investment in science which affects value; contribution to wages falling below the value of labour power, through the provision of de-commodified services). Secondly, it tends to take steps to stop the violation of the law of commodity exchange. Thirdly, in certain cases, it itself enforces unequal exchange (or it tolerates or encourages unequal exchange on the part of commodity producers), when it is necessary in the immediate interest of capitalist class as a whole, or in the interest of a hegemonic fraction of that class, or when the long-term interest of capitalist society is at stake. Colonialism/imperialism is an expression of this tendency.

At a concrete level and generally speaking, capitalism is indifferent to whether a worker is a male or a female, a Black or a white, a Brahmin or an ex-untouchable, and so on, as long as they all produce an average level of surplus value and are not trouble-makers. Capitalists may exclude men here and women there from employment or pay lower wages to workers of some social background than to others. Among many social relations racism is an important oppressive relation. Racism allows capitalists to divide the working class, and elements of the working class may make use of racism to achieve success in the competitive labour market, and if racism benefits capitalists as it does, the capitalist state, including through bourgeois political parties, tends to reproduce racism. As Gordon says, 'the constitution of the racialised as an object of administration typically involves their exclusion from, not inclusion into, full citizenship rights' (p. 25). But that does not mean that the state is fundamentally racist in the way that it is fundamentally capitalist. So I cannot agree with Gordon (2007: 24) who says that

> racism is not a mere policy option pursued by the state: it is part of the state form. As the state is capitalist, so it is racial. It is an integral moment in the state's effort to constitute a market in wage labour and ensure the expanded reproduction of capitalist social relations and, as such, race is deeply embedded in the state's institutions.

As we have seen, in capitalism, whichever product has more exchange value will get produced, not what people need. The state, which claims to represent the general interests of society, fails to make sure that there are enough of the things that people, irrespective of their gender, race, and the like, need (e.g. food and shelter, protective equipment during a deadly pandemic). The dominant aim of capitalist production is not to directly meet the needs of people. In a sense, this motive of capitalist production – incessant pursuit of exchange value, of money – 'imposes constraint' on what the state can do for common people, those who do the work of production. The state can do little even if toxic and useless commodities are produced that are not useful to the vast majority of the people. It is therefore impossible to agree with David Harvey (2019) when he says:

> a socialist program, or an anti-capitalist program, of the sort that I would want is one about trying to manage this capitalist system in such a way that we stop it being too monstrous to survive at the same time as we organize the capitalist system so that it becomes less and less dependent upon profitability and becomes more and more organized so that it delivers the use values to the whole of the world's population.

The idea that capitalism can be made to depend less and less on profitable production and that it can be organized in such a way that *use-values* will be produced, amounts to a most fundamental distortion of the very core of Marxist view of capitalism as Marx laid out in *Capital volume 1* and Lenin (1899) did in his *Development of capitalism*. Marx begins *Capital volume 1* with these lines: '[t]he wealth of societies in which the capitalist mode of production prevails, presents itself as "an immense accumulation of commodities"'. And in terms of capitalism being made to be dependent less on profits, Marx is very clear: capitalists have the '*boundless greed after riches*' and the '*passionate chase* after value' (ibid.; stress added) (Marx, 1887: 107). Further,

> it is only in so far as the appropriation of ever more wealth in the abstract is the sole driving force behind his operations that he functions as a capitalist . . . *Use-values must therefore never be treated as the real [or immediate] aim of*

> *the capitalist,* neither *must the profit on any single transaction. The restless never-ending process of profit-making alone is what he aims at.*
>
> (ibid.; italics added)

There is a major political implication of the relation between the state and the law of value in the context of the struggle for socialism. Two aspects of the law of value are worth noting here. One is that commodity exchange presupposes a complex division of labour: different countries (just as different enterprises in a country) produce different commodities, at varying level of development of productive forces. Another is that the value of commodities changes as the development of productive forces – productiveness of labour – changes. In relation to both, the role of the state in protecting a country against the law of value is limited.

Let's start with the uneven productiveness of labour. As I have mentioned, the state can help a given enterprise under its jurisdiction to close the gap between its own value and the social value (or the gap between the value of all commodities produced in a country and the value of all these commodities produced globally). In fact, the extent to which a state can protect its economy against the law of value is a major contributory factor to the economic development of that country, under the limits of global capitalism. By investing in science and technology and through other measures the state can create a situation where the value of commodities produced by capital under its jurisdiction is reduced below the global average and enhance competitiveness.

There is, however, a limit to the extent to which the state can protect the enterprises (e.g. small-scale producers) that produce above the social value. First of all, the capitalist state must maintain commodity relations (the law of value). Besides, the *nation*-state's own economic health, *to the extent that* it operates under capitalism, depends on social value and total social wealth. A given country needs resources to pay for the commodities it needs, so it must itself commodities produce competitively to be able to sell them. The state can regulate the law of value operating in terms of how it affects the country under its jurisdiction but cannot *eliminate* it because a given state as well as the economy under its jurisdiction are parts of a bigger whole (the world-economy). That is why, 'Marxism takes its point of departure from world economy', but it sees the world economy 'not as a sum of national parts but as a mighty and independent reality which has been created by the international division of labour and the world market, and which in our epoch imperiously dominates the national markets' (Trotsky, 1931a). The capitalist world economy subjugates its component parts (e.g. national economies and their states). As commodities are circulated at a global scale, an introduction of a machine in one country can affect the value of commodities in another country: the value of commodities is affected by society-wide labour productivity. No country can remain competitive if its labour productivity per hour does not rise to the global average. 'The strength and stability of regimes are determined in the long run by the relative productivity of their labor' (Trotsky,

1991: 41). And it is ultimately the state's responsibility to ensure the strength and stability of the economic system.

If a socialist revolution occurs in a country surrounded by capitalist countries, there are two ways in which the latter can influence the new state. One is military threat. Another is the global law of value supported by the guardians of law of exchange (nation-states) and the guardians of the guardians (imperialist states). The importance of the military threat should not be over-emphasized at the expense of the law of value. There are two processes involved. Firstly, 'by the rapid improvement of all instruments of production, by the immensely facilitated means of communication' the capitalist class draws all the countries, including the less developed ones into one world market. Secondly, cheaper commodities produced in advanced countries break into the markets of LDCs and break their protected economies (Marx and Engels, 1848: 16).

In fact, the world market is a major means of imperialist penetration (more on this in the last chapter). In a world of uneven and combined development, where countries are different in terms of the dominance of bourgeois relations and in terms of the level of capitalist development, the bourgeoisie of the advanced nations using its state power 'compels all nations, on pain of extinction, to adopt the bourgeois mode of production; it compels them to introduce what it calls civilisation into their midst, i.e., to become bourgeois themselves', to adopt the techniques of development it (the bourgeoisie of the advanced countries) prefers (Marx and Engels, 1848: 16).

'All nations' means all nations, including the ones where the capitalist class has been overthrown (temporarily). In the context of the post-1917 Russia, this is what Trotsky said, in his *Third international after Lenin*, critiquing those who believed in the idea and practice of socialism in one country, that it is possible for the state to construct socialism in a single isolated country:

> To the extent that productivity of labor and the productivity of a social system as a whole are measured on the market by the correlation of prices, it is not so much military intervention [by the state of an advanced country] as the intervention of cheaper capitalist commodities that constitutes perhaps the greatest immediate menace to [the new state of a post-revolution society]. This alone shows that it is by no means merely a question of an isolated economic victory over 'one's own' bourgeoisie.
>
> (Trotsky, 1996: 71–2)

To the extent that greater level of productiveness affects the value of commodities and enhances the competitiveness of a country, it is important to remember that an advanced country may enjoy greater productiveness, which acts as a threat:

> [A] Ford tractor is just as dangerous as a Creusot gun, with the sole difference that while the gun can function only from time to time, the tractor

brings its pressure to bear upon us constantly. Besides, the tractor knows that a gun [i.e. coercive powers of the state] stands behind it, as a last resort.

(ibid.)

A new post-revolution transitional state will 'depend on world capital':

If we were producing at the prices of the world market, our dependence on the latter, without ceasing to be a dependence, would be of a much less severe character than it is now. But unfortunately this is not the case.

(ibid.)

Of course, the new state can exercise its monopoly over foreign trade trying to regulate the impact of the global law of value on the country. But a state's 'monopoly of foreign trade itself is evidence of the severity and the dangerous character of our dependence' in a context of existing unfavourable correlation of forces: '[W]e must not forget for a moment that the [state] monopoly of foreign trade only regulates our dependence upon the world market, but does not eliminate it' (ibid.)

Then there is the second aspect of the value: international division of labour. A given country, whether it is more or less developed, is affected by the division of labour at the international scale. In capitalism, there is an 'incompatibility between the present productive forces and the national boundaries' (Trotsky, 1996: 78), which means that productive forces are being developed at a global scale, while the political system of capitalism is still more or less dominated by nation-states. This implies that even if a country is more developed and the value of its commodities is lower than that in other countries, that country and therefore its state are no less dependent on other countries than the LDCs and their states. Every state, developed or not, must depend on imports and exports. This means that

highly developed productive forces are by no means a lesser obstacle to the construction of socialism in one country than low productive forces, although for the reverse reason, namely, that while the latter are insufficient to serve as the basis, it is the basis which will prove inadequate for the former.

(ibid.: 83)

In other words, one cannot forget the importance of the law of uneven development. The branches of the economy that are less developed (i.e. which produce above the global value) cannot be developed if the more developed sectors cannot export.

The impossibility of building an isolated socialist society . . . in the concrete geographical and historical conditions of our terrestrial economy, is determined for various countries in different ways – by the insufficient development of some branches as well as by the 'excessive' development of others.

(ibid.: 83)

'On the whole, this means that the modern productive forces are incompatible with national boundaries', that is, the boundaries controlled by particular nation-states (ibid.). If, thanks to the global law of value, the construction of socialism by a state in an isolated country is difficult, the same law of value also limits the extent to which the capitalist state can take steps to improve the conditions of the majority in a significant and durable manner.

Notes

1 For example, in 2020, the Indian government has introduced three farm laws which would strengthen the market power of agri-business at the expense of farmers and consumers. The new legislation would allow large corporations to be involved in commodity relations with farmers, in the name of providing farmers with the *freedom* to sell and purchase produce. It would allow farmers to deal with large corporations outside the Agricultural Produce Market Committee (APMC), which guarantees a minimum support price (MSP) to the farm producers. Companies dealing with farmers outside the APMC could get around MSP. The laws would also encourage hoarding without any limits on quantity or time. Futures contracts would be also facilitated, through which all types of speculative vultures would be welcomed into the sector (Ghani, 2020). The three laws faced widespread farmers' protests for a year. Under the pressure of these protests, the Indian government was forced to repeal them in November, 2021. Of course, there is the possibility of the laws returning in a modified form when a suitable political condition arises. This is simply because the *mechanism* behind the introduction of the laws – i.e. the pro-corporate character of the regime – remains.
2 'Pashukanis's theory does imply coercion and politics, but does not imply the necessity of a particular form of organisation of that coercion. The state certainly 'injects clarity and stability into the legal structure', but that is a secondary function' (Mieville, 2005: 128).
3 On 8 November 2016 at 8 p.m., the Indian prime minister gave a surprise address to the nation, saying that as of midnight on that day, all Rupees 500 and Rupees 1,000 notes (which together accounted for 86.2% of all currency in circulation) would no longer be valid currency and that people would get fifty days to deposit the demonetized currency into their accounts, with the expectation being that those holding onto untaxed 'black money' will be caught. No black money (unaccounted-for money) was caught, of course. This had a catastrophic effect, especially in rural areas and small towns 'where banks or even an exchange mechanism do not exist' and where people heavily depend on commodity relations. Workers and small-scale producers were 'unable to purchase daily necessities' and small-scale producers could not sell their perishable produce to traders, 'since these transactions are almost always conducted in cash' (Kumara and Kumar, 2020). The main aim of the government was to replenish cash in the hands of the banks (which were not able to get back the money they had loaned to the private companies; in fact, the pro-business government has been forgiving these loans). And the e-enterprises also benefitted from millions of e-transactions that ensued. The move also forced people to open bank accounts. It thus helped strengthen the public sector banking system and deepen commodity relations. Large parts of the banking system will be privatized in due course by the government.

4 Marx and Engels (1845) say in *German ideology*:

> Customs duties which originated from the tributes which the feudal lords exacted as protective levies against robbery from merchants passing through their territories, tributes later imposed likewise by the towns, and which, with the rise of the modern states, were the Treasury's most obvious means of raising money.

5 The British state 'sponsored monopolies headed by the East India Company, state expenditures on equipping the armed forces, especially the navy'. In fact, '[a] very long spell of state sponsorship, of "mercantilism", was necessary for British capitalism to develop sufficiently to be able to dominate the world on the basis of the free trade urged by Smith' (Harman, 1991).

> The newer centres of capital accumulation [e.g. Germany, the US and Italy] that emerged alongside Britain in the 19th century were as dependent upon national state support as British capitalism had been previously German, Italian and Yankee capitalists all looked to a national state which would use its power to impose protectionist measures against outside competition: the rise of indigenous capitalist firms in these countries was closely tied to the establishment of unitary states prepared to accede to their demands (the unification of Italy, the victory of the North in the American Civil War, the establishment of the German Empire under Bismarck). (ibid.)

6 The amount of money laundered globally in any given year could be as high as 2–5% of global GDP (White, L., 2017).

7 Friendly (2019: 9) says that '[i]n a market model, child care is treated as a commodity, not a right or an entitlement or a systematically planned and developed public good'. If it is not a commodity, then the state is more or less directly involved in its provision.

8 What is assumed here is that in producing a commodity, 'no more time [is spent] than is needed on an average, no more than is socially necessary' (Marx, 1887: 29). If an average shirt needs 10 minutes to produce, and if the shirt produced by given producer takes 20 minutes, then their short will be sold *as if* it is produced in 10 minutes.

9 If one laptop is exchanged for 100 pens (worth $1000), this means that if 100 minutes of homogenous labour are necessary to produce a laptop, only 1 minute of such labour is necessary to produce a pen, on an average.

10 For example, the same amount of labour in favourable environmental conditions is embodied in x tons of corn, and in unfavourable, only in, say, $x/2$ tons. With 'richer mines, the same quantity of labour would embody itself in more diamonds', and therefore, 'their value would fall' (Marx, 1887: 29).

11 Labour power as a commodity exists when a person has no direct (i.e. market-unmediated or state-mediated) access either to the other means of production with which they can produce their means of subsistence or to the means of subsistence, to any significant extent.

12 For a contrast, consider the cases (e.g. India) where scavenging is considered a polluting/inferior kind of work, relative to the priestly work or writing poetry, so scavengers – like performers of manual labour as such – necessarily enjoy a low social status, while there is no objective reason for this (see Chattopadhyay, 2013, on how the origin of the devaluation of manual labour is causally linked with the emergence of class relations in India).

13 In the US, there are 50.8 million US households that cannot afford a basic monthly budget, including housing, food, child care, healthcare, transportation, and a smart phone in 2017. In 2017, 4 in 10 US adults, 'if faced with an unexpected expense of $400, would either be unable to cover it or would pay for it by selling a possession or borrowing money' (Randall, 2018).

14 'In 2018, almost 8 per cent of the world's workers and their families lived on less than US$1.90 per person per day' (UN, n.d.). That effectively means that at least 8% does not have enough food to eat.

15 'The world's largest retailer, Walmart, pays its workers so little that thousands of them in the US are forced to rely on public assistance programs such as food stamps, Medicaid and subsidized housing, which are funded by American taxpayers. '[A] single Walmart Supercenter is estimated to cost taxpayers between $904,542 and $1.74 million per year in public assistance money. For Walmart, this represents tens of millions of dollars in savings, all on the backs of America's taxpayers and workers'. (Sheppard, 2017). This is called Walmart tax.

16 Their total income $(I) = (w_h) (h)$, which is the per hour wage (w_h) times number of hours worked in a day or a month (h).

17 Commodity fetishism is reinforced by capital fetishism where workers falsely attribute to machines or constant capital, a power which really belongs to them (Dimoulis and Milios, 2004).

18 Marx treats 'the labour of those who are physically and legally minors' which can play an important role as 'a specially striking example of labour exploitation' (Marx, 1887: 194) where, in some contexts, the adult male acting as a free agent 'sells [his] wife and child. He has become a slave-dealer. The demand for children's labour often resembles in form the inquiries for . . . slaves [as in America]' (Marx, 1887: 272).

19 Capitalism 'assumes and requires *general* labor mobility, but "general" does not mean "universal," and individual capitalists can employ, have employed, and continue to employ unfree labor' (Davidson, 2016: 209). This will not be possible without the state's assistance to capitalists.

20 Article 19 of the Indian Constitution is about the '[p]rotection of certain rights regarding freedom of speech, etc.' and says that all citizens shall have the right 'to move freely throughout the territory of India', 'to reside and settle in any part of the territory of India', and 'to practise any profession, or to carry on any occupation, trade or business' (Human Rights Watch, 1999).

21 'In former times, capital resorted to legislation, whenever necessary, to enforce its proprietary rights over the free labourer' and this meant geographical restriction: 'For instance, down to 1815, the emigration of mechanics employed in machine making was, in England, forbidden, under grievous pains and penalties' (Marx, 1887: 405).

22 There are 30 million American workers – one in five – who are covered by non-compete agreements which 'are in many cases less about protecting trade secrets than they are about tying workers to their current employers, unable to bargain for better wages or quit to take better jobs' (Krugman, 2017). These agreements allow companies to assert 'assert ownership over work experience as well as work' (Dougherty, 2017). Add to these 30 million the 50 million or so workers with pre-existing health conditions who might be effectively unable to buy individual health insurance, so they are stuck with their current employers (Krugman, 2017).

23 Between 1970 and 2015, the share of national income paid out to workers has decreased from about 55% to below 40% in advanced countries and from more than 50% to less than 40% in emerging economies (Dao et al., 2017).

24 More specifically, this happened until the time of the fully developed manufacture period when 'the capitalist mode of production had become sufficiently strong to render legal regulation of wages as impracticable as it was unnecessary; but the ruling classes were unwilling in case of necessity to be without the weapons of the old arsenal in case some emergency should arise' (p. 524).

25 Commenting on the trade union activity in the current times, an ILO (2017) report says:

> In some cases union membership is repressed for political or investment considerations. Some governments have 'adopted a restrictive policy with regard to recognising unions in the hope of attracting foreign investment.' In addition, restrictions of various kinds and officially sanctioned, or ignored, anti-union activities remain

pervasive in a large number of countries as reflected by the numerous complaints filed each year and examined by the ILO's Committee on Freedom of Association.

26 In Marx's (1880) proposed workers' enquiry, the question #91 reads: 'Do you know of cases when the government made unfair use of the armed forces, to place them at the disposal of the employers against their wage workers?'

27 The Maruti car workers' struggle in India is a clear testimony to this: these workers have been punished basically because they have fought to establish a trade union organization that is independent of company influence (Krishnan, 2017; White, J., 2017).

28 The provisions of the labour statutes as to contracts between master and workman, as to giving notice and the like, which only allow of a civil action against the contract-breaking master, but on the contrary permit a criminal action against the contract-breaking workman, are to this hour (1873) in full force. (Marx, 1887: 525)

29 And the body – women's body in the current society – is also the *producer* of future labour power.

6 The state and capitalist property relations

As we have seen, the sphere of the exchange of commodities, including labour power, is one where not only Freedom, Equality, Bentham rule but also where Property does (Marx, 1887: 123). Why property? 'Property, because each disposes only of what is his own' (ibid.). There is a need for state intervention to make sure this rule is protected. Not just that. The state is involved in the very creation of specific property rights by virtue of which 'each disposes only of what is his own' (ibid.).

In this chapter, I will begin with a typology of private property and then discuss the role of the state in relation to the production of private property in capitalism. I will conclude with a discussion on how it is that many contemporary Marxists under-emphasize the importance of private property and the Marxist proposal for the abolition of private property.

1 Forms of private property

Private property comes in various forms (Figure 6.1). The state is inevitably connected to these forms. A distinction is to be made between private property in one's labour (or in one's labour power, the ability to perform labour) and private property in 'things' (= non-labour use-values). Things can be of different types, so another distinction to be made is between private property in the means of subsistence (e.g. vaccine, food, videos) and private property in the means of production (e.g. land, an industrial enterprise).

Private property in the means of production is of different types, depending on the form of labour (Marx, 1887: 541). The first type of private property is where one person or family uses their own abilities and own means of production (some of which may be in the form of commodities) to produce a commodity which they sell to another person who produces a different commodity in the same way. Here private property is the materialization of one's own labour (or surplus labour or surplus labour product, that is, the difference between what one produces and what one absolutely needs to live).[1] Some sort of state intervention is necessary to make sure there is no unequal exchange between and, among owners of this form of private property (usually, small-scale producers), that one only parts with what one has.

DOI: 10.4324/9781351168007-6

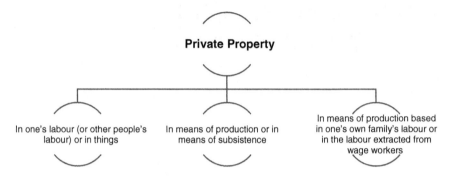

Figure 6.1 Forms of private property

The second type of private property in the means of production is exploitative property. Here private property is the materialization of the surplus product appropriated by the exploiting class from direct producers. Under pre-capitalist private property relations, direct producers (e.g. small-scale producers or peasants) are not free to work for whoever they wish to (serfs only partially owned their labour and slaves did not own it at all), while in capitalism, direct producers, who are wage workers, are (nominally) free. Both unfreedom in pre-capitalist societies and freedom in capitalist society are defended by the state. Capitalist private property is the material form of surplus labour appropriated by capitalists, and the state defends both the surplus appropriation and its result, i.e. capitalist property. Both the state and the capitalist class justify the existence of capitalist property on the basis of conflation between the capitalist form of property and property based in one's own labour.

Capitalism requires that direct producers, more or less, sell not their labour (i.e. products of their labour such as corn or a computer code) but the power to do labour. This in turn requires that they must not have direct (= non-market) access to (a) the means of production that are necessary for them to engage in social production and (b) the means of subsistence that they need to be able to live. Unless people with rights in the products of their own labour are separated from their property on a large enough scale (or unless serfs and slaves are transformed into free wage workers directly), there can be no capitalist property. There are two ways in which the separation of direct producers from property – the production of capitalist form of private property in the means of production – happens. Both of these are state-mediated.

2 State-mediated class differentiation as a basis for capitalist private property

One is class differentiation, a process that Lenin, including in *Development of Capitalism in Russia* (Lenin, 1899), analysed in greater details than Marx and other classical Marxists. This is a process where under the rule of equal exchange of commodities, some commodity producers gradually lose their property because other commodity producers produce more efficiently. Class differentiation of commodity producers results in the formation of capitalists and proto-capitalists, but also independent non-exploiting producers and semi-proletarians (the latter two groups constitute what I call small-scale producers).[2] Small-scale producers are adversely impacted by the capitalist class in at least three different but connected ways. Firstly, when they work as wage labourers for a part of the year, they are exploited like full-time wage labourers. Secondly, they are dispossessed of their property by the capitalist class and its state through primitive accumulation. Thirdly, they do not receive the full price of the products of their labour from the capitalist class and its state, so they are exploited in the commodity market; they may also pay a high price for the things they need (inputs; insurance, bank-loans, etc.). Apart from being impacted by the capitalist class, small-scale producers are also exploited by the landlords/money-lenders (on the basis of appropriation of ground rent and usurious interest).

Exploitation of small-scale producers by elements of the ruling class cannot happen without the support of the state: this fact Lenin under-emphasized. It is the state that codifies the rules of the commodity exchange. The state also codifies and defends the rights of the propertied classes (e.g. moneylenders and merchants) to alienate direct producers from their property when, for example, the latter fail to pay back their loan. Small-scale producers often go into debt because the cost of the means of production and subsistence produced by capitalists is too high. The terms of trade between small-scale commodity production and large-scale commodity production being against the former can be countered by the state, and yet the state allows small-scale producers to incur a loss and go into a debt.[3] They lose their property until they become property-less (pauperization is followed by proletarianization).[4] Capitalist private property is based on the state-mediated negation of small-scale private property based in own labour or family labour. The market-based process of class-differentiation can involve violence as well: if an independent producer (e.g. a peasant) owes a loan to a moneylender or to a bank and if they do not surrender their assets in return for the loan because they wish to protect their livelihood, then violence is used against the independent producers.

An important question to ask: why can the state not socialize the debt of small-scale producers (all those who are not net buyers of other people's labour power)? After all, the state routinely forgives billions of dollars that big businesses owe to state-owned banks or otherwise makes available to the big business free money. This is important to ask in order to understand where the state's necessary bias lies and to see that commodity exchange based on private property is partly a political (state-mediated) process.[5]

State's taxes on subsistence goods (indirect taxes in general) – an extra-economic intervention – can contribute to the expropriation of small-scale producers, including peasants (Cleaver, 2019: 82). Indeed, tax on workers and small-scale producers is an indirect form of 'exploitation' by the state, a state which fails to look after the common interests of these classes. To understand the relation between the state and small-scale producers, one might ask: why does the state not exempt them from taxation (while it gives billions of dollars of tax exemption to the big business)?

It is also important to note that state's defence of commodity relations on the basis of equality and freedom produces unfreedom and inequality in the sphere of property relations which the state defends; unfreedom because those who have private property in labour but not in means of production and have become the net sellers of labour power are *not free* not to sell that property to the capitalist class; inequality because those who are owners of private property in labour and owners of the products of their labour (i.e. small-scale producers), when unable to pay their bills, lose their property; some of them come to have more property than others, and some of them become net buyers of labour power, and others become net sellers of labour power (Lenin, 1899: chapter 2).

3 State-assisted extra-economic 'production' of capitalist private property

The second process in which small-scale producers lose their property giving rise to the emergence of capitalist property rights holders is what Marx calls primitive accumulation, which involves the state (this is the subject of my detailed theoretical study in the sequel to this book). The state typically enables the forcible separation of direct producers from their private property and from access to communal property and contributes to the emergence of private property in its capitalist form. The state thus produces an important condition for capitalism, that is, 'the owner of money [finds] labour-power in the market as a commodity' (Marx, 1887: 119). This means that 'instead of being in the position to sell commodities in which his [or her] labour is incorporated', a person 'must be obliged to offer for sale as a commodity that very labour-power, which exists only in his [or her] living self' (ibid.). The state must reproduce, and it does reproduce, a significant section of people as sellers of labour power, that is, as wage workers, and not as people who can sell goods and services that they produce by using their labour power.

In modern times, one can observe a 'property circuit' (somewhat similar to capital circuit and labour circuit I have mentioned earlier). It can be represented as P-S-C. The state takes property from small-scale producers (P) through a combination market mechanisms and extra-market mechanisms. The market mechanisms include two. One is that the systemic neglect of rural areas and the rural periphery of city-regions by the state, especially, in the South, drives down the price of land, allowing the state (and/or capitalists) to buy it cheap. This is akin to a massive gentrification process. Another is that rural impoverishment due to the systemic neglect by the state and exploitation by different property-owning strata can induce some small-scale producers to sell their land 'voluntarily'. In any case, after obtaining the property, the state holds it as state property (S) temporarily as a bank holds money. And then state property is turned over to capitalists at a cheaper rate, and thus it becomes capitalist private property (C). Of course, sometimes, P-S-C can be shortened to P-C, when capitalists directly buy/obtain property from small-scale producers, with the help of the state (including its police and judiciary).

The transition from P to C takes time, in part because of small-scale producers/owners' opposition to alienation/dispossession of their property as such or alienation/ dispossession for a given compensation. The more the time, the greater the loss of potential profit for capitalists, including from speculation on the property following alienation. State coercion is needed to shorten the transition time. One reason why many small-scale producers are reluctant to part with their property is that while capitalists (and their state) wish to get the land at a cheaper rate, small-scale producers wish to get a higher price – higher relative to current market conditions and higher relative to what the price of the property would be in the near future due to speculative rise in the price. Another reason is that after losing their property, they are not sure that they can obtain decent and secure employment in the capitalist enterprises that might be established (as an alternative to the current self-employment on their own property). Whether property is transferred, and at what price, partly depends on the balance of power between small-scale owners on the one hand and the state/capitalists on the other. Capital does not always get what it wants, but it generally does, thanks to the role of the state.

Following the coercive dispossession from their property (and/or alienation from property through market mechanisms), the direct producers are now turned into new class subjects (workers for capitalists). The state then subjects them to a series of processes: statistical investigation and classification (they are classified on the basis of occupation, location, income, and so on), a degree of economic consolation (e.g. policies aimed at poverty alleviation or poor relief), and ideological, including religious indoctrination. They are also subjected to physical coercion, criminalization,[6] and disciplinary action. It is indeed not enough that the state forcibly separates direct producers from their means of production (and subsistence such as homestead or cottages) and creates a proletariat. Marx says that following 'the forcible creation of a class of outlawed proletarians', it was the 'bloody discipline that turned them into wage-labourers' (Marx, 1887: 528). They were subjected to 'disgraceful action of the State which employed the police to accelerate the accumulation of capital by increasing the degree of exploitation of labour' (ibid.). The newly created class of workers must be made to be accustomed to working for the capitalists and must be used to working for long hours.

Being forced to choose between starving and working for a wage, and thus being compelled to choose the latter, people begin to agree to – that is, give consent to – living like wage workers. This indicates that coercion, both economic and extra-economic, creates consent. Of course, notions of equality, freedom, and the like contribute to the consent-process as did notion of (colonial-style) paternalism, especially, in the South.[7]

The process of primitive accumulation (or alienation from small-scale producers' property), which is state-aided, creates two things: (a) the wage-labour class, a class of people which lives as long as it can sell its only commodity (labour power), and (b) owner of private property in its capitalist form. As we have already seen, the capitalist form of private property is different from other forms in that 'determined by big industry and universal competition', it is 'pure private property, which has cast off all semblance of a communal institution and has shut out the State from any influence on the development of property' (Marx and Engels, 1845). Marx's 'any influence', of course, exaggerates the separation between the state and capitalist private property a bit.

While the state has to ensure separation of small-scale producers from their means of production and subsistence on a significant scale, this separation is not necessarily a once-and-for-all process. Note that not all small-scale owners must be dispossessed and become wage workers for capitalism (to begin) to work. This means that there are always small-scale owners who may need to be dispossessed because capital needs their wage-labour and/or their means of production (farm land, water bodies, forested land, mining land, and so on). So, the state must continuously be involved in the act of separating small-scale owners from their property on behalf of capital as per its need. The state must also continuously stop workers from having direct – non-market – access to means of subsistence (and not just to means of production). This act is made possible in many ways. For one thing, even if the state has enough food under its control, it would not make it available to the poor for free, on the ground that, for example, such an action would promote idleness and create labour shortage. For another, there are laws against begging and vagabondage.[8]

The world produces enough food, and yet close to a billion people go without food. Food riots represent people's demand to have direct (affordable) access to food.[9] Similarly, when people squat on vacant urban land and empty buildings as in Brazil where there is a powerful landless rural workers movement, they are demanding access to land and shelter. The state ensures that people do not have direct access to what they need, so not surprisingly, the state heavily suppresses people's action. Such suppression is not a happenstance. It is the essence of the state: it is to keep a significant number of direct producers separated from means of production and subsistence forcing them to work for a wage. So such a separation cannot happen without another separation: people being separated from state's coercive apparatuses and powers. Political suppression of people's demand for direct access to means of subsistence is a condition for capitalist mode of production.

Partly because of struggle from below in different forms, there came to exist state provision of means of subsistence (e.g. public housing, healthcare and education, subsidized nutrition programme), and state-directed/-owned productive enterprises, including in ex-'communist' countries or in post-colonial societies. These state-provided means of subsistence or state-controlled means of production (state's enterprises) are partly or wholly in the form of non-commodities (or property which is not capitalist in form proper). They form the social commons akin to communal means of subsistence in pre-capitalist societies and contributed to partial 'de-proletarianization'.[10] They therefore offer opportunities for primitive accumulation in contemporary times via their privatization and transfer to the hands of the capitalist class. This Marx did not quite encounter. Such a modern form of primitive accumulation ensures that a class of property-less direct producers, separated from means of production and subsistence, continues to exist, and this ensures uninterrupted sale and purchase of labour power as a commodity.

As mentioned earlier, an entire population does not have to lose its property for capitalism to exist. Indeed, sometimes, a limited amount of means of production and subsistence in the hands of workers might help contribute to the cost of their reproduction and thus reduce the wages that capitalists have to pay. Also sometimes, when capitalism fails to address the problem of unemployment, the state encourages petty business, even by giving small loans to workers and small-scale producers, including women.[11] Consider micro-credit policies and state assistance to micro-enterprises. Thus, a 'reverse primitive accumulation' can happen with the support of the state: this can take the form of poor people given some land taken from large-scale owners or small government loans to set up small businesses.

The foregoing discussion shows that the absolutely fundamental purpose of the capitalist state, as a class-state, is to defend the capitalist form of private property (not necessarily private property as such) on the basis of threat and actual use of the means of violence. As mentioned earlier, the social relations of production between classes (and intra-capitalist relations) are codified in the form of state laws, producing what are strictly called property relations or juridical relations. The right to charge an interest and rent and the right to appropriate surplus value are juridically defended by the state, in the overall interest of the capitalist property owners. Of course, all this does not mean that the state cannot and does not go against the short-term or long-term interests of individual members of the capitalist class or indeed against certain short-term economic interests of the class as a whole in order to preserve its class rule. As Engels says, 'rarely it happens that a code of law is the blunt, unmitigated, unadulterated expression of the domination of a class' (in Marx and Engels, 1975: 399–400).

Whether the owner of labour power or of any other commodity, everyone is a commodity owner and seller. In addition, all are regarded as equal before the law irrespective of what capital each owns: whether they own land as private property or whether they are poor people who own nothing but their labour power. Indeed, '[a]s the *rule of law*, the bourgeois state treats its citizens as free and equal owners of private property . . . one only acquires property by endowment, inheritance, exchange, or purchase' (Heinrich, 2004: 204–5).[12] So state's neutrality – as the realm of extra-economic coercion – is not an illusion. Rather, it is precisely by means of this neutrality that 'the state secures the foundations of capitalist relations of domination and exploitation' (p. 205). The defence of property of *everyone* in a *neutral* manner implies that 'those who possess no relevant property beyond their own labour-power *must* sell their labour-power . . . and submit to capital' (ibid.).

4 Capitalism, theft, and anti–theft laws

The entire capitalist mode of production itself is based on stealing and 'theft' (note that this theft does not include appropriation of surplus value on the basis of law of value supported by the state). Consider the following examples that Marx himself provides.

Capital steals people: 'Nothing is more characteristic than their system of stealing men' (slaves) (Marx, 1887: 534). The genesis of capitalism is itself based on 'colossal scale thefts of state lands' (p. 512). Laws exist which serve as 'the instrument of the theft of the people's land' (p. 513). Capital engages in 'the systematic robbery of the Communal lands helped especially, next to the theft of the State domains' (ibid.). In pursuit of cheap labour, it is engaged in 'child-stealing' (p. 537). Capital 'steals the time required for the consumption of fresh air and sunlight' (p. 179). There are ' "small thefts" of capital from the labourer's meal and recreation time, the factory inspectors also designate as "petty pilfer-ings of minutes" ' (p. 167).

In other words, capital steals people's life (e.g. slave labour) and people's wealth (small-scale property). Capital also steals people's labour ('extra' surplus labour) in the sense, for example, that people's need to enjoy a meal is not respected (haggling over meal times). This happens with – and cannot hap-pen without – the full support of the state. Yet it is the same state that uses force against stealing by poor workers (or small-scale producers), stopping them from obtaining direct access to the necessaries of life. Economically deprived and poor, common people do engage in theft. For example, there were '[t]he whole series of thefts, outrages, and popular misery, that accompanied the for-cible expropriation of the people, from the last third of the 15th to the end of the 18th century' (Marx, 1887: 514). The capitalist state has many laws against theft.[13]

Anti-theft laws represent the state's way of stopping people from having direct (= extra-economic) access to means of subsistence (and production). These laws make no distinction between the forms of property being stolen: a person stealing food or such necessaries from a capitalist is not distinguished from a person stealing from a slightly better-off person who is not a capitalist or a landlord.[14] While the state takes action against stealing (or robbing) on the part of common people, consider how it is that the state is fully in support of the capitalist, who has 'bought the use of the labour-power for a definite period' and who 'insists upon his rights', and who therefore 'has no intention of being robbed' (Marx, 1887: 137) by workers (workers can rob when they work less than the usual working day or when they work with less than normal intensity or when they waste any resource). The capitalist has 'a penal code of his own' (ibid.), a penal code to stop any such robbery, a penal code that, ulti-mately, cannot exist without the state's support.

5 Summary, and theoretical and political implications

The state is a necessary precondition for value relations and for capitalist property relations. The state makes sure that commodity exchange happens on the basis of the principle of 'the equivalent for the equivalent'. And, it takes steps to stop the violation of the law of commodity exchange. In certain cases, it itself enforces – or tolerates – unequal exchange as well (in the interest of a hegemonic fraction of the capitalist class, or when the long-term interest of capitalist society is at stake), including at the global scale. In fact, by using extra-economic coercion against small-scale producers and by supporting commodity relations that subject small-scale producers to class differentiation, the state supports the creation of the two basic classes: a class which owns/sells labour power as a commodity and a class that is the (net) buyer of this commodity and that owns the means of production in their commodity form. To the extent that small-scale property owners do remain (they are a substantial presence in rural areas of the South and urban areas of the North), the state fails to meet their needs. They are exploited by both capitalists and all those property owners who appropriate rent and interest, a process that the state also defends.

For capitalism to exist and to continue to exist, the state must separate (and continue to separate) direct producers from the means of production and subsistence. And it must ensure that the separated means of production are turned into capital. It must make sure that capitalists as the new ruling class can, like the older ruling classes, appropriate unpaid surplus labour from direct producers. Capitalists do this even while paying the full value of the commodity they purchase (i.e. labour power). The money with which labour power is bought is actually the surplus value that has already been appropriated from workers. That means that the outer limit of the state intervention is this: it must do no more than making sure that commodities are exchanged at value (wages must cover at least the value of labour power) and that there are enough people with a reasonable amount of health and education to work for the capitalists for a wage.

In terms of freedom, the situation is better in capitalism than in pre-capitalist societies which lack the kind of equality and freedom that nominally exist under capitalism. Yet one cannot fetishize freedom in the sphere of capitalist exchange that the state protects. But this is exactly what most people do: prompted by the surface appearances of free exchange, they fetishize the idea that there is freedom and equality and that there is respect for private property (private property is sacrosanct), even if millions of small-scale producers lose their property through commodity exchange every year in major capitalist countries. In fact, the Heritage Foundation (2020) speaks for many when it equates economic freedom to freedom *from* government regulation, which means freedom *to* buy and sell without government intervention. Ultimately, this freedom to buy and sell is the freedom of large-scale businesses to (a) buy labour power from its owners (the working class), (b) to buy commodities (e.g. raw materials) from small-scale producers, and (c) to sell commodities to small-scale producers *and* wage workers (e.g. means of production to the former, and means of subsistence to both), *in a way that affects these classes adversely.* The state protects *this specific* economic freedom, the freedom of capitalists that exists at the expense of the masses.

It is important to note that the ideas about the state and capitalist property presented here go against several prevailing views within Marxism. For example, Fred Block (2019) rejects Marxism's emphasis on the property-based definition of capitalism. He rejects the Marxist idea that 'the key factor in understanding any given society is the nature of the property system', the question of who controls property (p. 1167). He suggests that one must 'avoid characterizing any particular society as being capitalist' (p. 1173), that is, a society 'defined as a regime of private property in which producers seek to profit in competitive markets' (p. 1167). The property-based view of capitalism cannot explain 'the huge differences in income inequality' among capitalist countries. The factors that explain all these differences 'lie outside of the system of property and production' (ibid.). He rejects therefore Marxism's view that '[w]ithout transforming that core relationship by ending private ownership of the means of production, reforms that were won today would be reversed tomorrow' (p. 1167). Block advocates for 'the Polanyian view of socialism' which 'is not tied to property, but rather to the ability of the citizenry, through democratic means, to exercise sovereignty over the market' (p. 1173). Block assumes that there is no internal relation between capitalist class relation and the legal and political system (i.e. the state), so the latter can be used to meet the needs of the masses.

In the post-modernist Marxist view, 'the ownership of property (whether in means of production or more generally) is neither a necessary nor a sufficient condition for the wielding of power and vice versa' (Resnick and Wolff, 2006: 119). In this view, communism, which, in Marxism, requires that exploitative private property be abolished, is also a class society because the society as a whole will appropriate and distribute surplus labour from individuals.

From the Analytical Marxism camp, Wright is also sceptical of revolutions against capitalist property relations. Echoing the post-modernist view, he says that 'Anticapitalist revolutions attempt to eliminate the distinctively capitalist form of exploitation', by putting the means of production in the hands of the state (nationalization), but nationalization would not necessarily affect non-capitalistic exploitation, that is, exploitation based on unequal ownership of such assets as skills/credentials, and nationalization may in fact increase bureaucratic control over people's lives (Wright, 1989: 20).

All these views neglect the fact that Marx and Engels (1871) draw our attention to the 'economical subjection of the man of labour to the monopolizer of the means of labour; that is, the sources of life lies at the bottom of servitude in all its forms, of all social misery, mental degradation, and political dependence'. In addition, for Marxism, '1917' (the Russian revolution) actually vindicates the Marxist claim that while nationalization of property is the first necessary step, it is not sufficient at all for socialism to be built. Indeed,

> [i]n order to become social, private property must as inevitably pass through the state stage as the caterpillar in order to become a butterfly must pass through the pupal stage. But the pupa is not a butterfly. Myriads of pupae perish without ever becoming butterflies. State property becomes the property of 'the whole people' only to the degree that social privilege and differentiation disappear, and therewith the necessity of the state.
>
> (Trotsky, 1991: 201–2)

State property *itself* is not socialism. Marxism knows it. State property is necessary but not sufficient. State property is to be 'converted into socialist property in proportion as it ceases to be state property'. And the higher the post-revolution state 'rises above the people, and the more fiercely it opposes itself as the guardian of property to the people as its squanderer, the more obviously does it testify against the socialist character of this state property' (ibid.).

In any case, it is important to reiterate the importance of private property which is closely connected to the state. Property has to be seen as a process and not just a thing. The expansion of wealth or property in capitalism is constituted by a set of state-mediated processes. The first is the commodity production (site of primary exploitation), which operates in relation to and alongside four other processes. One is the realm of commodity exchange and financialization, the site of secondary exploitation, that is, exploitation in the market for consumer goods, in the rental and mortgage market and in the sphere of money-lending, including by the loan sharks as well as big banks. The second is class differentiation (and the tendency towards proletarianization) among commodity producers. This results in the transfer of non-capitalist private property to capitalist private property (or the transfer of private property from weaker capitalists to stronger capitalists more or less on the basis of law of value). The third is ongoing primitive accumulation or dispossession of non-capitalist producers, which also results in the transfer of private property to the capitalist class. Finally, commodity production in its advanced stage tends to develop into imperialism which results in transfer of value and wealth from poorer nations to the richer nations (Das, 2020a).

As we have seen, there are at least two main sources of capitalist private property. One form of capitalist private property is from non-capitalist sources: this is when the state takes away the private property of non-capitalist owners and lands it in the hands of the pro-capitalists or capitalists. The other form of capitalist private property, the dominant form in the modern society, is based on capitalist accumulation (as Marx discusses in chapter 25 of *Capital volume 1* in great details): this is when surplus value appropriated by capitalists from property-less direct producers (proletarians and semi-proletarians) is reinvested by capitalists to make their business bigger. Thus, the second form of capitalist private property is the form that surplus value takes when the private property of ordinary men and women – private property in labour power – is put to use by the capitalist class. Here as well, the state's contribution is enormous, including in terms of not only maintaining the already-existing capitalist property but also maintaining and protecting the capitalist right to exploit and to reinvest in order to expand the existing private property (discussed in a later section).

Indeed, while the fundamental purpose of the capitalist state is to defend private property in its capitalist form, merely creating and protecting private property as a thing – existing mines, land, plantations, factories, service sector enterprise, banks, capitalist form of knowledge (and intellectual property), and so on – is not enough. Private property seen as a relation and a process, and not a thing, represents the process of materialization of exploitation and accumulation. Capital is value in motion. Money has to be constantly made from private property based on exploitation of labour, and that money must be converted into private property, and the state must ensure this. Therefore, the state's *economic* interventions emanate from the state's fundamental *political* purpose – the protection of capitalist private property and its augmentation, against any threat from direct producers who must be subjugated. The economic intervention, beyond creation and augmentation of private property through primitive accumulation and class differentiation, takes the form of its contribution to the process of production of value and surplus value, which we will now discuss in Chapter 7.

Notes

1 Private property based in one's labour, 'the property of petty artisan and of the small peasant, a form of property that preceded the bourgeois form', Marx says, 'is alleged to be the groundwork of all personal freedom, activity and independence' (Marx and Engels, 1848).

2

> The differentiation of the peasantry . . . creates two new types of rural inhabitants. The feature common to both types is the commodity, money character of their economy. The first new type is the rural bourgeoisie or the well-to-do peasantry. These include the independent farmers who carry on commercial agriculture in all its varied forms . . . , then come the owners of commercial and industrial establishments, the proprietors of commercial enterprises, etc. From among these well-to-do peasants a class of capitalist farmers is created.
>
> (Lenin, 1899)

> The other new type is the rural proletariat . . . This covers the poor peasants, including those that are completely landless . . . Insignificant farming on a patch of land, with the farm in a state of utter ruin (particularly evidenced by the leasing out of land), inability to exist without the sale of labour-power, . . . [and] an extremely low standard of living . . . are [among] the distinguishing features of this type.
>
> (ibid.)

3 'A 2018 study by the National Bank for Agriculture and Rural Development [of India] showed that 52.5 percent of all the agricultural households were indebted with an average debt of $1,470' (Purohit, 2019). Compare the latter figure to the per capita income of agricultural households of barely $600 (or Rs 40,000) (Sharma, 2019).

4 In India, every year, 2,000 farmers leave their farming business because they cannot pay their bills (Sainath, 2013). Thousands of micro-enterprises begin every year and thousands disappear every year. In Canada, if 100 such enterprises employing no more than four people start in a given year, by the 10th year, only 42% survive (Government of Canada, 2019). In the US, 20% of all new businesses fail during the first 2 years of being open and 65% during the first 10 years (Deane, 2020).

5 In 1918 the Usurious Loans Act was passed prohibiting excessive rates of interest. In the 1930s, laws to regulate moneylending were passed at the provincial level. There were also numerous laws under which borrowers could petition Debt Relief Boards to reduce their obligations (Roy and Swamy, 2016).

6 If people beg out of desperation, or if they engage in political protests, they are liable to criminalization by the state.

7 In colonial India, according to Chitra Joshi, there were public beatings and managerial attempts to police even the time spent in lavatories. Working days in the early 20th century still ranged between 12 and 15 hours. The management seemed to justify the long working hours in the old language of paternalism: it was better for boys to spend their days in the 'sanitary surroundings' of a 'well-managed mill' than to while away their time in 'a dirty bazaar'. (Chakravarty, 2020)

8 'Hence at the end of the 15th and during the whole of the 16th century, throughout Western Europe a bloody legislation against vagabondage' (Marx, 1887: 522).

In India, according to the Bombay Prevention of Begging Act, 1959, from which anti-begging laws at the provincial level have been derived, '[a]ny person who is found begging can be arrested by any police officer or by any person who is authorized in this behalf' (Shodhganga undated; Mukherjee, 2008).

9 In June 2016, 'in the rundown, garbage-strewn Caracas district of El Valle [in Venezuela], some 200 people pushed up against police guarding a supermarket as they chanted, "We want food!" and "Loot it!"' (Gupta and Ulmer, 2016).

10 This is in the sense that people who have access to state-provided means of subsistence in the commodity form or part-commodity form or who worked in the state-controlled enterprises with some security of tenure and benefits are a little less coerced by the commodity logic of capitalist class relation: their reliance on the market for means of subsistence and the labour market was a little weakened to the detriment of the interest of the global capitalist class.

11 In July 2019, the Indian government declares that it seeks to include at least one 'woman member from each rural poor household' in self-help groups (SHGs). On how SHGs have become a mechanism of financialization and debt accumulation, see Morgan and Olsen (2011) and Kalpana (2015). See Ramesh (2007), who was a government minister, for a more favourable view.

12 The state just makes sure that 'all members of society behave like owners of private property' (Heinrich, 2004: 204). It has to be independent because it has to force all members of society to recognize one another as private property owners.

13 Section 378 in the Indian Penal Code says that '[w]hoever, intending to take dishonestly any moveable property out of the possession of any person without that per-son's consent, moves that property in order to such taking, is said to commit theft'. Section 379 says, 'Whoever commits theft shall be punished with imprisonment of either description for a term which may extend to three years, or with fine, or with both' (Government of India, undated).

According to the Canadian criminal code (322 (1)):

Every one commits theft who fraudulently and without colour of right takes, or fraudulently and without colour of right converts to his use or to the use of another person, anything, whether animate or inanimate, with intent

(a) to deprive, temporarily or absolutely, the owner of it, or a person who has a special property or interest in it, of the thing or of his property or interest in it;

(b) to pledge it or deposit it as security;

(c) to part with it under a condition with respect to its return that the person who parts with it may be unable to perform; or

(d) to deal with it in such a manner that it cannot be restored in the condition in which it was at the time it was taken or converted. (Government of Canada, undated)

14 To the extent that un-employed and semi-employed people are necessary for capitalism to operate, if some of them can survive by stealing (which represents access to means of subsistence neither through the market nor through the state), this should be functional. But stealing could grow over into stealing *from* capitalists, and stealing could dilute the discipline of wage work that the state must support: it could soften up the idea that people must work for a wage to live.

7 The state, and capitalist production, exploitation, accumulation, and crisis

In the preface to the first German edition of *Capital volume 1*, Karl Marx says: 'It is the ultimate aim of this work [*Capital volume 1*], to lay bare the economic law of motion of modern society' (Marx, 1887: 7). There are economic laws that explain the 'spontaneous expansion of capital' (ibid.: 163) or 'the successive phases of its normal development' (ibid.: 7), and then there is state power, including 'legal enactments' and legislations or acts (ibid.). The economic laws of capitalism are modified by the laws and actions of state. The actual degree and importance of the modification is a conjunctural matter.

Following the completion of the sale and purchase of commodities, including labour power, the process of capitalist production (labour process) begins under the laws of motion of capital. It is a process in which the capitalist (or its agent) brings the means of production and the worker together to produce a use-value for sale: under capitalism, '[t]he labour-process is a process between things that the capitalist has purchased, things that have become his [or her] property' (Marx, 1887: 131). The workplace, the space of labour process, the hidden abode of production, is a sphere of certain rights of the exploiting class. These rights are defended by the state. Therefore, the sphere of production, including the workplace, reveals important attributes of the state. As in the last two chapters, I partly rely on *Capital 1* to show how the logic of capitalist social relations and production create a space, and produce an imperative, for the state to act, whether or not the state does act in a given situation or whether it acts satisfactorily or not from the standpoint of capitalists.

In society, fresh wealth (new wealth) cannot be produced *merely* on the basis of primitive accumulation or even class differentiation (the topics discussed earlier). Fresh wealth cannot also be produced merely on the basis of commodity circulation: surplus value (fresh wealth) cannot be produced inside circulation, although it cannot be produced outside of commodity circulation. Circulation, or the exchange of commodities, itself creates no value. On the basis of circulation and creation of capitalist property from pre-capitalist or non-capitalist (small-scale owners') property, fresh wealth is ultimately produced inside the hidden abode of production, and it is here that the state plays an important role.

The capitalist state is an economically powerful agent. In fact, the part of total social capital that is spent by the state keeps rising, including under

DOI: 10.4324/9781351168007-7

neoliberalism.[1] Using its economic power (including the power to create money), the state produces those conditions for capitalism which the profit-driven individual capitalists will not generally produce and may indeed destroy.

As argued before, capital is value in motion, so it is not enough for the state to merely defend capitalist property rights. Therefore, the state must take steps to promote capitalist accumulation in the long-term interests of the capitalist class and especially its economically and politically hegemonic fraction. The state behaves like a machine of social reproduction, from the standpoint of the social capital. And '[l]ike any other machine, it requires maintenance, amortization, new parts, and a continuous supply of fuel and energy'. So 'the social capital . . . must set aside a considerable portion of the value it realizes in order to continuously finance state activity' (Smith, 2018: 234):

> [L]ike unproductive capital in the sphere of circulation, the state carries out a range of tasks that are indispensable to maintaining the institutional framework of the valorization process. In this sense, it contributes 'indirectly' to the production of social surplus-value.
>
> (ibid.)

By appropriating more surplus labour, the state reduces the overhead costs for social capital.

To describe the nature of capitalism, Marx (1887) begins with the formula, M-C-M, which means 'the transformation of money into commodities, and the change of commodities back again into money; or buying in order to sell. Money that circulates in the latter manner is thereby transformed into, becomes capital, and is already potentially capital' (p. 104). But given that no one would exchange M for M ($100 for $100), Marx says that '[t]he exact form of this process [of circulation of commodities] is therefore M-C-M′', where M′ = M + D M = 'the original sum advanced, plus an increment' (ibid.: 106). 'This increment or excess over the original value' is called surplus value. 'It is this movement that converts it into capital' (ibid.).

M-C-M′ is actually M-C-P-C′-M′, which can be further expanded to M-C (MP+LP)-P-C′-M′. The state is connected to each phase of the circuit (Figure 7.1). The capital circuit in its expanded form can serve as a method of systematic presentation as well as a method of analysis of the role of the state.

In Sections 1–4, I discuss how the state is connected to the successive phases of the capital circuit. I discuss the state's role in relation to accumulation in Section 5 (which is connected to the previous section); here I closely follow Marx's discussion in Chapter 25 in *Capital volume 1*. In Section 6, I turn to the state's role in relation to tendencies *and* counter-tendencies towards economic crisis. In the last section, I summarize the discussion and reflect on the implications of my discussion for the concepts of state capitalism and socialism.

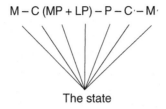

$$M - C (MP + LP) - P - C \cdot - M \cdot$$

The state

Figure 7.1 The capital circuit and the state

1 The state and the 'M-C(MP+. . .' phase of the capital circuit (the sphere of money and means of production)

The state makes liquid investible resources (M) available to capitalists (and especially to the big business), often at below-market rates, through various policies (e.g. low-interest loans, quantitative easing, loan waivers or forgiveness and various bailout packages). Some of these policies represent simple plundering of the state treasury. Liberalization of financial markets allows domestic businesses access foreign capital. Often the money received from the state (including by cheap credits) is used by capital to simply speculate rather than to invest to produce goods and services that people need, and in this case the state's connection to capital circuit is its connection to a shorter version of the circuit: the state helps capitalists increase their profit in the form of interest in the sphere of financialization, so M-C-P-C'-M' is shortened to M-M' (meaning money can simply be made from money, with assistance from the state).

For the production process, capitalists need actual commodities, including means of production (raw materials, land, energy, software, machines, the built environment or social and physical infrastructure, and so on). Means of production can exist in a collective form (publicly owned airport or railroads or mines) or in the form of privately owned assets.

The state makes commodities available to the capitalist class in the form of cheap raw materials and cheap land, water bodies (lakes), and forests, which have been obtained from people via ongoing primitive accumulation (often the latter process happens in areas inhabited by poverty-stricken indigenous communities). Land is a crucial means of production. It is necessary for locating any enterprise. It is directly necessary in land-based production (e.g. farming, forestry, fishing, eco-tourism, and the like). Capitalists' access to minerals for extractive industries requires their access to land. If all the land is owned by numerous private owners (including small-scale producers/owners), then assembling a big chunk of land for large-scale enterprises (e.g. laying out major railroads and railways, large-scale factories, and so on) would be a problem, so the state comes to own the land too. As mentioned earlier, the state uses its power to take control over privately owned land by paying a low price – lower than what the price would be when the land is fully developed and an enterprise begins to operate – and then makes this property available to capitalists at a rate suitable to them and sometimes for free. In part because a capitalist wishes to buy as cheap as possible and small-scale owners wish to get a better price, coercion by the state may be necessary to transcend their reluctance to part with their property. Where the state owns forested land or water resources, it also makes these available to private capitalists as and when they need.

The state may not always resort to primitive accumulation in the interest of capitalists or the big business. The state can try to make sure that small-scale commodity producers, including small-scale capitalists, produce commodities – as potential raw materials – for sale to the big business at a price suitable to the latter. The state can promote contract farming too (see Shrimali, 2021). The state can weaken its own erstwhile role in trading whereby the state would buy products from small-scale producers as a remunerative price. The state thus makes the small-scale producers depend entirely on private trading capital through which raw materials reach the production process.

As discussed earlier, it is the state that creates, or contributes to the production of, the geographically built environment that connects commodity owners located in different places and countries. A hierarchy of market centres (e.g. metros, smaller cities and towns, rural markets) is created including through urban and regional planning by the state that is behind the urbanization and ruralization of capitalist production and exchange. Means of transportation and communication are laid out by the state or with state's assistance. The state is involved in what David Harvey (1985) calls the production of space. The built environment or the produced space, which includes the means of transportation and communication, can often appear partly or wholly as a form of commodity for which common people have to pay in order to use them. The cost of geographical movement of a commodity is a part of the cost of production, so the state is under pressure to make it available. The value of commodities is thus reduced. The state 'engages in productive activities particularly with respect to investments in public goods and collective physical infrastructures such as roads, ports and harbours, water and sewage provision' (Harvey, 2018: 16).[2] It helps capital annihilate obstacles to social and geographical mobility.[3] The state-aided built environment can increase the rate of profit in the private sector producing heavy goods, and the like, and thus increase its national competitiveness (Mandel, 2008/1968: 502).[4] Marx (1973: 531) comments on the role of the state in the production of the physical infrastructure (public works) in *Grundrisse*: there may be a need for the development of railways, and so on, but specific capitalists may not invest because 'the direct advantage arising from them for production may be too small for the investment to appear as anything but sunk capital'. So

> capital shifts the burden on to the shoulders of the state; or, where the state traditionally still takes up a position superior to capital, it still possesses the

authority and the will to force the society of capitalists to put a part of their *revenue*, not of their capital, into such generally useful works, which appear at the same time as *general* conditions of production, and hence not as particular conditions for one capitalist or another.

As science becomes a productive force, the state socializes the cost of science. The state creates conditions for intellectual labour that is more directly connected to production: natural sciences and engineering as well as management (the 'science' of organization of capitalist enterprises taught in business schools).[5] If the state is involved in technological change, this can reduce the value of labour power by shortening the time taken to produce means of subsistence.

Anything that the state can do to reduce the costs of discovery of, for example, minerals will affect their value. The state spends money on research and development (R&D) in the public (including in the military sector), the results of which are enjoyed by the private sector (ibid.: 555).[6] As widely known, it was government research that created the internet from which all the companies could make money. In other words, R&D is socialized while its benefits are privatized.

In fact, as productivity rises, there is a tendency for more circulating capital to be converted into fixed capital which is invested in things that (unlike 'the machinery directly active in the direct production process') do not impact production immediately: 'railways, canals, aqueducts, telegraphs etc.' (Mandel, 1978: 484). As technical change becomes increasingly crucial to capitalism, and as investment in technology is expensive, the state shares responsibility for some of the costs of capital accumulation projects (ibid.).

The value of a commodity in capitalism = c + v + s. When the nationalized industry supplies a commodity to the private sector at a price that equals constant capital and variable capital (and not the surplus value that is extracted from worker), it is tantamount to the private sector receiving a free surplus value (Mandel, 1978: 554). This can increase the rate of profit in the private sector, other things constant.

As already indicated, there are different juridical ways in which the state makes available the means of production to capital for private sector accumulation (Figure 7.2). The state makes small-scale producers sell the raw materials (e.g. agri-products) at a cheaper rate to big business. Or the state buys from them raw materials and other resources at a cheap rate and makes them available to big business. It also provides means of production and transportation facilities through state-owned enterprises (railways, heavy industries), which is a concealed method of subsidizing the private capitalist sector. Nationalization of industries, especially in natural resources and in infrastructure – some of which could be unprofitable for the private sector at the initial stage of capitalist development – can provide means of production to the private sector such as power and transportation, and the like at reduced cost. The state also resorts to the opposite process: it turns over the commons, including erstwhile

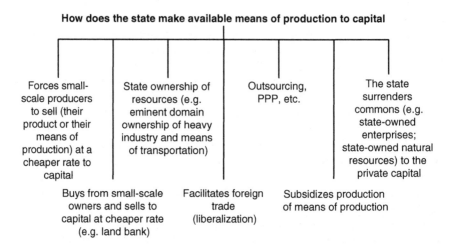

Figure 7.2 How does the state make available means of production to capital?

state-owned enterprises or state-owned natural resources, to the private hands at a low price. For example, where necessary, the state resorts to the reprivatization of erstwhile nationalized companies and establishments (e.g. museums, monuments) at a throw-away price which puts an enormous amount of assets at a low cost in the hands of the capitalist class. This represents unequal exchange reminiscent of colonial times. Through the liberalization of trade, the state makes foreign commodities available as intermediate goods.

The state also makes use of market mechanisms. One is PPP (public private partnership). The latter is a sweet name for the state openly subsidizing the private sector. Another is outsourcing whereby state-provided use-value is actually produced by a private company. While the capitalist class as a whole may not have an interest in building the built environment which all of its members need but cannot produce for their own benefit only, sections of the capitalist can make profit by building it on behalf of the state which acts on behalf of the capitalist class as a whole. By facilitating the provision of credit, the state allows concentration and centralization (of financial resources), without which infrastructural conditions such as railways requiring bulky investment would be difficult. The state sometimes gets the private companies to build infrastructure (e.g. railways) by guaranteeing a certain rate of profit (this happened in colonial India, for example).

2 The state and the 'C (. . . + LP)' phase of capital circuit (the sphere of labour power)

A special type of commodity that capitalists, whether bigger or smaller, need in the production process is labour power. The state's relation to commodity labour power has been discussed in a previous chapter, so a few points only may be recapitulated here.

Mainly by using the tax money from workers themselves, the state can collectivize a part of the value of labour power and provide subsidized education and healthcare. With state-funded commons (e.g. government-provided/-subsidized education and healthcare), the value of labour power – the value of necessaries in commodified forms that workers receive from private employers – can fall, and other things constant. This can increase the rate of exploitation.[7] Also certain kinds of commons – education – might make workers more productive, so more surplus value may be appropriated in its relative form. State investment in education and workforce retraining to produce a skilled workforce can benefit capital investment in high skills and high-wage industries in specific regions.

Facilitating the use of vulnerable groups of workers, and especially child labour and immigrants, is a method of ensuring low-cost labour. The owner of this special commodity can, of course, bargain for its price, but the state seeks to reduce its bargaining power in many ways: increasing the ease at which capital can hire and fire labour and resorting to identity politics to divide potential or actual organization of workers. The state sets the minimum wage at a very low level which has an adverse effect on workers' bargaining power and on the actual wages paid by private capital. In addition, the minimum wage laws tend not to be implemented seriously.

When the state makes available a given amount of means of subsistence as a part of its poverty-alleviation programme, it can potentially increase the bargaining power of workers by weakening their reliance on employers. But by defining the poverty level at a low level in order to restrict the number of eligible recipients of state assistance, the state reduces the total amount of assistance, thus minimizing any potentially positive impact of state's social policy not only on workers' economic condition but also on their political bargaining power. The non-implementation of a living wage and non-provision of a safety net – in a context where there is a massive and growing reserve army to which dispossession under neoliberalism contributes – drives wages below the cost of maintenance (i.e. the value of labour power). Further, the state, including the courts, suppresses the right to strike, including in the name of inviting foreign capital, as well as the right to work,[8] economic development, employment generation, and so on.

3 The state and the 'P' phase of capital circuit (the sphere of commodity production)

The main aim of capitalists is to increase their profit by reducing the cost of production, so what happens inside 'the hidden abode of production' (Marx, 1887: 123) crucially matters. The internal relation between capital and the state is forcefully expressed in the hidden abode of production. Apart from making available certain general conditions for production and exchange (built environment, natural resources, raw materials, scientific knowledge, and the like), the state defends the capitalist nature of labour process and capitalist exploitation. The sphere of production is a sphere of the political battle between capital and labour, one where capital exercises its despotic control (ibid.: 231–2). So all the interventions by the state aimed at reducing the bargaining power in the labour market also reduce workers' power on the shop floor.

Ensuring that private property rights are in place, the state has to support capitalist labour process. The capitalist 'has bought the use of the labour-power for a definite period, and he insists upon his rights. He has no intention of being robbed' (Marx, 1887: 137). In capitalism, money is converted into capital 'in the most exact accordance with the *economic laws of commodity production* and with the right of *property* derived from them' (ibid.: 413). This right is defended by the state.[9]

The product of labour 'is the property of the capitalist and not that of the labourer, its immediate producer', 'just as much as does the wine which is the product of a process of fermentation completed in his cellar' (Marx, 1887: 131). The state defends the capitalists' property right in the workplace. At best, as far as the state is concerned, the worker retains his or her labour power and can sell it anew if they can find a buyer.

Under capitalism, even if there is equal exchange (all commodities, including labour power, are paid at their value), 'the laws of appropriation or of private property, laws that are based on the production and circulation of commodities, become by their own inner and inexorable dialectic changed into their very opposite', that is, opposite of equal exchange (p. 412). This is for two reasons. Firstly, 'the capital which is exchanged for labour-power (as a commodity) is itself but a portion of the product of others' labour appropriated without an equivalent' (ibid.). Secondly, 'this capital must not only be replaced by its producer, but replaced together with an added surplus' (ibid.). In other words, 'what *really* takes place' between capitalists and workers is that 'the capitalist again and again appropriates, without equivalent, a portion of the previously materialised labour of others, and exchanges it for a greater quantity of living labour' (ibid.; italics added).

This economic law of capitalist exploitation – like the law of equal exchange between commodity sellers – is codified and defended by the laws of the capitalist state. If a worker is paid the full value of the things that the worker and their family need to live, and if society takes 3 hours to produce all those things, the state has to make sure that the worker works longer than those 3 hours, that the worker works, say, 8 hours, producing surplus value for capital. By maintaining the class status of the vast majority as workers, with little or no access to means of production, and of the minority as capitalists who monopolize the means of production, the state makes sure that workers surrender a large part of what they produce to the capitalists. So, in capitalism, 'property turns out to be the right, on the part of the capitalist, to appropriate the unpaid labour of others or its product, and to be *the* impossibility, on the part of the labourer, of appropriating his own product' (Marx, 1887: 412; italics added). And this sort of property right, the capitalist property right, must be coercively defended because between the right of the capitalist to the unpaid labour of the worker and the right of the worker to have full control over the entire product of their labour, between these two fundamental class interests, there is no compatibility. This incompatibility is indicated by '*the impossibility*, on the part of the labourer, of appropriating his own product' (p. 412). The state function cannot but be shaped by this characteristic of capitalism. If the worker leaves the workplace after 3 hours, the state will consider that illegal. The state has to ensure that 'the value of this product includes, besides the value of the capital advanced, a surplus-value which costs the worker labour but the capitalist nothing, and which none the less becomes the legitimate property of the capitalist' (p. 413).

In capitalism, product and labour power are commodities, but they are different types of commodity. Those who sell their labour power do not have the right to sell the products of their labour. If at the end of a day's labour, workers in a factory producing cell phones decide to sell all the phones they have made and share the profit – or most of it – among themselves, then the police will be at the door of the workplace and act against the worker.

If people receive only a part of the net product they produce under the control of capitalists, it is not injustice. But it is not injustice *if and only if* we accept the law of commodity exchange: labour power has been paid at its value, and therefore its use-value – what the capitalist, the buyer, makes of it – depends entirely on the capitalist. The state accepts this: capitalist exploitation is not necessarily unjust:

> The circumstance, that on the one hand the daily sustenance of labour-power costs only half a day's labour, while on the other hand the very same labour-power can work during a whole day . . . is, without doubt, a piece of good luck for the buyer' however, it is 'by no means an injury [injustice] to the seller.
>
> (Marx, 1887: 136)

Acting in the interest of the majority, the state, given its coercive power, *could* make sure that there is no exploitation in the workplace: that is, 'the [labour] process be not carried beyond the point, where the value paid by the capitalist for the labour-power is replaced by an exact equivalent' (ibid.: 137) and a little more in order to pay for the things society needs (all the deductions from the social product that will be necessary in a society beyond capital). But the state will not do this. On the contrary, it must juridically support the fact that the labour process 'be continued beyond that point' in order to become 'a process of creating surplus-value' (ibid.). 'The fact that half a day's labour is necessary to keep the labourer alive during 24 hours, does not in any way prevent him [or her] from working a whole day' (Marx, 1887: 135). The state defends this difference in time – that is, the difference between the time taken to produce the necessaries that people need and the time they spend in the workplace as workers, or the difference between what they get and what they make.

Everything in the social world exists as a product of human labour interacting with nature. The capitalist form of the wealth (value) is entirely a product of wage labour. Capitalists control property, so the world we live in *appears* to be one that has been created by capital in its own image, as per the logic of capitalist production. But, in actuality, this world is the world of ordinary people, the people who actually do the work (mostly as wage labour but also as small-scale producers). The world we live in is the world created by people's necessary labour (that is reflected in their consumption of necessaries) and by their surplus labour. The state does everything to suppress the people's image of the world and to prop up the capitalist image. This is evident when state policies are expected to not harm capitalists and also when capitalists are seen as employers or jobs providers, investors, and wealth creators. Underlying this view is the capitalist image: that they actually do something and are indispensable to people's lives.

Marx says that '[a]s soon as his labour actually begins, it has already ceased to belong to him; it can therefore no longer be sold by him' (Marx, 1887: 379). This happens in spite of the fact that *everything* he/she works on or with (e.g. raw materials, machines, software, and so on) has been produced by him. Even wages that the workers receive are paid from the money that the capitalist obtains by selling the products that the workers have earlier produced.

One can imagine a normal rate/process of exploitation in a society that an average worker is subjected to.[10] Apart from this, there are excesses that the capitalists inflict on workers: this is by lowering the wages below the average cost of maintenance of workers,[11] cutting down on spending for workplace safety (e.g. protective equipment during a pandemic, enough working space per worker, safety of chemicals),[12] and so on. Under some circumstances, the state can intervene, and it has intervened, to curb these excesses. But often it does much less than what workers need, given the 'limits' that capitalism 'imposes' (discussed later).

What is crucial to recognize is how the state sees exploitation. The normal process of exploitation is not what exploitation is in the eyes of the state; only the *excesses* of the capitalist system constitute exploitation. In the normal discourse, including that produced by most academics and other commentators on capitalism, which the state makes use of, exploitation happens when an employer uses a person's labour power by force and/or without a payment (or with a payment below the state-mandated minimum wage).[13] Even ILO (n.d.) has a grossly inadequate view about exploitation, as demonstrated in own document titled the 'Details of indicators of labour exploitation'. Workers' organizations also hold a similar view: this is influenced by the state and is legalistic. It is as if the state creates and defines capitalist exploitation.[14] The view of exploitation that is held, and acted on, by the state (and state-like institutions) does little to combat – let alone – eliminate – exploitation proper. Reducing the normal to the non-normal (the excess), the state protects the normal by virtue of which the non-normal forms of exploitation happen.

Capitalism is a free society relative to pre-capitalism. Unlike in pre-capitalist societies, no one can generally force a person to sell her/his labour power to this and that capitalist. After men and women have sold their labour power, and once they enter the workplace, they have, however, very little freedom, including over their own body. They play no role in decision-making with regard to production and accumulation. In the capitalist workplace, the worker works under the control of the capitalist, and the product of labour belongs to the capitalist. This is how the labour process in general – one that is common to all societies – becomes capitalist labour process.

The state codifies and defends the capitalist right to control the work of the worker: state action is necessary because such right of the capitalist to control the workplace is against the need and desire of the worker to perform free labour. 'The bargain concluded, it is discovered that he was no "free agent," that the time for which he is free to sell his labour-power is the time for which he is forced to sell it'. And this unfreedom is juridically justified and codified by the state. Without the state, as the realm of unfreedom, unfreedom of labour cannot exist.

In the workplace, control over workers is necessary to pre-emptively eliminate or reduce chances of resistance by workers: 'As the number of the co-operating labourers increases, so too does their resistance to the domination of capital, and with it, the necessity for capital to overcome this resistance by counterpressure' (Marx, 1887: 231). Thus, the people who do 'the work of directing, superintending, and adjusting' as agents of capital engage in despotic control over labourers subjecting them to oppressive power relations in order to increase exploitation and overcome resistance to that exploitation. Here unequal race/ethnic and gender relations between ordinary workers and managers further reinforce the despotic control of capital. The despotic control happens in the workplaces in general and those in so-called special economic zones (or 'special exploitation zones'), with the support of the state, which represents the society-wide concentration of political power of the exploiting classes.[15] The unfreedom of labour within the workplace, defended by the state, is every bit extra-economic. Marx's concept of 'despotic control' points to that. Thus, workers are not free to take control of the product they collectively produce in the workplace. To enforce this unfreedom and to make workers produce more surplus value, capitalism resorts to a form of unfreedom, which consists of the political control by capitalists over workers in the workplace.

There are two major ways in which capital can increase the rate of exploitation (the ratio of surplus product to necessary product) if we assume that wages cover the value of labour power (the topic of wages falling below the value of labour power and state's complicit in it has been discussed in an earlier chapter). One is technical change that raises labour productivity and makes workers produce more every hour. Here the state helps by supporting technical change including its funding for research and development, higher education, and so on. The other method is where some capitalists mainly rely on workers work-ing long hours (for low hourly wages); capitalists are directly affected if, for example, their access to cheaper labour is restricted by the state.

Other things constant, the longer the working day, the higher the profits. This relation is particularly strong in capitalism's infancy, given the absence of productivity-raising technology.[16] Acting on behalf of capital, the state forces workers to work long hours.[17] The capitalist 'can, under the pretense of paying "the normal price of labour," abnormally lengthens the working-day with-out any corresponding compensation to the labourer' (Marx, 1887: 385); 'the bourgeoisie, at its rise, wants and uses the power of the state . . . to lengthen the working-day' (p. 523). It lengthened the working day by compulsion (p. 181).

Even when during an economic crisis, production is interrupted and enter-prises work only a part of the week, the working day is not necessarily short-ened. Capitalists may have an incentive to increase working day: 'The less business there is, the more profit has to be made on the business done. The less time spent in work, the more of that time has to be turned into surplus labour-time' (Marx, 1887: 167). The state allows this.[18]

There are several reasons why workers are made to work long hours. For one, 'the capitalist has bought the labour-power at its day-rate. To him its use-value belongs during one working-day. He has thus acquired the [state-defended] right to make the labourer work for him during one day' (Marx, 1887: 163). From capital's angle, the 'spontaneous' operation of the laws of capitalist commodity relations imposes no limit to the length of the working day. From the opposite angle, that is, from labour's angle, matters are different: what might begin as equal exchange ends up being unequal. If a worker works excessively long hours (say, 15 hours a day) and if due to overwork, her longev-ity is reduced by, say, 20%, her total wage income during her working life is not increased by 20%: she still gets the wages as if she is going to live a life of normal longevity. In other words, the law of equal exchange supported by the state is violated *on the basis of* equal exchange, which is also supported by the state. Marx says, '[T]he nature of the exchange of commodities itself imposes no limit to the working day, no limit to surplus labour' which allows the capi-talist to maintain 'his rights as a purchaser when he tries to make the working day as long as possible'. Acting in their own interest, on the other hand, 'the labourer maintains his right as seller when he wishes to reduce the working day to one of definite normal duration'. So '[t]here is here . . . an antinomy, right against right, both equally bearing the seal of the law of exchanges. Between equal rights force decides' (Marx, 1887: 163–4). And this is ultimately the force of the capitalist state. The state often supports the longer working days.

Long working days as well as unhealthy working conditions, job insecurity, irregular or unpredictable work hours, and the like lead to various physical and mental illnesses.[19] Capitalism is literally killing people now as it did in Marx's time.[20] 'Capital cares nothing for the length of life of labour-power.' It shortens 'the extent of the labourer's life, as a greedy farmer snatches increased produce from the soil by robbing it of its fertility' (Marx, 1887: 179). Sufferings of workers inflicted by capital are contemptibly 'necessary conditions to the existence of capital' (p. 316).

The law of uneven development mediates in the way the state responds to the long working days. If capital subjects workers to excessive overwork and endangering health and cause people to die prematurely in one region/country, it can obtain fresh sources of labour from other regions/countries, especially those where capitalist development is at a lower level (e.g. rural areas or LDCs) so the degeneration of the workers in the former region is kept within limits: 'the degeneration of the industrial population is only retarded by the constant absorption of primitive and physically uncorrupted elements from the country' (Marx, 1887: 181). The state could stop capitalists from making use of uneven development to subject workers to overwork, but it does not, and this non-doing of the state is a necessary condition for what capitalists do to workers: exploitation.

In any case, with respect to the two major methods of labour exploitation, it can be said that if some capitalists make money by taking advantage of workers available to work for long hours (and for low wages), and other capitalists resort to technical change, the state may resort to legislations to restrict the working day and to increase wages, so a level-playing field is created.[21] State action driven by inter-capitalist competition (and class struggle) and by the interests of certain (hegemonic) capitalists or capitalist fractions can in turn affect capitalist accumulation as a whole. When the state shortens the working day, this action may put pressure on all capitalists to resort to technical change as a way of increasing surplus value in its relative form. Conversely, state's inability to shorten the working day allows many capitalists to resort to the appropriation of surplus value in its absolute form, producing a capitalism at a lower level of development, characterized by an absence of systemic increase in labour productivity per hour.

4 The state and the 'C′-M′' phase of capital circuit (the sphere of realization)

The state helps capital access foreign markets (C′). It also creates a domestic demand for what capital produces. While the state itself is a sphere of extra-commodity or extra-economic relations, it is a massive source of market itself – demand for commodities that are produced for a profit. For the state to exist, a large number of goods and services (e.g. legal advice, knowledge, information about citizens, technical expertise, digitalization, surveillance technology, military equipment, and so on) are necessary, and through state contracts and outsourcing, the state converts these use-values into commodities and thus creates a large market, a large opportunity for capitalist investment.

The state creates markets through its activities that aim to benefit those that are economically weaker or to benefit society at large. In the latter category are state contracts for the physical and social infrastructure and arms, which are actually produced by private companies for a profit on an outsourcing or PPP basis. Privatization of state services (e.g. education and healthcare) creates and expands markets for production of goods and services in the private sector. Even sensitive state activities such as consular services, where citizens' private information are in question, have been given over to private sector capital.[22] State's environmental regulations can create new industries and opportunities for eco-capitalism: waste management, recycling, toxic waste disposal, eco-tourism, and so on. An average amount of wastage in the production process – for example average amount of damage to the environment when the environment serves as a sink for polluted gases or water – is a part of the value of commodity, but an above average amount of wastage is not. The state may take steps to clean up the environment and fight global climate change, and this may create opportunities for accumulation (when, for example, the state outsources these tasks to the private businesses). Mention should be made of culture too: the state operates as a repository of culture, which in turn is physically expressed in the landscape. The production of the cultural landscape (e.g. statues of specific icons of the parties in power, museums, war memorials) by the state creates a market for capital when such production is outsourced to the private sector.

The state can create markets in the form of 'welfare-provision'. In this category are activities such as state-promoted insurance to selected groups of people (e.g. farmers; urban poor), which is sold by private companies and various welfare policies. The implementation of state's welfare policies creates a market for commodities including when the state implements these policies through private service providers (e.g. Medicare, public housing, vaccination programme) creates new opportunities for the private sector to maximize profits by supplying public services.[23] Anti-poverty policies create a market for goods and services produced by capitalists to be delivered to the poor on a subsidized basis by the state. Food subsidies for the poor domestically and food aid to poor countries create a market for agribusiness. To promote economic development in economically depressed areas, the state provides tax breaks. Consider opportunity zones (OZ) policy in the US that was introduced with bipartisan support under the Trump administration (Gose, 2020). When the value of an asset has gone up on paper, but has not yet been sold for a profit, then unrealized capital gains occur. At the end of 2017, a potential \$6.1 trillion in unrealized capital gains was available for reinvestment in the US. Taxes are triggered once the asset has been sold. The state makes it possible for investors to offset or defer these taxes by investing in opportunity zones (Neufeld, 2020).[24]

Tax breaks and similar incentives (e.g. tax reduction, tax deferral, write-off of tax arrears, export subsidies) mean two things. One is that the tax break means that capital does not pay for the collective services – transportation, educated workforce, security, and so on – provided for by the state, so its net M' (M' after tax) remains larger than it would otherwise be. These incentives also mean, in a context of uneven development, that the state makes sure that in those areas and sectors, where the rate of profit is below the national average, businesses receive financial benefits from the state in order to be able to reap at least the average rate of profit. Through these incentives, the state makes sure that the business world gets to keep much of the surplus it appropriates from workers and small-scale producers. This happens in the form of tax exemptions, tax reduction, write-off of tax arrears, export subsidies (especially in export-oriented zones), and so on, all in the name of promoting growth and helping common people. In addition, when a company does not earn enough surplus value, that is, when it incurs losses, the state often nationalizes the losses by temporarily nationalizing the company.[25] However, the state guarantees that profits ultimately remain in the private sector.

5 The state and capitalist accumulation

As already indicated, it is not enough that the state helps capitalists produce and realize surplus value. The surplus value has to be constantly reinvested. This is what accumulation means. We can now make some general comments on the relation between the state and accumulation, partly based on the discussion in the last section.

Accumulation is in two forms: in its 'primitive' or mainly extra-economic, form (primitive accumulation) and capitalist form proper. Methods of primitive accumulation include, to borrow Marx's words, 'the colonies, the national debt, the modern mode of taxation, and the protectionist system', and so on and involve coercive state power. The treasures that an advanced country captures in the South flow back into the former and are invested as capital. And this form of 'anti-value' transfer reinforces 'value-based' transfer, that is, transfer based on equal exchange.

Just as state-supported primitive accumulation happens globally, so does state-assisted accumulation in its specifically capitalist form. To extend their businesses, capitalists reinvest the surplus value they appropriate. This is concentration. Then, some capitalists acquire businesses from other capitalists, making their businesses grow bigger. This is centralization. Concentration and centralization, strictly speaking, are two forms of capitalist accumulation.

The state allows the development monopolies and large-scale companies including through mergers and acquisitions. It makes bulky investments in the physical infrastructure, including through its own large-scale companies. If credit 'soon becomes a new and terrible weapon in the battle of competition and is finally transformed into an enormous social mechanism for the centralisation of capitals' (Marx, 1887: 441), then cheap credit from the state – and injection of cash to financial markets through such things as quantitative easing[26] – can contribute to centralization: some companies use the cheap money to buy other companies. The state indeed supports changes in the re-distribution of means of production as long as the people who receive assets belong to the hegemonic fraction of the ruling class. The state supports the fact that some commodity producers – for example larger and more efficient capitalists – gain at the cost of other capitalists. If the c / v is higher for some enterprises than for others, then the commodities of the enterprises with the higher organic composition will be sold at prices of production higher than value, while commodities of the enterprise with lower c / v are sold at prices of production lower than value.

Capitalistic accumulation, with the rise in c / v and attendant technical change, produces a relatively redundant population of labourers, including globally (a global reserve army). As the ratio of constant to variable capital rises: capitalistic accumulation produces 'a relatively redundant population of labourers, *i.e.*, a population of greater extent than suffices for the average needs of the self-expansion of capital, and therefore a surplus-population' (Marx, 1887: 443). More efficient companies may swallow less efficient ones. In fact, centralization of capital also displaces people: when one company acquires another company, the new company generally employs fewer people than the number of people employed by the two erstwhile separate companies together. Capitalism 'forms a disposable industrial reserve army, that belongs to capital quite as absolutely as if the latter had bred it at its own cost' (Marx, 1887: 444), so the reserve army is very much a part of capitalism. 'Independently of the limits of the actual increase of population, it creates, for the changing needs of the self-expansion of capital, a mass of human material always ready for exploitation' (Marx, 1887: 444).

The state is connected to the relative surplus population (un- and underemployed people) in at least two ways by its doings and not-doings. (a) It *could* take steps to make sure everyone who loses their job due to technical change in one enterprise remains employed elsewhere. It does not. It does not act to significantly counter the reserve army. It does not make sure that everyone is able to work according to their abilities and for a decent wage. (b) It controls in- and out-migration generally in the long- and short-term interests of capital (or its hegemonic fractions), so capital has access to a reserve army, especially in the South, which puts pressure on wages there as well as in the North.

While state regulation of abuses in the workplace is partly a product of class struggle from below (workers' struggle), such regulation in turn shapes the nature of capitalism. This happens when capitalists respond to state regulation, for example, by introducing machinery, which represents class struggle from above. Capitalist accumulation based on machinery, or the industrial revolution, 'which takes place *spontaneously*, is *artificially* helped on by' state legislations such as 'the extension of the Factory Acts to all industries in which women, young persons and children are employed'. When the length of the working day is regulated by the state, this necessitates technological change 'in the place of muscles'. In addition, 'in order to make up for the loss of time' caused by the shortening of the working day, 'an expansion occurs of the means of production used in common, of the furnaces, buildings, &c., in one word, greater concentration of the means of production and a correspondingly greater concourse of workpeople' (Marx, 1887: 312–3; italics added).

Thus, state regulations contribute to the changes in the technical mode of production:

> While in each individual workshop it enforces uniformity, regularity, order, and economy, it increases by the immense spur which the limitation and regulation of the working-day [by the state] give to technical improvement, the anarchy and the catastrophes of capitalist production as a whole, the intensity of labour, and the competition of machinery with the labourer.
>
> (Marx, 1887: 329)

While an educated and healthy workforce is in the interest of the whole capitalist class, the short-term interests of capitalists are adversely affected, although in different ways by different capitalists (big capitalists versus smaller capitalists). Smaller capitalists are directly affected if their access to cheaper labour is restricted by the state: 'Unlimited exploitation of cheap labour-power is the sole foundation of their power to compete' (as in the Global South now generally but also in many parts of the North).[27] There is another way in which the state regulation can influence smaller capitalists. Because state regulation necessitates greater outlay of capital, smaller capitalists can be outcompeted by bigger capitalists: 'owing to the necessity they impose for greater outlay of capital', Factory Acts and similar other legislations 'hasten on the decline of the small masters, and the concentration of capital' (Marx, 1887: 314).[28]

For bigger capitalists, who are a little flexible with respect to the use of constant capital versus the use of cheap labour, state regulation means that they have to invest more in constant capital – investment in machinery, for example – to make up for the loss of cheaper labour (adults working long hours for low wages and children labour).[29] Of course, it is true that so soon as capital 'finds itself subject to legal control at one point, compensates itself all the more recklessly at other points' (Marx, 1887: 320). For example, if the working day is reduced, wages can be reduced, or mechanization can be introduced expanding unemployment, which puts pressure on wages. Similarly, if the working day is reduced here, workers can be made to work longer hours elsewhere, and if wages are higher here, workers can be made to work for lower wages there.

Factory Acts that seek to ensure workers' safety in the workplace, regulate the working day, and so on remain un- or under-implemented. This is in part because of the need to cut costs, one that is expressed by the nefarious nexus of state officials/politicians and the business world and the overall climate of free market ideology. With this, capital's despotic rule in the labour process becomes even more despotic, a despotic rule that is strengthened by the ease with which capital can hire and fire labour with the support of the state. The existing rules protecting nature and workers from the harmful effects of capitalist production are gutted as soon as there arises a slight political opportunity (e.g. weakness of anti-capital and anti-state organizations). All this makes for a heightened level of accumulation by exploitation.

Irrespective of the size of capital invested, certain enterprises can be more adversely affected by state regulation of the working day than other enterprises. For example, capitalists investing in chemical and metallurgical industries (e.g. earthenware trade, in bleaching, dyeing, baking, and in most of the metal industries where the discontinuity in the labour process will affect production adversely) can complain of state-legislated pauses in the working day.

When capitalists ignore the general laws of the state that seek to protect workers from excesses of capitalism and when the state does little, this *non*-action is a specific form of active state action. In parts of a country (e.g. special economic zones), the state makes it legal that its laws do not operate, that they are negated. This amounts to 'a state of exception', created by the state, in the economic sphere. The state protects the conditions for the production of value and surplus value. Appropriation of surplus value and countering any potential/actual resistance to exploitation require that the workplace be the site of capitalists' private legislation, of capitalists' despotic control. The state defends this, if necessary, through public (nationwide) legislation and its coercive powers. The state makes sure the worker has no control over surplus value and remains separated from it, the surplus value that can contribute to further accumulation and becomes a means of exploitation.[30]

6 The state and tendencies/counter-tendencies towards the crisis of accumulation

The literature on capitalist crisis tends to focus on the relevant ratios trying to prove that capitalism does go through the crisis of profitability.[31] In other words, a necessary focus has been on 'the economic'. This is, of course, fundamental, but the crisis-proneness of the capitalist economy – 'oscillations of the economic conjuncture (boom-depression-crisis)' – has palpable political implications for the state too:

> The revenues of possessing classes, the state budget, wages, unemployment, proportions of foreign trade, etc., are intimately bound up with the economic conjuncture, and in their turn exert the most direct influence on politics. This alone is enough to make one understand how important and fruitful it is to follow step by step the history of political parties, state institutions, etc., in relation to the cycles of capitalist development.
>
> (Trotsky, 1923)

In capitalism, there *is* an overall tendency towards the rate of technical change as expressed in the ratio of constant capital to variable capital rising faster than the rate of exploitation as expressed as the ratio of surplus value to variable capital. This causes a tendency of the rate of (average) profit to fall (TRPF) (Carchedi and Roberts, 2018; Smith, 2018; Smith et al., 2021). With the capitalist system experiencing a crisis of profitability, there is a crisis of investment in the production of goods and services. This crisis of profitability may

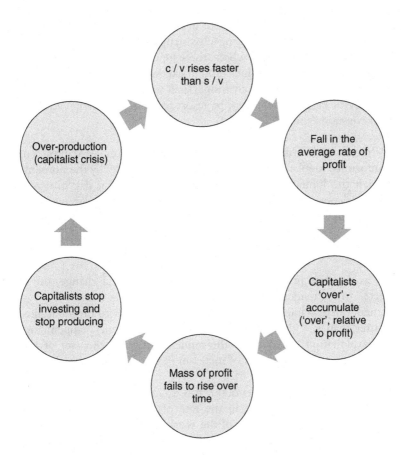

Figure 7.3 Marxist crisis theory

sectorally or geographically, or otherwise, *appear* as the crisis of over-production and over-accumulation, which the state seeks to counter (Hirsch, 1978: 97; Poulantzas, 2008: 306). Figure 7.3 shows the chain of causal links involved in the production of crisis.[32] The state takes several steps to respond to the recurrent economic crisis, the crisis of accumulation, and these steps aim to increase exploitation and/or cheapen elements of constant capital.

The state is connected to every stage in the formation of the crisis. First of all, the state helps capitalists increase the rate of exploitation. 'The degree of exploitation of labour, the appropriation of surplus-labour and surplus-value, is raised notably by lengthening the working-day and intensifying labour' (Marx, 1894: 165). This the state seeks to facilitate. Legislations prolong the working day, or the state does little to stop capitalists make workers work longer than the legal working day.

However, and as mentioned, there is a constant tendency towards technical change expressed in the form of a rise in c / v. To this, the state contributes. When, in part, because of working-class struggle and to serve the long-term interests of the capitalist class a whole, the state introduces legislation to restrict capitalists' greed for surplus value through excessive prolongation of the working day, and through other mechanisms, such state intervention forces capitalists, initially in bigger enterprises, to resort to technical change and to invest more in constant capital (Figure 7.3).

> While in each individual workshop it [pro-worker legislation] enforces uniformity, regularity, order, and *economy*, it increases by the immense spur which the limitation and regulation of the working day give *to technical improvement, the anarchy and the catastrophes of capitalist production* as a whole, the intensity of labour, and the competition of machinery with the labourer.
>
> (Marx, 1887: 329; italics added)

Insofar as the state policies contribute towards technical change, the state *is* connected to the tendency towards the formation of the crisis.

As mentioned, while the average rate of profit tends to drop because c / v rises faster than s/v, the opposite can also conjuncturally happen: increased rate of exploitation can counter the tendency towards the rate of profit to fall. There are various methods of increasing exploitation to which the state is connected.

Marx (1894) says that 'the tendency towards a reduction in the rate of profit is notably weakened by a rise in the rate of absolute surplus-value, which originates with the lengthening of the working-day'. The state helps capital prolong the working day.[33] Formal subsumption of labour (FSL) (employment of labour for long hours) is a method of appropriating absolute surplus value, and employers are able to engage in this especially when there is a massive reserve army of labour: when there are many un- or under-employed people around, one can be forced to work longer, and this is possible when the state does nothing to counter this. Marx develops this idea in *Capital volume 1* (see Das, 2017a: 340–90, 2012). The reserve army or the relative over-population, Marx says in *Capital volume 3*, 'is the reason why . . . the more or less imperfect subordination of labour to capital continues in many branches of production' (Marx, 1894: 167). Among the various other methods of increasing exploitation is 'the widespread introduction of female and child labour. Exploitation is increased because the whole family must now perform more surplus-labour for capital than before, even when the total amount of their wages increases' (Marx, 1894: 166). The rate of exploitation can be increased in the sphere of circulation by depressing the wages below the value of labour power (further than it already might be). And here the state plays an important role too, including by making it difficult for workers to strike, by reducing or denying economic support (e.g. unemployment insurance, food stamps, anti-poverty assistance, and so on) to the reserve army of labour, and by not forcing capital to pay a wage that at least conforms to the value of labour power.

The state can contribute towards the cheapening of elements of constant capital via its investment in science and technology and also through the liberalization of trade which brings cheaper means of production from abroad. It can facilitate foreign trade (liberalization of trade under neoliberalism): 'foreign trade partly cheapens the elements of constant capital, and partly the necessities of life for which the variable capital is exchanged', so 'it tends to raise the rate of profit by increasing the rate of surplus-value and lowering the value of constant capital' (Marx, 1894: 168). Grossman (1929) says, '[A]n injection of surplus value by means of foreign trade would raise the rate of profit and reduce the severity of the breakdown tendency' because 'the original surplus value expands by means of transfers from abroad'. Of course, often multiple states may experience crisis at a given point in time, so given their inter-dependency at the global level, competition among countries intensifies: every country tries to export the effect of the crisis to another country. When the state enables greater foreign trade and indeed foreign investment, the scope for extensive exploitation of labour expands. When capital is invested in the periphery (ex-colonies, and the like), this allows heightened level of 'exploitation of labour', at least, in part 'because of the use of unfree labour' (Marx, 1894: 168).

Several processes during what is called neoliberalism have countered falling profitability. Neoliberal reforms – anti-trade union legislation, privatization of state companies, cuts in pensions and government services, lowering of corporate taxes, and increase in taxes on spending – all have countered, and were meant to counter, the falling profitability in the post-war period until late 1970s (Roberts, 2016: 61). The rate of increase in surplus value has risen faster than the rise in c / v. The development of high-tech dot-com revolution in the 1990s, which was based on initial state investment, led to the cheapening of constant capital, making sure that c / v did not rise in many countries (ibid.). Often the state bails out bankrupt companies: the state bailed out the insurance company AIG in order to meet in full the insurance claims on losses on speculative investments made by the likes of Goldman Sachs' (ibid.: 67). This meant that 'taxpayers ended up fully compensating the big banks for the losses they incurred from their own recklessness and greed'. Bailout is followed by cut in government welfare spending, higher taxes on wage workers, and reduction in the cost of pensions (deferred wages) by extending retirement ages. In other words, in trying to counter the crisis, the state makes workers pay for the crisis. Capital does not come out of its recurrent crises spontaneously but through state assistance given to it. (See the short Appendix to this chapter that provides a very basic and provisional outline of how one can examine the crisis in relation to the state.)

7 Summary, and theoretical and political implications

In this chapter, I have examined the state's role in production by employing Marx's general formula for capital (M-CM'). It is clear that, the state, whether it is a so-called neoliberal state or not, connects to each phase of the capitalist circuit. It seeks to make sure capitalist accumulation, including concentration and centralization, occurs. By facilitating cheapening of constant capital and by helping capital increase the rate of exploitation, the state seeks to counter the tendency for the average rate of profit to fall.

It is in the very nature of capitalist state power that it will fundamentally protect the interests of the capitalist class. This fact sets limits on the state. One is the outer limit: the state must ensure the right of the capitalist class to own property in its *specifically capitalist* form: to buy and sell for profit, to appropriate surplus (whether in p-roduction or outside), to dispossess direct producers, and so on. One of the other (two) limits (apart from creating appropriate ideological conditions) is the one that is indicated by the fact that the state must ensure conditions for capitalist accumulation within the *framework of capitalist property relation*, in a country and globally (or at least it must not undermine these conditions). The significance of this outer limit is this: capital is a class *relation*, which is expressed as *things* (money, capital investment, machines, and so on) and which must keep moving, so it is useless for the capitalist class to just maintain its ownership of property, with the help of the state, if its property is not put to use to produce more money. For the state to contribute to such a process (i.e. accumulation of wealth for its sake), it is neither enough to create/sustain property rights nor is it enough that the state ensure free commodity exchange. The state must ensure that the separated means of production and subsistence are turned into capital and that the capitalists constituting the new ruling class are, like the older ruling classes, able to appropriate the unpaid surplus labour from direct producers, *even if* they pay the full value of the commodity they purchase (i.e. labour power). It must ensure that the money with which labour power is bought is actually the surplus value that has already been appropriated from workers. If commodities produced are not sold (realized) then the value of the commodities is lost, so the state tries to help capitalists with the realization of value by expanding markets for commodities. The chapter has a series of theoretical implications. I turn to these now.

Firstly, the state's role in relation to the capitalist circuit and in relation to capitalist accumulation and crisis must be seen as a tendency, and like any other tendency it is subject to counter-tendencies. The state cannot help capitalist accumulation beyond a point. There are many reasons for this. One major one is that the internal relations between the state and capitalists which define the outer limit means that the state must not generally have control over private capitalist investment decisions. There is also a contradiction between the socialized production process and the privatized appropriation of the benefits from such a process, thus creating conditions for recurrent economic crisis. So, there is a limit to the extent to which the capitalist state can help capitalist accumulation. There is also the contradiction between worldwide capitalist accumulation and nation-state political framework of capitalism. This contradiction restricts the state – that is, particular nation-states – from being able to resolve the problems that capitalist accumulation faces.

Secondly, while from one vantage point, there is a pressure on the state to seek to produce the general conditions for capitalist accumulation by spending the tax money, from another perspective, it is not *absolutely* necessary that the state will produce those conditions in a de-commodified manner. There is actually no *absolute* reason, from the standpoint of capital, why the state has to provide, for example, school education or public transportation: these conditions can be provided for in a more or less commodified manner by capital for a profit, as we have been seeing under what is called neoliberal capitalism. Consider these remarkable lines from Marx (1973: 532) from *Grundrisse*: 'The highest development of capital exists when the general conditions of the process of social production are not paid out of *deductions from the social revenue*, the state's taxes . . . but rather out of capital as capital.'[34] Yet the state is called upon to provide some of the general conditions for accumulation. This partly shows the potential 'weakness' of capitalist development.

Thirdly, in the light of the foregoing discussion on the state in relation to the capital circuit, it might be useful to reflect on the idea of state capitalism.[35] People use the term 'state capitalism' without making clear just what they mean by that. State railroads are state capitalism. On the basis of state subsidies, certain industries are said to represent state capitalism. Post-colonial state-led capitalist development is often called state capitalism. 'And the entire nationalized and plan-directed Soviet economy is supposedly also state capitalism [no matter that it was "the result of a revolution"]' (Trotsky, 1979: 340).

> The term 'state capitalism' originally arose to designate all the phenomena which arise when a bourgeois state takes direct charge of the means of transport or of industrial enterprises. The very necessity of such measures is one of the signs that the productive forces have outgrown capitalism and are bringing it to a partial self-negation in practice.
>
> (Trotsky, 1991: 208)

As indicated already, capitalism itself creates conditions for state's economic involvement:

> Monopoly capitalism has long since outgrown the private ownership of the means of production and the boundaries of the national state. Paralyzed, however, by its own organizations, the working class was unable to free in time the productive forces of society from their capitalist fetters. Hence arises the protracted epoch of economic and political convulsions. The productive forces pound against the barriers of private property and of national boundaries [that are defended by the state]. The bourgeois governments are obliged to pacify the mutiny of their own productive forces

with a police club. This is what constitutes the so-called planned economy. Insofar as the state attempts to harness and discipline capitalist anarchy, it may be called conditionally 'state capitalism.'

(Trotsky, 1933)

[U]nder state capitalism, in the strict sense of the word, we must understand the management of industrial and other enterprises by the bourgeois state on its own account, or the 'regulating' intervention of the bourgeois state into the workings of private capitalist enterprises.

(ibid.)

One has to adequately distinguish between state capitalism and state-ism, from the standpoint of property relations or class relations.

There are undoubtedly points of contact between state capitalism and 'state-ism', but taken as systems they are opposite rather than identical. State capitalism means the substitution of state property for private property, and for that very reason remains partial in character. State-ism . . . means state intervention on the basis of private property, and with the goal of preserving it. Whatever be the programs of the government, stateism inevitably leads to a transfer of the damages of the decaying system from strong shoulders to weak.

It 'rescues' the small proprietor from complete ruin only to the extent that his existence is necessary for the preservation of big property. The planned measures of stateism are dictated not by the demands of a development of the productive forces, but by a concern for the preservation of private property at the expense of the productive forces, which are in revolt against it. State-ism means applying brakes to the development of technique, supporting unviable enterprises, perpetuating parasitic social strata. In a word, state-ism is completely reactionary in character.

(Trotsky, 1991: 209)

Thus, the capitalist state can acquire attributes of 'state-capitalists', with state-managers effectively acting like capitalists.[36]

Fourthly, the state under neoliberalism is fundamentally capitalist in character. Given the usual portrayal of the state as neoliberal state in many circles, it is difficult to believe that the state is so closely linked to the businesses. Neoliberalism is the modern form of laissez-faire economy. And '*laissez-faire* too is a form of state "regulation", introduced and maintained by legislative and coercive means. It is a deliberate policy, conscious of its own ends, and not the spontaneous, automatic expression of economic facts' (Gramsci, 1971: 160). The neoliberal form of the state, just like the state as such, is connected to each phase of the capitalist circuit.

Fifthly, the capitalist state is a contradiction-ridden personification of illusory common interests. About the capitalist, Marx says, '[H]e is only capital personified. His soul is the soul of capital' (Marx, 1887: 163). 'As the conscious representative of this movement [advancing money to make more money], the possessor of money becomes a capitalist' (ibid.: 107). And the capitalist sees labour as a personification as well: from the standpoint of capital, 'The worker is here nothing more than personified labour-time' (ibid.: 168). Even labour has developed a habit of seeing things this way. And the state, the personification of illusory interests, supports both forms of personification, capital's as well as labour's. These forms are contradictory: capital wants people to work longer while labour wants to work shorter hours. That contradiction is represented in the heart of the state, which is partly represented in state legislation to shorten the working day under pressure from workers. Excessively long working days 'called forth a control on the part of Society which legally limits, regulates, and makes uniform the working-day and its pauses' (ibid.: 194). But state legislation makes numerous concessions to capital. The state sometimes prolongs the working day and sometimes restricts it.

The freely exchanged commodities are produced by workers who do not receive the full value of what they produce. The money with which the commodity labour power is bought today is, ultimately, the form of unpaid labour appropriated from workers yesterday, and therefore it properly belongs to workers. The equality and freedom that the capitalist state 'protects' (the idea that all commodity owners are equal and that workers are free to work for whoever they wish to) are the *capitalist* form of equality and freedom within the sphere of exchange relations. Such equality and freedom are transformed into their opposites, i.e. inequality and unfreedom, within the sphere of property relations and production relations. In fact, and as mentioned earlier, *even in* exchange relations, there are inequality and unfreedom. This is because: (a) workers are not free not to work for the capitalist class as a whole, a fact which the state as the state of the capitalist class *as a whole* absolutely cannot do anything about, and (b) often millions of workers do not get a wage that conforms to the value of labour power, and millions are not free to work for whoever they wish to, the facts which the state *can* do something but often fails to, because it works in the interests of *specific* capitalists who may be politically and/or economically important and who benefit from such a regime of low wages and unfreedom.

A legal system that corresponds to social relations where there are *equal* commodity producers can only support inequalities or injustice under capitalism: workers lack control over production and over the fruits of their labour. The state becomes a contradictory entity because the world of equality and freedom contradicts the world of unfreedom and inequality. While labour and capital are commodity owners, equal and free in the eyes of law, it is the case that underlying the freedom and equality in commodity exchange is the appropriation of unpaid labour from sellers–cum–owners of commodity labour power. The state supports such an unjust system. The state ensures conditions that produce substantial inequality (one between capital and labour, and between big business and small-scale producers). Given the exploitative nature of capitalist property rights defended by the state, it is futile to think about social justice, in the Proudhon style, on the basis of merely 'the juridical relations that correspond to the production of commodities' (Marx, 1887: 64) and on the basis of the idea that 'the production of commodities [by small-scale producers] is a form of production as everlasting as justice' (ibid.).

Sixthly, the state plays an immense role in the reproduction of capitalism, and yet the state in capitalism is not the main cause of people's economic and other problems or indeed of the class relations as such. Marx (1847) says:

> [I]f the bourgeoisie is politically, that is, by its state power, 'maintaining injustice in property relations', it is not *creating* it. The 'injustice in property relations' which is determined by the modern division of labour, the modern form of exchange, competition, concentration, etc., by no means arises from the political rule of the bourgeois class, but vice versa, the political rule of the bourgeois class arises from these modern relations of production which bourgeois economists proclaim to be necessary and eternal laws.

Engels presented two views (Marxist and anarchist). Theoretically speaking, the anarchist view (e.g. Bakunin) is that 'it is the *state* which has created capital, that the capitalist has his capital *only by favour of the state*', while in the Marxist view, 'state power is nothing more than the organisation with which the ruling classes, landlords and capitalists have provided themselves in order to protect their social prerogatives' (in Marx and Engels, 1975: 257). In the Marxist view, as we have seen, capitalism does not exist because of the capitalist state but the capitalist state exists because of capitalism, which then makes use of it.

As often is the case, these contrasting *theoretical* views are translated into contrasting *political* differences. This is the case even if Marxism and anarchism are united in that they hope to see a society without class and the state. For anarchism, Engels continues, 'the state is the chief evil, it is above all the state which must be done away with and then capitalism will go to hell of itself' (in Marx and Engels, 1975: 257). But Marxists think differently. Engels speaks for Marxists when says:

> We, on the contrary say: do away with capital, the appropriation of the whole means of production in the hands of the few, and the state will fall away of itself. The difference is an essential one. Without a previous social revolution the abolition of the state is nonsense; the abolition of capital is in itself the social revolution and involves a change in the whole method of production.

(ibid.: 257–8)

Finally, to some extent the capitalist state intervention can have a progressive character. Marx begins *Capital 1* with associated producers and ends it with a call to expropriate the expropriators. If Marx thought that the state can improve matters significantly, he would not do this. What the capitalist class does to the most vulnerable among workers – male and female children – sums up the nature of capitalism and of the conditions of the working class as a whole. If the state has failed to protect the children from the juggernaut of capitalism, it cannot be expected to do much for the working class as a whole.

Yet Marx points to the potentially progressive implications of state legislations, including those concerning education, health, etc. State regulation of the workplace, while it is an attack on capitalists' limitless power over workers, can also be an attack on power relations within the family, an attack that is generally favourable towards children and women. When state legislation seeks to regulate commodity-production at home where children are employed in large numbers producing goods for larger businesses, state legislation is seen as an attack on *parental authority*.[37] But the matter must be understood correctly:

> It was not . . . the misuse of parental authority that created the capitalistic exploitation, whether direct or indirect, of children's labour; but, on the contrary, it was the capitalistic mode of exploitation which, by sweeping away the economic basis of parental authority, made its exercise degenerate into a mischievous misuse of power.
>
> (Marx, 1887: 320)

And this points to what is possible in the future.

> However terrible and disgusting the dissolution, under the capitalist system, of the old family ties may appear, nevertheless, modern industry, by assigning as it does an important part in the process of production, outside the domestic sphere, to women, to young persons, and to children of both sexes, creates a new economic foundation for a higher form of the family and of the relations between the sexes.
>
> (ibid.)

If the state measures force capitalists to adopt normal working days, capitalists have to make money in other ways (investing in constant capital). This has implications for smaller-scale capitalists and thus capitalism as such. Making use of workers working long hours and exploitation of children cannot be the major basis for remaining competitive. Small enterprises are out-competed and are swallowed by bigger capitalist units. Centralization of capital happens. The general extension of state measures to all enterprises 'for the purpose of protecting the working-class both in mind and body . . . hastens on the general conversion of numerous isolated small industries into a few combined industries carried on upon a large scale' thus accelerating 'the concentration of capital and the exclusive predominance of the factory system' (Marx, 1887: 329). And large-scale production is a pre-condition for socialism where people work together using means of production on a large scale, which can only be used in common and which allow massive increase in productivity and therefore availability of leisure time.

Appendix
Studying the state-crisis relation

In studying the relation between the state and economic crisis, one may keep in mind the following points presented schematically.

There are definite causes of – tendencies towards – the economic crisis. There are also definite counter-tendencies. However, over a long period of time and over a large enough area of commodity circulation within the world economy (e.g. a bloc of countries from the North and the South), the tendencies overpower the counter-tendencies. This means that c / v will rise faster than the rate of exploitation. The state contributes to the crisis tendency when its activities directly or indirectly increase labour-productivity-enhancing technical change that can cause c / v to rise.

The counter-tendencies to the crisis are not automatic or spontaneous: at least some of these counter-tendencies could be actively mobilized by the state. This happens when the state contributes to increased capitalist exploitation of labour at the societal scale.

The ability of the state to mobilize counter-tendencies to the economic crisis is limited in part because of the crisis (which contributes to the state's fiscal crisis, for example) and will geographically vary across state-spaces (nations) as well as across regional/ sub-national economies.

One also needs to study the impact of the crisis on different classes and class fractions located in different sectors and regions, and of their subjective and objective response to the state's assistance, and so on. One needs to know whether the state responds to the causes of the crisis or to its effects.

A study of the crisis requires a prior empirical analysis of the economic crisis (including of the relevant value ratios) in a number of countries, some from the North and some from the South. Besides, given that economic crisis is global and given that a state exists in a system of states, how a state can respond to economic crisis under its jurisdiction depends on its location within a system of states. However, it must be understood that the state does not have the ability to remove the tendency of the rate of profit to fall (TRPF), but the constant recurrence of crisis does potentially create conditions for the working-class mobilization against capitalism and the state.

Notes

1

> Under ageing capitalism, the proportion of the total income of society passing through the hands of the state is usually much greater than income going directly to private capital as PROFITS, interest and rent. Investment directly undertaken by the state is often more than half total investment.
>
> (Harman, 1991)

State spending as a percentage of GDP has increased from about 20% in 1975 to 27% in 2018 for the entire world economy. The European figures are about 25% and 35% (World Bank, n.d.).

2

> The theory of anti-value has to embrace a whole range of activities which are not productive of value even though they are essential and necessary to the functioning of capital . . . Unproductive but socially necessary activities like . . . proper state regulation and law enforcement are not inherently anti-capitalist.
>
> (Harvey, 2018: 87)

3 'If the profit rate is to be equalized then both capital and labor must be highly mobile which means that the State must actively remove barriers to mobility when necessary' (Harvey, 2012/1978: 274).

4

> 'In [geo-economics], investment capital for industry provided or guided by the state is the equivalent of firepower; product development subsidized by the state is the equivalent of weapon innovation; and market penetration supported by the state replaces military bases and garrisons on foreign soil as well diplomatic influence.' (Luttwak in Davidson, 2016: 240–241)

5 Consider Indian Institute of Management (IIM) and Indian Institute of Technology; the many graduates (e.g. Sundar Pichai of Google) from these become a part of the capitalist businesses in India and in advanced countries to which they migrate. Consider also the business schools and science and engineering departments in state-funded universities in North America and Europe.

6 This is true even if it may be the case that 'research and development policies designed and funded by the state are by no means directed towards concrete beneficiaries' (Offe and Ronge, 1982: 252).

7

> To be absolutely accurate, it is the total state revenues minus that portion of them that flows back to the working class in terms of welfare benefits, subsidies etc. that is part of the total surplus value; and the value of labour power is total take home wages plus these benefits, subsidies etc.
>
> (Harman, 1991)

8 There are 28 right-to-work states in the US. In spite of the name, the right-to-work laws do not guarantee employment to those who seek it but are a government ban on contractual agreements between employers and union employees requiring workers to pay for the costs of union representation (Baird, 1998). These laws prohibit contracts that require workers to pay union dues or fees as a condition of employment. The rationale for this is that compulsory unionism contradicts the right-to-work principle – a fundamental human right. Compulsory union membership is also contrary to the U.S. concept of individual rights and freedom of association. The principal aim of the right-to-work laws is 'to undermine the ability of workers to organize collectively' (Kishore, 2013).

9 Marx approaches surplus value *'regardless of its particular* forms as profit, interest, ground rent, etc.' (Marx's Letter to Engels; 24 August 1867) (Marx and Engels, 1975: 180). The division of the surplus value into its component parts (profit and the like) requires state intervention: rules that regulate ground rent are different from those that regulate interest or profit. The state mediates among different fractions of capital: productive, financial, landed, and so on. Thus, the state does not only mediate between property rights of capital and those of labour.

10 When workers receive less than what they need in order to maintain themselves and their family members, this condition is workers' super-exploitation (= above-normal exploitation). Super-exploitation can result in the fact that 'the proper reproduction of his labour-power is crippled' (Marx, 1887: 221). 'Despite the important part which this method plays in actual practice', Marx assumes 'that all commodities, including labour-power, are bought and sold at their full value' (ibid.). His point is that *even if* wages cover the cost of maintenance, with a normal working day, workers are still exploited: they are alienated from much of the net product that they produce, a process that the state protects while it may take steps against super-exploitation.

11 'At the end of the 18th and during the first ten years of the 19th century, the English farmers and landlords enforced the absolute minimum of wage, by paying the agricultural labourers less than the minimum in the form of wages, and the remainder in the shape of parochial relief' (Marx, 1887: 422).

12 Workers of the world without the protection against work-related safety issues (accidents, illnesses, and so on) are the 'invisible victims of development' (AMRC, 2012). According to Mike Robinson, CEO of the British Safety Council (an NGO working on workers' issues), about 48,000 workers die in India annually due to occupational accidents of which 38 fatal accidents take place every day in the construction sector. Overall, workplace deaths are 20 times higher in India than UK. Only 20% of India's 450+ million workers are covered under any health and safety legal framework (Indian Express, 2017).

13 See Rijken (2011) on this. Consider how exploitation is seen in the Indian Constitution. There are six fundamental rights recognized by it. One of them is the right against exploitation which prohibits all forms of forced labour, child labour, and trafficking of human beings. The Right against Exploitation is specifically enshrined in Articles 23 and 24 of the Constitution which prohibit/restrict trafficking and child labour (GOI: n.d: 13).

Similarly, when the state in Canada says that it 'continues to promote and uphold the ILO's decent work agenda, and is committed to combatting labour exploitation and promoting strong labour inspection systems' (Newswire, 2019), clearly it does not intend to combat the actual exploitation of labour by capital in the sense of appropriation of surplus labour.

14 Migrant Workers Center (undated), a Canadian organization that works for 'justice for migrant workers by providing legal services, advocacy, research, public education and engaging in law and policy reform initiatives', pointedly asks: 'What is Labour Exploitation?' Below is the answer it provides: 'Labour exploitation occurs when employers treat workers in ways that break the law. This includes treatment that is against workers' legal rights, such as: Employments Standards rights around wages and working conditions.'

15 That this work of directing and controlling is given over to a special class of wage labour does not make that work any less capitalistic:

> An industrial army of workmen, under the command of a capitalist, requires, like a real army, officers (managers), and sergeants (foremen, overlookers), who, while the work is being done, command in the name of the capitalist. The work of supervision becomes their established and exclusive function.
>
> (Marx, 1887: 232)

In fact, the idea and practice of hierarchy of work in the capitalist workplaces inform the internal organization (or form) of the state itself, which is discussed in a later chapter.

16 'Legislation on wage-labour . . . is started in England by the Statute of Labourers, of Edward III., 1349. The ordinance of 1350 in France, issued in the name of King John, corresponds with it' (Marx, 1887: 524).

17 In England, 'from the middle of the 14th to the end of the 17th century', capital, by using the state measures, tried to impose 'the lengthening of the working-day' (p. 181).

18 Taking advantage of the ongoing coronavirus pandemic, many Indian states are making changes in the laws concerning the length of the working day, forcing workers to work several hours longer. A key change made by at least seven Indian states implementing the wish of the central government is to raise maximum working hours from 48 to 72 a week to compensate for the effect of the lockdown. While some state governments have 'magicked away the Factories Act of 1948 altogether for three years', other states have issued notifications which 'exempt workers from specific provisions of that Act' (Chakravarty, 2020).

19 A 2018 BBC report says: 'The workplace is making people sick and even killing them.' According to this report,

> there were 120,000 extra deaths annually in the US from harmful management prac-tices, and that extra health-care costs were $190bn each year. That would make the workplace the fifth leading cause of death, worse than kidney disease or Alzheimer's. In the UK, the Health and Safety Executive reported that 12.5 million working days were lost from work-related stress, depression or anxiety in 2016–2017.
>
> (Pfeffer, 2018)

20 According to a recent study, poor Americans are nearly twice as likely to die before they reach old age as rich Americans. The study examines a subset of Americans, those between 51 and 61 years old in 1992.

> Nearly half of those (48 percent) in the poorest quintile died before 2014, when they would have been between 73 and 83 years old. Of the wealthiest quintile, only a quarter (26 percent) died . . . The second-poorest fifth of the age group under study had the second-worst death rate, with 42 percent dead by 2014. The figures for the middle fifth and the second-highest fifth were 37 percent dead and 31 percent dead, respectively.
>
> (Martin, 2019)

21 'The capitalist state can regulate some of the most unpleasant fields of production not through any particular altruism, but simply to ensure level playing field and to enforce the domination of the most important forms of capitalist industry' (Choonara, 2019: 126).

22 Consider BLS International Services, which is listed at the National Stock Exchange in India and which handles visa and passport and related applications.

23 Barrow (1993: 41) says this about the US state:

> [A] welfare system has been created which responds to popular demands for eco-nomic and social reform, but which in its implementation must continually dis-tribute benefits to the corporate sector (e.g., urban renewal for private developers, health care for private hospitals) while distributing program costs to service recipi-ents (e.g., user fees, Social Security taxation).

24 Originating in the 2017 Tax Cuts and Jobs Act, they offer the potential to connect long-term capital with low-income communities across the country to drive return and impact. A total of 8,700 opportunity zones exist. An opportunity zone fund (OZF) has been created as an investment vehicle that provides tax benefits for private capital – operating businesses and real estate business (but mainly the latter) – to help revitalize

the low-income areas. For example, once the previously earned capital gains are channelled into a qualifying OZF, federal tax is deferred until 31 December 2026 or the date the investment is sold – whichever comes sooner. Also, 10% of the original capital gains will be excluded from federal taxes if an investment is held for 5 years. The federal tax on capital gains earned within the OZF is completely eliminated if an investment is held for 10 years (Neufeld, 2020; Gose, 2020).

25 Davidson (2016: 211) notes:

> [N]ationalisation of the insurance company AIG and the mortgage institutions Freddie Mac and Fannie Mae . . . demonstrates that state managers will usually act in what they perceive to be the interests of capital, rather than according to the dictates of whatever version of capitalist ideology currently happens to be dominant. Ideology will adapt in due course.

26 This may be in the form of the injection of cash to financial markets through such things as quantitative easing, which happens when a central bank purchases government bonds and other securities from the open market in order to increase the money supply and encourage lending and investment. That the policy has not quite succeeded is a different matter. Capitalists take the money and speculate on it rather than invest it to produce goods and services.

27 Marx writes: '[A]s regards labour in the so-called domestic industries and the intermediate forms between them and Manufacture, so soon as limits are put to the working-day and to the employment of children [by the state], those industries go to the wall' (Marx, 1887: 313).

28 Also

> While in each individual workshop it enforces uniformity, regularity, order, and economy, it increases by the immense spur which the limitation and regulation of the working-day give to technical improvement, the anarchy and the catastrophes of capitalist production as a whole, the intensity of labour, and the competition of machinery with the labourer.
>
> (Marx, 1887: 329)

29 'The chief objection, repeatedly and passionately urged on behalf of each manufacture threatened with the Factory Act, is in fact this, that in order to continue the business on the old scale a greater outlay of capital will be necessary' (Marx, 1887: 313).

30 In capitalism, a part of the value produced by workers is taken away from them in the form of net profit, interest, rent, and so on and in a way which they have no control over (they have no control over wages paid to them). They have also no control over the other part of the value that goes towards the replenishment of existing means of production and for society-wide expenditures. So exploitation *is* partly a political process. Workers have no access to state power so they do not control value and surplus value. They do not just lack control over means of production (see Foley, 1986).

31 The origin of Marx's discussion of the capitalist crisis is actually in *Capital volume 1* (especially chapter 25) but is developed in chapters 13–14 of *Capital volume 3* so I build on both *Capital volume 1* and *Capital volume 3*.

32 As Roberts (2010) says:

> the profitability of capitalist production does not stay stable, but is subject to an inexorable downward pressure (or tendency) [in some years the rate of profit may rise, but the general tendency is towards the fall in the profit rate]. That eventually leads to capitalists overinvesting (overaccumulating) relative to the profits they get out of [the exploitation of] the workers. At a certain point, overaccumulation relative to profit (i.e. a falling rate of profit) leads to the total or *mass of profit* no longer rising. Then capitalists stop investing and producing and we have overproduction, or a

capitalist crisis. So the falling rate of profit (and falling profits) causes overproduction, not vice versa. But a falling rate of profit does not directly lead to a crisis as long as the mass of profit can rise.

33 As I have said earlier, the ongoing pandemic which has slowed down the economy has prompted the state to prolong the working day in countries such as India.

34 Marx continues:

> This shows the degree to which capital has subjugated all conditions of social production to itself, on one side; and, on the other side, hence, the extent to which social reproductive wealth has been capitalized, and all needs are satisfied through the exchange form; as well as the extent to which the socially posited needs of the individual, i.e. those which he consumes and feels not as a single individual in society, but communally with others . . . are likewise not only consumed but also produced through exchange, individual exchange. (p. 532)

35 See Sperber (2019) for a critical survey of 120 years of reflections on state capitalism and read back through the prism of class-state relations. See also Alami (2021).

36 This is to be distinguished from the nationalization of industries following anti-capitalist revolutions in the early parts of the 20th century.

37

> So long as Factory legislation is confined to regulating the labour in factories, manufactories, &c., it is regarded as a mere interference with the exploiting rights of capital. But when it comes to regulating the so-called 'home-labour,' [where children are massively employed] it is immediately viewed as a direct attack . . . on parental authority.

(Marx, 1887: 319)

8   The state and the agency of capitalists and state actors

If a capitalist, or indeed even a very rich person, hurts a worker or a peasant, that it is almost impossible to get justice from the state is well known. This is especially the case in the periphery. A phone call or a courtesy visit by the perpetrator to a top politician and/or a bureaucrat would be enough to crush all illusion in the minds of the victim about their rights. During a strike, capitalists can wait out the workers (how long can workers survive without working?); similarly, for anything that capitalists and their hangers-on do, a court case can be dragged for years which involve a lot of money that common people cannot afford to spend, whether in rich or poor countries. When it comes to justice, state institutions work well when two equally big capitalists (or two large landowners) fight out, but for any vertical fight (the fight between capitalists or very rich people, and common people), the state is almost useless.

The state must protect capitalist private property, support commodity relations and the exploitation of labour, and create general and specific conditions for accumulation. But the ways in which the state performs these actions in support of the capitalist class are not automatic. They are shaped by the agency of the capitalist class, especially its ties with state actors (decision-making politicians and officials). They are also shaped by the agency of state actors.

A terminological clarification is in order. In the narrow sense, instrumentalist mechanisms that explain the nature of *the state in capitalist society* include individual and institutional connections between capitalists and politicians/officers. But in a wider sense, the state *is* an instrument – a weapon – of the capitalist class or of capitalism in that it must serve the long-term interests of the capitalist class. The instrumental connection in the narrow sense is more relevant with respect to the inner limit to state action (i.e. which indicates the imperative of the state promoting capitalist accumulation) than with respect to the outer limit (which indicates the imperative that the state must protect capitalist property rights and class relations).

I begin with some remarks on structure-agency relations in Section 1. In Sections 2–3, I discuss the capitalist agency and state actors agency respectively (working-class agency is the topic of Chapter 9). Section 4 discusses the limits to what state actors can do for capitalists. In the final section, I discuss the conceptual implications of the agentic aspects of the capitalist class and state actors.

DOI: 10.4324/9781351168007-8

1 Structure and agency

Agency (i.e. practices informed by certain ideas) presupposes a structure. A structure is a set of certain internal *relations* among various processes and objects, the relations that in turn set up certain *mechanisms* (ways of doing/ acting). An individual or a group acts as an agent when they make a difference in the face of the *constraints* that a structure imposes, including by utilizing *opportunities* provided by the structure of relations under which one acts. If under given structural conditions (S), one expects outcome (O_1) but if another outcome (O_2) is observed that is significantly different from O_1, then, other things constant, one may say that agency – certain agentic behaviour – has made a difference. Structural conditions are *inert*. They can only propel action, but they cannot act.

If history is understood in terms of changes in the structural conditions, it is easy to see that history itself does not act. (Similarly, the geographical organization of people's activities itself does little.) People – as classes/class fractions – operating in time-space – do the acting on the stage created by the structural conditions. '*History*' or time, and one might add geography (location, etc.), 'does *nothing*', and it does not fight. Much rather, '[i]t is *man*, real, living man who . . . fights'. Further, ' "history" is not . . . a person apart, using man as a means to achieve *its own* aims; history is *nothing but* the activity of man pursuing his aims' (Marx and Engels, 1845; italics added).

The materialist-dialectical standpoint of Marxism does not reify structures, so it does not ignore the role of human agency either, while it insists on the primary role of structural necessity in historical changes. Men and women do make their own history but, 'in the first place, under very definite antecedents [assumptions] and conditions' (Engels in Marx and Engels, 1975: 395). Making history (and geography) means exercising agency and will. Depending on its nature, agency can reproduce or transcend a structure.

Agency involves knowledge or consciousness which shapes the material practice of the agent under structural conditions, even if ultimately structural conditions set a limit to the nature of consciousness. To act, one needs to know what to act on and how, and that means that cognitive error is a possibility: one may not know fully. In part because of this possibility, even if a given agentic behaviour aims to materialize certain structural imperative, it may not succeed, or it may succeed unevenly in time-space: it may succeed here more than there, and now and not then. There can be conflicts between the agentic powers of different individuals and groups. Engels writes: '[T]here are innumerable intersecting forces, an infinite series of parallelograms of forces which give rise to one resultant – the historical event' (in Marx and Engels, 1975: 395–6). One can think about the agency of different capitalists and of state actors as 'innumerable intersecting forces' with wills between and among which there can be contradiction.

Given the capitalist *structure*, the state must perform certain functions (this is the level of relatively more abstract analysis), but the ways in which such functions are performed through the relevant agency belong to a relatively more concrete level of analysis. The present chapter deals with the agency of capitalists (individual capitalists or a group of capitalists) and of high-level state actors.

2 Capitalists' agency

State policies are indeed affected by the inter-penetration of personnel, including instrumentalist control.[1] Bukharin (1988: 242), a classical Marxist, says that in capitalism 'the bourgeoisie is in control of production and therefore also of the state'. He also says that 'the structure of the State itself reflects the economic structure, i.e. the same classes occupy relatively the same positions', meaning that higher positions in the state are filled by people from the bourgeoisie (ibid.). Capitalists cultivate special relations with politicians and top bureaucrats who then shower favours on them: so there is a degree of overlap between the class of capitalists and higher-level state personnel (Figure 8.1). A major goal of the capitalist institutions is to advocate for a given policy that is dominantly, if not exclusively, pro-market and pro-business (increasingly pro-big-business) relative to the interests of the common people.

The capitalist class is indeed connected to the state machine 'by thousands of threads' (Lenin's words). It uses the state in their own parochial interest and, generally, against the interests of the masses:

> Two institutions most characteristic of this state machine are the bureaucracy and the standing army. In their works, Marx and Engels repeatedly show that the bourgeoisie are *connected with these institutions by thousands of threads*. Every worker's experience illustrates *this connection* in an extremely

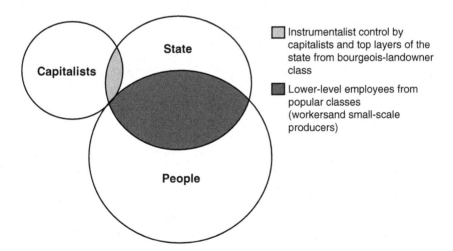

Figure 8.1 Capitalists and state employees

graphic and impressive manner. From its own bitter experience, the working class learns to recognize *this connection*.

(Lenin, 1949: 31; italics added)

Why does instrumentalist connection exist? This should be answered from
the standpoint of capital as a whole and from the standpoint of competing
capitalists.

There is a structural pressure on one arm of the capitalist social totality
(i.e. the state) to serve another arm (i.e. the capitalist class). The pressure
needs to be activated and manifested by capitalist agency. While an educated
and healthy workforce and a good physical environment are in the interest
of the whole capitalist class, ensuring that this actually happens – and note
anti-capitalist forces can counter/weaken the state imperative to act in the
capitalists interests as can ideas and actions of state actors themselves – may
require some capitalists or their associations to cultivate ties with the relevant
state personnel. The manifestation of the structural pressure can have a flexible
temporality and flexible spatiality: while the state, more or less, needs to serve
the fundamental interests of the bourgeoisie over a given period of time and
at the national scale, the agency of the capitalist class as a whole, or of specific hegemonic fractions is necessary in order to ensure the correct timing
of a pro-capitalist policy.[2] It is also necessary for the correct spacing of a pro-
capitalist policy (explained later).

The state is to look after not only long-term interests but long-term
common interests of the bourgeoisie. Common interests coexist with fractional interests. This fact prompts capitalists' agency. So the matter of capital versus capitals is important. Capital as a whole, the reality of common
interests, exists and functions through mutually competing capitals with
different needs and interests.[3] Capitalists' interests are different because they
differ in terms of their size of investment (smaller and bigger capitalists)
and sector (different capitalists produce different use-values). Capitalists are
different in terms of specific accumulation strategies: some rely on technical change as a way of increasing profit to a larger extent than others; some
are more integrated into the world economy and are export-oriented than
others.

Capitalists also differ in terms of location: some fractions (especially productive capital as opposed to money capital) are based in specific areas. Their profits
come from specific places, so they are more geographically dependent. Utilities
companies are fairly place-based, as are farm-based and mining enterprises.
Given place dependence of some capitals at multiple scales (local, sub-national,
national, and so on), what state institutions do in a given place matters a lot,
which means that ties to the state institutions are important, the ties that are
not spatially portable (Cox, 2002). This is why spacing of policy is important:
capitalists interests are regionally/locally specific (e.g. mining industry here,
utilities industry there), so the state must meet geographically circumscribed
capitalist interests and not just capitalist interests.

The question is, given that different capitalists have different interests and that they compete with one another, what are the ways in which inter-capitalist relation relates to capitalist agency? There are several.

1   While over the long term the state serves the common affairs of the capitalist class, an existing state policy may benefit certain capitalists and adversely affect their competing siblings. When a given policy is in place, capitalists seek to maximize its favourable impact and/or minimize its unfavourable impact, through their special ties with state actors. If the state has decided to introduce a policy to privatize state-owned companies and is looking for buyers, then it can favour some private capitalists – including those who might have offered financial help to the governing party, clandestinely or not – over others. Alternatively, a given regulation is countered through close ties, legal and illegal. This applies to not only domestic capital but also to foreign capital: 'the executive committees of the main institutions of globalization' and imperialism such as 'the International Monetary Fund (IMF) and the World Bank (WB) are composed of the finance ministers of the leading capitalist powers' and the finance ministers in turn have 'close ties with the chief transnational corporations' (Aronowitz and Bratsis, 2002: xxi).

2   At a given point in time, different – and often mutually contradictory – strategies of capitalist accumulation are possible, because of contradictions among capitalists and because the state itself may not exactly know what to do, so capitalists advocate for, through personal and institutional ties, certain state strategies in their favour. Strong ties between capitalists and the state personnel can also help capitalists to avoid existing unfavourable regulations and stop future regulations of profit-making and thus remain competitive. A capitalist or a group of capitalists can 'buy' an entire policy package (e.g. a policy that opens insurance industry to private investors or that allows contract farming whereby agribusiness has greater control over farm input/output markets). Harman (1991) writes: 'capitalists have always tried to boost their competitive positions by establishing alliances' with influential politicians, and such alliances are 'cemented by money but also by intermarriage, old boy networks, mutual socialising'.

3   The political turnover time is quickened: an application for certain required permissions is dealt with more quickly (e.g. permission to open a new firm or sell a newly created vaccine or drug and/or that allows the use of genetically modified seeds which have hitherto been opposed by large segments of the population). This is often done by ignoring existing rules; for example, a permission to open a factory is given without a proper environmental clearance or socio-economic impact assessment, thanks in particular to personal/institutional ties.

4   Personal ties are important not just in the context of competitive relations among capitalists. They can be important when the government introduces a measure or is planning to do so, under pressure of the masses. To the

extent that inter-capitalist competition sets the context for instrumental connection between capitalists and the state, the competition in question is the competition among capitalists over the surplus value to be appropriated from the masses. During periods of intense class struggle, certain capitalist fractions may be much less conciliatory – or more aggressive – towards the masses than other fractions. So they may try to influence state action through their ties to politicians and bureaucrats in the civil administration and the army. There is also a possibility of class struggle within the state, with some influential state actors representing the voice and interests of the masses. A large part of the totality of state apparatuses is indeed populated by common people (men and women from working class and small-scale producers background (Figure 8.1) who do not necessarily share a common ground with the top layers). This creates a need to use the instrumental connection with other state actors, especially the more powerful ones, to counter the 'reformist' elements unless they are countered spontaneously within the state.

The short-term interests of capitalists (e.g. capitalists paying very low wages and industries which pollute a lot) can be adversely affected if, for example, the state takes measures against the payment of low wages or excessive pollution, in part because of common people's struggles. Often big businesses support regulations concerning health and safety, especially if small businesses cannot afford them (Harvey, 2010a: 228). So they capture the state regulatory apparatuses to eliminate competition. It is widely known that the British colonial state introduced pro-worker measures at least partly in order to increase the cost of production in the enterprises owned by indigenous Indian capitalists competing with British capitalists. Because state regulation necessitates greater outlay of capital, smaller capitalists can be outcompeted by bigger capitalists.

Capitalists use their ties with state personnel not only to reap an advantage vis-à-vis their competitors but also to make sure that the threat from the masses remains minimized. If a state policy is nonetheless introduced, its actual implementation can be blunted through the same ties between capitalists and the state. For example, laws regarding fire safety can be conveniently ignored by capitalists seeking to reduce the cost of production and remain competitive. This happens on the basis of the ties between capitalists and state actors (e.g. factory inspectors and/or their immediate political bosses).

When masses engage in a struggle for concessions from capitalists (e.g. a rise in wages), having a good relation with the police officers and their political bosses comes in very handy. All states use the mechanism of intimidation to weaken people's struggle, and the proximate driving force for this mechanism, including how quickly it happens and with what intensity and so on, is often the ties between specific capitalists and state actors. By using their personal and institutional ties with the state, capitalists can buy their own safety; they can also get state actors to endanger the personal safety of militant trade union leaders and politically active rank-and-file workers, print/electronic media journalists who report abuse and injustice, and even judges, and indeed anyone, who is more vocal against capitalist beyond a given limit.

The greater the intensity of inter-capitalist competition, the greater the intensity of potential or actual class struggle of the masses, and the greater the dependence of capitalists on a given place (e.g. large farm or mineral-based factory), the more intense are the instrumental ties between capitalists and state actors. Whether the ties are legal or illegal does not matter. This is because by virtue of the ties, an illegal transaction/tie can be presented as legal.

Capitalists make use of their associations/institutions to exercise their agency in a society where they do have structural power by virtue of their control over the economy. The fact that business people 'require associations' cannot be used as an evidence to say, as liberals such as King (1986: 160) do, that they do not have structural power and that they are not 'inevitably privileged in the political systems of advanced capitalist societies'. Panitch and Gindin (2015: 8) say that capitalists 'come together as real social actors through institutions which play a crucial role in their formation, identity and behaviour' and which help them overcome their mutual divisions.

Apart from the institutions of bourgeois democracy (e.g. parliament, bourgeois parties, and so on, there are at least four major capitalist 'institutions' (including associations) that link capitalists to their instrument, the state.

Organizations of the capitalist class

Operating as *non-profit* entities, national and regional-scale trade organizations of the capitalist class actively connect capitalists' interests to the bourgeois political parties and bureaucracies. This indicates that monopolies with their immense economic power can have direct interaction with the state personnel (Mandel, 1978: 490).

In the US context, such organizations as the Council on Foreign Relations, the Committee for Economic Development, the Conference Board, the Business Council, and the Business Roundtable help the members of the capitalist community to transcend their interest-group consciousness and to develop an overall class consciousness, by identifying the long-term interests of the capitalist class as a whole (Barrow, 1993: 33).[4] They 'are usually financed through corporate contributions and draw the bulk of their membership directly from the capitalist class and act as the political inner circle of the capitalist class'. In India, such organizations include All India Organization of Employers and the Federation of Indian Chamber of Commerce and Industry.

Think tanks, opinion makers, and lobbyists

They survey the diverse business interests to acquire specific knowledge about what the different capitalists need in a concrete situation and suggest favourable compromise policies in support of the capitalist class or its hegemonic fractions.[5] University professors, retired civil servants, judges, and many others can lend their distinguished service, anonymously or not, and for a payment in cash or kind (e.g. appointment to a governmental commission/position and the like). These policy proposals are sugar-coated by an appeal to national development, people's welfare, and so on in order to create a belief that what is good for business is good for people, and that is, that capitalists' investment decisions even if they hurt people, and the state's economic policies, even if they benefit the businesses, are ultimately in the interest of the common people. In other words, the general *economic interests* of the tiny capitalist class are expressed as *concrete state policies* which are claimed to benefit *everyone*. So blatantly capitalist policies are de-classed. These think tanks, which provide crucial ideas to bureaucrats for drafting pro-business policy statements, often function as firms in the non-governmental sector, which some see as a progressive counter current to capitalists and to the state. The task of the production of such blatantly false perception of capitalist policies as pro-people on the part of think tanks and bureaucrats is complemented by a pliant pro-business media which often depends on governments' advertisements and which presents the sugar-coated policies and ideas as acceptable to the common people.[6]

Armed with the relevant knowledge produced by think tanks and the like, lobbyists do their work on behalf of individual capitalists or groups of them. Most recently in the US, business lobbyists are targeting a proposal to raise taxes on the wealthy to help cover costs for funding boosts in areas related to climate change, education, and so on. Justifiably annoyed at this, Senate Budget Committee Chairman Bernie Sanders has said:

> This is what oligarchy and a corrupt political system are all about. The rich and large corporations get richer, and their lobbyists do everything possible to protect their wealth and greed.
>
> (quoted in Folley, 2021)

Lobbying is one of the 'political processes' that 'are necessary "transmission belts" between capital and the state' (Barrow, 1993: 62). 'Experts in lobbying firms . . . do the work of conceiving and writing the documents that give direction and coherence to policy formulations' (Peet, 2007: 85). Peet even suggests that the notion of 'the state, "the government" or even "political institutions" has to be expanded to include these private bureaucracies' (ibid.).

People's organizations

No capitalists, especially larger capitalists, can afford to completely ignore the dissenting voices in society. Cultivating a good relation with trade union bureaucrats, liberal or critical-minded academics, moderate parts of Left parties and progressive grassroots ecological and other movements can contribute to the production of an image of a conscientious capitalist, a capitalist with a sense of corporate social responsibility.[7] (Some bourgeois politicians also maintain good relations with the 'progressive movements' in order to cultivate a good image and to give their actions a progressive cover.)

Instrumental ties are not merely 'sociological': capitalists do not just cultivate personal relations with state actors. They are deeply material as they involve in-cash transactions (e.g. open and secretive election funding, apart from bribing) and/or in-kind transactions (e.g. offer of private sector jobs to 'good' civil servants and politicians, providing helicopters for election campaign, vouching for civil servants for appointment to good posts within the government, public support for politicians during elections including by allowing their own media outlets to be used by them).

At a concrete level, the state is like a big real estate owned by top politicians and officers, which can be 'bought' in small parcels by capitalists, and yet the more that real estate is bought, the more it remains. It is not a massive exaggeration to say that different parts of the state (or different state actors) are in the pocket of different moneybags at different points in time. While in the LDCs, both politicians and officials are involved in the clandestine deals with the business world, in the advanced countries, civil servants may be less so while elected politicians are deeply connected to businesses through the money connection.[8]

As we know, capitalists engage in M-C-M': they invest money, buy commodities, and sell the same commodities or manufactured commodities for more money than invested. In terms of their political connection with state personnel, a political version of the capital circuit might be seen as functioning. Capitalists invest money (M_p) to influence state actors and buy favourable interventions/policies. The latter is capitalists' political commodity, C_p. C_p helps capitalists remain competitive and reduces the cost of doing business, including what they might otherwise have to spend on workers' safety and the like. So capitalists with connections to the state can make more money than they invest in their instrumentalist ties (M'_p). Thus, in the sphere of politics, or state-capital relation, capitalists engage in what can be called a political capital circuit: $M_p - C_p - M'_p$ (where the subscript 'p' stands for political).

3 State actors' agency

Capitalists use ties to state actors. But these ties are the ties with the state actors who have a degree of autonomy relative to a given capitalist or a group of capitalists. A major reason for state autonomy is what much of state theory has pointed out (as discussed in Chapter 2): the fact that individual capitalists generally do not need to exercise coercion against other capitalists or their workers in economic transactions contributes to the state enjoying a degree of autonomy vis-à-vis individual capitalists. Besides, as Creaven (2000: 267) says, 'the relative autonomy of polity from the direct control of the ruling class acquires a consistently high form, and its most stable form, in a developed capitalist society' because 'the productive forces are sufficiently advanced here to support an independent "unproductive" centralised administrative apparatus on a nationwide scale'.

The act of money-making and the act of governing represent a division of labour in society. Unless the state is given some autonomy, it cannot work for the common affairs of the money-making class and for hegemonic fractions of this class. Nor can it perform functions in support of the general affairs of society which are important whether or not a society is capitalist (e.g. dealing with a pandemic). Indeed, regardless of the class character of state actors, 'the role of the state in administering or overseeing a large-scale national community ensures that certain of its activities (e.g. upholding certain kinds of criminal law or traffic regulations such as the Highway Code) must be "classless" in the sense that they are indispensable to the running of any industrialised urban society' (Creaven, 2000: 268). The fact that a part of society – the capitalist state – needs to look after the common affairs of the society as a whole (these are not necessarily the same as the common affairs of the capitalist class) contributes to, and requires, a degree of autonomy of the state. This autonomy is then used by the ruling class and is given a class colour: when the state does operate on behalf of an entire capitalist society, this functioning is mediated by capitalist class interests. This is seen, for example, in the relation between the state's attempt to keep society 'crime free' and the prison-industrial complex, or between the state's attempt to defend a country against foreign enemies and the military-industrial complex, or indeed between the state's attempt to fight a pandemic and the healthcare-industrial complex that churns billionaires when millions die. The so-called class-neutral functions of the capitalist state end up having a class character, because the state is inherently the capitalist state.

Generally speaking, given the conflicts of interests among capitalists, self-interested capitalists *as capitalists* might not be great administrators to look after the common affairs of the capitalist class as a whole. There are all kinds of conflicts within the capitalist class within a country and globally. Within a country, there are different competing 'regional group interests, different industrial interests, antagonisms within an industry, rivalry between producers of consumers' and producers' goods, light and heavy industry, and so on, aside from religious, political, and other ideological differences' (Draper, 1977: 323). This fact 'makes it more difficult for any individual capitalist to be trusted as executor for the class as a whole' (ibid.). For example, during times of social upheavals from below, 'concessions may have to be made to the class enemy below, the working classes' (ibid.). But if concessions have to be made, who will pay for them? At a given point, to the extent that state's revenue is a given, if more goes to the masses, which section of the dominant class is made to sacrifice and how? It would be difficult for capitalists acting as state actors to decide. Therefore, a 'built-in characteristic of capitalism . . . minimizes the functioning of capitalists themselves as state administrators or managers', and there is a need for 'finding political leaders who can take, and stick to, an overall and farsighted view of the interests and needs of the system as a whole' (p. 324).

However, one should not have too dim a view of capitalists being able to manage the common affairs of society as well as functions in support of the capitalist class including its hegemonic fractions. One has to just consider how many capitalists increasingly occupy important positions within the state. So the inability of the capitalist class for its self-rule is only relative, just as the autonomy of the state actors qua state actors is relative.[9]

As indicated already, while the state's main task is to look after the common economic and political affairs of the capitalists, the very idea of common affairs implies that there are *different* interests too, and this implies a degree of autonomy on the part of the state. That is, to be able to manage the common affairs, the state has to have a degree of autonomy vis-à-vis short-term interests of capital as a whole and vis-à-vis short-term or long-term interests of specific capitalists (this is acknowledged even by scholars such as Miliband). The fact that there is competition in the economic sphere among capitalists (or indeed between capitalists and landlords as in many LDCs) does require that the state as a structure of relations have a degree of autonomy to be able to resolve conflicts among them.[10] It is the autonomy of this structure of relations that is enjoyed by state actors, the bearers of that structure, and their autonomy in turn influences state functions.

A bureaucrat/politician, who is a mere rolling stone, and who lacks his/her own voice, like a president of a chamber of commerce, would not be taken seriously. Even the most obedient servant needs a degree of autonomy which the master is happy to provide, because otherwise the master will be using much time and resource in directing the servant at every step. Indeed, to be able to function in a context where capitalists themselves may not agree on what a good policy might be when, for example, it comes to foreign investment in insurance or industrialization in indigenous areas and so on, a degree of autonomy on the part of the structure of the state and state actors *is* necessary. In fact, in certain conditions acting as representatives of the private property owners, the bureaucracy can create specific types of private property owners such as the capitalist class.[11]

It is not just that interests of competing capitalists are different. Capitalists' interests, at a fundamental level, are incompatible with those of the common people, so there is an objective need to represent what are the interests of capitalists as the interests of the nation as a whole. Here the ideas of influential state actors (officials and politicians) about the national interest and how it might overlap with the interest of the capitalist class are crucial. (In this context, Miliband's partnership idea is a useful one.)

For the state to operate in the interest of the capitalist class (and of society as a whole), it needs resources (in the form of taxes and the like). An enormous amount of value (social wealth) passes through the state (almost a third of the GDP of countries), giving enormous economic power to the state vis-à-vis any individual capitalist or group of capitalists. This economic power, which is a part of the basis for its autonomy, is enjoyed by the state actors.

While ultimately capitalists' action is driven by the fact that they have to make an average *rate* of profit and a significant *mass* of profit, state actors' action is driven by the fact that they must ensure reproduction of capitalist relations and help capitalists accumulate value. Yet, within these limits, state actors have their own interests to pursue too. These include careerism, accumulation of wealth in extra-economic ways – through collaboration with capitalists and large-scale landowners, winning elections, or obtaining some form of legiti-mation from common people in support of their rule.[12] Marx (1843) writes, 'As far as the individual bureaucrat is concerned, the end of the state becomes his private end: a pursuit of higher posts, the building of a career.' State actors do pursue their own interests because doing so is beneficial to them. They *can* pursue their interests because the structure of the state has given them some autonomy to. The state bureaucracy might seek to 'make gains for itself at the expense of others' (Harman, 1991), that is, capitalists and other groups. Of course, how far they can go in this direction depends on how well capitalists (and others) exercise their agency. In response to state actors actions that might hurt capitalists, capitalists might 'use their own special position – industrial capital its ability to postpone investment, money capital its ability to move overseas – to fight back' (Harman, 1991).

In pursuing their own interests, state actors may end up doing things that are not exactly in the capitalists' short-term interests, and indeed they can pur-sue their own interests which are relatively independent of capitalists' inter-ests.[13] There can be conflicts, within limits, between autonomously acting state actors and capitalists with their ultimate economic veto power. Certain actors can be a little reformist in relation to the masses and/or may pursue their own interests and may therefore implement policies which may be seen as a drain on the surplus value in the eyes of the capitalists.[14] State actors' perception of what is needed to promote capitalist accumulation may not exactly coincide with the objective interests of the capitalist class and of its individual segments.

State actors, and especially politicians, can be seen as being involved in an M-C-M'-like circuit in politics whereby politicians invest money (M) to bribe poor voters and opposition party representatives and on political propaganda and political violence (e.g. physical coercion against opponents) in order to manufacture a political commodity, called governmental power I which is then used as an instrument to make more money (M') than invested. Similarly, state officials (especially those at the higher echelons) invest money (in the form of bribing politicians and/or other officials) to occupy certain posts that can gen-erate a lot of rent (bribe). So they are also involved in an M-C-M'-like circuit. If capitalists and their political representatives as well as state bureaucrats make more money than invested, where is the money coming from: it ultimately comes from workers/voters not getting the money they need to meet their needs.

There is a limit to the state actors' self-interested actions; these actions can-not undermine conditions for accumulation too much and too long. These limits are set by capitalism as a structure of relations setting limit on the state as another structure of relations. Accumulation provides employment without which there might be a crisis of legitimation for specific regimes and indeed for the state. Accumulation is a source of taxes and loans for the state itself *as long as* the state remains bourgeois.[15] The consequent pressure on the state as a structure to earn its revenue is manifested as the pressure on the top layer of the bureaucracy: 'the directing layer in the state bureaucracy is dependent upon successful capitalist exploitation and accumulation' without which it cannot get the revenues it requires, including 'for its own privileges and its own functioning' (Harman, 1991). So state actors are forced to provide conditions that promote capital accumulation within the geographical boundaries of the state. Mandel (1969) says, the fact that capitalist class 'in large part fills the coffers of the state' and thus pays 'for the upkeep of the state' means that it 'will demand that the latter place itself completely at their service' through its laws and institutions.

Of course, I would argue, this financial reliance of the state is derivative and conjunctural. Institutional separation – of the state from the profit-oriented market economy (i.e. the fact that state institutions are not the headquarters of big companies) – does not mean processual separation between the state and the private sector. What the state does or does not do, either in the interest of a country as a whole (to the extent that economic growth benefits both capitalists and workers) or in the interests of the masses is fundamentally driven by state's class character – that is, its need to support economic and political interests of the exploiting class – and *not* primarily because of its own dependence on capitalists. Such dependence does exist. It exists at a more concrete level. And it does have important effects on capitalists and non-capitalist classes.

4 Limits to state function in support of capitalist interests

The state can create general conditions for capitalist development by connecting to every step in the M-C-M' circuit, as we have seen in Chapter 7. Conversely, its actions, intentionally or not, can impede the development of productive forces under capitalism. 'The state power has been able . . . to co-operate with capitalist development.'[16] Or it can 'put brakes on it' (Trotsky, 1991: 212).

While the state promotes capitalist accumulation in various ways, there are limits to the extent to which the state succeeds and can succeed in doing so. These limits are given in the concrete mechanisms creating conditions for capitalist accumulation. This is for various reasons.

Firstly, given its derivative dependence on the capitalist class for its survival (tax dependence), the state has limited resources in its hands at any given point in time, and this limits what state actors can do for capitalists (and in their own interests). The state can help capitalists – for example, it can help a relatively weak enterprise under its jurisdiction to close the gap between its own value and the social value – but there are strong limits to any given state doing this because the state is subordinated to the law of value operating at the global scale, the law that ultimately determines how much value (or, money) will pass through the state.

Secondly, since the state is 'separate' from the sphere of production, it only reacts to accumulation crisis.[17] Besides, specific policies may not be adequate to capitalist accumulation (Jessop, 2012: 340; Jessop, 2006: 418) because within structural limits (e.g. the limit to protect property rights, commodity relations, and so on), 'there will always be more than one possible 'accumulation strategy' (Jessop, 1990: 159). The different capitalists may have different interests and different ideas about their interests, and they might contradict each other. Accumulation strategies must advance the immediate interests of the different fractions of capital (located in different territories) and must secure the long-term interests of the hegemonic fraction, at least, which must, in turn, sacrifice some of its short-term economic interests. It is not an easy task to figure out what these will be in a context where different fractions of capital have different interests and where capitalists and workers are antagonistically related. No capitalist fraction knows exactly what policies are needed at the level of the whole economy, especially if the economy is constantly crisis-prone. Trial and error is one of the methods in which *specific* pro-business policies are arrived at. But the bureaucratic state is not always equipped to innovatively think about new actions that are needed as it is best designed to follow fixed legal structures in processing certain inputs (Offe, 1984).

Thirdly, a given intervention can be contradictory: certain positive impacts of an action might be nullified by its negative impacts. Some people think that military expenditures are good for capitalist accumulation. Luxemburg (1913) says: militarism is a 'pre-eminent means for the realisation of surplus-value; it is in itself a province of accumulation'. For Harvey (2008b), the importance of the wars is that value is destroyed creating opportunities for the production of new value. From a class fractional approach (from the standpoint of certain capitalists), this might sound reasonable: the favourable impact of militarism on capitalist accumulation 'is how things may appear from the standpoint of individual capital as military supplies have always been the occasion for rapid enrichment' (Grossman, 1929). But from the standpoint of capital as a whole, 'militarism is a sphere of unproductive consumption' in the sense that '[i]nstead of being saved, values are pulverised'. This means that '[f]ar from being a sphere of accumulation, militarism slows down accumulation' as 'a major share of the income of the working class' which the state secures through indirect taxation and which 'might have gone into the hands of the capitalists as surplus value is seized by the state and spent mainly for unproductive purposes' (ibid.).

Similarly, if the state reduces/eliminates support for the unemployed (unemployment insurance), it may reduce its expenses to the delight of capitalists who are always for austerity, and it may reduce the wages by weakening the bargaining power of workers, but without the state support, unemployed people may not be available in a place for capitalists to take advantage of them. The reserve army must be in situ. To cite another instance, if the state invests more in support of capital it is good for capital, but increased state borrowing may raise interest rate which adversely affects capital (and not just capital) (Resnick and Wolff, 2006: 319).

Fourthly, the more intense demands on the state can threaten to overburden it. Policies of the state can pose a threat to the dominance of the capitalist exchange relations. The more the state is involved in the economy, the less the investment opportunities for certain segments of capital there are, and the greater is the proportion of the social surplus product that it absorbs, which could otherwise be in the hands of the capitalist class.[18] While the economic purpose – maintaining conditions for capitalist economic development – is a prime motive of the state, the state does engage in various non-economic activities that can undermine conditions for capitalist development.

Fifthly, the capitalist state cannot be solely concerned with benefitting the capitalist class. A hegemonic class must ensure that there is a space within which the state meets the interests of non-capitalist classes and class fractions, including large-scale landowners, and top layers of state actors. To be the capitalist state, the state does not have to be exclusively concerned with the capitalist class. In fact, the state has to relate to all the classes, to the totality of capitalist class society. The state seeks to meet the needs of non-capitalist classes from time to time, in howsoever limited a manner; it must meet the common social-ecological needs of all classes (laws of marriage, traffic lights, pandemic, global warming), even if the ways in which it meets the common needs are shaped by its capitalist character. To the extent that the interests of the capitalist class are fundamentally incompatible with those of the workers (as well as small-scale producers), the fact that the state must meet the needs of the non-capitalist classes puts a limit to the extent to which the state can meet the needs of the capitalist class at a point in time, even if welfare policies create a market for capitalists. After all, every deduction from the surplus value that does not go to the capitalist class is considered to be a loss to that class, other things constant.

Sixthly, the capitalist class needs to make money, and for this to happen certain cultural-political conditions need to be created, and these conditions may not be necessarily conducive to profit-making in any direct sense. If to divert attention from the failure of capitalists and their state to better the working and living conditions of the masses, the state run by a right-wing party supported by its own bigoted supporters decides to spend its energy on cultural and sentimental matters, then creating general conditions for capitalist accumulation may be compromised. In India, the state under a right-wing fascistic party *is* indeed often more concerned about promoting the religious nationalist agenda than creating general conditions for capitalist development. Such an agenda involves strategies and interventions that are more or less useless from the standpoint of the common affairs of the capitalist class.

Seventhly, the ultimate limit is the tendency for the rate of profit to fall as the organic composition of capital rises. As there is less surplus value to play with, the state's ability to intervene (including on behalf of labour) is diminished. The recurrent economic crisis, over which the state has little control, causes unemployment. And '[g]rowing unemployment, in its turn, deepens

the financial crisis of the state and undermines the unstable monetary systems'
(Trotsky, 1938a).

5 Summary, and theoretical and political implications

It is partly because of the capitalist *structure* that capitalists need to exercise
their agency by making use of instrumentalist connection to state actors: the
structural imperative on the state to do certain things has no guarantee that
a given policy will be adequate and will always happen on time. Capitalists
have their associations and organizations (including chambers of commerce,
bourgeois parties, and so on) through which their class agency is exercised and
through which they launch class struggle (blocking pro-people measures and
repressing people's struggles). Panitch and Gindin (2015: 9) say that capitalist
institutions 'like employers' associations, confederations of industry, chambers
of commerce, think tanks, consultancies, law firms, foundations and philan-
thropies mediate and fashion 'capital's collective class interests'. Of course, the
state itself is the most trustworthy organization of the capitalist class (if not a
specific regional or social fraction of the class). Instrumentalism is an important
mechanism, in other words.

It is also the capitalist structure that leaves a space for the autonomy of the
state as a structure, and its autonomy is enjoyed by state actors. Their autonomy
is a double-edged sword. It allows the state (actors) to manage the common
affairs of the various fractions of the capitalist class (apart from the interests of
society as a whole), and yet state actors can pursue their own interests.

Views of state actors, including how they *see* accumulation in relation to
the 'national interest', are important. Their own interests in accumulation of
power and wealth (and their own interests may not always coincide with those
of capitalist class as a whole) might influence how (well) the state promotes
capitalist economic interests. The struggles of the masses have an impact on
the thinking and interventions of the state as well: sometimes the state might
grant concessions, and at other times, it might not. Some state actors, like some
capitalists, can be compassionate and philanthropic, but qua state actors, they
cannot do much. State actors may not always succeed in ensuring conditions
for capitalist profit-making, and not every state action is pro-capitalist, but that
does not mean that the state is *not* inherently capitalist. Just because a piece of
art produced by a poor artist living in a remote village may be sold for a million,
that does not invalidate the law of value.

On the one hand, it is mistaken to think that the close relation between
state actors and capitalists makes little difference to the state's functioning. On
the other hand, such close relation is not the essence of the state as a structure.
There has to be the state in the first place for the capitalists to make use of it
by cultivating close relations with those who manage the affairs of the state.
Given the capitalist structure, the state structure has to perform certain functions. That is true at a relatively abstract level. At a concrete level, however,
personal and institutional ties between capitalists and state actors are a reality,

as are the autonomous actions of state actors in their own interests. From their own experience, masses are aware of the 'thousands of threads' that connect capitalists to the state.

The facts that there are close relations between state actors and capitalists and that top state actors and capitalists may have similar standard of living lead some to think that they are the same, or they belong to, one class. For example, Davidson (2016: 213) says that state managers' incomes, that are 'paid from state revenues ultimately derive from the total surplus value produced by the working class, as do the profits, interest, and rent received by different types of private capitalist'. The fact that capitalists' profit as well as 'the relatively high levels of remuneration, security, and prestige enjoyed by these officials depend on the continued exploitation of wage labor' means that 'the interests of state managers and capitalists are the same' (ibid.).

> At the most fundamental level, the common interest between capitalists and state managers stems from their *common class position*. Both are part of the bourgeoisie: 'departmental permanent secretaries in the British home civil service as much as, say, the chief executive officers of major companies.
> (Davidson, 2016: 212; italics added)

Davidson invites us to 'visualise the bourgeoisie as a series of concentric circles' where 'the capitalist class as such (actual owners and controllers of capital) occupies the centre and a series of other layers radiates outwards' (p. 213). He says the groups that are 'closer to the periphery' are 'progressively less directly connected to the core capitalist economic activities of production, and so on, and are more involved in the 'ideological, administrative, or technical' tasks that are, however, 'essential to the reproduction of capitalism' (p. 213). This view, although it sounds super-radical, is dangerously close to a power view of society, where capital is one form of power and the state is another form of power, even if both are said to be closely connected.

Chris Harman (1991) also has a similar view:

> [S]tate revenues *are comparable to* the other revenues that accrue to different sections of capital . . . Just as there is continual conflict between the different sections of capital over the sizes of these different revenues, so there is continual conflict between the state bureaucracy and *the rest of* the capitalist class over the size of its cut from the total surplus value.
> (italics added)

Even in non-economic terms, 'the interests of state managers and capitalists are not dissimilar', and this is because '[a] shared background in institutions like schools, universities, and clubs helps to consolidate a class consciousness that articulates . . . [the] interests in both groups' (Davidson, 2016: 213). Here the assumption is that ideological position of a group of people determines their class position.

Similarly, arguing for 'a certain flexibility in drawing and redrawing class lines', and 'in order to capture the distinctive character of Japanese capitalism', Ollman (2003: 199) has found it 'necessary to extend the notion of capitalist class to include the higher state bureaucrats and the leading politicians in the ruling party' (p. 199). In Japan:

> some capitalists work in what are formally state institutions and others in what are formally private ones, though . . . most of the leading members of this class divide their lives between the two. The essential thing is that they all function as embodiments of capital, serving its (and, consequently, their own) best interests in whatever way their current positions allow. They all work to expand surplus-value and benefit materially when that happens, though *when* they are bureaucrats and politicians this is not immediately apparent.
>
> (Ollman, 2003: 199)

> [T]he process of becoming a capitalist for most of the leading members of that class begins with their entry into the state bureaucracy. Recognizing that Japan's top bureaucrats belong to the capitalist class does not mean that we can no longer distinguish them as that part of the class that functions (at present) in the state bureaucracy.
>
> (ibid.)[19]

Ollman says that there is the need for a new 'category for the peculiar case of Japan. That category is "collective capitalist". . . . It is the collective capitalist, which divides its time between bureaucratic, business, and governmental functions' (p. 200).

The mistaken parallel being drawn here between capitalists and powerful pro-capitalist officials qua officials is based on a subjective definition of capital divorced from its underlying objective trait. Capitalists are capitalists because of an objective relationship and not merely because they *wish to* make money. The bureaucracy can indeed play a very active and independent role promoting capitalist interests, but there has to be a state in the first place for there to be a state bureaucracy, and the state is there because there are opposed classes, and bureaucracy qua bureaucracy is not one of them. It would be a mistake to conflate capitalists with pro-capitalist state actors *as* state actors, just as it is a mistake to treat the bureaucracy of a post-revolution transitional society as a capitalist class.

Capitalists are those who command a huge amount of exchange value, control over private property and production, and who appropriate surplus value, and in whose interests the coercive powers of the state are primarily used. Workers lack these traits. It is the class relation and it is capitalism as class relation that explain the nature of the capitalist state as a structure of relations. And the nature of the state as a structure of relations explains the action of state actors, those who manage the affairs of the state in the common interests of the capitalist class (and large-scale landowners). Trotsky (1933) says:

> The class has . . . a scientifically restricted meaning to a Marxist. A class is defined not by its participation in the distribution of the national income alone, but by its independent role in the general structure of economy and by its independent roots in the economic foundations of society.

'The bureaucracy lacks all these social traits' of a class (ibid.). 'It has no independent position in the process of production and distribution. It has no independent property roots. Its functions relate basically to the political technique of class rule', and it 'derives its privileges not from any special property relations, peculiar to it as a "class"' (ibid.). Of course, bureaucracy can be exploitative. But 'insofar as the bureaucracy robs the people. . . , we have to deal not with class exploitation, in the scientific sense of the word, but with social parasitism, although on a very large scale' (ibid.). It is similar to the present-day clergy:

> During the middle ages the clergy constituted a class or an estate, insofar as its rule depended upon a specific system of land property and forced labor. The present day church constitutes not an exploiting class but a parasitic corporation. It would be silly to actually speak of the American clergy as a special ruling class; yet, it is indubitable that the priests of the different colors and denominations devour in the United States a big portion of the surplus value. In its traits of parasitism, the bureaucracy, as well as the clergy, approximates to the lumpen-proletariat, which likewise does not represent, as is well known, an independent 'class'.
>
> (ibid.)

Given the active role of bureaucrats in relation to capitalist development, it is indeed easy to think that they are almost like capitalist property owners or that they belong to the same class as capitalist property owners rather than the ones who make sure that capitalists continue to have their property and augment it. Marx and Engels (1845) say that 'since the bourgeois have organised the defence of their own property in the state', it is easy to believe that 'the state has the factory as property, the manufacturer holds it only in fee, as possession'. They mockingly retort:

> In exactly the same way when a dog guards my house it 'has' the house 'as property', and I hold it only 'in fee, as possession' from the dog.

Notes

1 According to Domhoff, 'business organizations' first and overriding goal is to secure special tax breaks and tax loopholes that reduce the tax burden of an individual firm or industry' (in Barrow, 1993: 30–31). They also want 'to funnel self-serving advice

and information selectively to state officials to influence which facts are available to government decision-makers'. And they also wish to 'secure favorable legislation for a particular company or industry (e.g., antitrust exemptions, tariffs) through legislative bodies'. 'All these objectives, in Domhoff's analysis, constitute the short-term interests of capitalists in maintaining or increasing the immediate profitability of their particular company or business sector' (ibid.).

2 Instrumentalist connections that capitalists have with the state 'can at least influence the timing of policy responses to fluctuations in business confidence and the types of policy adjustments that are forthcoming, and they can affect whether or not the state exerts its full capacities on behalf of capital' (Barrow, 1993: 62–63).

3 'The bourgeoisie as a class, and its interests, are not identical with the identity or ideas of a particular group of business leaders at a particular point in time' (Therborn, 1980: 243).

4

> A competing policy grouping is anchored by the National Association of Man-
> ufacturers (NAM) and the U.S. Chamber of Commerce (CC). This policy
> grouping represents an ultraconservative wing of the power elite and is sup-
> ported by smaller corporations (i.e., medium-sized competitive capital) and small
> businesses. The major strength of the ultraconservatives has typically been in
> Congress, although during the last decade they have increasingly captured the
> executive branch.
>
> (Barrow, 1993: 39)

5 Indeed, 'before business can communicate its interests to the state, it must at some level know what it needs from the state, that is, what policies will impact it negatively and what policies will satisfy its requirements' (Barrow, 1993: 62).

6

> The capitalist inner circle. . . [that the capitalists'] organizations represent is assisted
> in the technical aspects of policy planning by academic advisors and technical experts
> who are occasionally invited to join the planning organizations and to become mem-
> ber of the power elite. These advisors are usually drawn from well-known 'ideologi-
> cal satellites' such as major universities, foundations, and privately financed research
> institutes or think tanks. These 'intellectuals' are offered other inducements to assist
> the capitalist class, such as lucrative speaking honoraria, endowed university profes-
> sorships, mission specific research grants, positions as corporate consultants, positions
> on boards of directors, and lobbying fees. Likewise, high-ranking state managers
> and emerging legislators are often invited into the planning network, where they
> are trained and socialized to become the spokespersons, allies, and future executive
> leaders of the power elite.
>
> (Barrow, 1993: 36)

7 This image is often associated with one of the biggest capitalist conglomerates in India, the Tata group. In 2014, India became the first country to legally mandate corporate social responsibility (CSR). The new rules in Section 135 of India's Companies Act make it mandatory for companies with a net worth of ₹500 crore or more, or turnover of ₹1,000 crore or more, or a net profit of ₹5 crore or more during the immediately preceding financial year, to spend 2% of the average net profits of the immediately preceding 3 years on CSR activities. The objective of CSR is for large-scale private companies to share the burden of the government in providing social services (Nangia, 2021).

8 Consider the secretive electoral funding in India that the right-wing BJP-led government has introduced. One of the public sector banks sells bonds which corporates buy and donate to various parties, and the BJP is the dominant beneficiary of this.

9 'The interlocking directorships of corporate boards may be more important in bridging the various fractions of capital than in playing any directly functional role in the corporation' (Panitch and Gindin, 2015: 9).

10

> [T]he nature of the competition among owners of the means of production will tend to give each capitalist an active interest in having a state apparatus that enforces the rules of the game without being captured directly by any specific capitalist or group of capitalists. The institutional separation of state and property thus becomes not only possible, but desirable from the point of view of capitalists.
>
> (Wright, 1985: 122)

11 Ollman (2003: 196) says that 'the new Japanese state created capitalists in a manner not very different from how the feudal state in Europe had created knights and barons'. Similarly, it has been said that the state contributed to the creation of the capitalist class in Russia.

12 Wetherly (2005: 24) says that business confidence is not an on-off variable but is defined by a spectrum within which there may conceivably be a range that is acceptable for state managers. The room for manoeuvre equates to policy discretion and allows the possibility that some policies may even be at odds with business confidence (or the confidence of specific sectors of business) within an overall policy package that maintains business confidence at an acceptable level.

13

> [T]he very fact that the mode of production of capitalist society does allow a separation of its 'political' and 'economic' functions, ensures that a certain (though tightly circumscribed) conflict space is opened up for a differentiation of interest between the state and capital to develop. The state elite does have a real interest in attempting to concentrate in its own hands a greater share of the total surplus value pumped out of the direct producers against capital.
>
> (Creaven, 2000: 268)

14 'Indeed, the behavioral mechanisms driving the actions of state managers certainly involve noneconomic considerations, even the achievement of what one might call reformist objectives, in which support for national capitals is merely a means to an end' (Davidson, 2016: 214–215).

15 'A certain portion of value and surplus value is appropriated by the state in the form of taxes' (Harvey, 2018: 15).

16

> It is the state bureaucracy, and not the owners of industry or their much-touted managers and workers, who are primarily responsible for what Japan, Inc. is today. Rather than simply tell businessmen what to do, Japan's ministries have perfected the old Mafia tactic of making people an offer that they can't refuse. They call it 'administrative guidance'.
>
> (Ollman, 2003: 196)

> The *samurai* [hereditary military nobility and officer caste and warriors of medieval and early-modern Japan] who made the Meiji Revolution refused to become new feudal rulers. . . , opting instead to make themselves into a capitalist ruling class. But before they could do that they had to create capitalism and a capitalist class of which they could be part. Their success in establishing this new social formation with themselves as the core of its ruling class is undoubtedly one of the greatest feats of social engineering in human history.
>
> (Ollman, 2003: 200)

17 The state has no authority to order production or to control it so it cannot command economic performance; it can only induce investment and employment by offering incentives to capitalists (Offe, 1984).

18 Discussing Trotsky's ideas, Whitehouse (2005) says: 'By claiming a large portion of Russia's surplus product for its own projects, the state "lived at the expense of the privileged classes," including the bourgeoisie.' This process retarded the capitalists' independent class development at the same time that it created hothouse conditions for the growth of capitalist production.

19

> If in this situation the bureaucracy is generally allowed to take the initiative for the entire class, it is only because the other members of this class recognize that those currently working in state ministries have the best overview and clearest focus on the interests of the class as a whole. Their view is not compromised by the interests of a particular corporation or industry (as happens with managers and directors) or by those of a party or faction (as happens with government leaders). Freed from such temporary distractions, the bureaucrats are in the best position to serve the general as well as the long-term interests of Japanese capitalism and to mediate between rival factions of the ruling class whenever that is necessary.
>
> (Ollman, 2003: 199)

9 The state and the agency of the working class

Karl Marx (1887: 316) asks in *Capital volume 1*: 'What could possibly show better the character of the capitalist mode of production, than the necessity that exists for forcing upon it, by Acts of Parliament', the simplest of measures in the interest of workers such as the 'appliances for maintaining cleanliness and health'? Marx gives many reasons for these measures.

One is that capital needs men and women with the suitable physical and mental abilities to work and to produce surplus value, so the state steps in to ensure this. If this is the case, then why is it that so many people live with their very basic needs, including for food and healthcare, remaining unmet? To what extent can the state actually meet people's needs? Is capital's need a sufficient reason for state's pro-worker measures when these occur? What role does the working class play? In this chapter, the focus is on how the state functions to 'help' the working class in part as a response to the working-class politics.

Partly by building on the arguments about the state's role concerning commodity and property relations in Chapters 4–5, I discuss, in Section 1, the state's pro-worker interventions and the labour circuit. In Section 2, I turn to the driving forces behind the state's pro-worker measures. I argue that there is an objective pressure on the state (e.g. general and long-term interests of capital) to intervene on behalf of workers and that this pressure is mediated by working-class struggle. In Section 3, I discuss the limits to what the state can do for workers under capitalism, the limits that exist because of the capitalist control over property and production, nature of capitalist accumulation and its crisis-proneness, and the capitalist state's bureaucratic functioning and its anti-worker politics. In Section 4, I offer general theoretical reflections on the ways in which the state is connected to working-class interests and struggle. Section 5 discusses the practical implications of the ideas discussed in the chapter.

1 State's pro-worker interventions and the labour circuit (C-M-C'-R-C)

As suggested in Chapter 4, the state connects to each phase of what I have called the labour circuit (C-M-C'-R-C). The state is, to some extent, involved in the determination of the value of the commodity labour power (C). It

DOI: 10.4324/9781351168007-9

influences whether, how and to what extent labour power can be sold through its policies concerning, for example, the rate of employment and the freedom of labour in the labour market. It is involved in the determination of the monetary value of labour power, or wage (M), via the minimum wage policy, and it also supplements the private wage with a social wage. The state influences how much food and other things (C′) people can buy with the money wage that they receive, because the state has an impact on inflation through its monetary policy. It also has an impact on the sphere of reproduction (R) through its policies concerning, say childcare or family relations, which contribute to the (re)production of the commodity labour power (C). The concept of the labour circuit can now be expanded in order to shed light on state's pro-worker interventions, particularly, in the labour-market and the workplace. I will also briefly discuss state's policies in favour of small-scale producers.

The state fixes '[r]easonable wages' and 'the limits of the working-day' (Marx, 1887: 182) apart from various other measures. The minimum wage legislation, if properly implemented, can benefit workers who receive very low wages.[1] If the mandated minimum wage is significantly above the market rate in many sectors, the minimum wage legislation could have a positive impact on the determination of the value of labour power as it puts a floor on the wage level and indeed on the actual wages paid. A lower minimum wage would have the opposite effect.

In part because workers do not receive the cost of production of labour power from private employers, millions are in poverty who receive some state assistance (e.g. subsidized food), which really amounts to subsidizing capitalist companies who fail to ensure the reproduction of their workforce. The state constructs the poverty line to target welfare provision to the population below the poverty line. The poverty line represents state's perception of what people absolutely need to live, a perception that is determined by capitalists' interests. The state's poverty line, like the state-defined minimum wage, will have an impact on the value of labour power and on its monetary expression. A higher poverty line, if implemented, will put pressure on the buyers of labour power to pay higher wages. This will reduce the extent of the violation of the principle of 'exchange equivalent for equivalent' (Marx, 1887: 123).

During the infancy of capitalism, the state makes workers work long hours or supports capitalists making workers work long hours. As capitalism progresses, the state limits the working day (especially when technical change allows employers to extra more labour every hour): 'The legal limitation of the working-day puts an end to such mischief' (Marx, 1887: 385).[2] Indeed, Factory Acts came into force both in advanced countries and in the periphery.[3]

There has been a need for the state to make unfree labour illegal, including by acting against regulations characteristic of pre-capitalist societies. State intervention has included laws against bonded labour, and laws that restrict child labour, and prohibits child labour below certain age.[4] The fact that millions of people, including children, work as forced labour means that the state has not succeeded, thanks to the power of the capitalist buyers of the labour power.

The state may 'make elementary education a compulsory condition to the "productive" employment of children' (Marx, 1887: 274) under a certain age.[5] The state sometimes provides small loans or subsidized necessaries to workers and small-scale producers, but this intervention is inadequate. The state has policies against adulterated food.[6] Through its land reforms programme, the state may also weaken the power of rent-receiving landlords because of whom the ground rent exists which in turn directly or indirectly affects the economic conditions (e.g. cost of food) of the workers and small-scale producers. In addition, the state in some countries has 'tried to' guarantee that the produce of farmers will be bought at a minimum support price by the government, thus protecting them against the uncertainties in the market demand and market price.

The state seeks to feed the reserve army in situ, including the technologically induced floating population,[7] sometimes by helping people set up microenterprises, thus ensuring that the unemployed stay where they are just in case they are needed by the big business. It also invests in public works to create some employment and provides tax breaks to companies to attract them to create jobs in poverty-stricken areas (e.g. opportunity zones policy in the US discussed earlier).

All in all, some of the state's interventions aim to 'protect the workers' and can be '*against* the interests of the employers'. There is no doubt that the workers, especially in advanced countries, have enjoyed some benefits from these policies. These legislations tend to weaken some of the worse abuses (or excesses).[8] In the sectors and areas/countries that are not regulated, works suffer more, and this suggests that state regulation has made some difference. The working class of the world as a whole is more educated and healthier, and it lives longer now than it did 300 years ago. Of course, there is enormous geographical variation across jurisdictions of nation-states and between socially privileged and socially under-privileged groups inside a country (e.g. African-Americans in the US, ex-untouchables in India, indigenous peoples in Canada).

State intervention in favour of non-capitalist groups – the working-class people (both the employed and under/un-employed) and small-scale producers – can be of different types. One can think about state policies along two dimensions: (a) whether the intervention is primarily at the level of circulation (market-based) or production and (b) whether the intervention is commodified or de-commodified (Wright, 1985: 298). Taking these two dimensions together, we can produce the following four-fold typology of state interventions (as shown in Table 9.1) (ibid.).

To illustrate the differences between these types, state interventions to deal with the problem of malnutrition or food insecurity could be used as an example (Wright, 1985: 299). Food stamps would be a commodified-circulation intervention (CC): the state simply redistributes a targeted income to certain groups to be spent in the open market for the acquisition of food. Free distribution of surplus food to the poor would be a de-commodified-circulation

Table 9.1 Typology of state intervention in favour of the working class

	Circulation-based	Production-based
Commodified	CC	CP
De-commodified	DC	DP

Source: Based on Wright (1985)
Note: CC: commodified circulation; CP: commodified production; DC: de-commodified circulation; DP: de-commodified production.

intervention (DC). Government subsidies to farmers to encourage them to produce certain food products for poor people which otherwise might not be profitable to produce would be a commodified production intervention (CP). The minimum support price policy falls in this category too. State-run farms to produce food for the poor would be a de-commodified production intervention (DP).

2 Driving forces behind state action in favour of workers (and small-scale producers)

The question is this: why does the state, the state of capitalists (and large-scale landowners), intervene on behalf of the masses? The answer must be from multiple vantage points, including working-class revolt and the capitalist class society (general, long-term) interests of the capitalist as a whole and various capitalist groups. Also, in thinking about the state, a distinction has to be made between pretext for state action and its cause. A state action in the interest of workers and small-scale producers tends to find its immediate pretext (not its cause) in such things as a society-wide health crisis (e.g. pandemic) that decimates the people making it difficult for capitalists to have access to enough workers at reasonable wages.[9]

Class struggle

Given the immanent potential for class conflict within the exploitative capitalist system, the capitalist state granting material concessions is an attempt to produce common people's consent to the system and to subdue the intensity of actual class struggle as well as pre-empt future class struggle. State interventions in relation to working conditions – for example, Parliamentary Acts – are partly a result of class struggle between the two main classes and not 'the products of Parliamentary fancy' (Marx, 1887: 187). 'Their formulation, official recognition, and proclamation by the State, were the result of a long struggle of classes' (ibid.).

Clearly, '[t]he history of this struggle shows two opposed tendencies' (Marx, 1887: 181). This is in the sense that, for example, during the earliest stage in capitalism's history, and with respect to the working-day, the statutes of the state 'tried to lengthen it by compulsion', '[w]hilst the modern Factory Acts compulsorily shortened the working-day' (ibid.). Indeed, 'in its adult condition', with workers' organization getting stronger, they have received 'the concessions that, growling and struggling, it [i.e. capital] has to make' (ibid.; italics added). Indeed, *acting in its own collective interest*, the working class has demanded such things as the reduction in the working day: 'The establishment of a normal working-day is the result of centuries of struggle between capitalist and labourer' (ibid.: 181).[10] Of course, while class struggle contributes to the introduction of pro-worker measures at sub-national and national scales, the nature and the impacts of the legislations can vary geographically. There were important differences between the measures taken by the French state and those by the English state, for example.[11]

The laws of commodity exchange impose no limit to how much capitalists exploit workers, and because of the same laws, the state can do little except under 'compulsion from society' (Marx, 1887: 181). This compulsion is in the form of labour struggle: '[I]n the history of capitalist production, the determination of what is a working day, presents itself as the result of a struggle, a struggle between collective capital, i.e., the class of capitalists, and collective labour, i.e., the working-class' (Marx, 1887: 164).

In fact, both wages and the working day are a function of the relative balance of power. Marx (1865) writes in *Value, price and profit* that the upper limit to profit is 'limited by the physical minimum of wages and the physical maximum of the working day' and that, therefore, how much profit capitalists make 'is only settled by the continuous struggle between capital and labour, the capitalist constantly tending to reduce wages to their physical minimum, and to extend the working day to its physical maximum, while the working man constantly presses in the opposite direction. 'The matter resolves itself into a question of the respective powers of the combatants,' Marx says.

It is not just that the state grants concessions (e.g. shorter working days) because of the workers' struggle. In fact, because of the political pressure from below, the state grants to the workers their unionization right itself, and unionization in turn puts pressure on the state (and capital): 'only against its will and under the pressure of the masses' did the British state (in the form of the parliament) 'give up the laws against Strikes and Trades' Unions, after it had itself, for 500 years, held, with shameless egoism, the position of a permanent Trades' Union of the capitalists against the labourers' (Marx, 1887: 525). The struggle to establish unions, and especially the unions that are independent of the enterprise management, continues as the recent history of India's Maruti workers struggle shows (White, J., 2017).

While concessions are promised and granted by the state due to reform-oriented struggles, the connection between the two – concessions and struggles – is stronger, however, if/when there is a threat to capitalist property interests (a threat to public order) from people's struggles.[12] In the US context, historically, according to Piven and Cloward (1974: 147):

> relief arrangements are initiated or expanded during the occasional out-breaks of civil disorder produced by mass unemployment, and are then abolished or contracted when political stability is restored. . . . [E]expan-sive relief policies are designed to mute civil disorder, and restrictive ones to reinforce work norms. In other words, relief policies are cyclical-liberal or restrictive depending on the problems of regulation in the larger society with which government must contend.

While the capitalists and the state do not grant anything without a struggle by the masses, it is also the case that capitalism creates conditions for class struggle. It does this by promoting transportation and communication technologies and removing geographical barriers to working-class unity through the spatial con-centration of workers in specific localities and cities, all in its own economic interest (easy access to a labour pool). Capitalism – 'the direct and open sway of capital' – also removes non- or pre-capitalist social relations 'behind which the dominion of capital is still in part concealed'. With the 'destruction of petty and domestic industries', gone is 'the sole remaining safety-valve of the whole social mechanism', and this in turn 'generalises the direct opposition' of the masses to capital (Marx, 1887: 329). In fact, as non-capitalist ways of repro-duction (e.g. family-based production, access to common property resources) vanish, workers increasingly depend on the state to meet the gap between what they need and what they receive from employers. And since the state work-ing on behalf of capital will not give anything automatically, that is, without a struggle, people fight for concessions.

Capital's interests (coinciding with workers' interests)

There is more to the story of pro-worker measures than just working-class struggle forcing the state to intervene on behalf of labour. Behind the pro-worker legislations, there are often long-term capitalist interests: 'Apart from the working-class movement that daily grew more threatening, the limiting of factory labour [by the state] was dictated by the same necessity which spread guano over the English fields.' In other words, '[t]he same blind eagerness for plunder that in the one case exhausted the soil, had, in the other, torn up by the roots the living force of the nation' (Marx, 1887: 166).

Capital engages in the normal process of exploitation when workers sur-render to capital a large part of the net product. And then there is exces-sive (= above-normal) exploitation, causing the degeneration of the working population. The excesses (abuses) inflicted on workers are a product of the mutually competing capitalists when they lower the wages below the aver-age cost of maintenance of workers, make workers work excessively long hours of work, cut down on spending for workplace safety (e.g. protective equipment during a pandemic, enough working space per worker, safety of chemicals), and so on. 'Free competition brings out the inherent laws of capitalist production, in the shape of external coercive laws having power over every individual capitalist' (Marx, 1887: 181). These external laws of capitalist production meet with the extra-economic laws: 'Capital is reckless of the health or length of life of the labourer, *unless under compulsion from society*' (ibid.; italics added). This compulsion from society is represented by pro-worker state interventions against capital's recklessness of workers' health and well-being and against the violation of equal exchange in the labour market (p. 181). In general, the measures regulating the working conditions develop 'gradually out of circumstances as natural laws of the modern mode of production'(Marx, 1887: 187) in the sense that excesses of capitalism (e.g. long working day, low wages) would result in a crippled reproduction of the only source of surplus value (i.e. labour).

Thus, short working day is not entirely due to class struggle from below: long-term interests are important explanations, especially when 'the living force of the nation' (Marx, 1887: 166) is endangered including during a society-wide economic crisis and/or ecological crisis (pandemic). It is important to note that

> the mere fear of contagious diseases which do not spare even 'respectability' [that is, the bourgeoisie and well-off strata close to it] brought into existence from 1847 to 1864 no less than 10 Acts of Parliament on sanitation, and that the frightened bourgeois in some towns . . . took strenuous measures through their municipalities.
>
> (ibid.: 458)

Individual capitalists are cogs in the wheel of competition. Their short-term interests – capitalists 'recklessness' – directly destroy workers' health (and they cause the destruction of the environment which in turn affects workers' bodies/health). This fact undermines long-term interests of capitalists, thus prompting the state to intervene. The regulation of the working day is in the interest of capital and not just labour: if due to overwork and adverse working lives (and environmental pollution), people die faster, then they have to be replaced quicker (the value of labour power will thus go up), and this has a cost for the user of this labouring body, that is, the capitalist class.[13] The fact that 'the forces used up have to be replaced at a more rapid rate and the sum of the expenses for the reproduction of labour-power will be greater' implies that 'the interest of capital itself points in the direction of a normal working-day' (Marx, 1887: 179). If in place of 'the unnatural extension of the working-day', and the like that Marx talks about, we put environmental damage, the logic mentioned earlier will still hold. Capitalist production leads to unfavourable effects which need state regulation:

> Factory legislation, that first conscious and methodical reaction of society against the spontaneously developed form of the process of production,

is . . . just as much the necessary product of modern industry as cotton yam, self-actors, and the electric telegraph.

(Marx, 1887: 315)

In other words, the state is prompted by capitalists' long-term interests to implement certain policies in favour of workers and the environment, curbing capital's passion for profit. These policies are *ultimately* in favour of the capitalist class as a whole, more or less; or they are implemented in such a way that the capitalist class as a whole or some dominant sections of the class benefit from them.[14] So the *general* interest of the capitalist class is crucial to the understanding of pro-worker state policies. The adverse conditions under which workers work and live and which cause illnesses and the crisis of bodily reproduction mean that capitalists can find it difficult to obtain enough people at a wage rate at which enough surplus value can be made (p. 181). The regulation of capitalist production is a political act on the part of capitalist society against spontaneous economic laws and shapes those economic processes.

Similarly, to the extent that the state also allows, however reluctantly, a degree of trade union activity, one reason is the pressure of the masses, as mentioned before. Another reason, once again, is the self-interest of capital: trade union activity 'has expansionary effects on the market and therefore on the profitability of business' (Cox, 2002: 249). Besides, a slightly reconciliatory section of the bourgeoisie may use trade unions to subordinate the working class (and small-scale producers), through its collaboration with the trade union leaders, to their party and thus to the state. Indeed, it may promote unions to garner votes and thus political legitimacy for pro-capitalist actions. The current Biden-led government in the US is an example.

The state looks after non-capitalist classes when their interests do not go against, or when they match with, the interests of the capitalist class or its dominant fraction. State policies aimed at providing education and healthcare as well as higher minimum wages can, apart from buying peace, create a market for the capitalist class and thus respond to temporary realization problem within specific sectors and areas. Likewise, the state assistance to farmers would also create rural purchasing power to the benefit of the capitalist class.[15] The long-term interests in industrial peace and in the market clearance could partly explain why sometimes sections of the capitalist class ('patriotic billionaires') might actually advocate, or tolerate, 'pro-worker' reforms (including higher taxes on them and use of the taxes for workers' welfare).

The ruling class as a whole has certain long-term economic and political interests. Then elements within the ruling class have certain specific interests, and these can be mutually conflicting. Conflicts within the ruling class can help the lower-class struggle in certain cases.[16] If a section of the capitalist class needs the support of workers in its battle with, say, landowners, capitalists may support pro-worker legislations.[17] Also, inter-capitalist competition contributes to the universalization of the application of government regulations. 'The first birthright of capital is equal exploitation of labour-power by all capitalists' (Marx, 1887: 320). In addition, there is 'the cry of the [bigger] capitalists for equality in the conditions of competition, i.e., for equal restrain on all exploitation of labour' (ibid.).[18] Whenever a law (e.g. a law that limits the labour of children to 6 hours) is applicable to certain enterprises and not to other enterprises, manufacturers in the first category complain against this 'discrimination'.[19] Implied here is a general point about capitalism: 'since capital is by nature a leveller, since it exacts in every sphere of production equality in the conditions of the exploitation of labour, the limitation by law of' such things as 'children's labour, in one branch of industry, becomes the cause of its limitation in others' (Marx, 1887: 273).

It is the case that 'there are major differences and disputes' among the different branches of the state and within each one of them. These differences, more or less, reflect the different capitalist interests as well as different perceptions by state actors of what needs to be done to maintain conditions for capitalist accumulation and for industrial peace. And, 'subaltern classes can occasionally use this disarray to score minor victories in some of the state's more distant outposts' (Ollman, 2003: 203).

Apart from capital's common and mutually conflicting interests, there is also state's 'own' interest behind its pro-worker interventions. If common people live and work under adverse conditions, and if their physical fitness suffers, this is not good for the state from the standpoint of, for example, war-making (the latter, of course, is ultimately in the interest of the capitalist class as well). The capitalist state needs plenty of able-bodied people for the battlefield just as capitalist employers need them for the workplace.[20] Pro-poor attitude of some state actors might also contribute to the people getting some concessions, within limits. Of course, it is a moot point whether the concessions are funded by taxes from the people (workers and small-scale producers) or from the surplus appropriated by capitalists (and large-scale landowners).

3 Limits to state's pro-worker interventions, and why?

What has been said in the last two sections should be seen in terms of a tendency: under certain conditions, the state tends to grant some concessions, but whether in fact it will and, if it will, how adequate are the concessions, are a contingent matter. In fact, what is promised in the form of pro-worker interventions is usually much bigger than what is delivered.[21] There is a limit to the extent to which the state can limit the adverse impacts of capitalism on people. Pro-worker policies are in place, but they are often not fully implemented.[22]

That the state provides only limited benefits can be seen by looking at the social wage. The social wage, or overall net subsidy, is usually positive (but a very small positive amount) in some of the rich countries (Australia, Canada, Germany, Sweden, and United Kingdom),[23] while it is generally negative (that is, a net tax) in the US even during the boom years, and 'this meant that wage and salary earner paid out more in taxes than they received – they helped reduce any existing fiscal deficit'. In contrast, 'Over the same interval in Sweden, the net social wage was roughly zero, indicating that its generous social welfare expenditures were actually self-financed' (p. 538).[24] A more recent research reached a similar conclusion:

> [I]n almost all advanced capitalist countries, the great bulk of [their] social spending (and especially the part which constitutes labor benefits or the gross social wage) necessarily comes from gross labor income, that is, from personal income taxes, social security contributions, and other personal and property taxes that are levied on labor. To the extent that indirect business taxes or consumption taxes are assumed to be levied on labor, they finance and usually exceed the remaining part of the gross social wage even in the advanced capitalist countries with more developed welfare states than the United States. Therefore, if we assume that indirect taxes are partly paid by labor, the net social wage is significantly negative in the United States (-6.0 percent to -7.5 percent of GDP over the entire postwar period) and from modestly negative to close to zero in other countries.
>
> (Maniatis, 2014: 33)

The working class indeed receives only limited benefits from the state, relative to the assistance that the capitalist class does. It is interesting that the share of labour in national income has been decreasing: it has declined in advanced countries, from about 55% in 1970 to about 40% in 2015, and in emerging market and developing economies, from about 50% in mid-1990s to below 40% in 2015 (Roberts, 2017).

Even if the regulation of capitalist excesses inflicted on workers (very low wages, very long hours of work) is in the interest of long-term interests of capitalists, the latter do not still accept this 'except "under the pressure of a General Act of Parliament"' (Marx, 1887: 315). When capitalists reluctantly give in, granting such things as 'the compulsory regulation of the hours of labour', they do not give in much (ibid.). Pro-worker interventions are only a 'meagre concession wrung from capital' (Marx, 1887: 319), and in the case of England's Factory Act, it was 'limited to combining elementary education with work in the factory' (ibid.). Note that this was the case when capitalism was in a progressive phase relative to its current terminal decline stage. The state indeed continues to fail to implement its own legislation. For example, it fails to enforce the freedom of labourers as sellers of labour power: millions of unfree labourers, including children, work in slave-like conditions. The minimum wage policy is not enforced either, and where it is, usually, the government-legislated minimum wage is lower than a wage floor set within collective agreements (Boeri, 2012).[25]

All in all, to the extent that the state functions in support of long-term interests of capital, such intervention is more likely when (a) people fight against the effect of exploitation and (b) there are conflicts among the ruling-class elements which means that (c) interests of the working class coincide with interests of *some* elements of the capitalist class. State's, or state actors', own interests and ideas also play a role. Yet the state fails to meet the needs of the working men and women in a significant and durable manner.

Capitalist agency

While pro-worker interventions are due to long-term interests of capital and class struggle, the nature and scope of these interventions are also affected by capitalist class response to these interventions. The capitalist class aims to dilute and/or negate the actual impact of pro-workers policies after they are in put in place. They do this in many ways.

In order to preserve their own competitive advantage, some enterprise owners complain that if a given legislation does not apply to *all* enterprises, it will advantage those that are not covered by it.[26] Capitalists also fight welfare legislation on the ground that *it is against workers*, so they mobilize especially the right-wing politicians to make their case.

> The right-wing argument is that unemployment arises when laborers put too high a reserve price on their labour [power]. Labourers create unemployment by refusing to work below a certain minimum wage! This typically happens when welfare is too generous! Ergo, the best way to get rid of unemployment is to reduce welfare to zero.[27]
>
> (Harvey, 2010a: 281)

When a legislation is imposed on capitalists, they fight this, including through courts and political parties, on the ground that it is an 'interference with the exploiting rights of capital' (Marx, 1887: 319). Individual capitalists treat their private property rights as sacrosanct and beyond challenge, so mild actions against them are used to produce hyperbolic catastrophizing notion of the spectre of revolution: 'They [capitalists] denounced the Factory Inspectors as a kind of revolutionary commissioners' (Marx, 1887: 188).[28] The capitalist tradition of perceiving, and making common people perceive, some slightly reform-mindedly liberals (e.g. Nehru, Obama, Biden) as socialists and even as sympathizers of Marxism continues. This is the same tradition of socialist/Left fear-mongering that treats the Democratic party of the US as being on the Left. Considering what are blatantly bourgeois views and actions as Marxist, socialist and leftists, which are then presented as a threat to everything a nation stands for, is a great way of pre-empting/avoiding any pro-worker measure.

When laws regulating the capitalists do exist, capitalists can get around these laws or make it difficult for the state to enforce them, given their control over the process of production and exchange. After all, the workplace is the site of capitalists' private legislation. This is the site of capitalists' despotic control which is needed partly to counter potential and actual workers' resistance inside the workplace. Consider how capitalists respond to the legislation restricting the length of the working day, the use of child labour, and so on. Capitalists resort to multiple mechanisms to get around the pro-worker laws.

Firstly, capitalists make changes in the labour process. For example, they increase the speed of work, leading to increased injury to workers. Capital, more or less, goes unpunished by the state.[29] They introduce a relay system: individual (child) workers come to work at different points in time in a 24-hour-day, and this makes it difficult for state officials (inspectors) to monitor whether any worker is working longer than the law allows.[30]

Secondly, a specific form of change in the labour process is resorting to a technological fix (mechanization), which has two adverse effects on workers. One is that it is a weapon against workers' struggle: machinery replaces workers weakening their bargaining power. In addition, by enabling 'the excessive addition of women and children to the ranks of the workers, machinery . . . breaks down the resistance which the male operatives in the manufacturing period continued to oppose to the despotism of capital' (Marx, 1887: 276). Besides, capital uses more efficient machines to squeeze out as much labour during the reduced working day as during the longer one.

Thirdly, capitalists resort to spatial fix or threaten to do so. If laws to restrict capitalists' freedom to exploit are in place in one country, capitalists threaten to move their capital elsewhere in order to 'intimidate' the state and the workers.

Fourthly, capitalists resort to what can be called a temporal fix. The application of the laws that restrict capitalists' freedom to exploit is staggered. For example, if the state seeks to raise the minimum wages, the process of increase happens over a long period of time. In the US, the Raise the Wage Act proposed to raise the federal minimum wage to $15 per hour from the current $7.25 in stages: 2021: $9.50; 2022: $11; 2023: 12.50; 2024: 14; 2025: $15.[31] Similarly, laws to prevent capitalists from hiring young children (e.g. education clauses of English Factory Acts) are often staggered: these laws can allow capitalists to continue to hire younger children for a number of years, which means that the maximum age at which a child can be hired is not legally enforceable until after many years since the initial introduction of the laws.[32] In other words, if adults' working day is restricted, children are used.

Consider laws aiming to restrict the working day. If there are n number of workers and an average worker works for h hour, then there is $(n * h)$ hour of work from which surplus value will be extracted. But if, thanks to the laws that shorten the working day, the average worker works for $h - x$ hour (where $x > 0$), then the total amount of work possible is $n(h - x)$– where $n(h - x) < (n * h)$. This means that capital has access to less amount of total labour time of society. So n (number of available workers) has to be increased. One way of doing this is to use those sections of the working class which have not been hitherto used: children and women (and peasants and semi-proletarians as a part of the latent surplus population).

The state form and functioning

The nature of the functioning of the state itself limits the effectivity of pro-worker policies. Given that pro-worker policies will adversely affect capitalists, various processes (loopholes) are put in place to restrict the positive impact of good policies on workers. Political representatives of capital within the state who, more or less, work on behalf of capital and who share ideas that reflect capitalist interests make every effort, along with capitalists, to dilute the pro-worker laws and/or block their proper implementation. Every law is designed in such a way that it has many exceptions, which weaken the law.[33] Pro-worker laws can also be mutually contradictory thanks to the fact that they partly reflect the contradictor interests of capital and labour. For example, one law shortens the working day, and another law makes available more children for exploitation by lowering the minimum wage a child can work.

The wording of the laws itself is produced in such a way that it makes it easy for the capitalists to evade them; in addition, the scope of the laws remains limited.[34] If the state makes 'elementary education a compulsory condition to the "productive" employment of children' (Marx, 1887: 274) under a certain age, capitalists put pressure for the laws to be relaxed in order to increase the supply of labour. If the state defines, for example, the age at which a child can work for a given number of hours, then capitalists fight to reduce that age (for them, children must work for a wage at, say, 8 and not 9) and for longer hours than shorter hours.[35]

The state can introduce a legislation without making available adequate resources to implement it, while it has the money for the propertied class.[36] If a law exists restricting the number of hours that children can work and mandating that they must receive education but if there is no mechanism to implement this law, then the law has little material effect.[37] Without an adequate administrative machinery which costs money, and capitalists want a 'cheap state', laws are only dead letters.[38] A large number of government departments, especially those that look after welfare and environmental issues, remain typically understaffed. To the extent that an administrative machinery is created, several mechanisms can impede the implementation of pro-worker laws. For one, while statistical information is so important for state interventions, there are officials responsible for collecting social statistics, but they might not be given 'plenary powers to get at the truth' (Marx, 1887: 7). Sometimes, statistical data carefully collected by state workers are withheld if they reveal governmental failure.[39] There might not be enough people who are 'as competent' and who are 'free from partisanship' (ibid.).[40] Indeed, state officials, influenced by capitalist thinking, may not always perform their duties.[41]

Under neoliberal capitalism, this partisanship has reached a high level. The top layers of the state bureaucracy openly advocate for pro-business policies. In the neoliberal capitalist state, the personnel 'are closely aligned to the views of the Bretton Woods institutions' and are '*deeply enmeshed with the world of finance and big business*' (Patnaik, 2010). Their 'motivation is no different from that of the big bourgeoisie and financial interests' and they have 'no compunctions about being closely integrated with the latter' (ibid.).

The non-implementation of pro-worker laws is because of a distinct feature of state form: those who formulate laws are not responsible for their execution, and the common people are not involved in the ways the state works; in other words, the state works bureaucratically. And the state has to be bureaucratic: if every person participates in the everyday functioning of the state, there will be no state.

Capitalists can even bribe state officials and politicians to ignore the violation of state regulations on their (capitalists') part, including those concerning workplace safety. The bribe is after all a small proportion of their saving that accrues due to compromise on workers' safety. Capitalists simply may not submit to a law.[42] Capitalists can and do knowingly violate safety and other regulations, fully confident that any penalty the state might impose (after long legal battles that most workers as workers or as consumers can ill-afford) is a small deduction from the extra money they have made.

While there are strong limits to state spending for workers, a similar limit with respect to the financial assistance (including tax breaks) to capitalists does not usually exist. They receive a massive amount of state revenue, both during an economic crisis (so-called bailout package) and when certain segments of capital are judged to be too big to fail. There is little limit put on state spending on coercion (military and policing) needed to threaten workers and crush their resistance domestically as well as to counter any resistance to 'its' interests in foreign countries (and this shows that a mere increase in taxes on the super-rich and consequent increase in state *revenue* will not necessarily benefit the masses as they have little control over the state's *spending*). The so-called democratic form of the state is no barrier at all to how the state works for the capitalists. If capitalists cannot make money, the state's help arrives. However, if the masses do not have enough food and shelter or money to pay school fees, a similar approach does not exist.

Anti-working-class intervention by the state and lack of proletarian power

The introduction of a pro-labour measure and its actual implementation, generally speaking, depend on the intensity of class struggle of the masses. They depend on, within limits, the balance of power between capital and labour in society and within the state.

Unionization (greater union density) used to have some positive impact on social expenditure by the government (see Hooghe and Oser, 2016). Once a pro-worker measure is introduced, unions and workplace committees can have a positive impact on their actual implementation too. No wonder unions have been under attack by the capitalist class and their state, in forms that are direct or indirect. These include police attacks on unions, firing union leaders and some of the unionized workers, restrictions on trade union rights, influencing and corrupting union leaders, contractualization, making it easy for capital to hire and fire, and the threat of geographical relocation. In addition, the state (along with capitalist employers) promote and make use of divisions within the working class (on the basis of race, gender, location, nationality, and so on) – the divisions which are also promoted by the relatively educated and well-off sections of the wage-earning class trying to better their own situation on the basis of their special status defined by race, gender, and the like. These divisions – often mistakenly seen as the primary cleavages that are more fundamental than class divisions – weaken class consciousness and organization. In many cases, well-paid union leaders, capitalists, and state apparatuses form a bloc which fundamentally goes against rank-and-file workers' interest. So the relation between workers' trade union power and pro-worker measures has been weakened.

The sphere of production is a sphere of the political battle between capital and labour. So all the interventions by the state aimed at reducing the bargaining power in the labour market also reduce workers' power on the shop floor. The Taft-Hartley Act passed in 1947 in the US is an example of class struggle from above (Figure 9.1): it restricts organizing capacities of unions and allows state-level 'right to work' legislation. Austerity measures are an example of class struggle from above as well (Cockburn, 2004).

It is incontrovertible that the working class lacks power at the site of production and often in the labour market as well. Such lack of power is expressed in the fact that the capitalist class can pay a wage which does not cover the cost of reproduction of workers. Workers are often compelled to accept whatever wage that is offered by the masters. But the working class also lacks power to control the state, that is, to control the common affairs of society as a whole. Above all, it has no control over the coercive power of the state. Workers are 'slaves of the bourgeois class, and of the bourgeois State' (Marx and Engels, 1848: 18). Besides, given its lack of control over means of production and subsistence, how long can workers go on a strike and live on their limited savings? 'The capitalist can live longer without the worker than can the worker without

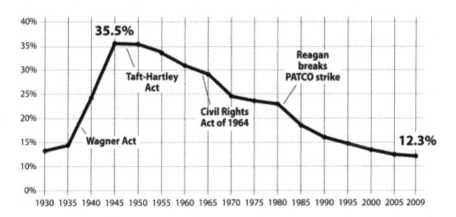

Figure 9.1 The Hartley Act, and class struggle from above

Source: www.faireconomy.org/enews/class_race_the_attacks_on_public_employees

the capitalist' (Marx, 1977a/1844: 21). So, in terms of the ongoing context between capital and labour, ultimately, '[v]ictory goes necessarily to the capitalist' (ibid.). But victory will *not* go to the capitalist if the state, for example, feeds the workers during their strike. But the state will not do this because, in spite of its appearance, the state is *inherently* capitalists' and not workers'.

Capitalist control over economy and crisis-prone accumulation process

As we have seen, the relations of equal exchange impose no limit on how long individual capitalists can make people work in a day: if capitalists have bought the commodity (labour power), they can use it as much as they wish to, according to the law of commodity, which the state itself supports. And even if the state introduces pro-worker measures (e.g. 'legal limitation of the working day') due to the pressure from below, the state, which is a class-state, cannot generally do much about macro-economic features of capitalist society which adversely impact workers. These include 'the diminution of employment caused by the competition of machinery' or indeed 'by changes in the quality of the labourers employed' (Marx, 1887: 385). The *state* cannot do anything about these features because it is *capitalists'* right to use machines or a particular kind of labour (e.g. child labour, immigrant labour, and so on). There is, of course, nothing natural about the state's inability mentioned earlier: for example, when the length of the working day is shortened, forced idleness (= unemployment) could be checked by spreading the working time (across workers from different sectors and areas) throughout the year, but this does not happen. This could happen if the state really was the state of the majority.

The interests of capitalists and those of workers contradict each other. There are fundamental conflicts, rooted in private property and production relations, over wealth and income or value and surplus value. Consider the limit to the rise in wages. There are two scenarios here. In one scenario, and as Marx says in chapter 25 of *Capital volume 1*, if investment ($c + v$) increases, without c / v increasing (much), wages can rise.[43] As soon as living standards increase via an increase in real wages per hour worked, other things constant, the normal rate of profit (or of exploitation) will be affected. This will put a stop to the rise in wages. Instead of $c + v$, and departing from Marx a little bit, we can use state policy in favour of workers and arrive at the same conclusion: the state policy can raise wages but not beyond a point (Figure 9.2). Note also that state policy can contribute to a rise in $c + v$. In another scenario, when $c + v$ increases and c / v also increases, the situation is worse: when c / v rises, with mechanization displacing labour, a relative surplus population is produced which adversely affects the bargaining power of the employed segments of the working class and reduces their wages: 'The constant generation of a relative surplus-population keeps the law of supply and demand of labour, and therefore keeps wages, in a rut that corresponds with the wants of capital' (Marx, 1887: 523).

Of course, and once again, there is nothing absolutely natural here (in the purely economic sense): an increase in $c + v$ combined with an increase in c / v

will not adversely affect the workers, *if* the relative surplus population's needs are fully met by the state on the basis of adequate unemployment insurance and/or if they are employed by the state with decent wages, and so on, but the state does not do this (Figure 9.2). For the state to do that would be to counter the very mechanism by which accumulation happens, wages are determined and the rate of exploitation kept at an acceptable level: in that sense the 'surplus population becomes . . . the lever of capitalistic accumulation, nay, a condition of existence of the capitalist mode of production' (ibid.: 444).

If workers belong to one of the oppressed groups (women, children, low caste, Blacks, and so on), their situation is even worse. In fact, when c + v rises, wages can rise and do rise, but the state policy often increases unemployment (through an appropriate interest rate policy, for example) and reduces workers' bargaining power by suppressing strikes (Figure 9.2). So the accumulation interests of capitalists, supported by the state, limit the extent to which state can benefit the workers.

Similarly, if small-scale producer's marketed surplus is given a remunerative price by the state (cost price plus a revenue that is necessary for a decent living), the cost of production, including of raw materials and wage goods, will go up and will hurt the capitalist profits, so small-scale producers do not receive a good price for their produce.[44] In other words, a large segment of the working population has to live a life of poverty or semi-poverty and economic insecurity so an average rate of profit for capital is guaranteed, and it is the state's responsibility to ensure this if normal market mechanisms fail to.[45] The state cannot be in the business of undermining the 'condition of existence of the capitalist mode of production'.

The financial means for state social welfare measures ultimately originate in the capital accumulation process, regardless of whether these measures are financed by social insurance contributions, taxes, and the like. A portion of total social value is used by the state in order to improve the conditions of the working class. This means that the mass of surplus value is reduced in the hands of capitalists for reinvestment. It is usually the case that the more the state gives to the people, the less there is for the ruling classes (and for top layers within the state itself, who are very close to the ruling classes). A state policy can reduce workers' access to state-provided services in order to, for example, reduce the tax burden on the capitalist class. Every dollar that the state spends on military – in the interest of the military-industrial complex, if not the capitalist class as a whole – could be spent by it on workers' welfare, but it is not.

As we have seen in an earlier chapter, the state is the personification of illusory common interests and supports the two other forms of personification (capital's as well as labour's), which are mutually contradictory. For example, while capital wants people to work longer and pay a lower wage, and labour wants to work shorter hours and get a higher wage. This contradiction is represented within the state. This is partly reflected in the state legislations that seek to help workers a bit but make numerous deliberate concessions to capital in the body of given legislations themselves.

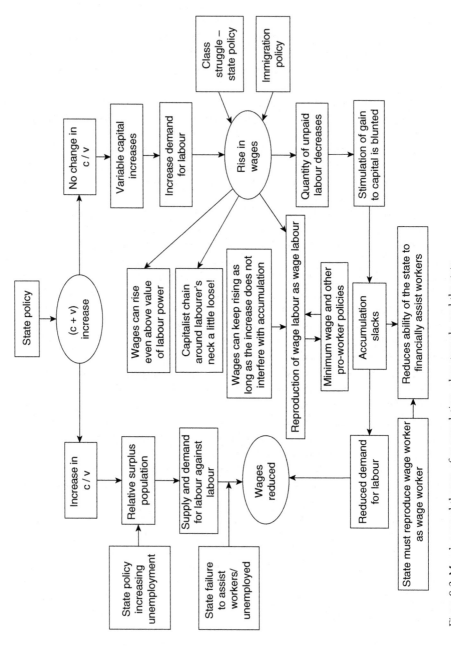

Figure 9.2 Marx's general theory of accumulation, class struggle, and the state

Even if the state somehow makes sure that wages rise, that fact, more or less, means that pro-worker legislations, just like an increase in accumulation with c / v constant, only reproduce workers as 'better-fed slaves' (Figure 9.2): a rise in wages 'only means, in fact, that the length and weight of the golden chain the wage worker has already forged for himself [or herself], allow of a relaxation of the tension of it' (Marx, 1887: 436). This would be the case whether the rise in wages is 'a consequence of accumulation of capital' or of state policy. In other words, 'just as little as better clothing, food, and treatment, and a larger peculium, do away with the exploitation of the slave, so little do they set aside that of the wage worker' (ibid.).

Like an increase in c + v raising wages, pro-worker interventions can only diminish the impact of the golden chain. The welfare measures 'safeguard the existence of workers in a manner consistent with capitalism, namely as wage-labourers' (Heinrich, 2004: 208). Even if wages rise, workers still are not free not to sell their labour power to a capitalist, and they still have little control over what happens in a workplace and over their product.

Given the antagonism between capital's interest and common people's interest, state social welfare measures (e.g. social security, unemployment insurance, old-age pension) are usually contingent not only upon a good pace of accumulation (rise in c + v) but also upon the sale of labour power or the willingness to sell labour power or prior labour-market participation, and, this means that these measures act as a disciplining force (Figure 9.2). The payment of unemployment insurance or welfare is also contingent upon their active effort to sell their labour power, or else benefits will be reduced or suspended. Therefore, '[t]he benefits of the welfare state . . . do not free one from the compulsion to sell one's labour power' (Heinrich, 2004: 208).

Because the state must reproduce workers as workers, this fact sets the limits to what it can do for them (i.e. how much improvement can be granted) (Figure 9.2). Given capitalist class relations which the state must defend, long-term economic *interests* of capital (e.g. the need to earn an average rate of profit) cannot be significantly undermined by the state over a long period of time. The state must maintain enough people separated from means of production and subsistence. They cannot provide things for free to people even if they need them badly and even if things are available in society. Too high a level of wage − which the state *could* ensure by using its coercive or legislative power against private employers − could allow a worker to convert their savings into capital. Too much benefit from the state (social wage) could weaken the commodity status of labour power and increase its bargaining power vis-à-vis capital. The main goal of the state is to reproduce capitalist class relations by suppressing class struggle from below, and therefore state's concessions cannot override this imperative. The ongoing pandemic that began in early 2020 provides evidence for this.[46]

There is an important relation between the state and the (gendered) reproduction of the working-class families. Kollontai (1920) recognizes that '[t]he more the workers became conscious of their rights and the better they were organised, the more society had to relieve the family of the care of the children', and that '[e]ven in capitalist society the education of the child in primary schools and later in secondary and higher educational establishments became the responsibility of the state'. However, she says, 'bourgeois society [is] afraid of going too far towards meeting the interests of the working class, lest this contribute to the break-up of the family'. Why? Kollontai (1920) provides an answer:

> For the capitalists are well aware that the old type of family, where the woman is a slave and where the husband is responsible for the well-being of his wife and children, constitutes the best weapon in the struggle to stifle the desire of the working class for freedom and to weaken the revolutionary spirit of the working man and working woman. The worker is weighed down by his family cares and is obliged to compromise with capital. The father and mother are ready to agree to any terms when their children are hungry.

The aforementioned idea, more or less, applies to families where both parents or primary care-givers are wage workers. In any case, the general conclusion is that '[c]apitalist society has not been able to transform education', and other areas of social reproduction of people such as health, including public health 'into a truly social and state matter because the property owners, the bourgeoisie, have been against this' (ibid.).

While an educated and healthy workforce is in the interest of capitalism and while that need prompts state measures in favour of workers, there is a limit to what is possible within capitalism, this irrational system of social production: '[T]he capitalist mode of production, owing to its very nature, excludes all rational improvement beyond a certain point.' (Marx, 1887: 316). It is impossible to wring from capital what labour needs for a safe and healthy working condition and healthy life, beyond a minimum level. In fact, unhealthy life and unsafe working conditions, just like un- and under-employment and precarity, 'are necessary conditions to the existence of capital' (ibid.).[47] Any significant pro-worker state policy means that '[t]he very root of the capitalist mode of production, i.e., the self-expansion of all capital, large or small, by means of the "free" purchase and consumption of labour-power, would be attacked' so such a policy is 'brought to a deadlock' (ibid.).

So the state is seen as a source of rationality (it is expected to intervene if workers are subjected to excessive abuses), but that rationality is irrational as it will not go beyond the rationality of the minority class; the state must create conditions for profit-making at the expense of the masses. It is true that state welfare measures happen in part because of workers' struggle, but, as mentioned already, the workers that are reproduced through state welfare – just like the workers reproduced through a regime of increased wages due to a rise in $c + v$, with c /− constant – are the workers that ultimately produce surplus value for the capitalists. Even if workers' struggle is allowed and tolerated, the state and capital make sure that 'the struggle between capital and labour [is confined] within limits comfortable for capital' (Marx, 1887: 525).

> Labour legislation is enacted as much in the immediate interest of the capitalist class as in the interest of society in general. But this harmony endures only up to a certain point of capitalist development. When capitalist development has reached a certain level, the interests of the bourgeoisie, as a class, and the needs of economic progress [i.e. workers' interests] begin to clash even in the capitalist sense.
>
> (Luxemburg, 2008/1938: 61)

Capitalist accumulation always happens in a specific geographical context – within a city and a nation. So there is a constant flow of capital across cities, provinces, and nations. To obtain some concessions, trade unions have had to often support – or they have to make sure they do not significantly undermine the conditions for – national- and regional-level capitalist accumulation. The fact that capitalist investment can move across state's territorial jurisdictions at national and sub-national scales and that state institutions at these scales are (increasingly) competing with one another for capital imposes a limit on workers' receiving significant concessions in particular places/countries.[48]

During normal times, the imperative of capitalist accumulation sets a limit on what the state can do for workers. When we consider the geographical mobility as an aspect of accumulation, we see that it also imposes some 'constraint', at a concrete level, on what the state can do for workers. The other aspect of the limit to what the state can do for the people is the crisis-proneness of capitalist accumulation. Capitalism is characterized by the tendency of the rate of profit to fall (TRPF), leading to reduced investment and employment. This mechanism puts a stop to the rise in wages and contributes to absolute and/or relative immiserization. Increasing the rate of exploitation, including by depressing wages below the value of labour, is a major way to counter the TRPF, and the state aids capital here. Indeed, some of the state interventions to counter the falling rate of profit aim to (help capital) increase labour exploitation. Some of the state interventions seek to bailout companies in crisis, and these are ultimately paid for by the working class and small-scale producers, in the form of austerity and the like. The fact that the state cannot fundamentally rescue capitalism *from its* crisis-proneness affects workers adversely: the state indeed has little control over 'crises partial or general' which cause unemployment' (Marx, 1887: 385). Or, more generally, the state qua capitalist state has little real and long-term control over the average rate of profit to fall and therefore over the extent to which it can help the workers.

4 Bringing it all together: broader theoretical reflections on the state and forms of working-class struggle

As we have seen, through its legislations and policies, the state seeks to force the capitalist class to reduce the length of the working day; it has tried to put a floor below which wages are not to fall. It contributes to the reproduction of segments of the reserve army through unemployment insurance and similar measures. There have been legislations concerning health and safety at work. The working class has also received benefits in the form of subsidized health and education. The state allows, or helps, people to freely sell their labour power and small-scale producers to freely sell products of their labour. The state can positively affect the value of labour power itself.[49] The state may also weaken the power of rent-receiving landlords because of whom the ground rent exists and directly or indirectly affects workers and small-scale producers. Certain general theoretical conclusions can now be made from these facts about the relation between the state and class struggle in the light of the foregoing discussion in Sections 1–3.

Long-term capitalist interests coinciding with workers' everyday interests

The long-term interests of the capitalist class (or of its hegemonic fraction) (and of the capitalist state) may coincide with those of workers, and this partly drives state functions in favour of the working class. Recklessly pursuing wealth in its abstract form, the capitalist class or individual capitalists can destroy the dual sources of all wealth (labour and nature), subjecting both to a dual metabolic rift, extracting far more out of them than what it gives them. In the long-term interest of capital, the state, as the idea collective capitalist, intervenes.

> The present state . . . assumes functions favouring social developments specifically because, and in the measure that, these interests and social developments coincide, in a general fashion, with the interests of the dominant class.
>
> (Luxemburg, 2008/1938: 61)

The state has to make sure that capital has access to the worker it needs, the worker which is the sole source of surplus value (which is supplemented by the labour product of small-scale producers). Capitalists need workers (and other elements of the workforce such as small-scale producers) in two forms. Objectively, capitalists need workers with healthy bodies and with certain mental and physical abilities that are productive of capitalist wealth, the workers who, because of their property-lessness that is (coercively) protected by the state, are 'forced to' voluntarily work for a wage under the despotic control of the capitalist and/or hired agent. Culturally/subjectively, capitalists need men and women who accept capitalist rules of the game as more or less natural. Capitalism requires 'a working class, which by education, tradition, habit, looks upon the conditions of that mode of production as self-evident laws of Nature' (Marx, 1887: 523). Here the state plays an active role, although Marx neglects to say this: the state contributes towards the development of a working class, which accepts capitalism as natural, through its cultural apparatuses that disseminate the ideas of the capitalist class as ruling ideas (e.g. educational system, propaganda system, and so on).

Objective class interests, the two forms of class struggle, and state action

Objective conditions and objective interests (capital's need for a suitable work-force, removal of feudal or semi-feudal-type constraints, workers' needs) do not act. People 'in so far as they are the personifications of economic catego-ries, embodiments of particular class relations and class-interests classes' (Marx, 1887: 7) exist as classes and class fractions (which identities are mediated by other identities) and engage in struggles in support of their economic and political class interests.

As a structure of relations itself that is internally connected to the structure of capitalist relations, the state is intimately and necessarily connected to class struggle: class struggle (or balance of power between the two basic classes) and the state shape each other. Epistemologically speaking, class struggle is the mediating term between the abstract analysis of capitalist reproduction and the concept of the state (Clarke, 1983: 110). Class struggle from below (struggle of the masses) coexists with class struggle from above:

> [T]he State and its Apparatuses only have meaning from the point of view of the class struggle, as an apparatus of class struggle [i.e. class struggle from above] ensuring class oppression and guaranteeing the conditions of exploitation and its reproduction. But there is no class struggle without antagonistic classes. Whoever says class struggle of the ruling class says resistance, revolt and class struggle of the ruled class [i.e. class struggle from below].
>
> (Althusser, 2001: 125)

Just because concessions can work in the long-term interests of capital and just because concessions can produce consent of the masses, that does not necessar-ily mean concessions are granted. Active class struggle from below is needed. Common people fight for their interests, with a consciousness that is variable over time and that varies across regions and countries. The general point is that the impact of objective conditions (e.g. capital's interest in a healthy and edu-cated workforce) on the state's pro-worker interventions is mediated by class struggle, including the struggle of workers. The need for consent, that is, need for workers to see capitalism as self-evident laws of nature, arises *because* there is potential/actual class struggle from below. And that consent is not produced automatically by economic processes of capitalism.

The struggle of the proletariat against the capitalist class and its state always goes on – literally every month, there is a strike in some part of the world – and it takes many forms. In its trade union form, the struggle of the proletariat aims to obtain concessions from the capitalist class and its state, within the bounds of the capitalist class system. Concessions are both political and economic, and people fight for both. Political concessions are about democratic rights and 'are made in the sphere of legislation concerning' such things as police brutality, discrimination against religious minorities, oppression of women and racialized minorities, censorship, and so on (Lenin, 1901). The fight for trade union rights is a part of the fight for political concessions.

Economic concessions involve improvements in the economic conditions of people, including in wages, conditions of work and state-provided services.[50] A part of this struggle is the struggle against the commodity status of use-values (e.g. demand for subsidized food, shelter, or child care). The commodity status of things is contested in part under pressure from common people who lack the means of exchange to buy the use-values that they need, so the state is partly involved in the determination of what is, and what is not, a commodity.

There is then class struggle from above. This is in the form of what capitalists do to the working class, including through their instrumentalist ties to the state and through its own associations (e.g. chambers of commerce and the like). It is also in the form of the state's anti-worker economic policies and the suppression of strikes against these policies, on behalf of the capitalist class. The state is the biggest and most trusted trade union of the capitalist class that counters the trade unions and other organizations of workers. The neo-liberal welfare cut is an instance of class struggle launched by capital and its state against the social wage that the working class had successfully fought for after the war.[51] As an arm of the capitalist class, the state supremely signifies class struggle from above by suppressing any significant potential or actual threat from workers to commodity relations, relations of property, and capitalist profit-making. When 'adverse circumstances prevent the creation of the industrial reserve army and, with it, the absolute dependence of the working class upon the capitalist class', capital 'rebels against the "sacred" law of supply and demand' (Marx, 1887: 448). Capital engages in its own methods of class struggle as it relies on 'forcible means', including 'State interference' (ibid.). This is class struggle from above. When the capitalist class hires goons to kill trade union leaders or hires strike-breakers during a strike, or when the business bosses use court orders to stop a strike, that is class struggle on their part too. When 'through their press, agents, and spies the capitalists labor to frighten and demoralize the strikers' (Trotsky, 1938b) that is an example of class struggle from above. Class struggle from above is supported/aided by the state.

Class struggle from below over state form

Class struggle takes place not just over policies (e.g. some economic benefits – that is, content of state policy). It also takes place over the 'separation' of the political from the economic, that is, over the very existence of the state in its capitalist form. This means that the working-class struggle for *economic* concessions can be *political*. People's fight for concessions in the form of social wage politicizes their economic struggle against private employers: after all, social wage is needed in part because private wage is grossly inadequate. Besides, the coercive forces of the state 'often take the initiative in lending the economic struggle a political character' (e.g. when they use force against strikers) (Lenin, 1901). When police suppress strikers, 'the workers themselves learn to understand whom the government supports' (ibid.). Workers' struggle for reforms has two aspects: it is narrowly economic, and it is political. It is economic when workers fight against this or that capitalist. And, here the state intervenes, including sometimes by mediating between capital and labour, and often sending police to crush strikes. Workers' struggle is political when they push for pro-worker legislations:

> [T]he movement to force an eight-hour day, etc., *law* is a *political* movement. And in this way, out of the separate economic movements of the workers there grows up everywhere a *political* movement, that is to say a movement of the *class*, with the object of achieving its interests in a general form, in a form possessing a general social force of compulsion.
>
> (Marx, 1871b)

When the exploited class struggles against economic exploitation, that struggle, combined with the political struggle in the sense just mentioned, can create conditions for the struggle against the state itself that defends property rights. That is, conditions are created for a *higher* form of political struggle. The exploited class experiences its 'exploitation not simply as economic, but as inseparably economic and political, with, for example, the threat of the bailiff and eviction standing behind the landlord' (Clarke, 1991: 32). Or when during a strike, the working class remains uncompromising and the police arrive or a court order is served making the strike illegal, that reveals the class and political nature of the state. The dominated classes *tend* to fuse them together in the manner suggested earlier (Clarke, 1991; see also Rothstein, 1990).

The relation between struggle for concessions and the actual concessions is, ultimately, a function of a revolutionary threat to the system: 'We have always said that reforms are a by-product of the revolutionary class struggle' (Lenin, 1921). So, to the extent that the working class obtains concessions from the state, the durability and magnitude of these concessions are directly related to the extent to which the working class acts in a revolutionary manner. The importance of class struggle also means that irrespective of the state possessing its relative autonomy (which much existing state theory is concerned with), the state will be forced to grant some concessions in response to class struggle in order to, as Marx and Engels (1850) would say, 'bribe the workers with a more or less disguised form of alms and to break their revolutionary strength by temporarily rendering their situation tolerable'.

State autonomy not automatically reproduced

In the light of the aforementioned discussion, it can be said that the state's apparent autonomy from the economic is not automatically reproduced. That is, the separation of workers from means of production, and correspondingly, the apparent separation of the state from the economy, is not a one-time event.

This separation is contingent on, and is reproduced in and through, class struggle. Thus, there is a dialectical relation between the state and class struggle.

> The wage contract between individual worker and capitalist is a very solid reality if the capitalist has the power to enforce that contract, but dissolves into pure illusion if the workers are able to counter-pose their collective power to that of capital. [Similarly] The majesty of the law can inspire awe when it confronts the isolated individual, while becoming an object of ridicule in the face of collective resistance.
>
> (Clarke, 1991: 45)

This also applies to state workers. Welfare state expansion has created new layers of workers in the public sector whose pay depends on state's ability to raise taxes. Apart from the struggle between private sector wages and profits that capital has been concerned about, there is now another struggle: the struggle over the sharing of the tax burden and access to public services furnished by these taxes (Schmidt, 2017: 29).[52] The four-way struggles over wages, profits, taxes, and welfare provision could trigger inflation and fiscal crises (ibid.) and could reveal to the masses the massive political biases of the state in favour of the tiny capitalist class.

Separation of the economic from the political aspects of capitalism by the state

The state, like capital, does not give any concession without a struggle. When there is a struggle for concession, the state may give concessions by separating the economic from the political. There are multiple aspects of the state's response.

Firstly, in giving concessions to the people, the state does go against the short-term or long-term interests of individual members of the capitalist class or indeed against certain short-term economic interests of the class as a whole in order to preserve the capitalist class rule.

Secondly,

> the state seeks to enforce the rights of property on the dominated classes individually through the courts, fragmenting collective resistance to the social power of property and ensuring that such power will be imposed on dominated classes individually through the 'market', decomposing class forces, and recomposing them as 'interest groups.'
>
> (Clarke, 1991: 33)

so that masses are prevented from struggling as a class. Whenever class struggle tends to overstep the constitutional boundaries of politics and law, and to challenge the rights of property, the state makes economic concessions in an attempt to re-establish the rule of money and law and to restore the separation of the two spheres. Once again, the state action is a form of class struggle from above.

Because of the threat from people's struggles to the immediate economic interests and long-term political interests of the capitalist class, the state, in order to defend capitalist property, resorts to the actual or potential use of violence, which is the single most important obstacle to both struggle for reforms (as evident when police attacks striking workers) and revolutionary struggle.

Thirdly, to petty-bourgeoisie and rural popular classes, the state gives concessions, including government jobs, which ensure that members of the popular classes are allowed entry into the state (educational institutions, army, and so on) (Poulantzas, 2008: 311–2).

> It [the state] is, however, only the political culmination of a social system whose other elements include the ideological separation of economics and politics, the creation of a bureaucratic state apparatus which gives large sections of the petty bourgeoisie a material and moral interest in the stability of the state, a bourgeois party system, press, schools' system, religion, etc.
>
> (Lukacs, 2005: 56)

The state gives concessions to petty-bourgeois strata 'in order to set them up as supporting classes of the power bloc and short-circuit their alliance with the working class' (ibid.: 311). States' concessions contribute to the depoliticization of the masses and blunting of their class consciousness. Poulantzas says that by giving concession even against the interests of capitalists, the state aims precisely at the political disorganization of the dominated classes: the economic concessions help prevent the dominated classes from attacking the political basis of capitalist exploitation, that is, state power itself (Poulantzas, 1968: 188, 1978: 127). This is the case whether or not the state is liberal-democratic. 'Every minority rule is . . . socially organized both to concentrate the ruling class, equipping it for united and cohesive action, and simultaneously to split and disorganize the oppressed classes' (Lukacs, 2005: 56).

Economic concessions that workers and small-scale producers may gain from the state from time to time help the state and the capitalist class produce consent of the masses to the rule of capital in an economically cheap manner, where possible. They are 'the cheapest and most advantageous from the government's point of view, because by these means the state hopes to win the confidence of the working masses' (Lenin, 1901). The state must take into account some of the interests of the masses – that is, interests in a better existence as workers (and small-scale producers) within capitalism. Of course, the extent to which this happens depends on how well their interests are represented within political parties, state apparatuses, media, academia, and so on.

Limits to state's pro-workers' action

Even if the state gives concessions and sometimes has to do so in order to separate the economic from the political aspects of capitalist class relation, there are strong limits to what it can do for the masses, given its own class character and internal relation to the capitalist class (and its allies). A given policy reflects contradictions among propertied strata and between them and the dominated classes (Poulantzas, 2008: 312), and these contradictions limit how much common people can benefit from state interventions.

There is a limit to what these interventions can do to restrict capitalist exploitation of workers (similarly, there is a limit to the extent to which it can protect the relatively less efficient small-scale producers who produce at an individual value that is above the social value, as we have seen). Ill will or good will, more or less, is immaterial/irrelevant. Even if there are philanthropic – or conscious – capitalists, there is a limit to how much the state can help. Capitalist control over property and production, which the state must defend, ultimately leads to the state serving the masses. As Joan Robinson noted:

> In the present age, any government which had both the power and the will to remedy the major defects of the capitalist system would have the will and the power to abolish it altogether, while governments which have the power to retain the system lack the will to remedy its defects.
>
> (quoted in Dowd, 2002: 129)

If state's pro-poor policy enables workers' significant access to means of subsistence in a way that is unmediated by the market, that may reduce the class power of capitalists. The state does not guarantee employment to wage-dependent families, nor does it ensure that small-scale producers receive a price that is needed for their families' reproduction, and this is the case in spite of the state's tall promises in the form of, say, minimum-wage and farmers' legislations. But the state seeks to make sure that capitalists have access to exploitable masses, that they can sell their unsold commodities and that they earn an average rate of profit or, at least, a significant amount of mass of profit.

The interests of capitalists and those of masses are fundamentally incompatible. Significant and durable improvements in their conditions of living and working cannot happen because they do not control either society's major means of production or the coercive power of the state. Without the state's coercive power over the working class, the control over the economy will not be in the hands of the capitalist class.

> [T]here can be no discussion of systematic social reforms and the raising of the masses' living standards; when every serious demand of the proletariat and even every serious demand of the petty bourgeoisie inevitably reaches beyond the limits of capitalist property relations and of the bourgeois state.
>
> (Trotsky, 1938a)

As mentioned, the state has sought to improve the conditions of common people. Yet it is the case that the state fails to meet their need in a significant and durable manner. This failure is actually the state's success in keeping the masses in their place. Its failure is internally connected to what the state is.

In relation to the working class, the state falls short in two major ways (Figure 9.3). Surplus value ultimately comes from the deduction of the value of labour power from the total net value produced by the worker. State's pro-worker laws can only aim to make sure that workers get back at least as much as it takes to reproduce their labour power, that there are enough workers with adequate physical ability and skills, available for exploitation by the employer, that is, that 'the worker has retained his labour-power and can sell it anew if he can find a buyer' (Marx, 1887: 413).[53] This means that the state's pro-worker laws can only be against *excesses* of capitalism. This constitutes the lower limit of state action. State laws cannot be fundamentally against the capitalist property relations, by virtue of which the excesses exist. Even then, the state falls short: it fails to eliminate the excesses, because it must meet the needs of capital. A capitalist class in a society *without* millions of people who are already in (near-)poverty and/or face the risk of being in poverty, would be a class *without* its necessary political guarantee too. This is because it would face a situation where those who are *not* poor (e.g. well-paid workers) would have a lot of bargaining power, which, in turn, would increase the

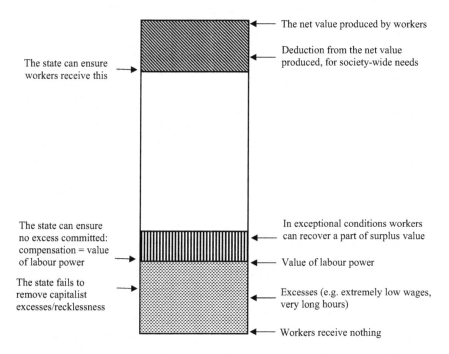

Figure 9.3 The state and value

bargaining power of those who *are* poor, and therefore, of *all* sections of the exploited class.

The state *could* ensure that workers receive the entire value of what they produce minus the usual deductions necessary for meeting society-wide needs.[54] But the state does not and cannot, because it is the state of the capitalist class and not the workers and small-scale producers.

There are 'layers' of the logic of state's limited success in improving the conditions of the masses. During normal times, the imperative of capitalist accumulation sets a limit on what the state can do for workers: as soon as the amount of total value of society that goes to the hands of the masses adversely affects the amount of the average rate of surplus value to be appropriated by the capitalist class, there will generally be a stop to any further improvement. When we consider the geographical mobility as an aspect of accumulation, we see that it imposes a further layer of constraint on what the state can do for workers. Finally, the crisis-proneness of capitalist accumulation, and indeed the fact that capitalism is in its relative terminal decline stage, with the productive forces retarded, constrains how much concession the masses can receive from the state. In relation to the decline stage of capitalism, imperialism (that is, capitalism at the world-scale) is a crucial process:

> Imperialist capitalism is no longer capable of developing the productive forces of humanity. For this reason it can grant the workers neither material concessions nor effective social reforms.
>
> (Trotsky, 1937)

In spite of many limits, the working class does receive the positive results of its struggle in specific sectors and regions:

> All this is correct. But it is only correct on the scale of an entire epoch. There are branches of industry . . . with prodigious force . . . Moreover, this decrepit economy has its ebbs and flows. The workers are almost continually passing from one struggle to another, and sometimes they are victorious.
>
> (Trotsky, 1937)

But that does not mean that the general tendency – that there are limits to what the workers can get – is nullified. Trotsky adds: 'Of course, capitalism takes from the workers with its right hand what it has given them with its left' (ibid.). In other words, there are limits to what the state can do for the masses and win consent through material concessions. If this is the case, then it follows that apart from consent production by means of ideological deception, methods of coercive action (actual and/or threatened), the methods that are heavily under-stressed in existing theory, are other ways in which the state maintains the capitalist class rule.

5 Summary, and theoretical and political implications

One implication of the class character of the state is that apart from the state having to meet the fundamental needs of the capitalist class, it must also respond to the struggle of the masses for concessions. We have seen that the masses get little without a fight and that there is a limit to how much they can get even with a fight, especially during the imperialist stage dominated by world monopolies, associated with the relative decline in the development of productive forces. It is also the case that to obtain some concessions, trade unions have to often support – or they have to make sure they do not undermine conditions for – national- and regional-level capitalist accumulation. The fact that capitalist investment in many sectors can move across state's territorial jurisdictions at national and sub-national scales imposes a limit on workers' receiving significant concessions. All these facts together have specific political implications. One is that trade union struggle is not *un-important* in spite of these facts:

> [I]n spite of the progressive degeneration of trade unions . . . , the work within the trade unions not only does not lose any of its importance but remains as before and becomes in a certain sense even more important work than ever for every revolutionary party. The matter at issue is essentially the struggle for influence over the working class [including communist caucuses within trade unions].
>
> (Trotsky, 1940)

Therefore,

> Every organization, every party, every faction which permits itself an ultimatistic position in relation to the trade union, i.e., in essence turns its back upon the working class, merely because of displeasure with its organizations, every such organization is destined to perish. And it must be said it deserves to perish.
>
> (ibid.)

Althusser (2001: 54) notes:

> Marx . . . proves irrefutably that the working class cannot hope to gain from the modern growth of productivity before it has overthrown capitalism and seized State power in a socialist revolution. He proves that from here to the revolutionary seizure of power which opens the road to socialism, the working class can have no other objective, and hence no other resource, than to struggle *against* the effects of exploitation produced by the growth of productivity, in order to *limit* these effects (struggle *against* speed-up, *against* arbitrary productivity bonuses, *against* overtime, *against* redundancies, *against* 'automation unemployment').

All in all, the state and the capitalist economic system cannot meet the needs of the people, and pro-worker interventions are only a 'meagre concession wrung from capital' (Marx, 1887: 319). The political aim of the proletarian movement therefore must be, as Marx, Engels, Lenin, Luxemburg, and Trotsky have said, 'the conquest of power by the proletariat for the purpose of expropriating the bourgeoisie' (Trotsky, 1938a). The ultimate aim of the labour movement is not to continue to fight merely for better conditions under which people can sell their labour power but to abolish the conditions for such sale, that is, to abolish wage labour itself, and this cannot be done without overthrowing the state that defends wage labour:

> The political movement of the working class has as its object, of course, the conquest of political power for the working class, and for this it is naturally necessary that a previous organisation of the working class, itself arising from their economic struggles, should have been developed up to a certain point.
>
> (Marx, 1871b)

> Where the working class is not yet far enough advanced in its organisation to undertake a decisive campaign against the collective power, i.e., the political power of the ruling classes, it must at any rate be trained for this by continual agitation against and a hostile attitude towards the policy of the ruling classes.
>
> (ibid.)

It would indeed be mistaken to ignore/under-stress 'the organisation of the working class as a class through the medium of trade unions' even if unions fight for concessions only, because through the unions the proletariat 'fights its daily battles with capital, in which it trains itself' (Engels in Marx and Engels, 1975: 275).

The struggle for economic and political reforms is important, not only because some concessions may be obtained which can improve the desperate conditions of the masses temporarily. An improvement in the conditions of the masses might also facilitate further struggle: it is easier for literate and healthier people living in cities and in villages well connected with modern means of communication, enjoying a certain amount of democratic rights, to struggle for self-emancipation, than for the illiterate, hungry, and ill people living in areas without any means of communication or culture or democratic rights. Also, the fighting for economic and political concessions can lead the masses to discover the limits, through practice, to what the state can actually do to help the masses, and therefore the real class-political nature of the state, which falsely represents itself as the state of and for everyone. Marx indeed says that if Marxism denies the importance of such struggles, then 'what is certain is that I myself am not a Marxist'

(Marx and Guesde, 1880). Fighting for economic and political reforms under appropriate conditions (e.g. education about theory and history of the working-class movement and capitalism) can have a positive effect on worker's political capacity.

But workers cannot fight only for economic concessions. If there are limits to the state's concessions, there are limits to the struggles that are only for concessions from the state. As we have seen, through economic concessions the state 'hopes to win the confidence of the working masses' (Lenin, 1901). 'For this very reason', communists '*must not* under any circumstances or in any way whatever create grounds for the belief (or the misunderstanding) that we attach greater value to economic reforms, or that we regard them as being particularly important, etc.' (ibid.).

If the state seeks to disorganize the working class, the working class must try 'to counteract this process of disorganization. It must first of all constitute itself as a class' (Lukacs, 2005: 57). And the working class must be conscious of the following fact: if the increased access to use-values via a rise in wages from employers can, at best, lead to a relaxation of the golden chain around the neck of the working class, so increased public wage in the form of government benefits can only have a similar effect as long as the working class has no direct control over the means of production and over the very purpose of production of wealth (satisfaction of human needs versus profit for a few) and over how the state works. Such control cannot occur without the masses creating their own transitional state, after replacing the current state. The fusion of economic and political struggle should neither be shaped by mere spontaneity nor by the desire to obtain more concessions. It has to be based on class consciousness, which, in its fully developed form, is the idea that capitalist interests and masses' interest are fundamentally incompatible, and that this incompatibility cannot be abolished until the capitalist state is overthrown.

It is true that in mobilizing workers for reforms, trade unions often lose their independence vis-à-vis the capitalist state, especially during the imperialist stage. But:

> Does this mean that in the epoch of imperialism independent trade unions are generally impossible? It would be fundamentally incorrect to pose the question this way. Impossible are the independent or semi-independent reformist trade unions. Wholly possible are revolutionary trade unions which not only are not stockholders of imperialist policy but which set as their task the direct overthrow of the rule of capitalism.
>
> (Trotsky, 1940)[55]

Trade unions (and other organizations of the masses such as factory committees) must remain independent of the state (and of bourgeois parties) to play a revolutionary role. For this to happen, they need to employ democratic slogans (e.g. right to unionize) and combine them with the transitional demands as well as minimum economic demands (e.g. a rise in wages).

> In the epoch of imperialist decay the trade unions can be really independ-
> ent only to the extent that they are conscious of being, in action, the
> organs of proletarian revolution. In this sense, the program of transitional
> demands . . . in its fundamental features is the program for the activ-
> ity of the trade unions [and not just for that of the communist political
> movement].
>
> (Trotsky, 1940)

Transitional demands are of a different type than the usual trade union (or partial) demand such as a rise in money wages which the system *can* accommodate.
Transitional demands include housing for all, indexed wages ('an automatic
rise in wages in relation to the increase in price of consumer goods'), and the
right to employment, including on public works (Trotsky, 1938a). The essence
of transitional demands 'is contained in the fact that ever more openly and
decisively they will be directed against the very bases of the bourgeois regime'
(ibid.). Transitional demands are those that stem 'from today's conditions and
from today's consciousness of wide layers of the working class and unalter-
ably leading to one final conclusion: the conquest of power by the proletariat'
(ibid.).

The need for transitional demand is to be connected to a need for solidarity across the social-cultural divides within the working class. Concessions are
granted partly because workers struggle for them. However, racial and other
divisions undermine workers' unity; the state, including the bourgeois parties, promotes such division and non-class identities. So the fight against racial
oppression and the efforts to create racial unity must be parts of people's struggle against capital, including that which demands concessions. Marx (1887:
195) was aware of the matter: 'In the United States of North America, every
independent movement of the workers was paralysed so long as slavery disfig-
ured a part of the Republic. Labour cannot emancipate itself in the white skin
where in the black it is branded' (ibid.). Besides, there is a need for solidarity
between currently employed workers and unemployed workers in cities, and
between all of them and small-scale producers.

Workers' successful struggle for concessions points to a possibility of a society
beyond capitalism:

> Though the Factory Act, that first and meagre concession wrung from
> capital, is limited to combining elementary education with work in the
> factory, there can be no doubt that when the working-class comes into
> power, as inevitably it must, technical instruction, both theoretical and
> practical, will take its proper place in the working-class schools. There is
> also no doubt that such revolutionary ferments, the final result of which is
> the abolition of the old division of labour, are diametrically opposed to the

capitalistic form of production, and to the economic status of the labourer corresponding to that form.

(Marx, 1887: 319)

Capital volume 1 not only reveals the economic laws of motion of capitalism but also sheds light on the conditions for, and the barriers to, the development of the working class. Capitalists' 'own most important interests dictate' that 'all *legally* removable hindrances' (e.g. the crippling of the quality of labour power due to overwork) 'to the free development of the working class' be removed. Partly for this reason, Marx (1887: 7) says, he gives 'so large a space in this volume to the history, the details, and the results of English factory legislation'. And this is why it is important to re-examine Marx's discussion of the workplace legislation and to reflect on what the state does for the workers' welfare.

The state has given concessions improving the health and education of the workers. What this means is that to the extent that capitalism, in its own interest, creates an educated workforce, such a workforce is also being trained to manage the affairs of society on their own without the interference of capitalists or bureaucratic state actors. Capitalism not only matures the material conditions (e.g. large-scale production, technical improvements, and so one), that are partly spurred on by the pro-worker action, for socialism. It also matures various contradictions inside it. These contradictions are economic, which are expressed in the form of periodic crises, prompting state action. These contradictions are also political: contradictions between (a) the image that the state is for all and (b) the reality of its structurally inscribed inherent 'biases' in favour of the propertied classes. Given these contradictions, a new force is created that can, under proper conditions, overthrow the state along with the capitalist property relation that it defends, and begin to create a new society by utilizing the conditions already maturing under capitalism:

> By maturing the material conditions, and the combination on a social scale of the processes of production, it [pro-worker state intervention] matures the contradictions and antagonisms of the capitalist form of production, and thereby provides, along with the elements for the formation of a new society, the forces for exploding the old one.

(Marx, 1887: 329)

Notes

1 India's Supreme Court in 1982 held that paying workers less than the minimum wage amounts to forced labour. It said that the Constitution recognized the right to a living wage. This includes not only enough to purchase bare necessities but 'frugal comforts' such as children's education, medical requirement, minimum recreation including festivals/ceremonies, and provision for old age, marriages, and the like (Kumar, 2019).

This means that the minimum wage is to be computed only on the basic needs of workers in each region and that it need not be based on the type of work being performed. What the executive institution of the state has actually done contradicts this line of thinking.

2 Excessively long working days 'called forth a control on the part of Society which legally limits, regulates, and makes uniform the working-day and its pauses. This control appears, therefore, during the first half of the nineteenth century simply as exceptional legislation' (Marx, 1887: 194).

'A normal working-day for modern industry only dates from the Factory Act of 1833, which included cotton, wool, flax, and silk factories' (Marx, 1887: 184). Compulsory laws for the extension of the working-day were put in place from the middle of the 14th to the end of the 17th century (ibid.).

3 In colonial India,

> The Factories Act of 1881 granted workers the grand concession of a 12-hour day. About half a century later, in 1921, India's colonial government would be among the first to ratify the ILO's eight-hour workday convention. The years in between had seen a world war and at least two pandemics that ravaged India.
>
> (Chakravarty, 2020)

4 Article 23(1) of the Indian constitution says: 'Traffic in human beings and begar and other similar forms of forced labour are prohibited and any contravention of this provision shall be an offence punishable in accordance with law.' And Article 24 says: 'No child below the age of fourteen years shall be employed to work in any factory or mine or engaged in any other hazardous employment' (Indian government, undated). In pursuance of Article 24, various laws have been passed.

These include the Factories Act, 1948, that sets a minimum age limit for the employment of children in factories; the Mines Act of 1952 that prohibits the employment of people under the age of 18 years in mines; as well as the Child Labour (Prohibition and Regulation) Act, 1986; Child Labour (Prohibition & Regulation) Amendment Act, 2016; and Child Labour (Prohibition and Regulation) Amendment Rules, 2017, all of which aim to regulate the use of child labour.

5

> [T]he intellectual desolation artificially produced by converting immature human beings into mere machines for the fabrication of surplus-value, a state of mind clearly distinguishable from that natural ignorance which keeps the mind fallow without destroying its capacity for development, its natural fertility, this desolation finally compelled even the English Parliament to make elementary education a compulsory condition to the 'productive' employment of children under 14 years, in every industry subject to the Factory Acts.
>
> (Marx, 1887: 274)

6 Section 272 of Indian Penal Code says:

> Whoever adulterates any article of food or drink, so as to make such article noxious as food or drink, intending to sell such article as food or drink, or knowing it to be likely that the same will be sold as food or drink, shall be punished with imprisonment of either description for a term which may extend to six months, or with fine which may extend to one thousand rupees, or with both. (in Dudeja et al., 2017)

7 The state has to look after, and does assist, the floating population – technologically induced unemployment whereby the unemployed compete with the employed, 'but this is less significant now given the trend towards neoliberalization' (Harvey, 2010b: 281).

8

> In those factories that have been longest subject to the Factory Acts, with their compulsory limitation of the hours of labour, and other regulations, many of the

older abuses have vanished. The very improvement of the machinery demands to a certain extent 'improved construction of the buildings,' and this is an advantage to the workpeople.

(Marx, 1887: 343–344)

In contrast, '[i]n those factories and manufactories that are not yet subject to the Factory Acts, the most fearful over-work prevails periodically during what is called the season, in consequence of sudden orders' (Marx, 1887: 314–315).

9 'The first "Statute of Labourers" (23 Edward III., 1349) found its immediate *pretext* (not its *cause*, for legislation of this kind lasts centuries after the pretext for it has disappeared) in the great plague that decimated the people' (italics added) (Marx, 1887: 181).

10

The Congress of the International Working Men's Association at Geneva, on the proposition of the London General Council, resolved that 'the limitation of the working-day is a preliminary condition without which all further attempts at improvement and emancipation must prove abortive . . . the Congress proposes eight hours as the legal limit of the working-day'.

(Marx, 1887: 195)

11

France limps slowly behind England. The February revolution was necessary to bring into the world the 12 hours' law, which is much more deficient than its English original. . . . It once for all commands the same limit to the working-day in all shops and factories without distinction, whilst English legislation reluctantly yields to the pressure of circumstances, now on this point, now on that, and is getting lost in a hopelessly bewildering tangle of contradictory enactments. On the other hand, the French law proclaims as a principle that which in England was only won in the name of children, minors, and women, and has been only recently for the first time claimed as a general right. (Marx, 1887: 195)

12 The Chief Justice of the U.S. Supreme Court Charles Evans Hughes sustained a crucial piece of New Deal legislation as a means of containing 'the paralyzing consequences of industrial warfare' (National Labor Relations Board v. Jones and Laughlin Steel). This is when 'an important aspect of Marx's theory came to the aid of the majority in the highest court in a very capitalist country' (Miller, 1991: 68).

13 This is 'just as in a machine the part of its value to be reproduced every day is greater the more rapidly the machine is worn out' (Marx, 1887: 179).

14 In England, the first statue of labourers was put in place in 1839. The state interventions in the form of the Factory Acts as in England 'curb the passion of capital for a limitless draining of labour-power, by forcibly limiting the working-day by state regulations, made by a state that is ruled by capitalist-and landlord' (Marx, 1887: 166).

In colonial India, '[o]fficials writing on the mills took note of the "physical wear and tear of the employed" and, in a burst of paternalistic regard, recommended shortening the 14-hour days' (Chakravarty, 2020).

15 In the post-1929 period, as Barrow says based on the work of Finegold, 'the intensification of the U.S. agricultural depression when coupled with a general economic downturn "proved an economic danger to big business as well, since the continued weakness of rural purchasing power served as a barrier to industrial recovery"'. This then opened political avenues 'for government experts to launch an interventionist agricultural policy' in ways that did not challenge the position of the dominant class interests within agriculture (Barrow, 1993: 142).

16
> The Inquiry Commission of 1862 also proposed a new regulation of the mining industry, an industry distinguished from others by the exceptional characteristic that the interests of landlord and capitalist there join hands. The antagonism of these two interests had been favourable to Factory legislation, while on the other hand the absence of that antagonism is sufficient to explain the delays and chicanery of the legislation on mines.
>
> (Marx, 1887: 323)

17 In England:
> [H]owever much the individual manufacturer might give the rein to his old lust for gain, the spokesmen and political leaders of the manufacturing class ordered a change of front and of speech towards the workpeople. They had entered upon the contest for the repeal of the Corn Laws [against the resistance of landowners], and needed the workers to help them to victory. They promised therefore, not only a double-sized loaf of bread, but the enactment of the Ten Hours' Bill in the Free-trade millennium. Thus they still less dared to oppose a measure intended only to make the law of 1833 a reality.
>
> (Marx, 1887: 186)

> The years 1846–47 are epoch-making in the economic history of England. The Repeal of the Corn Laws, and of the duties on cotton and other raw material; Free-trade proclaimed as the guiding star of legislation. . . . [In] the same years, the Chartist movement and the 10 hours' agitation reached their highest point. They found allies in the Tories panting for revenge. Despite the fanatical opposition of the army of perjured Free-traders, . . . the Ten Hours' Bill, struggled for so long, went through Parliament.
>
> (Marx, 1887: 187)

18 Marx quotes the Children Employment Commission which says that the Factory Act is unjust to the larger businesses, and by giving a stimulus to the multiplication of small workplaces, the legislation is against the 'general improvement of the people' (Marx, 1887: 321):
> It would be unjust to the larger employers that their factories should be placed under regulation, while the hours of labour in the smaller places in their own branch of business were under no legislative restriction. And to the injustice arising from the unfair conditions of competition, in regard to hours, that would be created if the smaller places of work were exempt, would be added the disadvantage to the larger manufacturers, of finding their supply of juvenile and female labour drawn off to the places of work exempt from legislation. Further, a stimulus would be given to the multiplication of the smaller places of work, which are almost invariably the least favourable to the health, comfort, education, and general improvement of the people.
>
> (Marx, 1887: 320–321)

19 For example:
> They allege that numbers of the parents withdraw their children from the industry brought under the Act, in order to sell them where 'freedom of labour' still rules, i.e., where children under 13 years are compelled to work like grown-up people, and therefore can be got rid of at a higher price.
>
> (Marx, 1887: 273)

20 'Periodical epidemics speak on this point as clearly as the diminishing military standard in Germany and France' (Marx, 1887: 166).

21 The existence of a thing, whether or not and how it functions, and the effects it produces: these are not the same thing.

22 That this is a possibility is demonstrated by some of Marx's (1880) questions (e.g. #93) in his proposed Workers' enquiry: '93. Does the government strive to secure the observance of the existing factory laws against the interests of the employers? Do its inspectors do their duty?'.

Also, referring to the English legislation of 1867, Marx (1887: 322) says that it faced 'the hesitation, the repugnance, and the bad faith, with which it lent itself' to the actual task of implementing these pro-worker measures, which the parliament was forced to adopt.

23 Shaikh says that in these countries,

> [B]etween 1960 and 1987, the difference between the value of total social benefits received [from the state] and total taxes directly paid (the net social wage) remains between 1 and 2 percent of GDP . . . in almost every year. [This] implies that wage and salary earners received more than they paid. But this overall net subsidy is clearly small.
>
> (Shaikh, 2003: 537–538)

24 Shaikh adds:

> In neither the United States nor Sweden, therefore, can welfare expenditures be indicted as the cause of fiscal deficits or consequent economic stagnation. However, in Germany the net social wage was generally positive in the boom years, on the order of 4 percent of GDP.
>
> (ibid.)

25 In India, in 2018, an expert committee set up by the Indian government recommended setting the national minimum wage for India at Rupees 375 a day to allow for expenditure on a balanced diet, shelter, clothing, and other essentials, based on the minimum per capita consumption expenditure per household. This is slightly higher than the existing rate of over Rupees 321 for agriculture or unskilled workers and Rupees 371 for semi-skilled workers.

The trade unions have demanded that a minimum wage of Rupees 660 per day (Rupees 20,000/month) be fixed and that any payment below this amount be considered illegal. The government has rejected these demands. The average wage in India is below Rupees 400/day.

The minimum wage violation is especially blatant in case of vulnerable workers (women, racialized, and low-caste workers).

26

> Some of the manufacturers, even, who had managed their factories in conformity with [an earlier regulation] overwhelmed Parliament with memorials on the immoral competition of their false brethren whom greater impudence, or more fortunate local circumstances, enabled to break the law. (Marx, 1887: 186)

27 It does not matter that such a policy 'makes it hard for the floating population to remain a labor reserve' (ibid.). And if the labour reserve diminishes because of the absence of state support for the unemployed, then wages might increase.

28 'This manoeuvre also failed. Factory Inspector Leonard Horner conducted in his own person, and through his sub-inspectors, many examinations of witnesses in the factories of Lancashire' (Marx, 1887: 188).

29 In England,

> Although, . . . the Factory Inspectors unceasingly and with justice, commend the results of the Acts of 1844 and 1850, yet they admit that the shortening of the hours

of labour has already called forth such an intensification of the labour as is injurious to the health of the workman and to his capacity for work.

(Marx, 1887: 283)

30

In the ten years during which it regulated factory work, first in part, and then entirely, the official reports of the factory inspectors teem with complaints as to the impossibility of putting the Act into force. As the law of 1833 left it optional with the lords of capital during the 15 hours, from 5.30 a.m. to 8.30 p.m., to make every 'young person,' and 'every child' begin, break off, resume, or end his 12 or 8 hours at any moment they liked, and also permitted them to assign to different persons, different times for meals, these gentlemen soon discovered a new 'system of relays,' by which the labour-horses were not changed at fixed stations, but were constantly re-harnessed at changing stations. . . . [T]his system annulled the whole Factory Act, not only in the spirit, but in the letter. How could factory inspectors, with this complex bookkeeping in respect to each individual child or young person, enforce the legally determined work-time and the granting of the legal mealtimes?

(Marx, 1887: 186)

31 The bill failed to be passed, even if the wage increase was to be staggered and even if the proposed new minimum wage of $15 was too low: if a person has a minimum wage job and works 40 hours a week for 52 weeks, they would earn just $15,080, which is below the $17,420 poverty line in 2021 for families of two. In line with inflation and productivity gains since 1968, the minimum wage would now be about $24, so $15 is really low.

32 For example, the English 'Parliament decreed that after March 1st, 1834, no child under 11, after March 1st 1835, no child under 12, and after March 1st, 1836, no child under 13 was to work more than eight hours in a factory' (Marx, 1887: 185).

33 'The Factory Acts Extension Act, which affects the large establishments, derogates from the Factory Act by a crowd of vicious exceptions and cowardly compromises with the masters' (Marx, 1887: 322).

34

Apart from their wording, which makes it easy for the capitalist to evade them, the sanitary clauses are extremely meagre, and, in fact, limited to provisions for white-washing the walls, for insuring cleanliness in some other matters, for ventilation, and for protection against dangerous machinery. . . . [There was] the fanatical opposition of the masters to those clauses which imposed upon them a slight expenditure on appliances for protecting the limbs of their workpeople, an opposition that throws a fresh and glaring light on the Free-trade dogma, according to which, in a society with conflicting interests, each individual necessarily furthers the common weal by seeking nothing but his own personal advantage!

(Marx, 1887: 315–316)

35 In England, capitalists engaged in 'a noisy agitation that went on for several years', which

turned chiefly on the age of those who, under the name of children, were limited to 8 hours' work, and were subject to a certain amount of compulsory education. According to capitalistic anthropology, the age of childhood ended at 10, or at the outside, at 11. The more nearly the time approached for the coming into full force of the Factory Act, . . . the more wildly raged the mob of manufacturers. They managed, in fact, to intimidate the government to such an extent that . . . it proposed to lower the limit of the age of childhood from 13 to 12. In the meantime the pressure from without grew more threatening. Courage failed the House of Commons. It refused to throw children of 13 under the Juggernaut Car of capital for more than 8 hours a day.

(Marx, 1887: 185–186)

An act came into full operation. That was not the whole story though. Marx further writes:

At their [manufacturers'] instigation the House of Commons reduced the minimum age for exploitable children from 9 to 8, in order to assure that additional supply of factory children which is due to capitalists, according to divine and human law.

(Marx, 1887: 187)

36 The English 'Parliament passed 5 labour Laws between 1802 and 1833, but was shrewd enough not to vote a penny for their carrying out, for the requisite officials, &c' (Marx, 1887: 184).

Parliament did not vote a single farthing in aid of emigration, but simply passed some Acts empowering the municipal corporations to keep the operatives in a half-starved state, *i.e.*, to exploit them at less than the normal wages. On the other hand, when 3 years later, the cattle disease broke out, Parliament broke wildly through its usages and voted, straight off, millions for indemnifying the millionaire landlords, whose farmers in any event came off without loss, owing to the rise in the price of meat. The bull-like bellow of the landed proprietors at the opening of Parliament, in 1866, showed that a man can worship the cow Sabala without being a Hindu, and can change himself into an ox without being a Jupiter.

(Marx, 1887: 409)

37

For this the legislature is alone to blame, by having passed a delusive law, which, while it would seem to provide that the children employed in factories shall be *educated,* contains no enactment by which that professed end can be secured.

(Marx, 1887: 274)

Consider another example:

The Mines' Inspecting Act of 1860 . . . provides that mines shall be inspected by public officers nominated specially for that purpose, and that boys between the ages of 10 and 12 years shall not be employed, unless they have a school certificate, or go to school for a certain number of hours. This Act was a complete dead letter owing to the ridiculously small number of inspectors . . . [and] the meagreness of their powers.

(Marx, 1887: 323)

38

The spirit of capitalist production stands out clearly in the ludicrous wording of the so-called education clauses in the Factory Acts, in the absence of an administrative machinery, an absence that again makes the compulsion illusory, in the opposition of the manufacturers themselves to these education clauses, and in the tricks and dodges they put in practice for evading them.

(ibid.: 274)

In the year 1865 there were 3,217 coal mines in Great Britain, and 12 inspectors. A Yorkshire mine-owner himself calculates . . . that putting on one side their office work, which absorbs all their time, each mine can be visited but once in ten years by an inspector. No wonder that explosions have increased progressively, both in number and extent (sometimes with a loss of 200–300 men), during the last ten years. These are the beauties of 'free' capitalist production!

(Marx, 1887: 328)

The Workshops' Regulation Act, wretched in all its details, remained a dead letter in the hands of the municipal and local authorities who were charged with its execution. When, in 1871, Parliament withdrew from them this power, in order to confer it on the Factory Inspectors, to whose province it thus added by a single stroke more than one hundred thousand workshops, and three hundred brickworks, care was taken at the same time not to add more than eight assistants to their already undermanned staff.

(p. 322)

39   Bad news on the job front can always have an adverse impact on election result. So, prior to the 2019 general election, India's Modi government suppressed an official report on the national unemployment rate that showed it had reached a 45-year high in 2017.
40   The English factory inspectors, whose reports Marx relied on so much, were exemplary though.
41   Marx talks about 'the certifying surgeons, who overstated the age of the children, agreeably to the capitalist's greed for exploitation, and the sordid trafficking needs of the parents' (Marx, 1887: 272).
42   That Marx (1880) clearly recognizes this was evident from the question #39 in his questionnaire. 'Has the government or municipality applied the laws regulating child labor? Do the employers submit to these laws?'
43   'For since in each year more labourers are employed than in its predecessor, sooner or later a point must be reached, at which the requirements of accumulation begin to surpass the customary supply of labour, and, therefore, a rise of wages takes place' (Marx, 1887: 434–435).
44   Many of them would join the working class if there was better employment and income prospect and better working conditions. Many of them are semi-proletarians – part-time workers.
45   Kalecki says, the push towards full employment would mean that business enterprises would begin to lose their managerial-authoritarian control over workers. It would mean the loss of control, not simply as represented by, say, demands for higher wages and better benefits, but also over the production process itself as well as over its exclusive power to make the pricing, investment, and wage-salary-dividend decisions (quoted in Dowd, 2002: 128).
46   During the pandemic, a limited amount of government support to workers has had some impact on labour supply: some workers have been able to stay at home instead of being forced to go to unsafe workplaces for what are poverty wages. This has led to capitalists complaining about government benefits. For example, the US Chamber of Commerce urged Congress to end the weekly $300 in federal unemployment benefit because 'paying people not to work is dampening what should be a stronger jobs market' (Austin, 2021).
47   Let's consider this example that Marx provides:

[T]he English doctors are unanimous in declaring that where the work is continuous, 500 cubic feet is the very least space that should be allowed for each person. . . . Now, if the Factory Acts, owing to their compulsory provisions, indirectly hasten on the conversion of small workshops into factories, thus indirectly attacking the proprietary rights of the smaller capitalists, and assuring a monopoly to the great ones, so, if it were made obligatory to provide the proper space for each workman in every workshop, thousands of small employers would, at one full swoop, be expropriated directly! . . . The sanitary officers, the industrial inquiry commissioners, the factory inspectors, all harp . . . upon the impossibility of wringing them [500 cubic feet] out of capital. They thus, in fact, declare that consumption and other lung diseases among the workpeople are necessary conditions to the existence of capital.

(Marx, 1887: 316)

48 The idea that capital mobility imposes a constraint on the state is only partly true, as discussed in an earlier chapter.

49 If the state accedes to the demand for a higher wage to allow the consumption of nutrition food or access to libraries, that need becomes a new component part of the value of labour power.

50

[T]he major social conflicts and political struggles that have taken place during the decade of the sixties did not take place within exchange relationships between labor and capital, but took place as conflicts over the control over the service organizations that serve the commodity form without themselves being part of the commodity nexus. Conflicts in schools, universities, prisons, military organizations, housing authorities and hospitals are cases in point. We suggest that an explanation of this fact can be based on the consideration that such organizations represent the most advanced forms of erosion of the commodity form within capitalist exchange relationships themselves.

(Offe and Ronge, 1982: 255)

51 A part of the wage that workers receive is the social wage benefits from the state paid from general taxation, which comes mainly from the total surplus value workers produce (Brooks, 2005). Now consider that the state provides such things as healthcare and education. Given that the labour involved in the production of these services does not directly produce surplus value, austerity can be seen as class struggle from above: struggle of capital for cuts in order to 'stop the drain on surplus value provided by the state spending' (ibid.). Such cuts can also be prompted by state's corporate welfare programme: when the state spends billions of dollars on corporate welfare, including to bail out criminal financiers that become bankrupt, a policy creates a massive deficit and then shifts the financial burden to workers in the form of cuts in welfare funding.

52 According to Schmidt (2017), the former struggle has been supplemented by the latter.

53 This is indeed the basis for so-called capability deprivation theory of bourgeois scholarship such as that of Amartya Sen (Sen, 1999; Hahnel, 2002).

54 Deductions will have to be made from the social product that people produce (Marx, 1875). Society will save resources for supporting people when they cannot or are not expected to work (e.g. women during pregnancy, children, older people, people who are ill, people who have met with an accident). A part of the total social product produced by people will need to be set aside towards the cost of the means of production (e.g. raw materials and machines and energy need to be replenished) and for the purpose of expanding the productive base (e.g. to establish new factories or labs or build a new bridge across a river). A part of the social product needs to be put aside for collective provisioning by the government (e.g. education, healthcare, and so on), for dealing with emergencies and natural calamities (e.g. storms, floods, earthquakes, pandemic) and for restoring ecological health.

55

[T]he trade unions in the present epoch cannot simply be the organs of [liberal-capitalist] democracy as they were in the epoch of free capitalism and they cannot any longer remain politically neutral, that is, limit themselves to serving the daily needs of the working class. They cannot any longer be anarchistic, i.e. ignore the decisive influence of the state on the life of peoples and classes. They can no longer be reformist, because the objective conditions leave no room for any serious and lasting reforms. The trade unions of our time can either serve as secondary instruments of imperialist capitalism for the subordination and disciplining of workers and for obstructing the revolution, or, on the contrary, the trade unions can become the instruments of the revolutionary movement of the proletariat.

(Trotsky, 1940)

10 State forms

Geographic and bureaucratic

The distinction between form and content is very important to Marx's *histori-cal* materialist method. He criticizes in *Capital 1*, 'The bourgeois economist whose narrow mind is unable to separate the form of appearance from the thing that appears' (Marx, 1887: 402). In his preface to the first German edition of *Capital 1*, Marx says that 'in bourgeois society, the commodity-form of the product of labour – or value-form of the commodity – is the economic cell-form' (p. 6). In fact, and as mentioned earlier, Marx begins his *Capital 1* by saying that while all societies need wealth (use-values), in capitalism, wealth takes the *form* of commodities. He says: 'Use values . . . constitute the sub-stance [content] of all wealth, whatever may be the social form of that wealth' (p. 27).[1] The form-content distinction, an important aspect of Marx's dialecti-cal method (see Chapter 1), has been used in this book to distinguish between class society and capitalist form of class society, and to distinguish between class-state and the capitalist form of it.[2]

In this chapter, I use 'state form' not at the level of class society (i.e. state form in terms of feudal state or capitalist state) but at the level of a particular class society, that is, capitalist class society. In relation to the capitalist state, I use 'state form' in the following sense: all capitalist states have geographical and bureaucratic forms in terms of their internal structure (this means that the *content* of state-society relations takes geographical and bureaucratic *forms*), and these forms serve capitalist accumulation, but can also problematize that process. While the state is a social relation/process, like all social relations/processes, it has a geographical (spatial and scalar) form. While the state is a relation/process of class domination, this mechanism of class domination is effected through its specific form. So, form, in this chapter, refers to particular expressions of a given content, or to the mechanisms through which a structure of relations actually operates. In other words, the term/concept 'form' will be used less in the historical sense and more in the 'substantive' sense. The claim that the capitalist state is a form of class-state employs the form-content dis-tinction historically. The claim that the capitalist state has geographical form and bureaucratic form applies to all historical phases of the capitalist state. But there is a common ground between Marx's use of form in the historical sense and the way form is used in the chapter: what is referred to as form is more

DOI: 10.4324/9781351168007-10

concrete than the object of whose form is in question. This is in the following specific sense: while all capitalist states serve the capitalist class, their particular geographical forms and the extent to which they are bureaucratic will
vary. While social relations/processes/objects necessarily have spatial forms, the
actual causal significance of the latter will depend on the processes/relations/
objects in question (Sayer, 1985). And, in terms of causal priority, it is the social
relations and, more specifically, class relations that have priority over their spatial forms (Das, 2017b).

In Section 1, I discuss the geographical form of the state, including the
scale division of labour within the state between more local and more central branches of the state. The local branches of the state are said to be more
accessible to common people. Section 2 discusses the bureaucratic form – the
question of bureaucratism and how the latter is a form of domination over
common people.

1 Geographical forms of the state and capitalist accumulation

As we have seen, the state is rooted in economic relations. Economic relations
not only include economic development but also the geography of economic
development. Engels says: 'The economic relations comprise . . . the *geographical basis* on which they operate and those remnants of earlier stages of economic
development which have actually been transmitted and have survived – often
only as a result of tradition or inertia', the remnants that combine with modern
features to produce combined development (more on this in Chapter 11). Economic relations comprise 'also the external milieu which surrounds this form
of society' (in Marx and Engels, 1975: 441) and thus refer to the fact that what
happens in a place/country can only be adequately understood in terms of its
relations to other places/countries. This fact points to the matter of geographical scale too: if the state and capital in Canada are what they are because of
their relations to those in India, the US, and many others, and vice versa, then
Canada or the US belongs to one scale (say, the national scale) on top of which
sits a higher scale, where all the different countries exist (say, the global scale).
This is the mighty independent scale of the world-market.

If economic development processes are geographical, so is the state geographical. It is geographical in many ways. One is that its rules, more or less,
operate within a specific territory. It has always been the case:

> In contrast to the old gentile organization, the state is distinguished firstly
> by the grouping of its members on a territorial basis. The old gentile bod-
> ies, formed and held together by ties of blood, had . . . become inadequate
> largely because they presupposed that the gentile members were bound to
> one particular locality, whereas this had long ago ceased to be the case. The
> territory was still there, but the people had become mobile. The territorial
> division was therefore taken as the starting point and the system introduced

by which citizens exercised their public rights and duties where they took up residence, without regard to gens or tribe. This organization of the citizens of the state according to domicile is common to all states.

(Engels, 1884)

The state is also geographical or territorial in an 'imperial sense': a given state exists as one of many states, some more powerful than others. This means that individual states seek to improve their competitive position – competitive position of economic actors under their jurisdiction – vis-à-vis other states.

To the extent that the state is a relation expressed as things, their presence is etched in the landscape ('state-space'): police stations, prisons, army headquarters and barracks, court houses, government buildings, border fences, memorials celebrating wars, and so on, which are often built at great expenses even while the state says it has little money for the masses.[3] There are also state-funded universities and radio/TV stations as parts of the state-space. The state-space serves to intimidate, and gain consent from, the masses.

An important geographical aspect of the state is its scalarity. The *scale* of the territorial reach of the state, or of the state's interaction with, and penetration into, society, has expanded over time, which corresponds to the scaling up of capitalist accumulation and development of technologies of transportation, communication, and surveillance. Lenin (1919a) says that

society and the state were [earlier] . . . on a much smaller scale than they are now, they possessed incomparably poorer means of communication – Mountains, rivers and seas were immeasurably greater obstacles than they are now, and the state took shape within far narrower geographical boundaries. A technically weak state apparatus served a state confined within relatively narrow boundaries and with a narrow range of action.

Capitalist accumulation is subject to mobility and fixity. This has implications for the state. More than pre-capitalist societies, it is the capitalist society that actively produces space through the annihilation of distance, and in this process the state plays a very important role as we have seen (consider state investment in physical infrastructures). Yet, no matter how mobile capital is, capitalist interests possess an element of place-specificity and fixity. One part of capital is more fixed than mobile. Money capital tends to be more mobile than productive capital. Resource-based productive capital tends to be less mobile than other forms of productive capital. Capital not only has to make a profit. Profit has also to be made here as opposed to there. Capitalism requires commodity exchanges, and these exchanges happen within, and across, specific territories. The state has to support not only profitability but profitability in particular places. This is expressed in the territorial aspects of the state (see Brenner, 1998, 1999; Clark and Dear, 1984; Harvey, 1985; Slater, 1989).

State power exists at multiple scales. In the history of class society, 'there is nothing inherently privileged about the national scale as a spatial unit of political organisation' (Smith, 2006: 190). In the past, and especially in the pre-capitalist times, the state took the form of 'city states and kingdoms, duchies and provinces, shires and cantons, and the like' (ibid.). In fact, the national division of the globe is very much the twin of capitalism's globalizing (universalizing) ambition as 'it performed a crucial yet very specific function in the evolution of capitalism' (Smith, 2006: 190). Just as social relations of capitalism act as a fetter on the development of productive forces, similarly, with the expansion of the scale of capital accumulation beyond geographically circumscribed localities, 'the inherited political and territorial units of social, cultural and military organisation' (that is, local-scale form of state power), are 'no longer capable of administering economics that [have] outstripped old boundaries' (ibid.). This is in the sense that

> [t]he expanded scale of economic power required expanded polities for helping to organise the process of capital accumulation, and it fell to emergent national states to create a new geography of more or less homogenous conditions internally – labour and tax laws, transportation systems, media, systems of social reproduction, state subsidy of capital, etc. The national state effectively organised a solution to the inherent contradiction between the need for socio-economic cooperation on the one side and economic competition, now implanted at the centre of the global economy, on the other.
>
> (Smith, 2006: 190–1)

Or Harvey has explained:

> The more the bourgeoisie lost control over urban centers, the more it asserted the dominant role of the nation state. It reinforced the authority of the spaces it could control over the places it could not. This was the political lesson that the bourgeoisie learned from the rise of the industrial city as a powerhouse of accumulation and a crucible of class struggle.
>
> (Harvey, 1985: 200–1)

'Politically, this meant increasing ruling-class reliance upon national and, ultimately, international power sources and the gradual reduction of the sphere of relative autonomy of urban-based class alliances' (ibid.). State power under capitalism exists at national and global scales as well as sub-national scales.

From the standpoint of state power, the national scale remains the most important scale in part because of the concentration of the coercive state power at the national scale (and the ideological force of nationalism), while the *world economy* is ultimately the most important scale from the standpoint of capitalist accumulation and the law of value which constrains the operation of the nation-state. (This scalar difference that is characteristic of capitalism means that as capitalist accumulation has increasingly transcended the national scale and has become more global, there has arisen a contradiction between global-scale capitalist accumulation and its nation-state-based political framework.)

Corresponding to the scale of the capitalist world economy, its 'specific political form' is 'the modern *system of nation states*' (Barker, 2006: 83). Hirsch and Kannankulam (2011: 14) say that 'the plurality of states is . . . an essential precondition for the reproduction and existence of modern capitalism'. Or, as Davidson (2016) says, competitive accumulation based on wage labour needs multiple states for different reasons. One is 'the need for capitals to be territorially aggregated for competitive purposes', as capitalist accumulation within self-contained isolated localities is not competitive (ibid.: 219–20). Another is 'the need for that territory to have an ideological basis – nationalism – that can be used to bind the working class to the state and hence to capital' (ibid.: 220). Capitalist competition has winners and losers. This fact has a geography: a winner may be in one country and a loser in another, because of uneven capitalist development at the international scale. This partly explains why 'the capitalist class in its constituent parts continues to retain territorial home bases, presided over by states': capitalists need the state 'to ensure that the effects of competition are experienced as far as possible by someone else' (ibid.).

> A global state could not do this. Indeed, in this respect it would be the same as having no state at all. For if everyone is protected, then no one is: unrestricted market relations would prevail, with all the risks that entails. The state . . . has to be able to distinguish between those capitals who will receive its protection and support, and those who will not.
>
> (Davidson, 2016: 220)[4]

And the latter means there are borders between states which need to be policed.[5]

It is also important to recognize that the multiplicity of states does not mean that all states are equally powerful. Imperialist states are a lot more powerful than other states, and this fact is an important aspect of the geographical form of the capitalist state, a form that in turn contributes to the reproduction of capitalism-under-imperialism. As the early Harvey (2012: 278), who took imperialism more seriously than he does now, puts it eloquently:

> In response to the organized power of labor within its borders, a particular nation-state may seek to export the worst elements of capitalist exploitation through imperialist domination of other countries. Imperialist domination has other functions also: facilitating capital export, preserving markets, maintaining access to an industrial reserve army, and the like. By these means a nation-state may purchase the allegiance of elements of the working class within its borders at the expense of labor in dependent countries.

It is important to stress that while state and capital interact universally, one capitalist state is not the same as another. Each state develops uniquely in relation to combined and uneven development within a national territory: nature of pre- and non-capitalist class relations, the balance between formal and real subsumption of labour by capital, and social (racial/gender) oppression and its relation to capitalism, and the degree to which and ways in which one country, including its various regions, is linked to other countries and to the world market. States are also different one from another because their territorial jurisdictions are different in terms of the balance among productive and non-productive forms of capital, balance among capitals in different sectors, the level of economic development, the level of cultural development (e.g. literacy), the previous history of state-capital interaction, history of common people's struggle, and the extent to which there is a relationship between capitalists and state personnel, that needs a lot of time to develop and is not geographically portable.

With the emergence of a world capitalist system along with transnational capitalist operations, the nation-state has not gone away, but some of its functions are scaled up or scaled down. This means that some of its tasks are performed more by sub-national institutions of the state, and other tasks are performed more by state or state-like institutions at the global scale constituting what Picciotto and Radice call a new state.[6]

The 'increasing scalarization' of state power – the fact that this power is increasingly exercised at extra-local scales – does not mean that state-society relation at a local scale has lost all its importance. The multiplicity of what can be called state-scales represents tendencies towards scalar decentralization and scalar concentration:

> Although the making of the national scale thus played a pivotal role in the early evolution of capitalism, it is not unique in proffering territorial solutions to the political economic contradictions between competition and cooperation, differentiation and equalisation, in capitalist societies. Parallel processes operate at other scales, equally if differently embedded in and transformed by the needs of capital accumulation. Across history, the urban scale has provided various social functions, centralising not just economic but military, religious, cultural and political power.
>
> (Smith, 2006: 191)

The urbanization of capital makes the urban scale, which may be defined in terms of an urban labour market (or what Harvey calls 'structured coherence'), an important scale (Harvey, 1985). Closely related to the urban scale is what I would call the city-region which includes a city and its surrounding rural or semi-rural areas. This scale, which is an important subnational scale, is where most of the *everyday* interaction happens in dominantly urban or even urbanizing societies. This represents the gradual expansion of urban capitalist accumulation into non-urban or semi-urban areas not only through real-estate development on the basis of the conversation of farm-land, but also what Lenin (1899) calls 'the transplantation of large-scale capitalist industry to the rural districts'. The city-region (or the urban scale) scale is where capitalist accumulation happens and labour power is reproduced. This is also where the exercise of state power is effected and experienced by people, as the state shapes both accumulation of capitalist wealth and reproduction of labour power. This is also the scale where labour resistance to capital and the state begins to form and tends to be concentrated. Not surprisingly, apart from the national borders, the city-region is where the coercive powers of the state are concentrated, as seen in its landscape. Indeed, specific parts of the city-region are devoted to the police and military apparatus of the state to protect the seats of capital and of state power against not only the urban working class, including recent rural-urban migrants, but also a potentially angry bloc of rural small-scale producers and workers waiting at the city border and beyond, a bloc which can be part of a politically explosive alliance with the urban working class.

There is a scale division of labour within the nation-state. This is indicated by the division of responsibilities between central/national organs and more regional/local branches (Cox, 2002: 250–1) which operate within a nested hierarchy.[7] Legislators commonly represent territorially defined populations (ibid.). More local branches (e.g. provincial and sub-provincial branches) can be more accessible to common people than the central branch. Some capitalist states are unitary states and other states are federal: Unitary states (e.g. the UK) and federal states (e.g. the US, India) are different in terms of the scale division of labour, although there is growing concentration of power in the central branches of the state and in the hands of the 'chief executive'.[8] At a given scale, state policies (e.g. minimum wage policy, or unemployment insurance policy) can geographically vary in part because of the specificity of state institutions in different city-regions/provinces. Such variation creates a geography of business climate and thus an important reason for capital mobility within the jurisdiction of, say, the national state.

Given that common people put pressure on the state and on capitalists for concessions and given that the state (as well as) capitalism operates at the local scale (as well as higher scales), it is important that we do not lose sight of the localness of social relations and class struggle. However, a distinction is to be made between 'spaces of dependence' and 'spaces of engagement' (Cox, 1998): '[I]n evaluating the strategies of individual agents and their organizations, as they construct the networks through which they hope to accomplish their ends, the spatial structure of the state, its scale division of labor, is an important consideration' (p. 15). The scales at which class struggle happens does not necessarily match the scales at which the state power is exercised. Locally dependent workers (workers living in a city) can make use of provincial and national-level political resources in their local struggles against the state and capital.

Capital does not just lobby for specific state policies but policies that benefit capitalist interests in *particular* places/cities, regions, and nations. Locally dependent or nationally dependent businesses may want protection from competition from capitalists located elsewhere. A given law may disadvantage or favour (some) businesses in region *x* as opposed to region *y*. If some firms are relocating from high-wage to low-wage areas, the more locally dependent firms (retailers, banks, utility companies, and so on) may want some intervention: they may want a more uniform national-scale law in support of workers (e.g. minimum wage law) rather than the laws according to which support for workers comes from the revenues from local jurisdictions. Sometimes fractions of labour and of capital of a given area come together for state support, and they do so in opposition to other such regionally based cross-class coalitions (Harvey, 1985; Cox, 1998).

State policies at a given scale (policies of the local state or provincial state) have territorial impacts (Duncan and Goodwin, 1987). For example, the state divides an area into various land use zones. It also establishes various geographically delimited, or territorialized, use-values for collective consumption such as national and local parks. Capitalism is known to produce uneven development at all scales (for example, uneven development between cities/city-regions and between provinces) in part due to the dialectic of geographical concentration of investment in some areas at the expense of other areas (causing differentiation) and the opposite process of equalization (movement of investment across areas) (Das, 2017b; Smith, 2008; Harvey, 2009). Under capitalism, at a given point in time, some areas become more developed than other areas; some areas are more profitable than other areas. Given the role of the state in assisting capitalist accumulation, state institutions at a given scale seek to attract businesses into their jurisdictions. The state provides special benefits to relatively less developed areas to attract capital – for example, 'opportunity zones' in the US, discussed earlier. The state also seeks to attract investment to special economic zones, which suggests that not all laws apply equally to all the areas inside the jurisdiction of the state. Consider the offshore centres: their existence suggests that 'a sovereign state offers foreign investors the ability to act economically on its territory under legal conditions that differ from those that apply to its own citizens', an offer that 'consists in a renunciation of the universality of law in the state territory' (Gerstenberger, 2009: 684). And 'in terms of state theory, it has made a fiction of the principle that the laws of a particular country apply to its territory [equally]. This has side-effects on the prospects for labour struggles' (ibid.: 684). In fact, the usual laws protecting trade unions rights do not apply in these offshore centres or special enterprise zones, which have 'greatly accelerated the international dynamic of deregulation' of businesses.

Capitalism is known for uneven and combined development (discussed in Chapter 11). Often uneven development gives rise to what is known as internal colonialism: areas and peoples (wage workers and small-scale producers) are politically prevented from being able to sell their labour power and other commodities at the market rate and are thus subjected to above-average exploitation. This happens in the interests of specific fractions of the capitalist class that control state power, often justified on the basis of its ethnicity, and so on.

2 Bureaucratic state form and political domination by the state

When Lenin (1919a) talks about a 'technically weak state apparatus' that operates 'within relatively narrow boundaries and with a narrow range of action', he appears to hint at what Michael Mann (2012: 13)) would call infrastructural power which is to be distinguished from despotic power:

> Despotic power is the ability of state elites to make arbitrary decisions without consultation with the representatives of major civil society groups. Infrastructural power is the capacity of a state (whether despotic or democratic) to actually penetrate society and implement logistically political decisions throughout the realm. . . . 'Infrastructural power' enables states to diffuse their power through or penetrate their societies ('power through'); while the exercise of 'despotic power' is by a state which has a degree of authoritative 'power over' society.

The implication of this is that 'states may be "strong" in either of two quite different ways'. That is, 'states can command anything they like of their citizens (despotic power) or they can actually get decisions implemented across their territories (infrastructural power)' (Mann, 2012: 13).

To say that the state exercises despotic and infrastructural power is to raise the issue of the agency that exercises these powers on behalf of the state. It is the (civilian and military) bureaucracy that exercises both forms of state power. As we have seen earlier, as a structure of relations, the state itself has a degree of autonomy, and state officials and politicians as bearers of that structure have their own autonomy. This autonomy exists within limits that are set by the fact that the state must look after the common interests of the exploiting class (and of society at large). Of course, the actual degree of autonomy enjoyed varies from one state to another. Indeed, it can also vary within the territorial jurisdiction of a nation-state across policy areas because of state's own organizational features.[9] It can also vary across regions within a country.

Bureaucratism is the trait of the state's bureaucratic form. It has several aspects, including red tapism that the bourgeoisie hates if it is a barrier to its freedom to make money.[10] Here I wish to emphasize bureaucratism as bureaucratic oppression of the masses, which compounds class-based oppression and exploitation. Bureaucratism – extreme form of the exercise of power of unelected officials (as well as the politicians with executive functions) over the masses – exists for various reasons.

Poverty and politics of workers and small-scale producers

Given the poverty and lack of (functional) education of workers and small-scale producers, there is a lack of adequate participation on their part.[11] 'Under capitalism, democracy is restricted, cramped, curtailed, mutilated by all the conditions of wage slavery, and the poverty and misery of the people' (Lenin, 1949). This causes bureaucratism within the state (and not just within the state).

Poverty of the masses is a part of a larger issue – inequality and scarcity of necessaries. The latter create a condition for bureaucratism which, in turn, stifles participation of the masses:

> The basis of bureaucratic rule is the poverty of society in objects of consumption, with the resulting struggle of each against all. When there is enough goods in a store, the purchasers can come whenever they want to. When there is little goods, the purchasers are compelled to stand in line. When the lines are very long, it is necessary to appoint a policeman [or some such state regulator] to keep order.
>
> (Trotsky, 1991: 96)

While, in ordinary times, large segments of the exploited class fail to actively participate in the affairs of the state thus contributing to bureaucratism within the state, that does not mean that the working class is never politically active. Advanced sections of the working class do remain politically engaged (pulling other sections behind them). This contributes to the emergence of working-class parties. As these parties enter the parliament, indicating a widening of the basis for class politics, and as there is increasing concentration and centralization of capital showing a narrower basis for capitalist accumulation, this contradiction between working class politics and capitalist concentration/centralization is resolved in a particular way. That is, the task of ensuring political dominance of the bourgeois class increasingly gets transferred from the parliament to successively higher levels of bureaucracy (Mandel, 1978: 482). This promotes bureaucratism within the state.

No matter what, there is always a possibility of class struggle of the masses. If the state is accessible to *everyone* or to the majority, it cannot perform its function in support of a tiny minority class, the class of exploiters. Bureaucratism is a political technique of keeping the masses under control. Such control is facilitated by the fact that the bureaucrats are *very* different from the masses and have an enormous amount of power. This is especially so in the LDCs which have massive economic and educational inequalities.

The bureaucratic state form does rely on lower classes: it 'provides the upper sections of the peasants, small artisans, tradesmen, and the like with comparatively comfortable, quiet, and respectable jobs raising the holders *above* the people' (Lenin, 1949: 31). But the top officials share, or come from, bourgeois (or large-scale landowner) social-economic background, or share bourgeois ideas/ideals. They often share membership in, or quietly sympathize with, one of the main bourgeois governing parties. Their formal wages, which are many times that an average wage of a (state) worker, are handsomely supplemented by various perks (free housing, servants, cars, and so on). Many get lucrative jobs in business after formal retirement, and that could not be happening without a prior history of pro-business credentials and loyalty. Their social being – high salaries and extremely comfortable living, intermingling and handshaking with capitalists and their allies/hangers-on, is such that they fail to share the world-view of the common people, including those who occupy lower positions within the state. In the US, where the cabinet consists of carefully selected officers and/or politicians, they normally have prior business connections or have credentials as pro-business politicians/officers. This is most recently demonstrated by the Biden Cabinet which is sold as being progressive because it includes women and racialized minorities.[12]

There is not only a massive difference in income and living standards between high-level state actors (officials and politicians) who live like kings and queens, and the men and women who are wage earners or small-scale producers. There are also enormous differences within the state structure: for example, economic and social differences among state employees. Given this, top level state actors

> have the same standard of living, as the big bourgeoisie, so that they are part of the same social and ideological climate. Then come the middle functionaries, the middle officials, who are on the same social level and have the same income as the petty and middle bourgeoisie. And finally, the mass of employees without titles, charwomen, community workers, who very often earn less than factory workers. Their standard of living clearly corresponds to that of the proletariat.
>
> (Mandel, 1969)

Thus, '*[t]he state apparatus is not a homogeneous instrument. It involves a structure that rather closely corresponds to the structure of bourgeois society, with a hierarchy of classes* and identical differences between them' (Mandel, 1969).[13]

Officials, who are 'divorced from the people and standing above the people', have a 'privileged position . . . as organs of state power' (Lenin, 1949: 15).

> 'Having public power and the right to levy taxes,' Engels writes, 'the officials now stand, as organs of society, above society. The free, voluntary respect that was accorded to the organs of the gentile [clan] constitution does not satisfy them, even if they could gain it. . . .' Special laws are enacted proclaiming the sanctity and immunity of the officials.
>
> (Lenin, 1949: 15)

That is how ' "[t]he shabbiest police servant" has more "authority" than the representative of the clan' (Engels in Lenin, 1949: 15).

It should also be noted that class struggle is partially 'present' within the state. A large part of the state is occupied by men and women who belong to working class and peasant background. Majority of state workers (here I am excluding those in the police and the army) are like the proletarians in the private sector: they have little control over their working life, and their wages are barely enough for their survival. Given the consequent class contradictions within state (top-level officers being in favour of the capitalist class versus lower-level officers who may sympathize with workers), there is a need for strict control over the latter. Bureaucratism serves this function.

Need for bureaucratic expertise

Managing the common affairs of the capitalist class and therefore of the state requires expertise. It is a different kind of work than the work of controlling/managing a capitalist company or indeed a political party. The state is partly 'an intellectual enterprise which draws upon the . . . skills of state officials to formulate policy goals and to administer, implement, and enforce those goals' (Barrow, 1993: 131–2). Enormous extension of state activities means that the politicians who come and go cannot understand the full significance of new interventions, so this work is done by permanent administration (Mandel, 1978: 490). Top state actors as part of permanent administration are therefore carefully chosen. In many countries, they are selected on the basis of competitive examinations. The more difficult it is to secure a top bureaucrat job (as in India or Japan), the more prestigious is the job – and the position – considered to be. The ways in which state actors are recruited – and this is an important part of state's bureaucratic form – shape how it performs its functions in relation to the two basic classes. State officials need to have a high level of education, and this means that common people are excluded from entering the decision-making layers of the state. Mandel (1969) writes:

> You have to have certain degrees, you have to have taken certain courses, to apply for certain positions, especially important positions. Such a system excludes a huge number of people who were not able to get a university education or its equivalent, because equality of educational opportunity doesn't really exist. Even if the civil service examination system is democratic on the surface, it is also a selective instrument.

Such a structure causes bureaucratism which is a source of oppression of the masses, who rely on the varying levels of financial support from the state, which is actually delivered by state actors. Such oppression is partly independent of the exploitation/oppression to which capitalism subjects the masses to. Bureaucratism is indeed a massive and sharp tool to keep the masses under control. It is rooted in class relations (even if it cannot be reduced to those relations). Autonomous power of state actors is a result of the autonomy of state power, and state's power is fundamentally rooted in the fact that it is a class institution, that is, that it must subjugate the workers and small-scale producers in order to defend the fundamental interests of the exploiting class. This idea can be expressed as follows:

Class power → state power → state actors' power over the masses = bureaucratism.

3 Summary, and theoretical and political implications

This chapter is focused on state form. It begins with the geographical form of the state, including the scale division of labour within the state between more local and more central branches of the state. It then turns to the bureaucratic form (the question of bureaucratism and how the latter is a form of domination over common people).

As we have seen in Chapter 7, at a concrete level, capitalism does impose constraints on the state. And this constraint can be reinforced due to the geographical form of the state. Just as capital exists in the forms of many capitals in a given region/country, so global capitalism exists in the form of many political jurisdictions across and within countries: this means that not only are there many nation-states, but also are there many 'national working classes' into which the nation-state system of global capitalism splits the global working class (even if in reality, the working class has no nation). 'In each national jurisdiction, the employment and welfare of the labor force depends on the profitability of each labor force in competition with all other labor forces on a world-market scale', the profitability that the state must ensure which is why: 'the political state is invariably a "planner" for the global competitiveness of "its" national labor force' (Bonefeld, 2021: 182). A similar process is at play at sub-national scales too.

The state is increasingly caught between the need to serve capitalist accumulation and the need to meet the needs of the masses. The state, of course, will attend to the former. This tends to create 'national state forms that are "fortress states" prone to using repressive measures to protect capital accumulation against democratic popular demands for protective regulations and social welfare provision' (Barrow, 2021: 174). And when a strong socialist movement is absent, 'fascism and dictatorship are now ever-present tendencies of the capitalist state, rather than exceptional circumstances, as once thought' (ibid.).

The geographical form of the state has several political implications for the masses. In bourgeois democracy, an electoral constituency is multi-class: there are workers and various kinds of property owners all combined into a constituency, and there are no class-based constituencies.[14] This fact is a barrier to workers and small-scale producers expressing their political choice and electing their own leaders. The state – or the ruling party – can resort to gerrymandering in order to blunt any potential class or 'class-like' polarization in terms of the division between politically progressive voters and politically conservative voters.[15] The bicameral system can check popular sovereignty.[16] In addition, territoriality of the state allows capital to weaken the working class and pro-worker interventions: capital plays state institutions of one city or province/region against those of another to extract concessions. Thus, state's territorial form becomes a terrain for the operation of the competitive logic of capital. Given the differences in working-class strength across cities and regions within a country, capital plays workers from one jurisdiction against those from others by threatening to move and/or by actually moving. Besides, the scalar division of labour allows the state itself to resort to spatial fix – or a scalar fix: to explain away its failure to meet the needs of the people (e.g. failure to deal with the pandemic or alleviate poverty), the central state blames it on regional/ provincial state institutions, and the latter on the former. As a result, the territoriality of the state form helps the state to hide the main cause of its failure which is, more or less, the fact that it must serve the needs of capitalists at the expense of those of the masses. What is ultimately a class relation mediated by the state becomes a matter of the relation between state institutions at different geographical scales.

While the state does many things, including for the common people, the way in which it does things is generally bureaucratic. Direct participation of the people in the affairs of the state does not usually happen. This is not an accident. If everyone is involved in the running of the state, as Lenin says, the state can*not* serve the interests of a tiny minority. So the bureaucratic form of the state[17] and the fact that state is fundamentally undemocratic while appearing to be democratic are connected. Marx (1871a: 23) indeed described the French state of his time in his *Civil War in France* as 'the centralized state power, with its ubiquitous organs of standing army, police, bureaucracy, clergy, and judicature – organs wrought after the plan of a systematic and hierarchic division of labor', a power that suffocates the social-cultural life of common people.

The state does many things for society as a whole and for the masses. It builds schools, universities, and hospitals. It constructs roads, railways, and electricity-generating plants. It builds the internet infrastructure. Marx, in fact, mocked those – the indifferentists – who thought that fighting for such things as state-funded education was too reformist an act. Marx said the following impersonating the indifferentists:

> Workers should even less desire that, as happens in the United States of America, the state whose budget is swollen by what is taken from the working class should be obliged to give primary education to the workers' children; for primary education is not complete education. It is better that working men and working women should not be able to read or write or do sums than that they should receive education from a teacher in a school run by the state.
>
> (Marx, 1873)

Yet there is a catch. There is something concealed behind such state functions and indeed behind any theoretical claim that show euphoric enthusiasm for such functions. We need to think about state form which reacts back on state function. David McNally (2019) says that according to Marx the state severs state's functioning, including pro-people actions, 'from the common interests of the people – *alienating* them from the people by ensconcing them in the hands of the state bureaucracy'. As a result, as Marx says,

> Every *common* interest was straightaway severed from society, counterposed to it as a higher, *general* interest, snatched from the activity of society's

members themselves and made an object of government activity, from a bridge, a schoolhouse and the communal property of the village community to the railways, the national wealth and the national university of France.

(in McNally, 2019)

That does not mean, of course, that 'Marx wants to "smash" railways and schools, provided by the state. But it does follow that dismantling the bureaucratic-military state involves *transforming* all state institutions into genuinely public ones' (ibid.). This involves the question about state form, once again.

The state form – the form of the content of state–society relation – is designed to exclude direct participation of the masses in their common affairs. Many pro-poor policies (e.g. policies that aim to distribute land to the peasantry, or provide employment to the workers) often fail because state funds and state functioning are captured by state actors and by affluent property owners, and consequently, the masses have no role in the implementation of these policies. The general point is that no matter how democratic the state is, no matter how many opportunities it provides for struggles by the masses, its form problematizes its function in the interests of the masses. That is partly why 'the working class cannot simply lay hold of the ready-made state machinery, and wield it for its own purposes' (Marx, 1871a: 23).

Notes

1 There are many other examples of the form-content distinction in *Capital 1*:

'the capitalist regime [is not to be] looked upon as the absolutely final form of social production' (p. 11); 'The value-form of commodities, money, is . . . now the end and aim of a sale' (p. 88); 'The first distinction we notice between money that is money only, and money that is capital, is nothing more than a difference in their form of circulation' (p. 104); 'Wages by the piece are nothing else than a converted form of wages by time, just as wages by time are a converted form of the value or price of labour-power' (p. 390); 'Variable capital is . . . only a particular historical form of appearance of the fund for providing the necessaries of life'. (p. 402)

2 Wright (1985: 296–297) says: '[L]iberal bourgeois democracies, fascist dictatorships, military juntas, social-democratic welfare states, and so on . . . all of these diverse forms of the state can be subsumed under the more general concept of the capitalist state.' Wright continues:

This aggregation process has the effect of transforming the concepts of each of the specific forms of the state being aggregated, for they are no longer defined solely in terms of formal political institutional characteristics, but in terms of their class character as well.

(ibid.)

Wright appears to be sceptical of the class basis of aggregation, when he says that '[o]f course, it goes without saying that this claim may be incorrect' and that all these different state forms 'may have no distinctive or common class character' (ibid.). I will defend and elaborate on such a class-based analysis of state forms.

3 Consider the construction of a new parliament building, a new prime minister's residence, and other such buildings in Delhi, India, as a part of central vista project, at a great cost during the ongoing pandemic while the state spends limited resources to prevent avoidable deaths and illness.

4 'Yet, curiously, neither Marx nor Engels seems ever to have explored the implications of this elementary fact. . . . Both tended to write about "the state" in the singular, and not about the relations *between* states' (ibid.), although on occasions Marx (1875) does talk about the multiplicity of states: '[T]he "present-day state" changes with a country's frontier. It is different in the Prusso-German Empire from what it is in Switzerland, and different in England from what it is in the United States. The 'present-day state' is therefore a fiction.' Marx hastens to add:

> Nevertheless, the various states of the different civilized countries, in spite of their motley diversity of form, all have this in common: that they are based on modern bourgeois society, only one more or less capitalistically developed. They have, therefore, also certain essential characteristics in common. In this sense, it is possible to speak of the 'present-day state'.

While I use 'the state' in the singular, I do recognize that at a concrete level the nature and functioning of the state varies across national boundaries. As Greg Albo says:

> In an international conjuncture with deep linkages between the advanced capitalist countries and in which national policy regimes appear to be diverging, it is all the more important to focus on any comparative institutional differences between the state in Canada and that in other advanced capitalist societies.
>
> (Albo and Jenson, 1989: 206)

William Robinson (2004) claims that a global capitalist state is in the process of coming into being through existing transnational state apparatuses, a process that corresponds to the rise of transnational capitalism and a transnational capitalist class.

5 'Sovereignty consists not only in a claim to authority over a state's subjects, but also in the maintenance of 'sovereign borders' (ibid.).

6

> The new state form will consist of transnational federations such as the European Economic Community, international parastatals such as the World Bank and the International Monetary Fund, international cooperative councils such as the Group of 7 and the Organization of Economic Cooperation and Development, and, finally, multinational private policy groups such as the Trilateral Commission. At the same time, the new state form will provide a framework in which to rationalize existing state structures by facilitating the coordination of functions between dominant capitalist states and by avoiding conflict between large blocs of multinational capital that are still nation-based. (in Barrow, 1993: 84)

7 As Cox says, local and central branches of the state internalize one another, and local branches are what they are by virtue of their relation to the central-level state institutions (Cox, 2018).

8 In India, the legislative tasks of the state fall in three categories: Union list (central government list), state list, and the concurrent list (which includes items on which both the central government and provincial governments can formulate laws). Often, the central government encroaches on the legislative jurisdiction of provincial governments, which is a sign of the concentration of power within the state that the big business demands.

9 These include 'patterns of centralization, elite recruitment, bureaucratic expertise, and ideological orientation' which 'may vary widely between policy sectors and even across subsectors' (Barrow, 1993: 134).

10 Red tapism refers to the fact that capitalists are subjected to certain regulation by the bureaucracy, and this often happens in order to reduce the amount of anarchy caused

by inter-capitalist competition and thus to ensure smoother operation of the capitalist market.

11 Whether in popular dramas or during everyday conversations with common people, one can hear this sort of statements: 'Having to look for roti [bread], kapda [clothes] and makaan [accommodation], we have little time for protesting against those who take away our rights'.

12 One might offer a few examples from the US under Biden (London, 2020):

> Avril Haines, a former CIA deputy director, is the first woman director of national intelligence. Haines was an architect of the Obama administration's drone assassination program, which killed thousands of impoverished Africans, Arabs and Central Asians, with no attention to the victims' gender. Janet Yellen is the first woman treasury secretary, after having helped implement the quantitative easing policy that transferred tens of billions of dollars to the banks on a monthly basis during the Bush and Obama administrations, while providing no support for millions of foreclosure victims. Linda Thomas-Greenfield, an African American, is the ambassador to the United Nations. Thomas-Greenfield worked in the State Department to help American oil and mining corporations extract resources from the world's most impoverished countries. Antony Blinken is the secretary of state. He helped orchestrate the wars in Syria, Libya and Yemen. He was a partner at a private equity firm and co-founded WestExec Advisors, which works with Israeli intelligence and helped develop Google's censorship tools.

And so on.

13

> [T]he participation of private individuals in state activities does not in fact shield those individuals from the class distinctions that constitute civil society. Instead, the individuals enter into political life with those class distinctions: 'The *class distinctions* of civil society thus become established as political distinctions [Marx]'. (Adam, 2010)

14 In fact, there is identity politics here too, as in India, where some constituencies are reserved for women or for low castes or for indigenous communities, but there is no working-class-only or peasants-only constituency.

15 This means re-drawing the boundary of an electoral constituency in order to reduce the importance of more politically progressive voters from one area by combining them with conservative voters from another (for example, some rural voters and some urban voters).

16 Consider how India's fascistic BJP rammed through anti-farmer laws in the Higher house of the parliament whose representatives are not directly elected.

17 This can sometimes adversely affect capitalists which is why they complain about red tapism.

11 Capitalism, imperialism, and the state in the global periphery

Marx (1887: 207) says in *Capital 1*: 'The nature of capital remains the same in its developed as it is in its undeveloped forms.' This means that at a fundamental level and at an international scale, class relations of advanced capitalism and those of the capitalist periphery (LDCs) must be similar. Partly because of this, the analysis of the state in the abstract and in the context of the advanced capitalist countries (as conducted in Chapters 4–10), more or less, applies to the state in the periphery. Yet periphery's class relations and economic development have certain specificities because of which the peripheral capitalist state cannot be exactly like the state under advanced capitalism.[1]

According to Marx's *Capital 1*, capitalism develops in historical stages. The first is the formal subsumption of labour (FSL), where labour is exploited on the basis of the appropriation of absolute surplus value, and capitalism is characterized by a relatively low level of the development of productive forces. The second is the real subsumption of labour (RSL), where capitalists resort to a systemic use of labour-productivity-enhancing technical change causing the appropriation of relative surplus value from labour. What if the periphery is characterized by a different kind of capitalism (relative dominance of the FSL) than the one that exists in the advanced countries, and what implication might this have for the state?

And what implication for the state might there be of the following facts: the periphery has a recent colonial past and continues to be impacted by imperialism; it experiences a (relative) under-development of productive forces and a low level of labour productivity; a large majority there do not earn enough to ensure a normal level of bodily reproduction; a large number of people still depend on land-based productive activities some of which are carried on within social relations that are not quite capitalist; and a high proportion of the workforce are small-scale producers in rural and urban areas.[2] Similarly, what implications are there for the state of the fact that the countries in periphery generally do not have the ability to produce the means of production (e.g. tools, machines, and the like) needed to produce the means of consumption and are more dependent on the economies of advanced countries than the latter are on them?[3]

DOI: 10.4324/9781351168007-11

In this chapter, I explore the specificity of the periphery's class structure and draw its implications for the objective pressure on 'the peripheral state' (see Figures 6.1, 7.1, and 7.2). The chapter begins, in Section 1, with a discussion on the extent to which production structure in the periphery is 'auto-centric'. Section 2 examines the specific character of capitalism in the periphery. Section 3 discusses imperialism from the standpoint of the periphery and its state. Sections 4–7 respectively discuss the class–alliance that holds state power, the state in relation to the struggle of the lower classes (proletarians, semi-proletarians, and small-scale producers), and failure of the state to meet their needs, the coercive nature of the peripheral state, and the potential threat to state's legitimacy. The final section concludes the chapter (and the book).

1 Disarticulated development of productive forces in the periphery

In an economy, one sector produces means of consumption, and another sector produces means of production. The latter sector has two sub-sectors: one produces means of production needed to produce consumption goods, and another produces other means of production.[4] 'In order to be auto-centered an economy must contain production at all of these levels and especially at the two highest levels of reproductive importance' which involve the production of the means of production (Ougaard, 1982: 389). In addition, the different sectors and subsectors must be articulated with one another, even if an auto-centred economy does not have to produce all the products in all the three major sectors (ibid.).

In the core, accumulation is autocentric: 'production of capital goods and the production of consumption goods' are articulated with one another, and foreign relations of central economies 'are subject to the requirements of this determinate articulation', and therefore generally 'labor's pay can follow the progress of productivity'[5] (Amin, 2009: 272). In contrast, the peripheral economy tends to be dominated more by the production of consumption goods and less by other types of production. A significant level of production in all the sectors/sub-sectors mentioned earlier is absent in a typical peripheral economy. An industrializing peripheral economy often assembles imported industrial parts, as it happens in many SEZs and Mexican maquiladoras. Or, some countries produce IT support, including in call-centres, for advanced countries. A major part of the periphery's IT industry is actually similar to its manufacturing assembly, where low-paid engineers such as those in India 'develop components or subpackages/assemblies/programmes that go into the final products made and marketed by US companies' (Bidwai, 2003). Bidwai says that 'a good proportion of the sub-programmes in Windows 95 and 98 were developed by Indian engineers. But it's Mr Bill Gates who skimmed off the profits!' (ibid.)

The lack of articulation between the main sectors blocks the periphery's economic development. Such an economy is also extraverted: internal linkages are not stronger than external ones. It remains export-oriented, or its production caters to the local elite (production of goods and services that workers and small-scale producers do not normally consume). Such a production system has, generally, little incentive, or need, to raise wages/income of the masses who are not the consumers of such a system (see Richards, 1986; De Janvry, 1981). Indeed, *distribution* of income/wealth does feed back into the nature of *production* system.

So, apart from the peripheral society where capitalism exists mainly in the sphere of exchange relations, there are two other types of peripheral society from the standpoint of production. In one type, there is capitalist production of consumer goods for the domestic (and foreign) market. This society is 'dependent on the import of means of production for its consumer industry'. Another type of peripheral society 'produces the means of production for its consumer industry' at least to a significant extent, but it is still 'dependent on imports of the means of production for its own producer goods industry' (Ougaard, 1982: 394). And 'since this dependency is located at the highest level of reproductive importance it can be expected to lead to an intensification of the conflicts with foreign capital' (ibid.).

What are the implications of all this for the peripheral state then? The state has a role in facilitating the transition from the first lower level of peripheral economy (capitalism in circulation, export of raw materials) to the form where 'a society can produce the means of production for its producer goods industry' and where this production covers a significant part of the society's needs and is reasonably integrated internally (Ougaard, 1982: 395–6). How well the state plays such a developmental role depends on a number of processes. These include which dominant class or class-strata (e.g. landlords, merchants, domestic capitalists, foreign capitalists, and so on) control state power; whether and to what extent the state can exercise autonomy vis-à-vis mutual competing capitalists and vis-à-vis conflicts between capital-owners and ground-rent receivers (landowners); and how well the state protects its capitalist (and small-scale) production from the globally operating law of value. The developmental state has reflected on some of these processes.[6]

Amin (2009: 273) says that '[i]n the periphery, constant adjustment in economies have to be made in relation to the economies of the core'. So, in the core, '[t]he state . . . fulfils the conditions that make possible autocentric accumulation and the dependence of foreign relations on the logic of that accumulation', but in contrast,

> the peripheral state . . . does not control local accumulation. It is thus objectively, an instrument for the adjustment of the local society to the requirements of globalized accumulation, the tendencies of which are determined by the requirements of the center.
>
> (ibid.)

This difference explains why the central state is a strong state and while the peripheral state is a weak state, says Amin. But to the extent that the periphery lacks economic dynamics associated with auto-centric production, the question is why? We need to turn to the very nature of capitalism in the periphery in terms of class relations and to imperialism as a form of class relation and explore their implications for the peripheral state.

2 Peripheral social formation dominated by 'backward' capitalism[7]

Whether in the global periphery or in the more economically advanced world, a society is capitalist if it is characterized by the dominance of the following features: commodity production, means of production confronting labour as capital, a class of nominally free labourers forced to work for a wage because they do not own sufficient means of production, and operation of the law of value (law of competition based on socially necessary labour time). When such conditions exist, then capitalist relation exists, at least in the sense of FSL. In FSL, lots of workers are hired to work for long hours on an enormous amount of raw materials with limited or little labour-shedding technical change used. There is hardly any place in the world which is not dominated by capitalism at least in this sense. While FSL is based on the appropriation of absolute surplus value, RSL is based on the appropriation of relative surplus value. RSL has all the features of FSL *and* an additional attribute – that is, the systematic tendency towards technical change. Then there is also hybrid subsumption, which is post-feudal and which does not involve wage labour; it involves exploitation by merchants and moneylenders of direct producers (see Das, 2017a: 340–90 for a detailed discussion on the subsumption of labour by capital).

Marx says in the Appendix to *Capital 1*: FSL is 'directly a process of the exploitation of the labour of others. . . . It is the general form of any capitalist production process' (i.e. production process under the rule of capitalist social relation) (Marx, 1977b: 1019). As the more general form of capitalist production, it 'can be found in the absence of the specifically capitalist mode of production', which is RSL for Marx (ibid.). The two forms of subsumption are similar in the sense of the general conditions for capitalism. But a dialectical approach also sees a difference.

Contrary to what Marx might (sometimes) have believed, the transition to RSL is not automatic, even if there *is* a long-term tendency towards the RSL, associated with a rise in the ratio of constant to variable capital (Das, 2017a). To me, the transition from FSL to RSL is contingent on the balance of power between the basis classes, which is expressed in the struggle of workers against the regime of long hours (and low wages). Class struggle (potential or actual) conditions the extent to which capitalists who are competing with one another cut costs of production through (a) the use of technology aimed at increasing labour productivity or (b) for example, FSL. And certain objective conditions can promote or constrain class struggle, and accordingly the transition to RSL can be quicker or be a prolonged process and geographically uneven.

Advanced capitalism is characterized by a successful transition to RSL and the resultant economic dynamism. This transition has been partly possible because of two factors such as colonial transfer, and class struggle against capitalists using labour for long hours and low wages. However, in most parts of the periphery (and especially in its vast rural areas and in small towns), the situation is a little different. There *are* the necessary conditions for capitalist relations. In some areas, property owners may be formally subsuming labour (e.g. capitalists use highly vulnerable and low-cost labour, including labour that is reproduced outside of capitalist reproduction as in indigenous communities).[8] In other areas, especially in selected large cities and villages near them, there do exist real subsumption. The state is connected to both, to the localized existence of RSL and to the obstacles to the transition to it.

Let's begin with localized existence of RSL. Backward countries can adopt technology from already-advanced countries, and this means that

> [t]he development of historically backward nations leads necessarily to a peculiar combination of different stages in the historic process' leading to combined development 'by which we mean a drawing together of the different stages of the journey, a combining of the separate steps, an amalgam of archaic with more contemporary forms.
>
> (Trotsky, 2008: 4–5)

By borrowing technology already developed in an advanced country, a peripheral country can skip some stages in the development process, thus producing combined development:

> The development of backward countries is characterized by its combined character. In other words, the last word of imperialist technology, economics, and politics is combined in these countries with traditional backwardness and primitiveness.
>
> (Trotsky, 1940)

This means that in an LDC, technologically backward 'peasant land-cultivation' can coexist with an industry which 'in its technique and capitalist structure' is 'at the level of the advanced countries', and in certain respects it can even surpass industry in advanced countries (ibid.: 8).

The peripheral capitalist state can be responsible for real subsumption, both by working with, and independently of, imperialism. Partly prompted by the struggles of the masses against low living standards and partly prompted by geopolitical rivalries (sometimes overlain by nationalist chauvinism with religious overtones), and in some cases, to protect their own capitals against imperialist competition (law of value), capitalist states in the periphery can give various forms of assistance to national capitals to introduce modern technologies and to increase labour productivity. This process may signal some kind of transition from formal to real subsumption.

To the extent that technological change in the periphery will create a market for products for the domestic (and foreign) companies and/or will increase relative surplus value, a part of which will be shared by imperialist countries, imperialism may not be inimical to technological change in the periphery. So a fundamental role of the peripheral state can be to mediate technological transfer from imperialist to imperialized countries:

> [O]fficials of the states with a subordinate position in the imperial state system will insist on the transfer of technological, management and marketing knowhow to strengthen the ability of their capitalists to compete and for them to make profit, extract rents and serve their 'national interest.'
>
> (Veltmeyer and Petras, 2015: 168)

There are limits to technical change in the periphery, however. This is partly because of its insertion into the imperialist world market and because of its relatively low level of cultural development (e.g. low level of education) (Trotsky, 2008: 4–5). As we have seen, for Trotsky, it is not just that capitalist development is *uneven* but also that capitalist relations are *combined* with pre-capitalist relations (e.g. serfdom). This is an advance over the perspective that focuses only on the unevenness of capitalist development (Harvey, 2008b/1982; Smith, 2008). Trotsky's perspective, however, has a problem: it homogenizes the capitalist class relation; it treats the different forms (and stages) of capitalism – subsumptions of labour – as one. It thus abstracts from the ways in which the balance of power between the basic classes intervenes in the transition from one form of capitalist class relation (FSL) to another form (RSL). Thus it abstracts from the obstacles to the transition *within* capitalism. In peripheral countries, it is not just that capitalism is combined with pre-capitalist relations existing in specific areas. The matter is more complex than that.

FSL can be a prolonged process when/where there is a massive army of un- and under-employed men and women whom the state does not have adequate support for nor does it do much to diminish the size of the reserve army. It is worth quoting Marx (from *Capital 3*) again: the reserve army or the relative over-population

> is the reason why, on the one hand, the more or less *imperfect* subordination of labour [read: FSL] to capital continues in many branches of production, and continues longer than seems at first glance compatible with the general stage of development. This is due to *the cheapness and abundance of disposable or unemployed wage-labourers*, and to the greater resistance, which some branches of production, by their very nature, render to the transformation of manual work into machine production.
>
> (Marx, 1894: 167; italics added)

This situation, I argue, holds specifically in the periphery, even though Marx did not think about this. In peripheral capitalism, there is a vast industrial reserve army of labour which owes its origin to colonialism and colonial state and is expanding under 'new imperialism' through, for example, primitive accumulation. During classical imperialism (colonialism), as widely known (Bagchi, 1976), a vast reserve army was created through deindustrialization caused by: coercive methods, including tariff on imports from colonies; cheaper machine-made exports to colonized countries; and primitive accumulation (dis-possession of small property owners, including peasants). In some parts of the ex-colonized world, the state actually took steps to break up the communal-type property into private property in order to stop ideas about communal (communist) property from taking root, and Marx commented on this (Anderson, 2010: 219–20). And, under current, 'new imperialism',[9] primitive accumulation is also happening on a big scale, thanks to the extra-economic (state-enabled) dispossession: this has been expanding the reserve army.[10] The reserve army is also expanding because of cheap exports from imperialist countries and lack of financial support from peripheral capitalist states for their relatively weak, small-scale property owners against international competition.

The massive and expanding reserve army of labour (never fully captured by official statistics) provides capital an ample opportunity for FSL, including of those who are oppressed on the basis of gender, race, ethnicity, age, caste, and the like. On the other hand, the reserve army adversely affects the bargaining power of employed labour and makes struggle against formal subsumption rather difficult. Many peripheral countries specialize in relatively low-skilled activities such as farming, mining and production of light industrial goods, as mentioned in the last section. These are potentially the 'branches of production', which 'by their very nature, can render relative resistance 'to the transformation of manual work into machine production' (Marx, 1894: 167).

The sporadic introduction of advanced techniques could strengthen not only the use of serfdom and other forms of extra-economic relations (as Trotsky says), but also relations of FSL that he fails to recognize. To enhance their competitiveness and to appropriate more surplus value, enterprises using advanced technology themselves and/or the small-scale firms they outsource some of their production to can – and do – resort to a regime of long hours (and low wages), just as they can and do use unfree labour. Besides, the peripheral state lacks the resources needed for systemic technological change. One reason for this, apart from colonialism-induced under-development, is the ongoing imperialistic transfer of resources in the form of debt payment, repatriation of profit, and so on from the periphery (Roberts, 2019). The peripheral capitalist state also lacks the resources because it is not allowed by imperialist institutions, which are obsessed with marketization and privatization, to use the resources where they may exist. As a result, it fails to develop the productive forces through technological change to any significant extent and on a nation-wide scale. It also fails to adequately augment the social wage through pro-labour policies in a way in which such policies can substantially increase the power of labour vis-à-vis private employers and enable them to demand a regime of higher wages. Such a regime, within limits, would contribute to an articulation between production and consumption. But the peripheral state fails to secure such a regime.

The system of capitalist class relation in the periphery then is marked by three main forms and logics of accumulation: accumulation by dispossession *of direct producers* (i.e. ongoing primitive accumulation); accumulation by exploitation of workers (proletarians and semi-proletarians), with its two moments of formal and real subsumption; and accumulation by class differentiation (Figure 11.1). These three forms of accumulation coexist with the (remnants of) pre-capitalist class relations and with class relations of hybrid subsumption. And then all these social relations of production are shaped by imperialism (see the next section). These different relations may exist in different areas within a peripheral country or even inside a given city-region, thus indicating uneven and combined development. Given this complexity of class relations, which impact the peripheral state, the latter has a certain specificity relative to the state in advanced capitalism.

An implication of the subsumption perspective is that the development process in the world in general and in peripheral capitalism in particular, with its attendant class relations, must be seen as multiple transitions: from pre-capitalist relations to hybrid subsumption, from pre-capitalist and hybrid relations to FSL under capital, from FSL to RSL, and finally, from the latter to cooperative labour of associated producers, nationally and at a global scale. So the role of the peripheral state must be seen in relation to these transitions. The democratic revolution against pre-capitalist relations has remained aborted or incomplete in the periphery, and this is in part because of capitalists' and their state's fear of anti-feudal struggle becoming the struggle against capitalism and the state. Massive concentration of land in the hands of a few and feudal remnants in the sphere of social relations of production as well as cultural and political spheres exist, which are partly behind undemocratic state practices (these issues are elaborated in Section 6).

3 Imperialism retarding development of productive forces in the periphery

Imperialism today

It is true that the periphery, like the core, is experiencing globalization. But there is a difference: for the periphery, globalization is generally expressed as imperialism. The multiple states system emphasized in the globalization literature is a system where some states are imperialist and other states are imperialized (see Callinicos, 2009). I define imperialism not mainly in terms of the unequal relations in the realm of exchange or in terms of income inequality between rich and poor countries, and so on, nor in terms of the bullying behaviour of rich states, although all these are important. I define imperialism fundamentally as the capitalist class relation at the international scale (i.e. at the level of the world market) supported by the powerful states of advanced countries. Imperialism is the economic exploitation of proletarians and of semi-proletarians (and other small-scale producers) of the peripheral capitalist countries by the monopolistic industrial-financial businesses of advanced countries, whereby the powerful, highly militarized states of advanced capitalist countries subjugate the militarily weak states of peripheral countries to ensure the business interests of the monopolies of advanced countries which are undergoing relative capitalist decay as seen in falling profitability. If the capitalist state, seen from a national angle or in the abstract, secures the general conditions for the capitalist accumulation, then the capitalist state, seen internationally (i.e. from the standpoint of imperialist world market and seen more concretely), secures the general conditions for accumulation of value in the hands of the imperialist businesses.

The imperialist state partly functions as the executive committee for different fractions of imperialist capital operating in the periphery. More accurately, the imperialist state, the state of imperialist countries, along with the various international state-like institutions it controls, is the executive committee for managing the common affairs of the different fractions of imperialist capital that are involved in accumulation within the periphery (and the core countries). The state in the periphery is, more or less, the junior partner of the imperialist state. The state is a fundamental aspect of the imperialist relation (it is surprising that Lenin's (1916) *Imperialism* hardly mentions the state).

Operating globally, the state of advanced countries turns imperialist in order to help its big business. To remain globally competitive and increase its rate of profit, imperialist capital makes use of political-military and diplomatic control over natural resources, markets for its goods and services, and over labour[11] of different LDCs which have militarily and economically weaker states. Imperialist capital also makes use of non-military processes such as ideas and practice of cooperation and assistance. So peripheral societies become the battle ground for inter-imperialist *rivalry*, which can become bloody from time to time. Sometimes even if a peripheral country has nothing to offer (in terms of resources or markets), its location itself could be attractive to imperialism:

> Once the race of imperial territory began in earnest during the closing decades of the nineteenth century, it became necessary for strategic reasons to seize territories that were often of no value in themselves – indeed, that were often net recipients of state expenditure – but that were necessary in order to protect those territories that *were* of economic value.
>
> (Davidson, 2016: 226)

Imperialist mechanisms and the peripheral state

Imperialism, as imperialist-state-enabled world-scale accumulation, is driven by specific mechanisms. These have implications for the peripheral state.

Protection of the capitalist rules of the game: In the global periphery, there is massive poverty which causes seething (molecular) anger against capitalism and imperialism. There can be a danger of the peripheral state weakening capitalist rules of the game. So the imperialist state has to guard the guardians (i.e. peripheral states) in reinforcing/defending the capitalist rules of the game globally and if necessary by creating conflicts among peripheral states and weakening any potential 'solidarity' among them.[12] Indeed, as Wood (2005) has stressed, imperialist power must be exercised to make sure that states and peoples in the periphery, more or less, adhere to the rules of the capitalist market. This implies, among other things, that the ability of the peripheral state to control the market (or value) relations is limited because of imperialism. Even state-mediated redistribution of small amount of land to the poor is sanctioned by imperialist institutions on the ground that it is an infringement of private property, as happened in Zimbabwe.[13]

Response to capitalist decay in advanced capitalism: There is relative stagnation in imperialist countries with falling profitability (long-term fall in the rate of profit). The relative stagnation is seen in the fall in the growth of investment, including in research and development, in the fall in the rate of growth, and so on. Imperialism is fundamentally a manifestation of the decay of capitalism in the advanced countries and not necessarily because of wrong government policies of an advanced country (Lenin, 1916). On behalf of globally operating imperialist businesses, imperialist states seek to use the periphery to alleviate the effects of declining profitability and capitalist decay. They do this in many ways.

Unequal trade: One is that the imperialist states compete with each other to make sure their own monopolies are able to use politically mediated access to the markets and resources of the periphery. Imperialism *is* about inter-imperialist rivalry, even if it is not always manifested:

> The drive to neutralise the breakdown tendency through increased valori-sation takes place at the cost of other capitalist states. The accumulation of capital produces an ever more destructive struggle among capitalist states.
>
> (Grossman, 1929)

In response to the attempt of imperialist states to defend the competitive position of their big business, the peripheral countries may wish to protect their own economies. As Grossman (1929) says, 'accumulation intensifies the drift to protectionism in the economically backward countries'. In this situation, the peripheral state will bear the consequences from the imperialist countries. Military intervention by imperialist states is one. Another is economic warfare: 'the cheap prices of commodities are the heavy artillery with which' an advanced country 'batters down all Chinese walls'. With this mechanism, imperialist countries force the less developed countries' 'intensely obstinate hatred of foreigners to capitulate' (Marx and Engels, 1848: 16).

While the state sustains commodity relations in various ways, it can enforce unequal exchange on behalf of the capitalist class operating under its own jurisdiction, where necessary. Imperialist states enforce unequal exchange in the world market. Colonialism/imperialism is an expression of this tendency. Unequal exchange happens in another way too. Given that c / v is higher in advanced countries than in poorer countries, the states of advanced countries and state-like institutions globally, by sustaining world trade, are actually complicit in the transfer of surplus in the form of 'the tribute levied by finance capital' and 'high monopoly profits for a handful of very rich countries' (Lenin, 1916) – from poor to rich countries. Here is Marx (1863):

> Profit can also be made by cheating, one person gaining what the other loses. Loss and gain within a *single* country cancel each other out. But not so with trade between different countries [peripheral countries, unlike core countries, depend more on unskilled labour]. . . . Here the law of value undergoes essential modification. . . . The relationship between labour days of different countries may be similar to that existing between skilled, complex labour and unskilled simple labour within a country.[14]

In this case, the richer country exploits the poorer one.[15] 'At advanced stages of accumulation', as the rate of profit (and eventually, its mass) drops, 'it becomes more and more difficult to valorise the enormously accumulated capital', and, therefore, transfers of surplus value through trade 'become a matter of life and death for capitalism. This explains the virulence of imperialist expansion in the late stage of capital accumulation' (Grossman, 1929).

An important unequal exchange is trade in agri-goods and natural resources. In the international division of labour, imperialist countries depend on raw materials produced in the periphery, and these must be produced and imported at extremely low prices, and this process in turn checks inflation in the imperialist countries (Patnaik and Patnaik, 2016). More specifically, certain use-values happen to be concentrated in what are peripheral countries. These use-values include crops produced in warmer climates (and these climate happen to be un-available in imperialist countries), oil, and minerals, including those needed for what is misnamed as a post-industrial economy (e.g. lithium needed for cell phones). To these use-values the big businesses of the North must have access at any cost, and this involves imperialist control over LDCs. This has an implication for the state: it is important that the capitalist state and a leading state maintain control over supplies of such scarce materials. To the extent that these tend be in LDCs, role of imperialism is crucial.

A new round of primitive accumulation: An important strategy used by imperialist capital to respond to falling profitability is investing capital not in production but in a new round of primitive accumulation. A lot of capital goes to the periphery to buy up assets, including of small-scale producers and state-owned companies, and if necessary by using its own force and the force of its junior partner (peripheral state) (Harvey, 2005). By forcing the peripheral states to open up their economies, imperialist capital also buys up assets of peripheral business owners, thus symbolizing a new round of centralization of capital at the international scale.

Cheap production: Apart from exploiting the periphery through unequal trade with advanced countries and a new round of primitive accumulation, imperialist capital makes use of cheap labour in the periphery. A massive reserve army allows FSL and production at a cheap cost. Marx (1894) himself says that when capital is invested in the less developed world, the rate of profit is higher there due to backward development, and likewise, because of the use of unfree labour such as 'slaves, coolies, etc.' Imperialist capital makes use of peripheral labour in at least two ways: export of productive capital to the periphery which results in production of goods and services by MNCs, including through joint ventures; and the production of commodities in the periphery through out-sourcing. Outsourcing is a more recent mechanism than capital export. As John Smith (2016) shows, production through outsourcing ensures that a very small part of the sale price of the commodities remains in the periphery with the major part going to the hands of imperialist businesses involved in various parts of the commodity chain including shipping, sale, advertisement, insurance, finance, design, and so on. Whether through direct investment by imperialist businesses in the periphery or through outsourcing, imperialism involves the exploitation of labour of the periphery by imperialist capital. The peripheral state must support this.

Imperialism is the objective condition under which the peripheral state, more or less, must work and reproduce the peripheral social formation not only as capitalist but also as imperialized. In fact, if any state in the periphery ever seeks to promote economic development, whether on the basis of capital-ism or non-capitalist relations or some combination of the two (e.g. China), by regulating the global law of value in its national interest, and if significantly hurts the interests of imperialist economy or politics, then imperialist state knows how to discipline the peripheral state, including through lies and decep-tion as well as coercion (military intervention aimed at regime change), and accusation that given peripheral countries go against the fundamental princi-ples of democracy, free market, freedom, world peace, and so on.

4 Class basis of the peripheral state, and peripheral state functions and form

Broadly speaking, there are two main proprietary classes which hold state power in the periphery. One is the urban bourgeoisie, especially the larger-scale owners of capital operating nationally and increasingly engaged in inter-national operations in part through collaboration with imperialist capital. The other major class is the class of large-scale landholders based in villages and small towns.[16] In this class alliance or power bloc, urban capitalists are not merely dominant but also increasingly so.[17] They demand state policies, includ-ing under both dirigisme and neoliberalism. It is the fundamental role of the

Theorizing peripheral capitalism

1. Capitalism as a class relation based on formal subsumption of labour (FSL) coexisting with subsumption (RSL); historically accumulating reserve army as a factor; islands of transition to RSL

2. Capitalism articulates with non-capitalist modes of production (e.g. remnants of pre-capitalism; petty commodity production)

3. Capitalism's disarticulation between production and consumption; incomplete transition to production of means of production (e.g. machinery); dependence on imperialist economies

4. Capitalist accumulation by dispossession/encroachment; dispossession of small-scale producers; privatization of commons; recommodification; privatization of post-colonial state enterprises

5. Capitalist imperialism impacting the periphery (e.g. surplus transfer directly impacting small-scale producers and wage workers); influence of capitalist decay in imperialist economies on the periphery; capital export and outsourcing from imperialist businesses; low prices for petty producers' products; obstacles to periphery's development

6. Peripheral capitalist state; its complicity in making the periphery a low-wage platform for global capitalist production (general FSL) and a market for global capitalist commodities, through repression and development discourse; executive committee for different fractions of imperialist capital

7. Capitalism is supported by non-capitalist relations (e.g. race, gender, indigenous identity, caste and religious identity, etc.); the non-capitalist relations dividing the bloc of workers and independent producers; 'political unity' (psychological wage) function and 'below-normal wages' function

Figure 11.1 Theorizing peripheral capitalism

Source: Adapted from Das (2017a: 388).

state in the periphery, as it is in the core, to serve the capitalist class.[18] During the initial decades of post-independence dirigisme, such a favourable relationship was often supported by not only the ideology of anti-imperialism but also the ideology of socialism (or socialistic patterns of society). The official names or constitutions of some states include the word 'socialism' or 'socialistic'. These ideologies did inform state practice to some extent as revealed in state regulation of businesses and state protection of domestic business vis-à-vis imperialist businesses until recently. The bureaucrats and politicians running the affairs of the state made use of capitalists' expertise, and the like. Capitalists joined various committees of the state. Capitalists made use of the state. Nothing major has been done to undermine capitalist private property as such. The state firmly protects *capitalist* property rights, not private property rights as such (consider the rights of small-scale producers, including the peasantry, that are being crushed by the state). This is necessary for the capitalist class to enlarge its property-base at the expense of self-exploiting small-scale property owners. To the extent that some nationalization has happened, it has had little to do with socialism. Trotsky's comments on nationalization in Mexico in the early decades of the 20th century have much contemporary relevance:

> The nationalization of railways and oil fields in Mexico has of course nothing in common with socialism. It is a measure of state capitalism in a backward country which in this way seeks to defend itself on the one hand against foreign imperialism and on the other against its own proletariat.
>
> (Trotsky, 1940)

The peripheral state has not only defended capitalist property rights and commodity relations. It has also protected and promoted capitalist profit-making in various ways. Domestic markets have been automatically protected from competition with imperialist capital (although increasingly less so), and state-owned industries have provided cheap capital goods and means of transportation, and state-owned banks continue to heap cheap money or indeed free money (loans given are pardoned) on private businesses. Concentration and centralization of capital have continued. The state has often provided subsidies to the emerging capitalist class or a group of capitalists in trouble, so it has the minimum sum necessary for investment. The state gives contracts to the private sector, helping it resolve its realization crisis. The strategy of locating industries in 'backward' areas (growth poles) in order to promote rural and/or regional development has been crucial: such an initiative has required the state to subsidize private businesses. Private sector companies (as well as public sector companies which have helped the former to grow) have benefited enormously from the huge reserve army of labour in rural and semi-rural areas, which has been kept alive at near-subsistence level through various 'development policies'.

Recently, the neoliberal method of primitive accumulation aided by the state has deposited an enormous quantity of exchange values in capitalist hands. This method includes the sale of public sector companies and privatization of government services (e.g. provisioning of water, education, healthcare, and the like) as well as the take-over of the land/assets of indigenous peoples and other small-scale producers by the urban capitalists at below-market prices.[19] Indeed, in the process, those members of the capitalist class who have enjoyed close relations with influential politicians and bureaucrats have benefited hugely by, for example, receiving state contracts. Such relations are the source of massive corruption and plundering of state resources, a form of primitive accumulation.

In some parts of the periphery, the state has taken on the form of the developmental state, which is obsessed with capitalist economic development. Such a state has to even discipline and coerce specific members of the capitalist class.[20] It typically keeps the workers in check. In the vast majority of cases, however, the state has not played such a developmental role. What Ron Herring (1999) calls 'embedded particularism' (state's links to specific capitalists) has been partly responsible for what he calls 'failed developmental state'. In addition, the world-market conditions favourable for exports, and the world-geopolitical conditions (American state's need to fight the communism threat in East Asia) that facilitated the emergence of developmental state with massive American support in that region, do not exist everywhere and always.

During more recent times, the peripheral state blatantly supports capital, and financial capital, over the interests of common people. About Brazil, Daniel Bin (2014) says that in the mid-1990s, the Brazilian state began removing state resources (tax money) earmarked from education and social security to essentially use them for servicing the public debt to the benefit of finance capital. This practical earmarking for finance was not guaranteed by the Constitution, as it had previously been earmarked for social security or education. This policy was a decision that clearly revealed the class character of the Brazilian state. It would prove to be the first step in granting an important advantage to the finance sector in the class struggle over surplus value transitionally appropriated by the state.

In large peripheral countries, a major component of the power bloc – class basis of the state – is foreign capital, including especially imperialist capital. The imperialist capital has had a relation of collaboration and conflict with 'national' sections of the capitalist class of the periphery. Its influence on the peripheral state, of course, varies geographically across the periphery: it is, traditionally, more in some countries (South America) than in other regions. Foreign capital possesses power based on its economic presence in a poor country: the simple fact of the periphery's economic dependence limits the possible economic and political actions of the nationally operating bourgeoisie (Ougaard, 1982: 401). The power of foreign capital that it actually exercises depends on the political activities of individual enterprises, including on the basis of their organizations operating in the periphery (ibid.). In addition, the exercise of the power of foreign capital in the periphery is based on the relations between the centre-state and the peripheral state and is enormously helped by such international agencies as the World bank, IMF, aid agencies of the advanced capitalist states, foreign embassies, western think-tanks, and so on, which force policy changes such as the expansion of commodification and privatization of state-owned companies (ibid.).[21]

The rural landholding families constitute another part of the power bloc or the class alliance that controls state power, and once again, its importance, like that of imperialist capital, is more in some countries than in others (see Das, 2020b: 233–81). The big latifundia owner of Latin America are much more powerful than an average large-scale landowner in the Indian Punjab or SE Asia. The large-scale land-owners are involved in the appropriation of capitalist profit: mainly from farming, but also from non-farming activities located in villages and small towns. Some of these rural landowners appropriate ground rent, as well as mercantile profit and usurious interest from poor rural labour and peasants. This process is enabled by the peripheral state: it considers it legitimate for the property-owners to extract extremely high rents, whether in cash or in labour or in kind (e.g. crop-share), and charge usurious interest rates on loans taken by small-scale producers and labourers in villages or even rural parts of the city-regions.

To some degree, the specifically capitalist elements of this class emerged in part due to what was predominantly a bourgeois land reform that, to some extent, removed some erstwhile pre-capitalist fetters (De Janvry, 1981; Djurfeldt and Sircar, 2017). Pre-capitalist cultural traits can coexist with capitalist values in the areas of influence of large landowners, and impact state-society relations. The capitalist class in rural areas has also benefited from the policy of exemption of taxation on agricultural incomes in some countries and from the state-enabled, regionally confined (and not nation-wide) introduction of technical changes which have included the Green Revolution. The Green Revolution was promoted by the state policy of providing cheap inputs and price support.[22] The rural propertied class still exercises substantial political power, through which it protects both its accumulation strategies and the sources of its capital/wealth.

Urban capital and the landed elements are inter-connected. An ally of the urban working class, rural masses (including those who have small plots of land) are an enormous potential threat to the propertied class, whether in rural or urban areas. What makes them a potent force is their role in production: if *they* stop working, there will be no surplus value. Given their potential as a threat to the propertied, it is important that they be prevented from launching any attack on the class character of the state or indeed on the urban capitalist class. The urban bourgeoisie indeed needs the landed to control the rural masses. The landed is therefore regarded as functional to the political interests of the bourgeoisie.

The act of controlling and disciplining of the rural masses by the landed also delivers an important *economic* advantage to the urban bourgeoisie. Food and agri-materials consumed by industries are produced cheaply, because rural workers are remunerated well below the value of their labour power. So these commodities are very 'competitively' priced as there are many producers, and this is to the benefit of urban capitalists. Besides, the continuing existence of rural landlords helps reproduce the idea of private property ownership and thereby the idea of capitalist private property, and this is beneficial to the urban capitalist class. So in terms of the defence of private property, rural landlords and urban capitalists have the same interest. It is important to note that just like most sections of the urban bourgeois class, the rural landowning capitalists (e.g. those in Brazil or India) have also supported the liberalization of trade that the urban capitalists have demanded because the rural capitalists, generally speaking, have eyed making money from exports of farm products.

Of course, class processes that benefit the landed class can go against the urban capitalist class. The class interest of the landed is in the ruthless exploitation of people with little or no land: as poor peasants via rental extractions and (increasingly) as labourers at below-subsistence wages, often under unfree conditions. Heavy rental extraction has meant that peasants have insufficient resources to invest in land. Super-exploitation of peasants and labourers also reduces the size of the home market. Besides, given the opportunity to earn revenue through these means of super-exploitation, property owners have little incentive to invest in land to increase labour productivity. Thus, to the extent that one can at all isolate national-scale factors of under-development, agrarian class relations have acted as a fetter on the development of productive forces, at least in specific regions. This situation goes against capitalists' interests in higher rates of profit which would have come from cheaper farm products for food and raw materials and a growing home market for large-scale production. So large-scale landowners are potential enemies of the urban capitalist class. Even if state policies against the landed (e.g. land redistribution) would help capitalists economically, the political interests of the latter (i.e. the need to control the rural masses) are a barrier to the implementation of such policies. Of course, urban capitalists, including MNCs, have begun to try relatively new strategies of accumulation in rural areas: they seek to control rural markets for inputs and outputs, and finance/insurance activities, and even production through contract farming. And, these strategies are sought to be codified/supported by the state's pro-corporate farm laws, as in India. Because such laws would work to the detriment of small-scale producers (and small-scale capitalists) as well as workers, so they protest against corporates' 'rural turn' (rural accumulation strategies) with the support of the state.

In the current epoch, the peripheral state functions to create conditions to make sure that the peripheral countries are a low-wage platform for the production of goods and services for domestic and imperialist capital. The state ensures this through coercive means (political control over labour when it protests). And the state ensures this by various pro-business policies, including flexible labour market policies as in India or Indonesia.[23] In many countries, the state allows capitalists to 'employ' labour on precarious terms.[24] This situation includes a large number of people being hired by labour contractors ('labour merchants') who then make them available to capitalists, so workers do not sell their labour power directly to capitalists. This means that those who productively consume labour power are not often its direct buyers, so if wages are low, workers cannot complain to the capitalists who actually use them. To the extent that low-wage production in these countries, in rural and urban areas, acts as a countervailing force towards the rate of profit to fall in imperialist countries, such a role of the state is objectively important. The state also makes sure that these countries absorb the commodities and finance from advanced and imperialist countries which experience the crisis of profitability and capitalist decay. And often such absorption is based on de-industrialization: import of foreign goods and services decimates peripheral enterprises.

Another beneficiary of peripheral state's policies is what might be termed 'state elites', composed of high-ranking members of the bureaucracy (in civilian administration and in the army) plus senior officials engaged in the industrial management of public sector enterprises. As in imperialist centre, so in the periphery, the capitalist form of exploitation is the dominant form of exploitation which is mainly based on economic coercion. This, in turn, allows the state to have a degree of autonomy vis-à-vis specific fractions of the capitalist class, an autonomy that allows the state elites to possess the flexibility with which to ensure the reproduction of the conditions of capitalist accumulation and, in the process, meets its own interests. In the periphery, state elites' autonomy could be a little more than in the core countries. One reason could be what Alavi calls the 'over-developed' nature of the state (over-developed in relation to its economic base).[25] But there are other reasons, as we will see. In the initial years of independence, state elites in the periphery had a slightly progressive stance and even exhibited a degree of anti-capitalist attitude. But over time, they have behaved as typical state elites acting in partnership with the propertied classes. Their bourgeois ideological orientation and coherence has helped the bourgeoisie. However, '[o]ften the organizational capabilities of the peripheral state's apparatuses are rather weak, which is why it might be said that the peripheral state is simultaneously underdeveloped and over-developed' (Ougaard, 1982: 400). This fact implies that their action may not perfectly coincide with the interests of capital. Yet state elites have ensured that state policies, more or less, benefit the capitalists. Of course, state elites' 'control over' state apparatuses, along with a relative absence of 'bureaucratic professionalization', is a massive source of rents (corruption): giving a license to a business person to set up a factory or ensuring a worker gets a water connection, is a source of bribe money for officials and politicians who work in concert. Peripheral states are the most corrupt in the world, and usually, the worst effects of corruption are borne by common people who are poor and lack relevant connections to officials and politicians.

If a government regulation is there (for example, one that disallows the use of child labour in a sector), civil servants can receive monetary compensation from the business class to look the other way: a certain part of the extra profit that a business person makes by violating the regulation is shared with the civil servants (who probably share a part of the bribe with their political masters in order to receive protection from them). Civil servants and politicians can also 'sell' a given policy (e.g. sale or leasing of state-owned enterprises) secretively (through the use of secret electoral bonds) to meet the specific needs of a given fraction of the capitalist class by presenting that policy as being in the interest of economic development and in the interest of the nation. What has changed since the neoliberal turn has happened?[26] Increasingly, civil servants are overseeing a market system, where animal spirits are highly encouraged, right from the prime minister's office. They need to ensure the success of the market system during their formal tenure (and after retirement when they work as so-called consultants for private companies). Now as before their power comes from their ability to favour the business class as such vis-à-vis the working masses. In particular, much of their power now comes from the ability to sell off public assets to private players at a throwaway price and from making land and other natural resources available to the business class that are taken away from unorganized small-scale producers. Their power also comes from connecting this or that fraction of the business class to the international circuit of capital and to powerful imperialist states on favourable terms, and so on. In playing this sort of 'compradore' role, they are helped by the fact that they may have worked for international institutions and have connections with them.

In contexts where the overwhelming majority of the population are illiterate or primary school dropouts and are poor, 'the educated elite' according to Bardhan (1998: 52), 'enjoy a high scarcity value (a rent) for their education and profession. By managing to direct educational investment away from the masses, the elite has protected its 'scarcity rent', which is seen in their salary increases and perks. State elites, especially from the dominant social-cultural groups (e.g. upper castes and dominant religious or ethnic groups), have benefited considerably from the expansion of educational and administrative functions and the nationalization of industries, which created jobs for managers in the public sector and subsidized collective consumption (which has actually made some of them members of an expanding consuming class). In short, state elites have economic resources, as well as social and cultural capital. Since they occupy crucial positions in the state apparatus, they use state's 'autonomy' to implement policies partly in their own interest, akin to exercising powers of patronage.

The state elite has personal connections with business groups, both inside a country and in its diaspora. Even before independence, it was also the repository of the intelligentsia, working out a development theory for capitalism, often restraining more intensely bourgeois objectives and formulating policies that appeared to be more reformist and universal (Kaviraj, 1988). Members of the state elite viewed 'their society as in need of basic change' (Kohli, 1987: 25) and charted a path of capitalist development that defied imperialist pressures, one that is consistent with a bourgeois conception of 'national' development. Much planning/policy discourse accordingly comes from them who are always in interaction with the organic intellectuals of the capitalist class, in their own country and in imperialist countries, working in the academia, media, private consultancies, and so on, and who help the capitalist class construct the accumulation strategies. Such interaction is materialized through the various institutions/apparatuses of the state, and through their rules, procedures, discourses, and strategies. The state elite governs, and exercises power over, the millions of development-hungry, illiterate, and semi-literate people in rural areas and in impoverished urban spaces, in the name of development. Often the promise of development stays on paper with the massive gap between development on paper and development proper. Development on paper serves as a big bourgeois state ideology in the periphery.

At the local scale of state-society relations, state elites (officials and political leaders, especially of ruling parties) represent the worst face of state power. Forming an alliance with the economically dominant classes at this level, they fail to implement policies that are supposed to benefit the common people and/or corner much of the development benefits that are supposed to go to the poor. Their high-handedness complements and reinforces that of the proprietary classes.

Whether they have much 'human capital' or not, state elites qua elites are not a class, however, so they cannot be considered a part of the class coalition holding state power.[27] Unlike landowners and private capitalists, they, as even the managers of state property, cannot transfer property to their heirs. It is the ownership/control of the means of production that decides who ultimately has power in a society and the state.[28] State elites do have a certain degree of autonomy, but this autonomy is that of the state as a structure in a dominantly bourgeois society. Their activities – including rent-seeking – must be seen as contingent on a state, the structure of which is designed to pursue capitalist interests. State elites as such are *not* a class and cannot therefore hold and exercise state power on their own behalf.[29] It is the logic of private sector profit in the hands of the (big) business houses that sets the limit within which specific economic development strategies are designed by state elites, based on their worldview which is more or less influenced by the interests of the bourgeoisie as a whole.[30] The actual nature of policies depends to some extent on the perception of their own economic/political interests, and their perception of what 'the nation' needs, and their ability to conceive these needs along the capitalist lines. In the early stage of the post-independence epoch, they conceived of national capitalist development to be relatively autonomous of imperialist pressures, but in more recent times, the elites have a penchant for neoliberal development without any pretention to counter imperialism.[31]

The dominant class base of the state changes over time (and over space). Since the late 1950–1960s, there has been an expansion of the capitalist class (although differently in different regions within a country). In more recent times, capitalist elements among the landed, relative to those landowners who used to appropriate ground-rent often using extra-economic coercion, have become more powerful and have been connected to urban capitalists. However, the economic and political importance of *rural* capitalists, in spite of their numerical dominance within the property-owning class, is declining relative to that of the city-based big-business, which includes foreign capital. There is also increasing integration between the periphery's capitalist class and imperialist capital.

5 The state, exploited classes, and class struggle from below in the periphery

The proprietary coalition is only part, albeit the dominant part, of the peripheral state's social conditioning. What the state is and does, and why, must also be investigated from the standpoint of the lower classes (the masses) and especially in terms of their struggle against the state and the propertied classes and against imperialism, no matter how weak and constrained that struggle is.

Which classes are the exploited classes in the periphery, and how are they exploited? This has been discussed in the last section on the nature of the dominant classes, but a brief re-articulation of the relevant ideas might be useful. In the rural context, the exploited classes are the small-scale producers. They include: middle peasants who do not hire labour, and poor peasants who may work on their own and/or rented land, and also as part-time wage-earners. The exploited classes also include agricultural and non-agricultural labourers. As a general rule, these classes/strata are exploited in the capitalist system, but they are subordinated by a wide variety of regionally specific production relations, extending from sharecropping and other kinds of tenancy arrangements which structure their conditional access to small plots of land. Such relations are additionally structured by the presence or absence of cash wages, debt, and freedom on the part of a worker personally to commodify his/her own labour power. Those compelled to rely mainly or wholly on the sale not of the product of their labour but rather of labour power itself – that is, labourers of various types – are exploited by property owners, who appropriate surplus labour in the form of profit as well as rent and interest. Many rural men and women and even children work as seasonal or migrant labourers in nearby city-regions and also in newly transplanted enterprises in rural areas. In the urban context, a small percentage of wage earners has access to a regular wage, tenure, and pension benefits. The vast majority of workers are precariously employed without regularity of employment or pension and other benefits. There are many men and women, who work as small-scale owners/producers, in part because of the lack of secure wage-employment with a decent wage. The miserable conditions of these classes prompt the struggle from below.

Forms of class struggle from below

Forms of class struggle from below vary and are often place-specific. One can observe four inter-connected forms. The first is the struggle by proletarian and semi-proletarian elements as full-time or part-time wage earners against capital, both in urban and rural areas. This 'from below' struggle includes struggle against pre-capitalist exploitation where it exists. More importantly, their struggle, which is generally in the form of strikes (work stoppage), is against the formal and RSL under capital: that is, it is against low wages, oppressive labour practices, long hours and poor working conditions, precarity, and the introduction of, or subordination to, labour-saving technology, and so on. This sort of struggle also aims at the state which supports the propertied class against 'from below' agency undertaken by workers and small-scale producers. Workers in rural and urban areas fight for concessions from the capitalist state, including in its role as an employer and as a provider of subsistence goods (e.g. food) that contribute to social reproduction. Also, workers (whether in South Africa or India, etc.) have not only struck work, and they have also defended the public sector (and fought against their privatization), and they have also built production and service-provision cooperatives as a means of building working-class power.

A second main form is 'from below' struggle against primitive accumulation: the state facilitating 'coercive depeasantization' (smallholders being coercively stripped of their means of production), the privatization of common property and public sector resources, and the withdrawal of state benefits meant for the poor. Here again 'from below' agency targets the state (and not just the propertied classes) for its support for primitive accumulation – for example, when it privatizes the commons. Connected to this form of struggles is the struggle, launched by small-scale commodity producers for better farm prices and lower farm inputs for protection from big business trying to extend its control over rural market, finance, and so on. Brazil's landless workers movement and Zapatista movement and numerous similar movements against modern forms of primitive accumulation in South Asia are the relevant examples.

In addition to these two forms of class struggle, there are other kinds of conflict that have their roots in class relations but have some autonomy: these struggles oppose ecological degradation and special oppression (i.e. oppression based on gender/caste/ethnic/national/religious/racial relations) that the state, including bourgeois parties promotes/sustains. Indeed, adverse environmental change and non-class forms of oppression have a disproportionate impact on the poor than on the better-off sections. To the degree that the propertied classes and the state bolster – either overtly or covertly – 'non-class' forms of oppression, they become the target of anti-oppression struggles. These are the struggles in which exploited classes participate, although they may not always be conscious of the role of capitalism in the creation of ecological problems and promotion/maintenance of social oppression.

There is also struggle which is most clearly 'political': for the democratization of the state. Workers and small-scale producers join with the broad mass of the population, not least because they are the ones who often experience in its most overt form the corrupt practices and patronizing attitudes of state elites, who treat them like slaves. Insofar as the undemocratic nature of the state – its lack of accountability to the exploited classes in terms of policies, programmes, and politics – derives from the fact that the main role of this capitalist apparatus is to reproduce dominance of the exploiting propertied classes, so struggles over democracy are centrally linked to the fact of class relations. In more recent times, struggles against the attack on democratic rights have focused on the assaults on religious and ethnic minorities from fascistic forces whether in Brazil, Turkey, India, or Sri Lanka. Anti-imperialist struggles, including in Pakistan, as well as struggles against fascistic tendencies as well as struggles against special oppression, are a part of the democratic movement in the periphery.

State's concessions as a response to class struggle from below

Struggles from below mean that both the propertied classes and the state find it necessary to make concessions from time to time. But these do not threaten capital. Even such state-enabled accumulation projects as the Green Revolution were driven in part by the fear that actual or potential famine conditions during the 1960s might constitute a threat to the political order. To the extent that the land reform policy has granted small amounts of land, taken from large landlords, to poor people, this has represented a reverse primitive accumulation.[32] But reverse primitive accumulation does not undermine capitalism. Capitalism does not require that *all* labour power become a commodity. As long as a sufficient amount of labour power is in the commodity form, capitalism's fundamental mechanisms (e.g. competition, appropriation of surplus value, and the like) can be in full force. In fact, the existence of a semi-commodified labour power is no barrier to capital's pursuit of surplus. Capital can benefit at the expense of small-scale producers in multiple ways.[33] Similarly, many states have provided limited wage employment on public works as well as small loans to poor people to set up small businesses, and this contributes towards their reproduction as potential wage labour (and as small-scale producers).[34]

However, the major interventions of the post-colonial state have failed to significantly improve the conditions of life of the poor, the conditions that are created by the ways in which the capitalist economic system works. The main, if not the sole, reason for state failure is the class character of the state and society. In most populous post-colonial countries, large landowners share state power with the urban bourgeoisie: this means that state policies have been dominantly in the interests of these classes and their international patrons. As already mentioned, the landowners perform the important role of economically and politically controlling the rural masses, including labourers, whose anger against landlordism could be potentially directed at the bourgeoisie of the country as well as their international patrons. Further, those who are responsible for the design and implementation of pro-poor policies, including judges and bureaucrats, come from the landed class or represent their interests.[35]

As explained earlier, the *economic* interest of the capitalist class, domestic and foreign, is such that it would not have had any problem if the land reform legislation had completely destroyed the pre-capitalist class, reviewing barriers to productivity. Such legislation would also have improved the material conditions of peasants and rural labourers. But the *political* interests of capitalists were such that they could not go against the feudals. What Marx said in 1852 (in a chapter in New York Daily Tribune) about the then–British bourgeoisie, is relevant to the late developing countries now:

> They prefer to compromise with the vanishing opponent [i.e. the feudals] rather than to strengthen the arising enemy [i.e. the working class], to whom the future belongs, by concessions of a more than apparent importance. Therefore, they strive to avoid every forcible collision with [them].
>
> (Marx, 1852b)

So, given the importance of the landowners, the state acting on behalf of the bourgeoisie cannot afford to hurt their (i.e. landowners') interest too much by properly implementing land reforms. This imperative of non-harm to the dominant classes is stronger under neoliberalism. This is seen in the attempted relaxation of ceiling laws to benefit the new rich. Existing ceilings on land holdings are being considered an obstacle to accumulation.

The Green Revolution, in a sense, represents a continuity with the earlier programme (i.e. the land reforms), once again revealing the class character of the state. The Green Revolution policy placed new means of production (e.g. the new technological package, state capital in the form of subsidies, and so on) *precisely* in the hands of the same class which was protected by the land reforms policy and allowed it an opportunity to accumulate capital, unfettered *and* untaxed. The landed elements continue to govern the conditions of existence of the poor. Neither the land reforms nor the Green Revolution has done anything to significantly undermine the economic and political power of large property owners (many of whom also invest in non-farm activities such as transportation, trading, and so on). I may add that since the onset of neo-liberal capitalist policies, land and water resources are increasingly being used to produce high value goods for a narrow domestic elite and for export. And one implication of this is a relative decline in the access to food on the part of millions of people in the periphery.

Also, given the overall capitalist class context, the amount of funding for the proper implementation of the policies on the scale that is necessary has to be limited. In the market system, the use of society's resources must be justified mainly on the basis of the profit logic. This logic puts severe limits on the amount of money the capitalist state can commit in the form of pro-poor policies, *relative* to the massive need of the hundreds of millions of the poor whom the system marginalizes (e.g. peasants increasingly losing access to land, people without secure employment for a living wage). The actual amount spent on the poor depends on, among other things, the balance of class forces as mediated by state-based mechanisms (e.g. judiciary, electoral power of different classes), and this balance is not in favour of the poor. But there are severe structural limits to what the state can do for the poor.[36] Note that these limits are expressed by the ruling class, directly or through its spokespersons, who have no qualms about milking the state to satisfy their appetite for profits. The situation of state spending for the poor relative to country's ability to spend is stark in neoliberal period with the state having shifted its path from welfare/interventionist state to laissez-faire neoliberal state (Tiwana and Singh, 2015). One of the (contradictory) aims of the latter is to shrink mass income and consumption at home in order to enable cheap exports and repayment of debt to imperialist finance capital (Patnaik, 1999).

When viewed in relation to policies for the exploited classes, within which the different strata belong to different castes/ethnic minorities, the state is a deeply contradictory entity. On the one hand, without the democratic grass-roots organization of these classes vis-à-vis the ruling classes and state elites, pro-poor policies will fail. Policies which aim to take land from landowners and give it to the poor, or which aim to ensure safety in the workplace and the payment of adequate wages, will not be implemented without the direct participation of the masses in their implementation, given the enormous power of the propertied classes to hide what they do. On the other hand, state's own actions and ideas and its own form, the form of anti-poverty policies, tend to fragment and *disorganize* the lower classes who compete for meagre resources. Not only must the state disorganize, it must also have a certain amount of social-political distance between itself and the lower classes. Indeed, *real direct democratic* control over the state's day-to-day operation by the lower classes contradicts state's function to reproduce *class* relations. In its day-to-day operation, the state is generally not accessible to lower classes the way it is to dominant classes. Therefore, the possibility of state officials properly implementing anti-poverty policies does not generally arise. If lack of power contributes to poverty, the state is a cause of powerlessness of the lower classes. It must therefore be seen as an important cause of poverty. One should therefore be critical of those who are sanguine about the talk of decentralization of state power as a solution to problems.

Many commentators, including Amartya Sen (1999), assume that by encouraging competition between parties and allowing a free press, democracy will lead to the implementation of pro-poor policies. He says that what the government does can be influenced by public pressures from below (Dreze and Sen, 1995). But much depends on what issues are politicised, and what is, or is not, politicized depends on the visions and pre-occupations of ruling as well as *opposition* parties. Non-communist *opposition* parties do not *oppose* ruling parties on crucial issues such as payment of compensation to landlords in the land reform laws or privatization of state-owned companies or periphery's subjugation to the imperialist military-economic framework. In other words, on class-related issues that do matter to the exploited classes, whose interests are fundamentally opposed to those of exploited classes, opposition parties do *not* matter. Parties in power and parties in opposition do not oppose the fundamental interests of the business class and its collaboration with imperialism. Both ruling and opposition parties work within the framework of a state that supports the fundamental interests of the propertied classes and share the ruling class ideology which, in turn, contributes to the de-politicization of the crucial issues. Dreze and Sen ignore the fact that the ideology of the propertied classes and the coercive character of the state, among other things, influence what enters into political debates and what does not. Sen's view is problematic because it is silent about the class character of the parties/regimes, which manage the common affairs of the state, which, in turn, manage the common affairs of the capitalist class. Sen's optimistic prognosis cannot answer the question of why it is that crucial development issues – such as unequal distribution of means of production (particularly land), extreme forms of income inequality, absence of high-quality and free state-provided healthcare and education, and employment for all at an inflation-adjusted living wage – do not become important election issues and are not much debated by competing mainstream parties. Democracy *can* help in the promulgation and implementation of policies favourable to the masses, but within limits. If the masses are to secure significant access to economic resources, including land and remuneration for their work, in the democratic process – so as to enjoy the health and educational freedoms which Sen rightly thinks all human beings should enjoy – then this requires, at least, the severe curtailment of political power exercised by dominant proprietary classes.

6 Coercive nature of the peripheral state's democratic form

It is a mistake, however, to assume that the *only* response the state can make to 'from below' struggle is a defensive one of concession, however limited. Hence the importance of understanding that the state response frequently is to launch *counter-revolutionary* action – a form of 'from above' class struggle – on behalf of capital and large landowners, and in the interest of maintaining political order. Hence the class character of society and the grassroots struggles arising from this influence the nature of the state *form* (especially in terms of whether it is democratic or not), which in turn influences state *actions*.

The existence of the democratic form does not mean that it is the only form of class rule: indeed, when necessary, the state will and does use coercion, and increasingly so, against the exploited classes if they resist its accumulation policies beyond a certain limit. The state turns coercive when people fight against domestic and imperialist capital. The capitalist state tends to be much less democratic in the periphery than the state in the metropolitan countries. In those peripheral countries, where the democratic state form exists, the amount of the gap between substantive economic inequality and formal political equality is much greater than in the imperialist countries. This is because of severe forms of economic inequality and high level of absolute poverty.

This fact is an aspect of a broader trend: in the LDCs, the normal effects of class relations on the common people are more extreme. Coercion is partly, and only partly, thanks to its colonial legacy.[37] There are strong anti-democratic pressures from society since independence from colonialism. Anti-democratic pressure emanates from geographically fixed land-based accumulation activities (e.g. latifundia, mining capital, and so on) that remain powerful in the villages and small towns: owners of farm-land or mines cannot leave a place with their property, so they must counter any resistance from the masses at all costs. Threats to formal democracy also come from those (e.g. fascistic forces) who are opposed to minority religions and women's rights. They also derive from the several other aspects of the capitalism that exists. One aspect is primitive accumulation which generally involves coercion.

In addition, in these countries, as we have seen, there is a backward form of capitalism. This form of capitalism potentially undermines the basis for democratic conduct. When capitalism is based on FSL, it is hardly conducive to democratic relations between state (officials) and citizens and between employers and employees. When profits come more or less from the naked exhaustion of the body of direct producers (or from their dispossession of property) rather than from increased productivity of their labour per hour of labour time spent in the workplaces based on the systemic logic of technological change in every sector and sub-sector, and when the very basic needs are not met by capital or the state, the relation between 'sovereignty and dependence', or the relation between the ruler and the ruled, tends to become a *coercive* relation, even if one is not tied to a given employer through extra-economic means. Several factors such as 'the feebleness of the national bourgeoisie, the absence of traditions of municipal self-government . . . cut the ground from under any kind of stable democratic regime' (Trotsky, 1940). So

> [t]he governments of backward, i.e., colonial and semi-colonial countries, by and large assume a Bonapartist or semi-Bonapartist character; and differ from one another in this, that some try to orient in a democratic direction, seeking support among workers and peasants, while others install a form close to military-police dictatorship.
>
> (Trotsky, 1940)

And if a peripheral country is dominated by foreign capital, there is an additional reason for the state to be coercive. Any struggle against capital invites coercion from the state.

> Inasmuch as the chief role in backward countries is not played by national but by foreign capitalism, the national bourgeoisie occupies, in the sense of its social position, a much more minor position than corresponds with the development of industry. Inasmuch as foreign capital . . . but proletarianizes the native population, the national proletariat soon begins playing the most important role in the life of the country. In these conditions the national government, to the extent that it tries to show resistance to foreign capital, is compelled to a greater or lesser degree to lean on the proletariat.

However,

> the governments of those backward countries which consider inescapable or more profitable for themselves to march shoulder to shoulder with

foreign capital, destroy the labor organizations and institute a more or less totalitarian regime.

(Trotsky, 1940)

Imperialism indeed directly contributes to a coercive state in peripheral countries in the face of anti-imperialist struggles. About the state in Pakistan, Azeem (2020) says, imperialism cannot rely on weak politicians to curb dissent against its global and regional concerns, and hence has propped up military regimes in the strategic contests of the Cold War and the 'War on Terror'. Pakistan's ruling classes were concerned that the communists could focus these uprisings into a counter-hegemonic politics; therefore, as in many other newly independent countries, US imperialism began to rely upon and bolster the bureaucracy, and especially the military, which became its seat of power through Ayub Khan's coup in 1958 (p. 1674). So the military is strong not because it has managed to pursue the self-interest of the state to its logical end but because imperialism has too often relied upon it as its seat of power.

The same process happened in Latin America. Here 'imperialism vis-à-vis the labour movement took the form of an armed struggle against "subversives"' that is, the left-leaning forces, a broad urban coalition of forces of resistance. This struggle 'was led by the armed forces of the Latin American state, particularly in Brazil and the southern cone of South America, . . . although financed by and (indirectly) under the strategic command of the United States' (Veltmeyer and Petras (2015: 172). The labour movement was more or less defeated by the 1970s 'under the combined weight of state repression and forces generated in the capitalist development process', thus creating conditions for 'the resurgence of the Right in the form of a counter-revolutionary political movement and an ideology of free market capitalism' (ibid.).

In the periphery, where, partly thanks to the kind of ('under-developed') capitalism it has, there are massive (near-)starvation, mass illiteracy, and enormous inequality in the means of consumption of what is required for a decent living. Such a situation promotes what is effectively an undemocratic state in its daily functioning (albeit disguised under democratic clothes). There is indeed a direct association between increasing inequality and increasing authoritarianism of the state in all societies. By virtue of its location in a poverty-stricken class-divided society, where the direct producers also experience enormous caste and gender oppression, and lack basic skills such as literacy, the peripheral state has much authoritarian power, some of which it acquired during colonial times for the purpose of carrying out the orders of the imperialist masters and keeping the 'natives' – the majority – in check. This power – the power of the state – is exercised by agents of the post-colonial state: the civil servants (and their political masters). Ordinary masses – the majority – bear the brunt of it.[38]

Officials' power comes from their power to intervene on behalf of, and at the behest of, business class people and landlords. Their power, dialectically seen, has another source: their role in relation to the masses. The economic elite uses civil servants as their foot soldiers to keep the masses under control, not only through naked physical and administrative force but also through deception, lies, trickery, mystification, and so on. They have to constantly 'tell' people that *elections*, and not protests/strikes, are a way of showing disapproval of a government and that government offices (e.g. magistrate's office or a police station or a court) are there basically to help ordinary people, that low-income toilers and rich property owners are all equal in the eyes of the law, that the profit-driven market system benefits everyone, that industrialization is in the interest of all, and so on. They (civil servants) have to work on a day-to-day basis *in line with these principles*. Coercion, trickery, and the like are not the civil servants' only role, which gives them power over the masses. In a society where economic and social development is a massive unfulfilled need, having to prostrate before the officials as a means of getting a few crumbs makes officials the semi-kings that they are. A colonial inheritance, this system of paternalistic power relations between civil servants and ordinary people, is one that serves the capitalist system as a whole very well. The undemocratic power of civil servants over the masses in the periphery's class-society supplements the role of the police and army as well as private armies of rural landlords, private security of urban capitalists, and paramilitary forces and vigilante groups, associated with certain social-cultural organizations, in keeping the masses in check. In fact, given the increasing influence of fascistic ideology on civil servants and police, they can and do look the other way when ordinary people are under physical attack from groups subscribing to that ideology.

What we have is a structure of relations among many elements (Figure 11.2): the practice and discourse of the pursuit of quick money and indeed fetishization of money and money-making at any cost; a system of capitalist production based on a regime of low wages and long hours; the need for the state to play a mediating role in relation to the market relations and (global) capitalism (or imperialism); the need for an undemocratic governance; privatization and cultural devaluation of education; and continuing colonial legacy/mentality. All these elements acting together produce an oppressive structure. More specifically, civil servants as they operate on the ground are one of the most important obstacles to the exercise of democratic rights by ordinary citizens. And civil servants exercising the power of the state as a structure in itself are one of the strongest fortresses around state power vis-à-vis workers, small-scale producers, and aboriginals (Figure 11.2).

Excessive coercion can, of course, adversely affect the political legitimacy of the parties in power, and even of the state itself. This is especially the case where the majority cannot meet their basic needs, and class anger is evident everywhere. Thus, the peripheral state, just like the state in the core, is required to balance three processes: (a) accumulation, (b) coercion, and (c) legitimation through material and non-material concessions, the democratic form (e.g. allowing the right to vote) as well as ideological deception (use of naked falsehood and myths, diverting attention of the masses to imaginary enemies, etc.). The actual intervention over a period of time and over space must be seen as a mix of these three, the nature of which depends on the intensity of

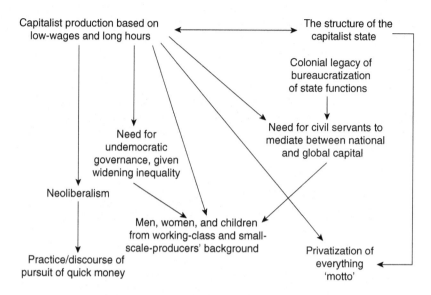

Figure 11.2 State elites and the peripheral state

class struggle both inside and outside the state, as well as on the requirements of accumulation in the hands of the capitalists and large landowners. The state deflects-suppresses class antagonism that inevitably arises out of the accumulation imperative which it must support. The state does this not only by means of coercion but also by means of (a) limited material concessions targeting individuals and non-class-based electorally advantageous strata (e.g. certain oppressed groups), (b) deception based on ideologies – ideology of religious or ethnic nationalism (which has nothing to do with, and which is actually friendly towards, imperialism) and ideology of religious or ethnic supremacism; and (c) periodic elections (democratic state form). A secular form of religion for the economically deprived masses, the capacity to exercise the vote at intervals provides them with the illusion that it is they who exercise control over the state and the dominant classes. Not only does this fuel the hope that they gain material benefits from electoral patronage, but it also perpetuates the belief that if not this party/leader then the next one in power will address their problems. The fetishistic worship of capitalist democracy is widely prevalent among the poor and among politicians and scholars.

The democratic state form also influences the shape taken by class struggle itself. On the one hand, it dissolves exploited *classes* into (juridical) *individuals*, and – further – into *voting individuals (individual voters)*, who are then *re-aggregated* into various non-class groups on the basis of well-cultivated non-class identities. Electoral success needs numbers. By giving opportunities for full expression to religious, indigenous, racist, casteist, ethnic, and regional identities, the democratic form of the state fragments the exploited classes into members of electoral groups (or, vote banks), and into supporters of this or that party (or fractions thereof). Deliberately ignored are their class position and interests. This process weakens the power and agency of common people *as classes*. Given the inability of the crisis-prone capitalist system to meet the needs of people, the politics of identity from the top (i.e. politics of identity of the majority community) are deployed by the fascistic forces as foot soldiers of reactionary capitalism. Currently, democracy has enabled the landowning class and elements of the bourgeois class to 'capture' specific parts of the state through liberal *democratic* elections. In parts of the periphery, therefore, proprietors are still able to compel the poor to vote as the politicians of the exploiting classes would like them to. Through their control over specific parts of the state – especially at the local/regional level – property owners appropriate the resources allocated by the state to the poor. On the other hand, by ensuring a limited degree of free association and speech, and through electoral procedures and the 'rule of law', the state in its democratic form has indeed allowed rural and urban workers (who form the majority of the population) to voice *some* opposition to political domination. Within limits, they are permitted to exert pressure on the capitalist state to create conditions for an egalitarian development pattern. The democratic state form has allowed competition between political parties, including the parties of the Left,[39] and this has contributed in varying degrees to the politicization of lower classes (as voters) and to the limited implementation of policies on their behalf. Yet the liberal democratic state form itself is a barrier to class politics from below in the periphery as well as the core.

7 Class contradictions of development and threat to peripheral state's legitimacy

From the standpoint of exploited classes, the colonial state did not discharge a developmental role; in part, therefore, the post-colonial state gained a degree of ideological legitimation from its promise to foster economic development, a break with the approach of the colonial state. About this Partha Chatterjee (1993: 203) observes:

> The new state represented the only legitimate form of the exercise of power because it was a necessary condition for the *development* of the nation . . . (it) acquired its representativeness by directing a program of economic *development* on behalf of the nation.

Like the colonial state, however, the current neoliberal post-colonial state is not fulfilling a developmental role. Hence the development process no longer discharges for the state the legitimizing role to the same extent it did earlier, in the more optimistic decades following Independence.[40] This is certainly true of the way the state is 'seen' by 'those below' in those areas where there exist very strong radical militant organizations of the rural poor (e.g. the Maoist movement in Asia). There the relative paucity of spending by the neoliberal state on anti-poverty policies – a process termed as 'the selective retreat of the state' – has indeed eroded its legitimacy in the eyes of the vast majority of the rural population in terms of promoting development. For lower classes, therefore, the state is not perceived as a 'caring' state to the same extent it was earlier, both materially and discursively.

Of additional relevance is that the ideological illegitimacy of the colonial state derived from its being 'other' economically: that is, it was seen as serving the external ('foreign') interests in furtherance of which it licensed the exploitation of workers and peasants. The ideological legitimacy of the post-independence state, and a central emplacement of the nationalist discourse, emanated from the fact that it would be independent of an international capitalism. Hence the legitimacy of the state, say in India, 'had to flow from the nationalistic criticism of colonialism as an alien and unrepresentative power' and from the expectation that 'an independent state . . . would promote national *development*' as 'the historical necessity' (Chatterjee, 1993: 205; italics added).[41]

But what is the post-colonial state doing? It is prostrating itself before the imperialism of the IMF, the World Bank, MNCs, and international 'aid' agencies. This is an imperialism that is justified and sold to ordinary people through the discourse of development and progress. The post-colonial neoliberal state itself has become a mechanism of new imperialism. The point is that now, as during colonial times, the state, as mentioned earlier, is creating the conditions for the transfer of profits to the foreign capital: indeed, the neoliberal state is actively encouraging international capital to exploit its own lower classes, a process in which domestic capitalists – urban and rural – are invited to participate. The nationalistic dream – the idea that there is a nation and what the state does is good for the nation – may be on the way out. Hence, there is a new national question for the masses: how to transcend the ongoing impact of imperialism which is predominantly practised through economic mechanisms and ultimately backed up by the threat of force?[42]

If the concept of nation has any significance, it must, first of all, be the 'nation' of workers and small-scale producers, yet the neoliberal-capitalist peripheral state is increasingly alienating itself from *this* 'nation'. And this is why, and given that the 'collaboration' of the peripheral ruling class with imperialism makes anti-imperialist nationalism an empty slogan, there is a need on the part of the ruling classes of the periphery to construct an alternative nation (and nationalism), one that is based on religious, racial, and ethnic identity. This strategy creates phoney internal enemies of the fake nation (the enemies being the religious and racialized minorities, people defending democratic rights and communists/Marxists). As a result, the real nation, the nation of workers and small-scale producers exploited by the ruling classes and subjugated by imperialism, is divided and weakened, and it fails to concentrate on the real enemies of the nation (i.e. capitalists, large-scale landowners, and imperialist forces). But this strategy of encouraging fascistic divisive tendencies however can contribute to delegitimization of (the democratic form of) the state.

Another contributory factor in this delegitimization process is that action by the neoliberal state is perceived to lack rationality. The colonial state was exporting food to the UK when in the colonies the population did not have sufficient food to eat. In a similar vein, the neoliberal state is now seen as irrational in promoting the production of luxury commodities (such as flowers, shrimps, and animal feed) or minerals and energy for export to imperialist/rich countries, when millions are malnourished/hungry at home and/or are without regular supply of energy and other industrially produced necessaries throughout the year. The state is under pressure from nationally operating and multi-national agribusiness to crush small-scale producers, which has been prompting mass protests. The state-promoted export of these commodities is itself based on cheap labour and cheap land. 'Cheap', however, hides the ecological and social conditions under which these commodities are produced by peasants and workers. Cheapness is not a characteristic innate to a country in the periphery, either to the (tattered) bodies of its workforce or to its (degraded) nature, both of which are deployed by neoliberal capitalist accumulation.

The perceived difference between the colonial state and its post-colonial counterpart – a crucial ideological one – thus no longer holds.[43] This is because the state is no longer able to sustain even the fiction of carrying out policies designed to benefit large swathes of the polity – the 'people' who form 'the nation', in other words. The failure is more drastic with the turn to neoliberalism and to right-wing politics associated with the rise of right-wing parties (e.g. Modi's Bharatiya Janata Party or National People's Party and Bolsanaro's Social Liberal Party of Brazil). In fact, the neoliberal state form and state intervention (the state's relative withdrawal from welfare provision and a certain degree of control over the business class) were justified on the basis that the neoliberal state is good for the masses, but this has turned out to be a lie. Neoliberalization has hurt the masses, including by dispossessing them of their small-scale property, so the neoliberal form of the state does not have the legitimacy in the minds of the ordinary people.[44]

Apart from the differences/contradictions between the colonial state and the post-colonial state, there are important differences/contradictions between the pre-neoliberal state and the neoliberal state. While the personnel of the state before the onset of neoliberalism, often drawn from lower strata of society (e.g. petty-bourgeois strata), maintained some distance between them and the capitalist class, now the personnel of the state revel in their connections with, and take pride from their work for, the business class. The social legitimacy of the state clearly is at stake because the state, at least, has to give the appearance that it is neutral, that it is for everyone, for all classes. But maintaining such an appearance is difficult because of a distinctive change in the class character of the personnel of the state. Prabhat Patnaik (2010) eloquently describes this pre-neoliberal process: 'The State was a bourgeois State, laying the foundations for capitalist development. But the motivation, the ideological inclinations, and the class background of the State personnel ensured that the State had a degree of autonomy both vis-à-vis imperialism and also vis-à-vis the domestic capitalists'.[45] This autonomy was there in the sense that state actors, drawn from the ranks of the petty-bourgeoisie, 'were generally skeptical about, and even to a degree hostile to, the capitalist class and were committed to State capitalism which they also saw as a means of self-advancement in the new situation of de-colonization' (ibid.). However, something has changed with the turn to neoliberalism. Patnaik (2010) explains:

> The 'neo-liberal State' too is a bourgeois State like the *dirigiste* State, but the personnel of the former differ fundamentally from the personnel of the latter, not just in their ideological predilections, which are closely aligned to the views of the Bretton Woods institutions, *but also in their being deeply enmeshed with the world of finance and big business.*

Therefore,

> What we find in today's State personnel is not just a different set of ideologues, World Bank ideologues, as distinct from the Nehruvian [i.e. secular bourgeois-nationalist] ideologues that manned the *dirigiste* bourgeois State, but a set whose motivation is no different from that of the big bourgeoisie and financial interests and which therefore has no compunctions about being closely integrated with the latter.

More specifically:

> The personnel of the neo-liberal State have little interest in running the public sector, which is one reason why the public sector becomes financially unviable over time, and provides grist to the mill of those who want it privatized. Even normal government functions are not carried out by the bureaucracy, which is more interested in networking with patrons in the world of corporates and foreign donors, or in attending World Bank-sponsored training programmes, than in the nitty-gritty of administration. More and more government functions as a result are 'outsourced' to private agencies, which promises profits for all.
>
> (Patnaik, 2010)

Partly as a result of this change in the personnel and in the mode of functioning of the state, there has been an 'undermining of the social legitimacy of the State', and this is happening 'especially in the context of the tremendous increase in wealth and income inequalities associated with the pursuit of the neo-liberal strategy' (Patnaik, 2010).

Whether all these structural conditions will actually result in a legitimation crisis, and to what extent, will, of course, depend on how the lower classes and their political parties and their organic intellectuals at home and internationally respond to these conditions politically. And to the degree that the crisis does take shape, much also will depend on how the state reacts, in particular its resort to coercive power at its disposal with the help of its imperialist mentors, and in turn how lower classes respond to this.

8 Summary, and theoretical and political implications

The main aim of this book has been to explicitly re-assert the class character of the state. The main aim of this chapter has been to explicitly re-assert the class character of the state in the *periphery*. The periphery is characterized by the combined coexistence of different modes of production under the dominance of capitalism and is under the impact of imperialism. So there is a greater number of classes and fractions than in the centre. This complicated class structure shapes the state. Class relations and the attendant material conditions – including imperialism – constitute the most important context for all forms of intervention by the state and for the very form (territorial and political form) of the state itself. Of course, within this class context other social relations – that is, those of caste, religion, ethnicity, region, and nation – operate and influence the state and its class character.

Because capitalism is the dominant mode of production in a typical peripheral country, the state is a capitalist state, and thus an agent of capitalist development, even if small-scale producers have a massive presence in the periphery. This is the case both in pre-neoliberal and neoliberal times and both in rural areas and city-regions. The relation of partnership between the two arms of the capitalist class relation – the state and the capitalist class – has been justified in terms of two major ideologies. One is of state control and socialism (many states such as India and Bangladesh, Sri Lanka, Tanzania, Nicaragua, and so on originally, were called socialist, or they have had references to socialism in their constitution). Another is one of free market. The ideology of state control over the business world in the early years of the post-independence period was not entirely a lie. There was a degree of state control. There was a degree of state intervention on behalf of the masses. Even the ruling class understood from the very beginning that a small degree of state control and a small degree of pro-poor re-distribution is a remedy to potential social upheaval against all forms of private property or against the danger of anti-feudal and anti-imperialist struggle growing over into anti-capitalist class relations. In the neoliberal times, the ideology of free market has justified serious intervention in the interest of capital and enabled by a change in the personnel.

It is however important not to over-emphasize this change in personnel. It is the capitalist class character of neoliberalism that has led to the state being managed by bourgeois personnel (people who either include members of the bourgeoisie or who are shaped by bourgeois ideas and aspirations), and that in turn is responsible for the ongoing reproduction of the capitalist-neoliberal order. The state has always worked, more or less, in the interest of the capitalist class. Its policies (as well its liberal democratic form where it exists) have been accordingly influenced by the interests/actions of the dominant classes, although they have also been, to some extent, shaped by the actuality/possibility of class struggle from below.

Like any capitalist state, the peripheral state must sustain the myth that capitalist accumulation (which goes by the name of 'growth') benefits not only the already-better-off entrepreneurs but also the poor. The myth needed is that the exploiters (misnamed as employers, wealth creators, and so on) and the exploited benefit from the same process. The legitimacy of the post-colonial state derived in no small measure from two assumptions: that, unlike colonial government which served 'foreign' interests, it would serve domestic ones; and that, to this end, it would promote economic development from which the nation as a whole would benefit. Increasingly, however, the distinction between the colonial and post-colonial development projects is being eroded, as the neoliberal state not only facilitates the dispossession and exploitation of the poor by international and domestic capital. Farm crops are once again being seen to be produced mainly for an elite (= 'foreign') market, much as they were during the colonial era. This can contribute to the broader process of delegitimizing the development state, a situation which in turn intensifies class struggle 'from below', and the repressive 'from above' response by the neoliberal state protecting the interests of the capitalist class.

The periphery should not be merely seen as having less income. It should be seen in terms of its class-capitalist character. To say that the peripheral social formation is decidedly capitalist has a different political implication, including for the relation between lower classes and the state, than the contrary view which is that (a) the social formation is not dominantly capitalist or that it is capitalist in limited ways and (b) obstacles to capitalist development are in pre- or non-capitalist relations. Implicit are two ideas here. One is that the capitalist class relation is everywhere and all times associated with higher level of development of productive forces. Another is that the obstacles to capitalist development are not in capitalism as a class relation as such and can be removed by forces other than those that seek to abolish capitalism. That is, a democratic state operating within the logic of capitalist relations can remove these barriers and promote a nicer form of capitalism, independent from capitalism.

If a peripheral country is dominantly semi-feudal or if it is not capitalist enough, then the radical strategy is one that is to be directed against semi-feudal landlords or at the creation of advanced capitalism somehow. This strategy licenses a long and indefinite wait for the fight for socialism (= abolition of class relations) to start and requires collaboration with some good (progressive = anti-feudal, nationalistic, democratic, and so on) capitalists. But if what is present is already capitalism, albeit one that is not very progressive,[46] and one that is not going to be very progressive for a long period of time because of all the constraints on the transition to RSL within the contemporary imperialist world market, and if there are forces that make the appropriation of absolute surplus value salient, then the nature of class politics in relation to the state must be seen in an entirely different manner: this means that revolution as the highest point of class struggle against capitalism and its state must be on the agenda right now, as in the core countries.

But does this mean that one cannot fight for reforms within capitalism? Or, more specifically, does this mean that, for example, small-scale producers' demand for access to means of production (e.g. land and/or credit) or workers' struggle for higher wages and public provisioning of use-values can be ignored? The answer is no: within limits, the fight for land and for other such concessions is a means of political mobilization of the masses, and under the pressure of mass mobilization, *some* land redistribution and *some* increase in private and public wages might even happen under a bourgeois (or bourgeois-landlord) state.

In the periphery and in the core, the masses must make a demand on the state around radical needs (as represented in transitional demands discussed earlier). Radical needs are the real needs of the masses, not the needs which the system says it can afford to meet, and are connected to the roots in the relations of production and exchange and in state power. The masses should democratically organize themselves over multiple 'rights': right to employment (including the right to more land and other farm inputs for poor peasants in agrarian economies), a living wage, a reduced working day, increased leisure, decent and affordable housing, high-quality healthcare and education as well as culture.[47] They should fight for the right-to-decent financial support for the elderly and the disabled, and the right to a healthy and safe environment at work and in neighbourhoods. Those who have small amounts of means of production must have access to more, and the state should ensure complete freedom from exploitation by landlords, merchants, and usurers (e.g. payday lenders in some advanced countries). The masses must fight for the defence of democratic rights, including those of aboriginal populations and religious and racialized minorities. They must demand democratic control over landed and financial aristocrats and over capitalist monopolies as an immediate step necessary to satisfy the fulfilment of their social needs, especially those monopolies which control the production of things and services (e.g. food items and seeds, medicines, houses, clothes, utilities, and so on) without which radical needs cannot be met and people cannot live like humans. It is, of course, clear that the poor masses cannot rely on the bourgeoisie and its state.[48]

In other words, to begin with, the masses as well as their organic intellectuals must re-imagine democracy as it originally was and as it should be: the democracy of the poor, who are the majority. Democracy is much more than being able to vote for this or that person or party once every few years to run the affairs of the capitalist state. It must be about the control over the ways society's resources are used and over the ways in which the state institutions work and deal with the majority, the exploited classes, the poor. At the minimum, the masses must demand a thorough democratization of the state *as a transitional political demand*. This means that excessive power (in the sense of 'power over') of the (secretive) civil servants and politicians must be stripped. Committees or councils of common citizens (workers, small-scale producers, and their organic intellectuals and political representatives) in different spheres of society must be formed. They must have direct oversight over the activity of the civil servants, including their income and daily interactions with politicians and business people as well as over politicians and state-owned and private enterprises. They must militantly defend democratic rights *against* fascistic attacks on minorities and anyone else. All the deals that the state makes with the capitalists must be subjected to popular scrutiny. This re-imagining of democracy must be a part of the project of conquest of state power and establishment of socialism.

The periphery, where most of the global population live, has its own specificities. Yet, increasingly, the mechanisms behind the conditions of wage earners and small-scale producers there and in the core are similar. Shrinking income and consumption of the toiling classes are the characteristic aspects of (neoliberal) capitalism *everywhere*. This means that there a potential basis for international solidarity of working class and small-scale self-employed producers against capital, including its neoliberal incarnation, everywhere and at all scales.

While the masses must struggle for all possible political and economic concessions, they cannot have any illusion that the current state, in the periphery and in the core, can return to a pre-neoliberal state which defends democratic rights, including of minorities. It is only a state under the control of the proletariat allied with small-scale producers, following a *socialist* revolution, that can meet the economic and political needs of the masses. Only such a state, in the context of the periphery, for example, can successfully carry out land redistribution *and* stop the beneficiaries from losing their land through coercive dispossession or market-based class differentiation.[49] Only such a state, freed from capitalists' control and the constraints of the law of value, can, both in the core and in the periphery, successfully create well-paying and secure jobs *for all*, invest in social and physical infrastructure, and secure ecological sustainability.

The capitalist state, in the periphery or in the core, cannot significantly and durably solve the problems created by capitalism, a system that the state must protect. So, the core of the political agenda, in imperialist and imperialized countries, must be the anti-capitalist struggle of the working class against the totality of capitalist class relation, including in its most general form (i.e. FSL). The working class must be politically allied with, and lead, small-scale producers who are adversely impacted by the capitalist class (and by its class partner, that is, rent-receiving landowners, where they exist) to overthrow the capitalist state. It is futile and mistaken to expect that this state will wither away under the pressure of the struggle for reforms. The withering idea in Marxism applies *not* to the capitalist state, but to the post-revolution, transitional proletarian state. The combined and common goal of the two toiling classes must be a socialist state in place of the existing capitalist state. The socialist state is a state of and for workers and small-scale producers, who constitute the majority of the population. By driving all propertied classes from their ruling positions and by stopping them from returning, such a state can create conditions for a higher level of development of productive forces, economic and geographical equality, and ecological sustainability. It will create conditions for a society without economic exploitation, social oppression, imperialism and the constant threat of war, a society where material and cultural needs of all men, women, and children are met. By creating these conditions, the proletarian state will ultimately make its own existence unnecessary. A global society without class exploitation does not require a state.

Notes

1 Poulantzas (2008: 407–408) says that given the increasing gulf between rich and poor countries, there is a need to develop a theory of the state in the latter. For Alavi (1972, 1982), because there are three dominant classes in the periphery rather than one, there is a need for a separate theory of the peripheral state.

   Apart from Alavi's work and the work discussed in this chapter, there is a large amount of literature on the peripheral state. This includes Bayart, 1993; Cox and Negi, 2010; Glassman and Samatar, 1997; Gulalp, 1987; Koo, 1984; Leftwich, 2000; Leys, 1976; Patnaik, 2010; Petras, 1982; Saul, 1974; and Ziemann and Lanzendorfer, 1977. This complements the developmental state literature cited later.

2 The small-scale production, of course, coexists with large-scale processes such as the central banking systems imposed by states, the increasing prevalence of high-tech finance, and the influence of multilateral development agencies (Breckenridge and James, 2021).

3 There is a large amount of literature on the class character of the periphery. This includes Anderson, 2010; Banaji, 2011; De Janvry, 1981; De Paula, 2015; Foster-Carter, 1978; Godelier, 1978; Marx, 1964; Larrain, 1991; Lindner, 2010; Meisenhelder, 1995; Mohri, 1979; Patnaik, 1990; Richards, 1986; Valencia, 2014; Weeks, 1997; Wolpe, 1980.

4 'The means of production for the producer-goods industry are of course the goods with the highest reproductive importance, since in principle anything can be produced by means of these' (Ougaard, 1982: 389).

5 In the US, this was the case for at least for 30 years or so. According to Economic Policy institute, between 1948 and 1979, the growth in productivity was 108% and growth in wages was 93%; however, between 1979 and 2019, while productivity increased by 70%, hourly compensation increased by barely 12% (quoted in World Economic Forum, 2020).

6 A lot of the literature on the peripheral state has been on the developmental state form of the peripheral state. This includes Canak, 1984; Chibber, 2006; Chu, 2016; Evans, 1995; Leftwich, 2000; Minns, 2001; Munck, 1979; Onis, 1991; Petras and Veltmeyer, 2007; Radice, 2008; Thompson, 1996; Wong, 2004; Woo-Cumings, 1999. Note that I have not dealt with the developmental state debate in this book in any detail because of lack of space (for some comments, see Chapter 2).

7 Parts of this section are based on Das (2017a: 345–366).

8 Capital also makes use of labour whose reproduction is only partly borne by the capitalist wage system (e.g. labouring households working seasonally for capital as migrant labourers may collect means of subsistence (fuel and the like) from common property for free and/or who may own some land. Capital also relies on the fact that those responsible for reproduction of the labouring households (especially women and girl children) spend many hours of unpaid labour at home and are often denied access to a normal amount of necessaries to consume, and all these processes in the realm of the private sphere of necessary labour (Vogel, 2014) reduce the social value of labour power that is bought and sold. This happens in rich countries, but this is especially true about the periphery.

9 Under new imperialism, market mechanisms are generally more significant relative to the coercive state power of advanced capitalist countries in implementing the imperialist project, although state power (sanctions and threat of or actual use of military power) is always the midwife of the imperialist project.

10

> Petty commodity production (PCP) is economic activity in which the household is the unit of production and consumption, a unit combining capital and labour in gendered roles. Unable to reproduce itself without engagement in the commodity economy, the PCP household may be found in production and in circulation.
>
> (Harriss-White, 2018: 357).

Harriss-White, 2018 (363): 'When the state engages in city beautification, when it invokes the law of eminent domain to seize land for public infrastructure or for corporate capital, it actively destroys PCP without compensation.'

11

> Given shrinking labour supply in advanced countries, Governments [of these countries] are slowly – and painfully – coming to confront the need for a permanent worker – and student – recruitment approach to world labour supply, and doing so in conditions of intensified competition for labour among most developed States. On the other hand, the emergence of significant diasporas of citizens living abroad confuses the old clarity of sovereign States and citizens.
>
> (Harris, 2018: 218–219).

In addition, the diaspora from the periphery experiences racist discrimination within the imperialist heartland on a regular basis.

12 Though trade deals such as NAFTA, states of powerful countries pit workers from LDCs against those from more developed ones (Cleaver, 2019: 80).

13 For example, as Mudimu et al. (2020) discuss, the Western states and international financial institutions imposed economic sanctions on the Zimbabwean state for property rights violations in relation to the land expropriations done by a state policy. These sanctions constrained the Zimbabwean state severely, as a result of which there was limited agrarian finance. The sanctions led the World Bank to increase the risk premium on investment for Zimbabwe from 3.4% in 2000 to 153% in 2004. Therefore, it became difficult to mobilize international capital to invest in Zimbabwe.

The Zimbabwe's state has therefore been giving more support to large-scale farming at the expense of the peasantry, so the state has been a tacit driver of the land dispossession. For instance, the state has been providing support to large-scale farming enterprise as a way of 'shoring up to the west' so that it is able to navigate the sanctions and can strike alliances with capital outside the West's control. Simultaneously, it has been promoting the leasing of huge pieces of land. This occurrence is connected to land dispossession in other parts of Africa, which is largely driven by the view that the peasantry is unable to produce enough food.

14 Here the assumption is that 1 hour of skilled labour is a n hour of unskilled labour (where $n > 0$).

15 Thus, there is no homogenous single Transnational Capitalist Class (TCC) (cf. Robinson, 2019; Robinson and Sprague, 2018): national differences between the segments of the world bourgeoisie – between less developed, imperialized countries and more developed imperialist countries – are significant.

16 This is contrary to the view that the state is a neutral arbiter between classes/groups and that the state is controlled by 'intermediate classes' located between the exploited and the dominant classes.

17 In some countries, a specific fraction of the bourgeois could be 'the comprador-bourgeoisie': it is engaged in a capitalist economic activity that is externally oriented as,

for instance, the export of raw materials. But it has a contradiction of interests with foreign capital regarding the export of profits from the extravert accumulation (Ougaard, 1982).

18 About Turkey, Gulalp (1987: 310) says: 'The role of the state is the same throughout the different phases of development: the reproduction of the system based on capital accumulation.'

19 The post-colonial neoliberal state in India has acquired land on behalf of private companies by virtue of eminent domain as outlined in the colonial-era Land Acquisition Act 1894. Several amendments to the 1894 Act have broadened the purview of the public purpose clause and have facilitated more state intervention in land acquisition on behalf of capitalists. The New Act of 2013 has expanded the ambit of public purpose to include public-private partnership projects (Mallick, 2018; see also Chakravorty, 2016).

20 One should not over-stress this point: it is problematic to assume that the state under capitalism could play a positive role in promoting development on a sustainable long-term basis, rural or urban. The positive role of the nation-state in, for example, East Asia has been overstated, and its negative role correspondingly understated (Burkett and Hart-Landsberg, 2003).

21 Privatization was thrust on Turkey by the structural dynamics, the World Bank, the IMF, and global capital (its implementation is contested both inside and outside of the state apparatus by the Turkish power bloc (i.e. fractions of capital) within the constitutive context of the prevailing strategies of the domestic capital accumulation regime of Turkey at the time (Zaifer, 2018)).

'By 1990 all but four major Latin American states had succumbed or joined the Washington Consensus in regard to a programme that was imposed on them as a conditionality of aid and access to capital markets to renegotiate the external debt' (Veltmeyer and Petras, 2015: 172).

> A comprehensive reform agenda was imposed by the IMF as part of its agreed bailout programme for Indonesia. At its peak, the IMF programme involved more than 500 conditions, mostly in the areas of controlling inflation, recapitalisation of failed banks and privatisation of state-owned enterprises.
>
> (Habibi and Juliawan, 2018: 661).

The neo-liberal reconfiguration steered the state to better serve the interests of international capital.

22 When landowners are able to increase profit by using improved technology, they rely less on rent and usury and are therefore encouraged to make productive investment, other things constant.

23 Habibi and Juliawan (2018: 666) say this about Indonesia:

> In the manufacturing sector the main strategy was to facilitate labour-intensive industries for export, powered by an abundant, cheap and politically repressed workforce. The annihilation of leftist ideologies and groups in the early Suharto regime and the tight control over labour and other potentially political forces in society tipped the balance of power towards the business and political cronies of the regime. The orientation to global markets also exposed the country to the economic crisis that was to destroy many of the gains of rapid growth.

24 Tjandraningsih (2013) discusses labour outsourcing as the main form of precarious work in Indonesia. Capitalists' demands for labour flexibility and the expansion of precarious work show that the state's role in protecting workers is being cast aside as Indonesia's peripheral position in global capitalism sees the state sponsoring a 'labor flexibility regime'. A 2003 law legalizing labour outsourcing came from an agreement between the government and the IMF. Labour outsourcing has created a new actor in industrial

relations: the labour agency. It is also fragmenting workers by work status and bringing harsh confrontations between labour unions and community members.

25 According to Alavi, the landed and capitalist classes in Pakistan are weak vis-à-vis the military (see McCartney and Zaidi, 2019 on an assessment of Alavi's theory of the state). Contrary to this argument, says Azeem (2020), these classes are to be understood much rather as being dependent and weak vis-à-vis imperialism. The dominant classes (including the landed) have not been cowed by the military, and they rather have cooperated with imperialism to protect and advance their own class interests. Even the military regimes have to operate through landed and capitalist elites.

26 Many people believe that with the so-called neoliberal turn, the state has less power. This is an utterly mistaken assumption. If the neoliberal state has less power, politicians will not spend millions to get elected in every election since the 1990s, neither will hundreds of thousands of people want to invest so much time and money to become bureaucrats. Nor will there be million-dollar scandals after scandals which signify the looting of public resources in the hands of the clique comprising civil servants, political leaders, and the business people.

27 The idea, held in progressive circles, that state elites are a dominant class, and the neoliberal idea that the activities of state elites are a reason for periphery's low level of development are two sides of the same coin. The problems of society are located in the political realm, rather than in the sphere of class relations of exploitation. To accept that state elites are a dominant class is also to accept that 'the rule of full-time corps of non-propertied officials is an unavoidable feature of modern society' (Post, 1999: 146; see also Pederson, 1992).

28 In the African literature, state elites controlling the public sector industries and business are called a state bourgeoisie or a managerial bourgeoisie (Leftwich, 2000: 91).

29 The political implication of this is that replacing one set of state actors with another leads to no fundamental changes in the conditions under which workers and peasants live.

30 This does not mean that every policy of the state perfectly looks after the interest of all capitalists. Different capitalists have different interests. Personal and institutional connection between state elites and business houses may also produce policies that may not exactly benefit the entire capitalist class at a given point in time. State elites also need to be mindful of public order: i.e. potential resistance to pro-business policies from lower classes (see the discussion that follows), and this consideration influences policies that may not immediately meet capitalist economic interests. Generally, over the long run, state policies tend to support capitalist class interests and especially interests of the dominant sections.

31 Top state elites as a 'consumption class', whose emergence state policies in the era before neoliberalism helped, along with the rural and urban propertied classes and their hangers-on, have acted as a great pressure for the liberalization of imported luxury items.

32 According to Mudimu et al. (2020), Zimbabwe's Fast Track Land Reform Program has resulted in re-peasantization and has a degree of accumulation from below by the resettled peasantry. Peasant resistance has countered full-scale dispossession. The state's ownership of land has also countered to some extent the tendency towards proletarianization of the peasantry.

33 Small-scale producers are adversely impacted by the capitalist class in at least three different but connected ways (see Chapter 6, Section 2).

34 'Yet, when the state seeks to develop small-farmer agricultural technology and extension services, implement land reforms, build micro-industrial estates and expand micro finance, it deliberately promotes PCP' (Barbara-Harriss White, 2018: 364). 'And when the state establishes safety nets of social protection, it protects PCP along with wage-labour' (ibid.). 'When it establishes municipal marketplaces and parking stands for carts and tempos, the state tolerates PCP' (p. 365).

Thus,

> PCP is also both sustained and disadvantaged through unintended outcomes – as when the rural employment guarantee scheme incentivises PCP by raising the formal wage floor, under which PCP competes, or disadvantages it by expanding and formalising credit for which PCP has no acceptable collateral.
>
> (p. 365)

35 If large landowners' farms were broken and their land was consequently redistributed among poorer peasants and the landless, and if the latter were provided technological and financial support by the state through cooperatives, land productivity would have increased, putting money in their hands creating a home market. This did not happen. This could not happen beyond a limit. This is because of the overall balance of class forces within the country and internationally (i.e. influence of imperialists).

36 These are ideologically expressed through such constructs as 'budget deficits go up' or 'government assistance makes people lazy' or that 'people should take initiatives to solve their problems'.

37 Talking about Egypt, Salem says that the colonial state did not have the hegemony because consent was outweighed by coercion (Salem, 2018: xii).

> While metropolitan nations – the colonizers – may have constructed hegemony in their own countries through consent – which did not mean there was an absence of coercion but rather that coercion was legitimized through consent – in the colonial state hegemony did not exist because consent was outweighed by coercion.
>
> (Ramachandra Guha, in Salem, 2018: xii)

38 The propertied class and all those with sufficient money can buy 'a bit of' democracy (including rule of law, decent treatment from officials, and the like.).

39 The lower classes have been able to win some concessions through their parties (Left parties) whose presence is much more visible in the periphery than in, say, North America.

   While left/radical/Marxist politics has lost some of its power at the central and provincial scales, there are literally hundreds of wards/hamlets, barrios, cities, city regions, villages, and so on where Marxists and radicals are relatively powerful, and they are exercising their power to make the state and employers do what they would otherwise not do.

40 Roy (2018) says that poor people are central to Indian politics in that the poor engage with their elected representatives, political mediators, and dominant classes in varied ways in order to advance their claims and that public policy and political parties, and development plans and elected representatives derive their legitimacy in the name of the poor. This is partly true: if the poor (lower classes) can be a source of legitimacy at one time, they can be a source of its opposite – the crisis of legitimacy – at another time too.

41 Some scholars say that the colonial state was characterized by a dominance without hegemony while the postcolonial state is characterized by a passive revolution (Chatterjee, 1993).

42 This force is evident partly through the presence of imperialist military bases throughout the periphery and through the so-called military collaboration between imperialist and peripheral states including their militaries. No peripheral country is a permanent friend of an imperialist power. Iraq is a recent example.

43 There are many other aspects of the difference between the colonial and the postcolonial state than those discussed here (see Murphy and Jammaulamadaka, 2017).

44 Chacko (2018) says that there is a long-term crisis of the state because successive governments have been unable to establish legitimacy for the post-1990s policies of neoliberalization. Similarly, Levien (2013) argues that while the pre-neoliberal state dispossessed small-scale producers like the neoliberal state does now, the latter has been unable to achieve the ideological legitimacy of its predecessor, leading to more widespread struggles against state-enabled dispossession.

45 A more correct interpretation would be that the autonomy of the state, structurally allowed by capitalism, was effected through the ideological inclination and petty-bourgeois background of the state personnel.

46 Progressive (non-monopoly capitalists) capitalists will develop productive forces and remove pre-capitalist or non-capitalist barriers to capitalist development.

47 This includes access to films, televisions programmes, music, museums, and the like that are not controlled by big business and its politicians.

48 They also cannot rely on those organizations which spend their energies mainly on electoral battles and which are focused almost entirely on immediate interests of the masses or on minimal demands (e.g. a small rise in wages), in abstract from the long-term goals (abolition of wage slavery and seizure of state power).

49 No government that still respects the rules of the capitalist market, whether or not there are capitalist monopolies, can protect wage earners' livelihood and small-scale producers against the loss of their property that is based on family labour. And it is only a socialist government that can create a situation where small-scale producers will voluntarily opt out of family-based production and join large-scale workers-controlled production units because only such a government can *drastically* expand the remuneration of workers by dispossessing the capitalist class and by cutting down on wasteful and unproductive expenditures that are the hallmarks of capitalist society.

Bibliography

Adam, D. (2010). Karl Marx and the state. Retrieved from: https://libcom.org/library/karl-marx-state

Alami, I. (2021). State theory in the age of state capitalism 3.0? *Science & Society*, *85*(2), 162–170.

Alavi, H. (1972). The state in post-colonial societies: Pakistan and Bangladesh. *New Left Review*, *74*, 59–81.

——. (1982). The structure of peripheral capitalism. In H. Alavi and T. Shanin (Eds.), *Introduction to the sociology of "developing societies". Sociology of "developing societies".* London: Palgrave Macmillan.

Albo, G. and Jenson, J. (1989). A contested concept: The relative autonomy of the state. In W. Clement and G. Williams (Eds.), *The new Canadian political economy*. Montreal and Kingston: McGill-Queens University Press.

Allen, P., Konzelmann, S., and Toporowski, J. (Eds.) (2015). *The Return of the State: Restructuring Britain for the Common Good.* New York: Columbia University Press.

Althusser, L. (2001). *Ideology and ideological state apparatuses, in his Lenin and philosophy and other essays* (B. Brewster, Trans.). New York: Monthly Review Press. (Original work published 1971).

Altvater, E. (1978) Some problems of state interventionism. In J. Holloway and S. Picciotto (Eds.), *State and capital: A Marxist debate*. Austin: University of Texas Press.

Amin, S. (2009). *Eurocentrism*. Second edition. New York. MR Press.

AMRC (Asia Monitor Resource Centre). (2012). *Invisible victims of development*. Asia Monitor Resource Centre. Retrieved from: www.amrc.org.hk/content/invisible-victims-development

Anderson, K. (2010). *Marx at the margins: On nationalism, ethnicity and non-western societies.* Chicago: The University of Chicago Press.

Aronowitz, S. and Bratsis, P. (2002). State power, global power. In S. Aronowitz and P. Bratsis (Eds.), *Paradigm lost: State theory reconsidered* (pp. xi–xxvii). Minneapolis: University of Minnesota Press.

Austin, T. (2021). US retail and food service industry complains of lack of workers. *WSWS*. Retrieved from: www.wsws.org/en/articles/2021/05/12/rafi-j01.html

Azeem, M. (2020). The state as a political practice: Pakistan's postcolonial state beyond dictatorship and Islam. *Third World Quarterly*, *41*(10), 1670–1686.

Baird, C. (1998). Right to work before and after 14 (b). *Journal of Labor Research*, *19*(3), 471–493.

Bagchi, A. (1976). De-industrialization in India in the nineteenth century: Some theoretical implications. *The Journal of Development Studies*, *12*(2), 135–164.

Banaji, J. (2011). *Theory as history*. Chicago: Haymarket.

Bardhan, P. (1998). *The political economy of development in India*. Delhi: Oxford University Press.

Barker, C. (2006). Beyond Trotsky: Extending combined and uneven development. In B. Dunn and H. Radice (Eds.), *100 years of permanent revolution: Results and prospects*. London: Pluto.

Barker, C. (2019). Marxism and state theory. *Marxist Left Review, 18*. Retrieved from: https://marxistleftreview.org/articles/marxism-and-state-theory/

Barrow, C. W. (1993). *Critical theories of the state: Marxist, Neo-Marxist, Post-Marxist*. Madison: The University of Wisconsin Press.

———. (2002). The Miliband-Poulantzas debate: An intellectual history. In S. Aronowitz and P. Bratsis (Eds.), *Paradigm lost: State theory reconsidered* (pp. 3–52). Minneapolis: University of Minnesota Press.

———. (2021). Globalization and the emergence of the fortress state. *Science & Society, 85*(2), 170–177.

Bayart, J-F. (1993). *The state in Africa: The politics of the belly*. London: Longman.

Bhattacharya, R. and Seda-Irizarry, I. (2015). Re-centering class in critical theory. *Review of Radical Political Economics, 47*(4), 669–678.

Bidet, J. (2009). *Exploring Marx's capital: Philosophical, economic and political dimensions*. Chicago: Haymarket.

Bidwai, P. (2003). Reality check on IT: Masters or cyber-coolies? *The Daily Star, 4*(42). http://archive.thedailystar.net/2003/07/08/d30708020419.htm

Bin, D. (2014). The class character of macroeconomic policies in Brazil of the real. *Critical Sociology, 40*(3), 431–449.

Bittle, S. (2015). Beyond corporate fundamentalism: A Marxian class analysis of corporate crime law reform. *Critical Sociology, 41*(1), 133–155.

Black, J. (2011). *Slavery: A new global history*. Philadelphia, PA: Running Press.

Bloch, M. (1983). *Marxism and anthropology*. Oxford: Oxford University Press.

Block, F. (1987). State theory in context. In F. Block (Ed.), *Revising state theory: Essays in politics and post-industrialism*. Philadelphia, PA: Temple University Press.

———. (2003). Karl Polanyi and the writing of the great transformation. *Theory and Society, 32*(3), 275–306.

———. (2011). Reinventing social democracy for the 21st century. *Journal of Australian Political Economy, 67*, 5–21.

———. (2019). Problems with the concept of capitalism in the social sciences. *Environment and Planning A: Economy and Space, 55*, 1166–1177.

Boeri T. (2012). Setting the minimum wage. *Labour Economics, 19*(3), 281–290.

Bonefeld, W. (2021). On the state as political form of society. *Science & Society, 85*(2), 177–184.

Brass, T. (2011). *Labour regime change in the twenty-first century: Unfreedom, capitalism and primitive accumulation*. Leiden: Brill.

Bratsis, P. (2002). Unthinking the state reification, ideology, and the state as a social fact. In S. Aronowitz and P. Bratsis (Eds.), *Paradigm lost: State theory reconsidered* (pp. 247–267). Minneapolis: University of Minnesota Press.

Breckenridge, K. and James, D. (2021). Recentering the margins: Theorizing African capitalism after 50 years. *Economy and Society, 50*(1), 1–8.

Brenner. N. (1998). Between fixity and motion: Accumulation, territorial organization and the historical geography of spatial scales. *Environment and Planning D: Social and Space, 16*(4), 459–481.

——. (1999). Beyond state-centrism? Space, territoriality, and geographical scale in globalization studies. *Theory and Society, 28*(1), 39–78.

Brenner, R. (1985a/2005a). Agrarian class structure and economic development in pre-industrial Europe in Brenner debate. In T. Aston and C. Philpin (Eds.), *The Brenner debate* (The first South Asian edition). Delhi: Aakar.

——. (1985b/2005b). The agrarian roots of European capitalism. In T. Aston and C. Philpin (Eds.), *The Brenner debate* (The first South Asian edition). Delhi: Aakar.

——. (2006). *The economics of global turbulence*. London: Verso.

Bridges, A. (1974). Nicos Poulantzas and the Marxist theory of the state. *Politics & Society, 4*(2), 161–190.

Brooks, M. (2005). Productive and unproductive labour. https://www.marxist.ca/article/productive-and-unproductive-labour

Bukharin, N. (1988). Dialectics and revolution. In D. McLellan (Ed.), *Marxism: Essential writings*. Oxford: Oxford University Press.

Burkett, P. and Hart-Landsberg, M. (2003). A critique of "catch-up" theories of development. *Journal of Contemporary Asia, 33*(2), 147–171.

Callinicos, A. (1987). Imperialism, capitalism and the state today. *International Socialism, 2*(35), 79–88.

——. (2009). *Imperialism and global political economy book*. Cambridge: Polity Press.

——. (2017). *The neoliberal order begins to crack*. International Socialism. Retrieved from: http://isj.org.uk/the-neoliberal-order-begins-to-crack/

Canak, W. (1984). The peripheral state debate: State capitalist and bureaucratic- authoritarian regimes in Latin America. *Latin American Research Review, 19*(1), 3–36.

Carchedi, G. and Roberts, M. (2018). *World in crisis*. Chicago: Haymarket.

Carrillo, S. (1977). *Eurocommunism and the state*. London: Lawrence and Wishart.

Carter, A. (1998). Fettering, development and revolution. *The Heythrop Journal, 39*(2), 170–188.

Chacko, P. (2018). India's right turn: Authoritarianism, populism and neoliberalisation. *Journal of Contemporary Asia, 48*(39), 1–25.

Chakravarty, I. (2020). Eight-hour day: States are using the pandemic to deny factory workers a hard-won right. *Scroll.in*. Retrieved from: https://scroll.in/article/961450/eight-hour-day-states-are-using-the-pandemic-to-deny-factory-workers-a-hard-won-right

Chakravorty, S. (2016). Land acquisition in India: The political-economy of changing the law. *Area Development and Policy, 1*(1), 48–62.

Chandra, B. (2009). *History of modern India*. Hyderabad: Orient Blackswan.

Chatterjee, P. (1993). *The nation and its fragments: Colonial and post-colonial histories*. Princeton: Princeton University Press.

Chattopadhyay, D. (2013). *Science and philosophy in ancient India*. Delhi: Aakar.

Chibber, V. (2006). *Locked in place: State-building and late industrialization in India*. Princeton: Princeton University Press.

Choonara, J. (2019). *A reader's guide to Marx's capital*. Chicago: Haymarket.

Chu, Y. (2016). *The Asian developmental state: Re-examinations and new departures*. Singapore: Springer.

Clark, G. and Dear, M. (1984). *State apparatus*. New York: Routledge.

Clarke, S. (1978). Capital, fractions of capital and the state: Neo-Marxists' analysis of the South African state. *Capital and Class, 5*, 33–77.

——. (1983). State, class struggle, and the reproduction of capital. *Kapitalistate, 10*(11), 113–130.

——. (1991). The state debate. In S. Clarke (Ed.), *The state debate*. New York: St. Martin's Press.

Cleaver, H. (2019). *Thirty-three lessons on capital: Reading Marx politically*. London: Pluto Press.

Cockburn, A. (2004). How many democrats voted for Taft-Hartley. *Counterpunch*. Retrieved from: www.counterpunch.org/2004/09/06/how-many-democrats-voted-for-taft-hartley/

Cox, K. (1998). Spaces of dependence, spaces of engagement and the politics of scale, or: Looking for local politics. *Political Geography*, *17*(1), 1–23.

——. (2002). *Political geography: Territory, state, and society*. Oxford: Blackwell.

——. (2018). Scale and territory, and the difference capitalism makes. In A. Paasi, J. Harrison, and M. Jones (Eds.), *Handbook on the geographies of regions and territories* (pp. 57–66). Cheltenham: Edward Elgar Publishing Limited.

Cox, K. and Negi, R. (2010). The state and the question of development in sub-Saharan Africa. *Review of African Political Economy*, *37*(123), 71–85.

Creaven, S. (2000). *Marxism and realism*. London: Routledge.

Dao, M. C., Das, M., Koczan, Z. and Lian, W. (2017). Drivers of declining labor share of income. *IMFBlog*. Retrieved from: https://blogs.imf.org/2017/04/12/drivers-of-declining-labor-share-of-income/

Das, G. (2003). Democracy and capitalism in India: What is unique about India's experience with democracy and capitalism? *The Globalist*. Retrieved from: www.theglobalist.com/democracy-and-capitalism-in-india/

Das, R. J. (1996). State theories: A critical analysis. *Science & Society*, *60*(1), 27–57.

——. (1999). Politicism and idealism in state theory. *Science & Society*, *63*(11), 97–104.

——. (2006). Marxist theories of the state. In S. Pressman (Ed.), *Alternative theories of the state* (pp. 64–90). New York: Palgrave Macmillan.

——. (2012). Forms of subsumption of labour under capital, class struggle and uneven development. *Review of Radical Political Economics*, *44*(2), 178–200.

——. (2013). Capitalism and regime change in the (globalizing) world of labour. *Journal of Contemporary Asia*, *43*(4), 709–723.

——. (2017a). *Marxist class theory for a skeptical world*. Leiden: Brill.

——. (2017b). David Harvey's theory of uneven geographical development: A Marxist critique. *Capital and Class*, *41*(3), 511–536.

——. (2020a). On the urgent need to re-engage classical Marxism. *Critical Sociology*, *46*(7–8), 965–985.

——. (2020b). *Critical reflections on economy and politics in India*. Leiden: Brill.

——. (2022a). On *the Communist Manifesto*: Ideas for the newly-radicalizing public. *World Review of Political Economy*. 13:2 (forthcoming).

——. (2022b). Social oppression, class relation, and capitalist accumulation. In D. Fasenfest (Ed.), *Marx matters*. Leiden: Brill.

Das, R. J. and Chen, A. (2019). Towards a theoretical framework for understanding capitalist violence against child labor. *World Review of Political Economy*, *10*(2), 191–219.

Davidson, N. (2016). *Nation-states: Consciousness and competition*. Chicago: Haymarket Books.

de Janvry, A. (1981). *The agrarian question and reformism in Latin America*. Baltimore: The John Hopkins University Press.

De Paula, P. (2015). Main interpretations of Marx's notion of development: A critical review. *Science & Society*, *79*(4), 582–609.

Deane, M. T. (2020). To 6 reasons new businesses fail. *Investopedia*. Retrieved from: www.investopedia.com/financial-edge/1010/top-6-reasons-new-businesses-fail.aspx

Dimoulis, D. and Milios, J. (2004). Commodity fetishism vs. capital fetishism Marxist interpretations vis-à-vis Marx's analyses in capital. *Historical Materialism*, *12*(3), 3–42.

Djurfeldt, G. and Sircar, S. (2017). Structural transformation and agrarian change in India. London: Taylor. & Francis Group.

Dooley, D., Prause, J. and Ham-Rowbottom, K. (2000). Underemployment and depression: Longitudinal relationships. *Journal of Health and Social Behavior*, *41*(4), 421–436.

Dougherty, C. (2017). How noncompete clauses keep workers locked. *New York Times*. Retrieved from: www.nytimes.com/2017/05/13/business/noncompete-clauses.html?mcubz=2&_r=0

Dowd, D. (2002). *Understanding capitalism: Critical analysis from Karl Marx to Amartya Sen*. London: Pluto.

Draper, H. (1977). *Karl Marx's theory of revolution volume 1: State and bureaucracy*. New York: Monthly Review Press.

Dreze, J. and Sen, A. (1995). *India, economic development and social opportunity*. Delhi: Oxford University Press.

Ducange, J., Keucheyan, R. and Broder, D. (2019). *The end of the democratic state: Nicos Poulantzas, Marxism for the 21st century*. Cham: Palgrave Macmillan.

Dudeja, P., Gupta, R. and Minhas, A. (2017). *Food safety in the 21st century: A public health perspective*. Cambridge, MA: Academic Press.

Duncan, S. and Goodwin, M. (1987). *The local state and uneven development*. New York: St. Martin's Press.

Eagleton, T. (1991). *Ideology*. London. Verso.

——. (2011). *Why Marx was right*. New Haven: Yale University Press.

The Economist. (2020). Global democracy has another bad year. *The Economist*, January 22.

Elliott, L. (2021). Progressive economic policies are back on the agenda – time for Starmer to catch up. *The Guardian*. Retrieved from: www.theguardian.com/commentisfree/2021/may/20/progressive-economic-policies-starmer-catch-up-state-intervention

Ellner, S. (2017). Implications of Marxist state theory and how they play out in Venezuela. *Historical Materialism*, *25*(2), 29–62.

Engels, F. (1884). Origins of the family, private property, and the state. IX. Barbarism and civilization. *Marxists.org*. Retrieved from: www.marxists.org/archive/marx/works/1884/origin-family/ch09.htm

——. (1877). Anti-Duhring. Herr Eugen Duhring's revolution in science. *Marxists.org*. Retrieved from: www.marxists.org/archive/marx/works/1877/anti-duhring/ch24.htm

——. (1886). Ludwig Feuerbach and the end of classical German philosophy. *Marxists.org*. Retrieved from: www.marxists.org/archive/marx/works/1886/ludwig-feuerbach/ch04.htm

Esping-Anderson, G., Friedland, R. and Wright, E. (1976). Modes of class struggle and the capitalist state. *Kapitalistate, 4–5*, 186–220.

Evans, P. (1995). *Embedded autonomy: States and industrial transformation*. Princeton: Princeton University Press.

Foley, D. (1986). *Understanding capital: Marx's economic theory*. Cambridge: Harvard University Press.

Folley, A. (2021). 'Not this time': Sanders blasts lobbyists plans targeting Democrats' spending bill. Retrieved from: https://thehill.com/policy/finance/570276-not-this-time-sanders-blasts-lobbyists-plans-targeting-democrats-spending-bill

Foster-Carter, A. (1978). The modes of production controversy. *New Left Review, 1*(107), 44–74.

Frankel, B. (1982). On the state of the state: Marxist theories of the state after Leninism. In A. Giddens and D. Held (Eds.), *Classes, power, and conflict: Classical and contemporary debates* (pp. 257–273). Berkeley: University of California Press.

Friendly, M. (2019). A bad bargain for us all: Why the market doesn't deliver child care that works for Canadian children and families. In *Child care Canada: Childcare resource and research unit*. Retrieved from: www.childcarecanada.org/sites/default/files/OP31-A-bad-bargain-for-us-all.pdf

Gerstenberger, H. (2009). *Impersonal power: History and theory of the bourgeois state* (D. F Fernbach, Trans.). Chicago: Haymarket Books. (Original work published 2007).

Ghani, A. (2020). India: Farmers rise up against reactionary agriculture bills. *In defense of Marxism*. Retrieved from: www.marxist.com/india-agriculture-bills-2020.htm

Glassman, J. and Samatar, A. I. (1997). Development geography and the third-world state. *Progress in Human*, *21*(2), 164–198.

Godelier, M. (1978). Concept of the 'Asiatic mode of production' and Marxist models of social evolution. In D. Cleary (Ed.), *Relations of production: Marxist approaches to economic anthropology* (pp. 209–254). London: Frank Cass.

Gordon, T. (2007). Towards an anti-racist Marxist state theory: A Canadian case study. *Capital & Class*, *31*(1), 1–29.

Gose, J. (2020). Despite challenges, opportunity zones provide much-needed capital. *The New York Times*. Retrieved from: www.nytimes.com/2020/11/24/business/opportunity-zones-funding-development.html

Government of Canada. (2019). Key small business statistics – January 2019. *Government of Canada*. Retrieved from: www.ic.gc.ca/eic/site/061.nsf/eng/h_03090.html

Government of Canada. (n.d. a). Part IX: Offences against rights of property (continued). *Government of Canada*. Retrieved from: https://laws-lois.justice.gc.ca/eng/acts/C-46/page-74.html?wbdisable=true

Government of India. (n.d. b). The constitution of India. *Government of India*. Retrieved from: www.india.gov.in/sites/upload_files/npi/files/coi_part_full.pdf

Gramsci. A. (1971). *Selections from the prison notebooks*. New York: International Publishers.

Grossman, H. (1929). Law of the accumulation and breakdown: 3. Modifying counter-tendencies introduction. *Marxists.org*. Retrieved from: www.marxists.org/archive/grossman/1929/breakdown/ch03.htm

Gulalp, H. (1987). Capital accumulation, classes and the relative autonomy of the state. *Science & Society*, *51*(3), 287–313.

Gupta, G. and Ulmer, A. (2016). 'We want food!' Looting and riots rock Venezuela daily. *Reuters*. Retrieved from: www.reuters.com/article/us-venezuela-looting-idUSKCN0YY0IR

Habib, I. (1995). *Essays in Indian history: Towards a Marxist perception*. Delhi: Tulika.

——. (2013). *Post-Mauryan India: 200 BC – AD 300. A political and economic history*. Delhi: Tulika Books.

——. (2016). *The Indus civilization: Including other copper age cultures and history of language change till c. 1500 BC*. Delhi: Tulika.

Habib, I. and Thakur, V. K. (2016). *The Vedic age and the coming of iron c. 1500–700BC*. Delhi: Tulika.

Habibi, M. and Juliawan, B. (2018). Creating surplus labour: Neo-liberal transformations and the development of relative surplus population in Indonesia. *Journal of Contemporary Asia*, *48*(4), 649–670.

Hahnel, R. (2002). Amartya Sen: Late twentieth century's greatest political economist? In D. Dowd (Ed.), *Understanding capitalism: Critical analysis from Karl Marx to Amartya Sen*. London: Pluto Press.

Harman, C. (1991). The state and capitalism today. *Marxists.org*. Retrieved from: www.marxists.org/archive/harman/1991/xx/statcap.htm

Harris, N. (2018). The rise and fall of the concept of 'national economic development'. In A. Shawki (Ed.), *Selected essays of Nigel Harris: From national liberation to globalisation* (pp. 212–226). Chicago: Haymarket Books.

Harriss-White, B. (2018). Awkward classes and India's development. *Review of Political Economy*, *30*(3), 355–376.

Harvey, D. (1985). *Urbanization of capital*. Baltimore: John Hopkins University Press.

——. (2005). *A brief history of neoliberalism*. Oxford: Oxford University Press.

——. (2008a). *Introduction to the Communist Manifesto*. London: Pluto Press.

——. (2008b/1982). *Limits to capital*. Chicago: Chicago University Press.

——. (2009). Notes towards a theory of uneven geographical development. In D. Harvey (Ed.), *Spaces of global capitalism* (pp. 69–116). London: Verso.

——. (2010a). *A companion to Marx's capital*. London: Pluto.

——. (2010b). *The enigma of capital*. London: Profile Books.

——. (2012/1978). *Spaces of capital*. London: Routledge.

——. (2014). *Seventeen contradictions and the end of capitalism*. London: Oxford University Press.

——. (2018). *Marx, capital, and the madness of economic reason*. New York: Oxford University Press.

——. (2019). Anti-capitalist chronicles. *Democracy at Work*. Retrieved from: www.democracyatwork.info/acc_global_unrest

Hay, I. (1999). Marxism and the state. In A. Gamble, D. Marsh, and T. Tant (Eds.), *Marxism and social science* (pp. 152–174). Urbana: University of Illinois Press.

Heinrich, M. (2004). *An introduction to the Three volumes of Karl Marx's capital*. New York: Monthly Review Press.

The Heritage Foundation. (2020). 2020 index of economic freedom. *The Heritage Foundation*. Retrieved from: www.heritage.org/index/pdf/2020/book/index_2020.pdf

Herring, R. (1999). Embedded particularism: India's failed developmental. State. In M. Woo-Cumings (Ed.), *The developmental state* (pp. 306–334). Ithaca: Cornell University Press.

Hirsch, J. (1978). The state apparatus and social reproduction: Elements of a theory of the bourgeois state. In J. Holloway and S. Picciotto (Eds.), *State and capital: A Marxist debate* (pp. 57–107). London: Arnold.

Hirsch, J. and Kannankulam, J. (2011). The spaces of capital: The political form of capitalism and the internationalization of the state. *Antipod*, *43*(1), 12–37.

Hoffman, J. (1995). *Beyond the state*. Cambridge: Polity Press.

Holmes, J. (n.d.). Losing 25,000 to hunger every day. *United Nations*. Retrieved from: www.un.org/en/chronicle/article/losing-25000-hunger-every-day

Holloway, J. (1991). The great bear: Post-Fordism and class struggle. A comment on Bonefeld and Jessop. In W. Bonefeld and J. Holloway (Eds.), *Post-Fordism and social form: A Marxist debate on the post-Fordist state*. London: Palgrave Macmillan.

Holloway, J. and Picciotto, S. (1978). *State and capital: A Marxist debate*. London: Arnold.

Hooghe, M. and Oser, J. (2016). Trade union density and social expenditure: A longitudinal analysis of policy feedback effects in OECD countries, 1980–2010. *Journal of European Public Policy*, *23*(10), 1520–1542.

Human Rights Watch. (1999). Appendix A: Selected articles of the Indian constitution. *Human Rights Watch*. Retrieved from: www.hrw.org/reports/1999/india/India994-15.htm

ILO. (n.d.). Details of indicators for labour exploitation. *International Labour Organization*. Retrieved from: www.ilo.org/wcmsp5/groups/public/ – ed_norm/ – declaration/documents/publication/wcms_105035.pdf

——. (2017). 40 million in modern slavery and 152 million in child labour around the world. *International Labour Organization.* Retrieved from: www.ilo.org/global/about-the-ilo/newsroom/news/WCMS_574717/lang-en/index.htm

——. (2018). New ILO figures show 164 million people are migrant workers. *International Labour Organization.* Retrieved from: www.ilo.org/global/about-the-ilo/newsroom/news/WCMS_652106/lang-en/index.htm

The Indian Express. (2017). *Accidents at workplaces in India 'under reported'; 38 per day in construction sector: Study.* Retrieved from: https://indianexpress.com/article/india/accidents-at-workplaces-in-india-under-reported-38-per-day-in-construction-sector-study-4947079/

Jeffries, S. (2012). Why Marxism is on the rise again. *The Guardian.* Retrieved from: www.theguardian.com/world/2012/jul/04/the-return-of-marxism

Jessop, B. (1982). *The capitalist state: Marxist theories and methods.* Oxford: Martin Robertson.

——. (1990). *State theory: Putting the capitalist state in its place.* Cambridge: Polity.

——. (2002). *The future of the capitalist state.* Cambridge: Polity.

——. (2006). States, state power, and state theory. In J. Bidet and S. Kouvelakis (Eds.), *Critical companion to contemporary Marxism* (pp. 413–429). Leiden: Brill.

——. (2008). *State power: A strategic-relational approach.* Cambridge: Polity.

——. (2012). The state. In B. Fine, A. Saad-Filho, and M. Boffo (Eds.), *The Elgar companion to Marxist economics* (pp. 333–340). Cheltenham: Edward Elgar.

——. (2016). *The state: Past, present, future.* Cambridge: Polity.

John, M. (2020). Capitalism seen doing "more harm than good" in global survey. Retrieved from: https://www.reuters.com/article/us-davos-meeting-trust-idUSKBN1ZJ0CW

Kalpana, K. (2015). Economic entitlements via entrepreneurial conduct? Women and financial inclusion in neoliberal India. *Semantic Scholar.* Retrieved from: https://pdfs.semanticscholar.org/2fbf/a663083baa5978a4aeb55b1623431e06820d.pdf

Kalyvas, A. (2002). The stateless theory: Poulantzas's challenge to postmodernism. In S. Aronowitz and P. Bratsis (Eds.), *Paradigm lost: State theory reconsidered* (pp. 105–142). Minneapolis: University of Minnesota Press.

Kautsky, K. (1892). The class struggle. *Marxists.org.* Retrieved from: www.marxists.org/archive/kautsky/1892/erfurt/ch05.htm

Kaviraj, S. (1988). A critique of the passive revolution. *Economic and Political Weekly, 23*(45/47).

Kim, Y. (1999). Neoliberalism and the decline of the developmental state. *Journal of Contemporary Asia, 29*(4), 441–461.

King, R. (1986). *State in Modern Society: New Directions in Political Sociology.* London: Macmillan

Kishore, J. (2013). The trade unions and Michigan's "right to work" law. *WSWS.* Retrieved from: www.wsws.org/en/articles/2013/03/28/pers-m28.html

Kohli, A. (1987). *The state and poverty in India: The politics of reform.* Cambridge: Cambridge University Press.

Kollontai, A. (1920). Communism and the family. *Marxists.org.* Retrieved from: www.marxists.org/archive/kollonta/1920/communism-family.htm

Koo, H. (1984). World system, class, and state in third-world development – toward an integrative framework of political-economy. *Sociological Perspectives, 27*(1), 33–52.

Kosambi, D. (2001). *The culture and civilization of ancient India in historical outline.* Noida, India: Vikash Publishing.

Kotz, D. M. and McDonough, T. (2010). A reconceptualization of social structure of accumulation theory. In T. McDonough, M. Reich, and D. Kotz (Eds.), *Contemporary capitalism and its crisis* (pp. 72–92). Cambridge: Cambridge University Press.

Krishnan, K. (2017). India: Why are Suzuki automobile workers in jail? *Links: International Journal of Socialist Renewal*. Retrieved from: http://links.org.au/india-why-are-suzuki-automobile-workers-in-jail

Krugman, P. (2017). The unfreezing of American workers. *New York Times*. Retrieved from: www.nytimes.com/2017/05/22/opinion/american-workers-noncompete-agreements.html

Kumar, A. (2019). India has a new code to simplify law on minimum wages – but it doesn't give workers any real benefit. *Scroll.in*. Retrieved from: https://scroll.in/article/939763/india-has-a-new-code-to-simplify-law-on-minimum-wages-but-it-doesnt-give-workers-any-real-benefit

Kumara, K. and Kumar, A. (2020). Indian government's demonetisation causes mass hardship and economic chaos. *WSWS*. Retrieved from: www.wsws.org/en/articles/2016/11/21/inde-n21.html

Larrain, J. (1991). Classical political economists and Marx on colonialism and 'backward' nations. *World Development, 19*(2/3), 225–243.

Lasslett, K. (2015). The state at the heart of capitalism: Marxist theory and Foucault's lectures on governmentality. *Critical Sociology, 41*(4–5), 641–658.

Lebowitz, M. (2009). *Situating the capitalist state, in his following Marx: Method, critique and crisis*. Chicago: Haymarket.

Leftwich, A. (2000). *States of development*. Cambridge: Polity Press.

Lenin, V. (1899). The development of capitalism in Russia. *Marxists.org*. Retrieved from: www.marxists.org/archive/lenin/works/1899/devel/index.htm#Chapter2

——. (1901). What is to be done? Burning questions of our movement. *Marxists.org*. Retrieved from: www.marxists.org/archive/lenin/works/1901/witbd/iii.htm

——. (1908). Marxism and revisionism. *Marxists.org*. Retrieved from: www.marxists.org/archive/lenin/works/1908/apr/03.htm

——. (1916). Imperialism, the highest stage of capitalism. *Marxists.org*. Retrieved from: www.marxists.org/archive/lenin/works/1916/imp-hsc/

——. (1917). The tasks of the proletariat in the present revolution. *Marxists.org*. Retrieved from: www.marxists.org/archive/lenin/works/1917/apr/04.htm

——. (1918). The proletarian revolution and the renegade Kautsky. *Marxists.org*. Retrieved from: www.marxists.org/archive/lenin/works/1918/prrk/equality.htm

——. (1919a). The state: A lecture delivered at the Sverdlov university. *Marxists.org*. Retrieved from: www.marxists.org/archive/lenin/works/1919/jul/11.htm

——. (1919b). A great beginning. *Marxists.org*. Retrieved from: www.marxists.org/archive/lenin/works/1919/jun/19.htm

——. (1921). Fourth anniversary of the October revolution. *Marxists.org*. Retrieved from: www.marxists.org/archive/lenin/works/1921/oct/14.htm

——. (1949). *The state and revolution*. Moscow: Progress.

Levien, M. (2013). Regimes of Dispossession: From Steel Towns to Special Economic Zones. *Development and Change. 44*(2): 381–407

Lewis, N. and Malone, J. (1996). *Introduction to Lenin's imperialism: The highest stage of capitalism*. London: Pluto Press.

Leys, C. (1976). The 'overdeveloped' post-colonial state: A re-evaluation. *Review of African Political Economy, 5*, 39–48.

Lindner, K. (2010). Marx's eurocentrism. Postcolonial studies and Marx scholarship. *Radical Philosophy*, *161*, 27–41.

Lukacs, G. (2005). *Lenin: A study in the unity of his thoughts*. Calcutta: Seagull Books.

Luxemburg, R. (1913). *Accumulation of capital* (Chapter 32). Retrieved from: www.marxists. org/archive/luxemburg/1913/accumulation-capital/ch32.htm

———. (2008/1937). Reform or revolution. In H. Scott (Ed.), *The essential Rosa Luxemburg: Reform or revolution and the mass strike* (pp. 41–104). Chicago: Haymarket Books.

Maher, S. and Khachaturian, R. (2021). Socialist strategy and the capitalist democratic state. *Science & Society*, *85*(3), 191–199.

Mallik, C. (2018). Public – private discord in the land acquisition law: Insights from Rajarhat in India. *Singapore Journal of Tropical Geography*, *39*(3), 401–420.

Mandel, E. (1969). Marxist theory of the state. *Marxists.org*. Retrieved from: www.marxists. org/archive/mandel/1969/xx/state.htm

———. (1978). *Late capitalism*. London: Verso.

———. (2008/1968). *Marxist economic theory* (Vol. 2). London: Merlin Press (2008 edition by Aakar, Delhi)

Maniatis, T. (2014). Does the state benefit labor? A cross-country comparison of the net social wage. *Review of Radical Political Economics*, *46*(1), 15–34.

Mann, M. (2012). *Sources of power* (Vol. 3). Cambridge: Cambridge University Press.

Martin, P. (2019). US study shows: Poverty and social inequality are killers. *WSWS*. Retrieved from: www.wsws.org/en/articles/2019/09/12/pers-s12.html

Marx, K. (1842). Debates on the law on thefts of wood. *Marxists.org*. Retrieved from: www. marxists.org/archive/marx/works/download/Marx_Rheinishe_Zeitung.pdf

———. (1843). Critique of Hegel's philosophy of right. *Marxists.org*. Retrieved from: www. marxists.org/archive/marx/works/1843/critique-hpr/ch03.htm

———. (1844). Critical notes on the article: "The King of Prussia and social reform. By a Prussian". *Marxists.org*. Retrieved from: www.marxists.org/archive/marx/works/1844/08/07.htm

———. (1847). *Moralising criticism and critical morality*. Retrieved from: https://marxists.architexturez.net/archive/marx/works/1847/10/31.htm

———. (1852a). The eighteenth Brumaire of Louis Napoleon. *Marxists.org*. Retrieved from: www.marxists.org/archive/marx/works/download/pdf/18th-Brumaire.pdf

———. (1852b). Free trade and the chartists. *Marxists.org*. Retrieved from: https://marxists.architexturez.net/archive/marx/works/1852/08/25.htm

———. (1857). Gundrisse: Notebook IV/V – The chapter on capital. *Marxists.org*. Retrieved from: www.marxists.org/archive/marx/works/1857/grundrisse/ch09.htm

———. (1863). Theories of surplus value. *Marxists.org*. Retrieved from: www.marxists.org/archive/marx/works/1863/theories-surplus-value/ch20.htm

———. (1865). General relations of profits, wages, and prices. *Marxists.org*. Retrieved from: www.marxists.org/archive/marx/works/1865/value-price-profit/ch03.htm

———. (1871a). The civil war in France. *Marxists.org*. Retrieved from: www.marxists.org/archive/marx/works/download/pdf/civil_war_france.pdf

———. (1871b). Letter to Friedrich Bolte. *Marxists.org*. Retrieved from: www.marxists.org/archive/marx/works/1871/letters/71_11_23.htm

———. (1873). Political indifferentism. *Marxists.org*. Retrieved from: https://www.marxists.org/archive/marx/works/1873/01/indifferentism.htm

———. (1875). Critique of the Gotha programme. *Marxists.org*. Retrieved from: www.marxists.org/archive/marx/works/1875/gotha/ch01.htm

——. (1880). A workers' inquiry. *Marxists.org*. Retrieved from: www.marxists.org/archive/marx/works/1880/04/20.htm

——. (1887). Capital volume 1. *Marxists.org*. Retrieved www.marxists.org/archive/marx/works/download/pdf/Capital-Volume-I.pdf

——. (1894). Capital: A critique of political economy, vol. 3. *Marxists.org*. Retrieved from: www.marxists.org/archive/marx/works/download/pdf/Capital-Volume-III.pdf

——. (1964). *Pre-capitalist economic formations*. London: Lawrence &Wishart.

——. (1973/1857). *Grundrisse*. London: Pelican Books.

——. (1977a/1844). *Economic and philosophical manuscripts*. Moscow: Progress Publishers.

——. (1977b). *Capital* (Vol. 1). New York: Vintage.

——. (1987). *Poverty of philosophy*. Moscow: Progress

Marx, K. and Engels, F. (1845). Absolute criticism's second campaign. *Marxists.org*. Retrieved from: www.marxists.org/archive/marx/works/1845/holy-family/ch06_2.htm

——. (1848). Manifesto of the community party. *Marxists.org*. Retrieved from: www.marxists.org/archive/marx/works/download/pdf/Manifesto.pdf

——. (1850). Address of the central committee to the communist league. *Marxists.org*. Retrieved from: www.marxists.org/archive/marx/works/1847/communist-league/1850-ad1.htm

——. (1871). General rules of the international working men's association. *Marxists.org*. Retrieved from: www.marxists.org/archive/marx/works/1871/10/24.htm

——. (1885). The German ideology. *Marxists.org*. Retrieved from: www.marxists.org/archive/marx/works/download/Marx_The_German_Ideology.pdf

——. (1975). *Selected correspondence*. Moscow: Progress.

Marx, K. and Guesde, J. (1880). The programme of the Parti Ouvrier. *Marxists.org*. Retrieved from: www.marxists.org/archive/marx/works/1880/05/parti-ouvrier.htm

Mayer, T. (1994). *Analytical Marxism* (Vol. 1). Thousand Oaks: Sage.

McCartney, M. and Zaidi, S. (Eds.). (2019). *New perspectives on Pakistan's political economy: State, class and social change*. Cambridge: Cambridge University Press.

McLellan, D. (2007). *Marx and Marxism*. New York: Palgrave Macmillan.

McNally, D. (2019). Thoughts on Marxism and the state. *Historical Materialism*. Retrieved from: www.historicalmaterialism.org/blog/thoughts-marxism-and-state

Meckstroth, T. (2000). Marx and the logic of social theory: The capitalist state. *Science & Society*, *64*(1), 55–86.

Meisenhelder, T. (1995). Marx, Engels, and Africa. *Science & Society*, *59*(2), 197–205.

Miéville, C. (2005). *Between equal rights: A Marxist theory of international law*. Chicago: Haymarket Books.

Migdal, J. (1988). *Strong societies and weak states: State-society relations and state capabilities in the third world*. Princeton: Princeton University Press.

Migrant Workers Centre. (n.d.). *Labour exploitation & trafficking in BC*. Migrant Workers Centre. Retrieved from: https://mwcbc.ca/labour-exploitation-trafficking-in-bc/

Miliband, R. (1969). *The state in capitalist society*. New York: Basic Books.

——. (1977). *Marxism and politics*. Oxford: Oxford University Press.

——. (1983). State power class interests. In R. Miliband (Ed.), *Class power and state power* (pp. 63–78). London: Verso.

Miller, R. W. (1991). Social and political theory: Class, state, revolution. In T. Carver (Ed.), *The Cambridge companion to Marx* (pp. 55–105). Cambridge: Cambridge University Press.

Minns, J. (2001). Of miracles and models: The rise and decline of the developmental state in South Korea. *Third World Quarterly*, *22*(6), 1025–1043.

Mohri, K. (1979). Marx and 'underdevelopment'. *Monthly Review*, *30*(11), 32–42.

Morgan, J. and Olsen, W. (2011). Aspiration problems for the Indian rural poor: Research on self-help groups and micro-finance. *Capital and Class*, *35*(2), 189–212.

Mudimu, G., Zuo, T. and Nalwimba, N. (2020). Inside an enclave: The dynamics of capitalism and rural politics in a post-land reform context. *The Journal of Peasant Studies*. doi:10.1080/03066150.2020.1722106

Mukherjee, D. (2008). Laws for beggars, justice for whom: A critical review of the Bombay prevention of begging act 1959. *The International Journal of Human Rights*, *12*(2), 279–288.

Munck, R. (1979). State and capital in dependent social formations: The Brazilian case. *Capital & Class*, *8*(1), 34–53.

Murphy, J. and Jammaulamadaka, N. (Eds.). (2017). *Governance, resistance and the post-colonial state*. London: Routledge.

Nangia, R. (2021). A closer look at CSR law. *BusinessLine*, February 21. Retrieved from: www.thehindubusinessline.com/business-laws/a-closer-look-at-csr-law/article33-897046.ece

Neufeld, D. (2020). Opportunity zones: Aligning public and private capital. *Visual Capitalists*. Retrieved from: www.visualcapitalist.com/opportunity-zones-aligning-public-and-private-capital/

Newswire. (2019). Canada commits to combating labour exploitation and promoting safer workplaces on 100th ILO anniversary. *Newswire*. Retrieved from: www.newswire.ca/news-releases/canada-commits-to-combating-labour-exploitation-and-promoting-safer-workplaces-on-100th-ilo-anniversary-897325899.html

Niemuth, N. (2017). Majority of young Americans prefer socialism or communism to capitalism. *WSWS*. Retrieved from: www.wsws.org/en/articles/2017/11/07/soci-n07.html

O'Kane, C. (2014). State violence, state control: Marxist state theory and the critique of political economy. *Viewpoint Magazine*. Retrieved from: www.viewpointmag.com/2014/10/29/state-violence-state-control-marxist-state-theory-and-the-critique-of-political-economy/

——. (2020). Capital, the state, and economic policy: Bringing open Marxist critical political economy back into contemporary Heterodox economics. *Review of Radical Political Economics*, *52*(4), 684–692.

——. (2021). Critical theory and the critique of capitalism: An immanent critique of Nancy Fraser's "systematic" "crisis critique" of capitalism as an "institutionalized social order". *Science & Society*, *85*(2), 207–235.

Offe, C. (1984). *Contradictions of the welfare state* (J. Keane, Ed.). Cambridge: MIT Press.

Offe, C. and Ronge, V. (1982). Theses on the theory of the state. In A. Giddens and D. Held (Eds.), *Classes, power, and conflict: Classical and contemporary debates* (pp. 249–256). Berkeley: University of California Press.

Ollman, B. (1976). *Alienation: Marx's conception of man in capitalist society*. Second edition. Cambridge: Cambridge University Press.

——. (1982). Theses on the State, *Monthly Review*, 34(7), pp. 41–46.

——. (2003). *Dance of the dialectic: Steps in Marx's method*. Urbana: University of Illinois Press.

Onis, Z. (1991). The logic of the developmental state. *Comparative Politics*, *24*(1), 109–126.

Ougaard, M. (1982). Some remarks concerning peripheral capitalism and the peripheral state. *Science & Society*, *46*(4), 385–404.

Panitch, L. (2002). The impoverishment of state theory. In S. Aronowitz and P. Bratsis (Eds.), *Paradigm lost: State theory reconsidered* (pp. 89–104). Minneapolis: University of Minnesota Press.

Panitch, L. and Gindin, S. (2015). Marxist theory and strategy: Getting somewhere better. *Historical Materialism*, *23*(2), 3–22.

Pashukanis, E. (1924). The general theory of law and Marxism. *Marxists.org*. Retrieved from: www.marxists.org/archive/pashukanis/1924/law/ch05.htm

Patnaik, P. (2010). The state under neo-liberalism. *Monthly Review Online*. Retrieved from: https://mronline.org/2010/08/10/the-state-under-neo-liberalism/(earlier published in Social Scientist 35, no. 1/2: 4–15).

Patnaik, U. (Ed.). (1990). *Agrarian relations and accumulation: The "mode of production" debate in India*. Bombay: Oxford University Press.

——. (1999). *Long transition*. New Delhi: Tulika.

Patnaik, U. and Patnaik, P. (2016). *A theory of imperialism*. New York: Columbia University Press.

Pedersen, J. (1992) State, bureaucracy and change in India, *The Journal of Development Studies, 28*:4, 616–639

Peet, R. (2007). *Geography of power: Making global economic policy*. London: Zed Books.

Petras, J. (1982). The "peripheral state": Continuity and change in the international division of labour. *Journal of Contemporary Asia, 12*(4), 415–431.

Petras, J. and Veltmeyer, H. (2007). The 'development' state in Latin America: Whose development, whose state? *Journal of Peasant Studies, 34*(4), 371–407.

Pfeffer, J. (2018). How your workplace is killing you. *BBC*. Retrieved from: www.bbc.com/worklife/article/20180502-how-your-workplace-is-killing-you

Piven, F. and Cloward, R. (1974). Reaffirming the regulation of the poor. *Social Service Review, 48*(2), 147–169.

Plender, J. (2008). The return of the state: How government is back at the heart of economic life. *Financial Times*, August 21.

Post, C. (1999). Ernest Mandel and the Marxist theory of bureaucracy. In G. Achcar (Ed.), *The legacy of Ernest Mandel*. London: Verso.

Poulantzas, N. (1968). *Political power and social classes*. London: New Left Books.

——. (1969). The problem of the capitalist state. *New Left Review*, 58, 67–78.

——. (1976). The capitalist state: A reply to Miliband and Laclau. *New Left Review, 95*, 63–83.

——. (1978). *State, power and socialism*. London: New Left Books.

——. (2008). *The Poulantzas reader: Marxism, law and the state* (J. Martin, Ed.). London: Verso.

Purohit, K. (2019). As debt grows, more Indian women farmers taking their lives. *Aljazeera*. Retrieved from: www.aljazeera.com/indepth/features/farm-debt-grows-indian-women-farmers-lives-191023193523782.html

Radice, H. (2008). The developmental state under global neoliberalism. *Third World Quarterly, 29*(6), 1153–1174.

Ramesh, J. (2007). Self-help groups revolution: What next? *Economic and Political Weekly, 42*(36), 3621–3624.

Randall, K. (2018). Fifty-one million US households cannot afford "survival budget". *World Socialist Web Site*. Retrieved from: www.wsws.org/en/articles/2018/05/26/ceos-m26.html

Resnick, S. and Wolff, R. (2006). *New departures in Marxian theory*. London: Routledge.

Richards, A. (1986). *Development and modes of production in Marxian economics*. New York: Routledge.

Rijken, C. (2011). *Combating trafficking in human beings for labour exploitation*. Wolf Legal Publishers. Retrieved from: www.ilo.org/wcmsp5/groups/public/–ed_norm/–declaration/documents/publication/wcms_155937.pdf

Roberts, M. (2010). Overproduction and capitalist crisis. *Michael Roberts Blog*. Retrieved https://thenextrecession.wordpress.com/2010/01/29/overproduction-and-capitalist-crisis/

——. (2016). *The long depression: Marxism and the global crisis of capitalism*. Chicago: Haymarket.

——. (2017). *Labours' share*. Retrieved from: https://thenextrecession.wordpress.com/2017/04/30/labours-share/

——. (2019). The economics of modern imperialism. *Michael Roberts Blog*. Retrieved from: https://thenextrecession.wordpress.com/2019/11/14/hm2-the-economics-of-modern-imperialism/

——. (2021). The rate and the mass of profit. *Michael Roberts Blog*. Retrieved from: https://thenextrecession.wordpress.com/2021/08/25/the-rate-and-the-mass-of-profit/

Roberts, W. (2017). *Marx's Inferno: The political theory of capital*. Princeton: Princeton University Press.

Robinson, W. I. (2004). *A theory of global capitalism: Production, class, and state in a transnational world*. Baltimore: Johns Hopkins University.

——. (2021). *Into the tempest: Essays on the new global capitalism*. Chicago: Haymarket Books.

Robinson, W. I. and Sprague, J. (2018). The transnational capitalist class. In M. Juergensmeyer, M. Steger, S. Sassen, and V. Faesse (Eds.), *The Oxford handbook of global studies* (pp. 309–327). Oxford, UK: Oxford University Press.

Rothstein, B. (1990). Marxism, institutional analysis, and working-class power: The Swedish Case. *Politics and Society, 18*(3), 317–345.

Roy, I. (2018). *Politics of the poor: Negotiating democracy in contemporary India*. Cambridge: Cambridge University Press.

——. (2021). India: From the World's Largest. *The India Forum: A Journal-magazine of contemporary Issues*. Retrieved from: https://www.theindiaforum.in/article/india-world-s-largest-democracy-ethnocracyDemocracy to an Ethnocracy

Roy, T. and Swamy, A. (2016). *Law and the economy in colonial India*. Chicago: University of Chicago Press.

Saad-Filho, A. (2019). *Value and crisis*. Leiden: Brill.

——. (2020). From COVID-19 to the end of neoliberalism. *Critical Sociology, 46*(4–5), 477–485.

Sainath, P. (2013). Over 2,000 fewer farmers every day. *The Hindu*. Retrieved from: www.thehindu.com/opinion/columns/sainath/over-2000-fewer-farmers-every-day/article4674190.ece

Salem, S. (2018). Reading Egypt's postcolonial state through Frantz Fanon: Hegemony, dependency and development. *Interventions: International Journal of Postcolonial Studies, 20*(3), 428–445.

Sartre, J. (1960). *Critique of dialectical reason* (Vol. 1, J. Rée, Ed., A. Sheridan-Smith, Trans.). London: Verso.

Saul, J. (1974). The state in post-colonial societies: Tanzania. *Socialist Register, 11*.

Sayer A. (1985). The difference that space makes. In D. Gregory and J. Urry (Eds.), *Social relations and spatial structures*. London: Palgrave Macmillan.

Schmidt, I. (2017). Capital and the history of class struggle. In I. Schmidt and C. Fanelli (Eds.), *Reading 'capital' today* (pp. 18–35). London: Pluto Press.

Science & Society. (2021). Marxist state theory today: A symposium. *Science & Society, 85*(2), 162–206.

Sen, A. 1999. *Development as freedom*. Delhi: Oxford University Press.

Shaikh, A. (2003). Who pays for the "welfare" in the welfare state? A multicountry study. *Social Research, 70*(2), 531–550.

Shandro, A. (2014). *Lenin and the logic of the hegemony: Political practice and theory in the class struggle*. Chicago: Haymarket Books.

Sharma, S. (2019). India's rural-urban divide: Village worker earns less than half of city peer. *Financial Express*. Retrieved from: www.financialexpress.com/economy/indias-rural -urban-divide-village-worker-earns-less-than-half-of-city-peer/1792245/

Sheppard, L. (2017). The Walmart tax every American taxpayer pays. *Commercial Appeal*. Retrieved from: www.commercialappeal.com/story/opinion/2017/04/08/ walmart-tax-every-american-taxpayer-pays/100188002/

Shodhganga. (n.d.). The Bombay prevention of begging act, 1959. *Shodhganga*. Retrieved from: https://shodhganga.inflibnet.ac.in/bitstream/10603/159933/21/21_bombay%20act.pdf

Shrimali, R. (2021). *Contract farming, capital and State corporatisation of Indian agriculture* Singapore: Springer.

Skidelsky, R. (2021). Rentier capitalism and the role of finance in the macroeconomy. In P. Allen, S. Konzelmann, and J. Toporowski (Eds.), *The return of the state: Restructuring Britain for the common good*. Newcastle: Agenda Publishing Limited.

Skocpol, T. (1979). *States and revolution*. Cambridge: Cambridge University Press.

——. (1985). Bringing the state back in: Strategies of analysis in current research. In P. Evans, D. Rueschemeyer and T. Skocpol *et al.* (Eds.), *Bringing the state back in*. New York: Cambridge University Press.

Slater, D. (1989). *Territory and state power in Latin America: The Peruvian case*. New York: St. Martin's Press.

Smith, J. (2016). *Imperialism in the twenty-first century: Globalization, super-exploitation, and capitalism's final crisis*. New York: Monthly Review Press.

Smith, M. (2018). *Invisible leviathan: Marx's law of value in the twilight of capitalism*. Leiden: Brill.

Smith, M., Butovsky, J. and Watterton, J. (2021). *Twilight capitalism: Karl Marx and decay of the profit system*. Black Point, Nova Scotia: Fernwood Press.

Smith, N. (2006). The geography of uneven development. In B. Dunn and H. Radice (Eds.), *100 years of permanent revolution* (pp. 180–195). London: Pluto Press.

——. (2008). (1992). *Uneven development*. Athens: University of Georgia Press.

Song, H.-Y. (2013). Marxist critiques of the developmental state and the fetishism of national development. *Antipode, 45*(5), 1254–1276.

Sperber, N. (2019). State capitalism and the state–class nexus. *Science & Society, 83*(3), 381–407.

Thapar, R. (2000). *The past and prejudice*. Delhi: National Book Trust.

Therborn, G. (1980). *The ideology of power and the power of ideology*. London: Verso.

Thomas, P. (1982). What does the ruling class do when it rules? In A. Giddens and D. Held (Eds.), *Classes, power, and conflict: Classical and contemporary debates* (pp. 224–248). Berkeley: University of California Press.

——. (2002). Bringing Poulantzas back. In S. Aronowitz and P. Bratsis (Eds.), *Paradigm lost: State theory reconsidered* (pp. 73–85). Minneapolis: University of Minnesota Press.

Thompson, M. (1996). Late industrialisers, late democratisers: Developmental states in the Asia pacific. *Third World Quarterly, 17*(4), 625–647.

Tiwana, B. and Singh, P. (2015). Nation state, marketization of social services and uncertainty of livelihood in India. *World Review of Political Economy, 6*(1), 33–57.

Tjandraningsih, I. (2013). State-sponsored precarious work in Indonesia. *American Behavioral Scientist, 57*(4), 403–419.

Trotsky, L. (1923). The curve of capitalist development. *Marxists.org*. Retrieved from: www. marxists.org/archive/trotsky/1923/04/capdevel.htm

——. (1927). Leon Trotsky – culture and socialism – 1927. *WSWS*. Retrieved from: www. wsws.org/articles/2008/oct2008/cult-o23.shtml

——. (1931a). The permanent revolution. *Marxists.org*. Retrieved from: www.marxists.org/archive/trotsky/1931/tpr/prge.htm

——. (1931b). Results and prospects. IV. Revolution and the proletariat. *Marxists.org*. Retrieved from: www.marxists.org/archive/trotsky/1931/tpr/rp04.htm

——. (1933). The class nature of the Soviet state. *Marxists.org*. Retrieved from: www.marxists.org/archive/trotsky/1933/10/sovstate.htm

——. (1937). Ultralefts in general and incurable ultralefts in particular. *Marxists.org*. Retrieved from: www.marxists.org/archive/trotsky/1937/1937-ultra.htm

——. (1938a). Transitional program (Part 1). *Marxists.org*. Retrieved from: www.marxists.org/archive/trotsky/1938/tp/tp-text.htm

——. (1938b). Their morals and ours. *Marxists.org*. Retrieved from: www.marxists.org/archive/trotsky/1938/morals/morals.htm

——. (1939). Marxism in our time. *Marxists.org*. Retrieved from: www.marxists.org/archive/trotsky/1939/04/marxism.htm

——. (1940). Trade unions in the epoch of imperialist decay. *Marxists.org*. Retrieved from: www.marxists.org/archive/trotsky/1940/xx/tu.htm

——. (1973). *Problems of everyday life*. New York: Pathfinder.

——. (1977). *Writings of Leon Trotsky [1935–36]* (N. Allen and G. Breitman, Eds.). New York: Pathfinder. (Original work published 1935–1936).

——. (1979). *Writings of Leon Trotsky supplement 1934–40*. New York: Pathfinder.

——. (1991). (1937). *The revolution betrayed: What is the soviet union and where is it going?* Detroit: Labor Publications, Inc.

——. (1996). (1928). *The third international after Lenin*. New York: Pathfinder.

——. (2008). *The history of the Russian revolution*. Chicago: Haymarket.

United Nations. (n.d.). Ending poverty. *United Nations*. Retrieved from: www.un.org/en/sections/issues-depth/poverty/

Valencia, A. (2014). Latin America: Dependency and super-exploitation. *Critical Sociology*, *40*(4), 539–549.

Veltmeyer, H. and Petras, J. (2015). Imperialism and capitalism: Rethinking an intimate relationship. *International Critical Thought*, *5*(2), 164–182.

Vogel, L. (2014). *Marxism and the oppression of women: Toward a unitary theory*. Leiden: Brill.

Watkins, S. (2021). Paradigm shifts. *New Left Review*, *128*. Retrieved from: https://newleftreview.org/issues/ii128/articles/susan-watkins-paradigm-shifts

Weeks, J. (1997). The law of value and the analysis of underdevelopment. *Historical Materialism*, *1*, 91–112.

Wetherly, P. (2002). Making sense of the 'relative autonomy' of the state. In M. Cowling and J. Martin (Eds.), *Marx's Eighteenth Brumaire; (Post)modern Interpretations* (pp. 195–208). London: Pluto Press.

——. (2005). *Marxism and the state: An analytical approach*. New York: Palgrave Macmillan.

White, J. (2017). What the Maruti Suzuki workers were fighting for. *World Socialist Web Site*. Retrieved from: www.wsws.org/en/articles/2017/04/12/mswu-a12.html

White, L. (2017). Accountants turn into white-collar crime stoppers. *Australian Financial Review*. Retrieved from: www.afr.com/companies/professional-services/what-to-do-about-fraud-20171124-gzrxup

Whitehouse, D. (2005). Classics of Marxism: Leon Trotsky: Results and prospects. *International Socialist Review*, *39*. Retrieved from: https://isreview.org/issues/39/results_prospects.shtml

Williams, R. (1976). *Culture and materialism*. London: Verso.

——. (1980). Advertising: The magic system. In R. Williams (Ed.), *Problems in materialism and culture* (pp. 170–195). London: Verso.

The Wire. (2018). BJP's Ram Madhav, state governor hail toppling of Lenin statue in Tripura. *The Wire*. Retrieved from: https://thewire.in/politics/tripura-bjp-lenin-cpm-rajnath-singh

Wolff, R. and Resnick, S. (2012). *Contending economic theories: Neoclassical, Keynesian, and Marxian*. Cambridge, MA: The MIT Press.

Wolpe, H. (1980). *The articulation of modes of production*. Boston: Routledge.

Wong, J. (2004). The adaptive developmental state in East Asia. *Journal of East Asian Studies*, *4*, 345–362.

Woo-Cumings, M. (Ed.). (1999). *The developmental state*. Ithaca: N.Y. Cornell University Press.

Wood, E. (1996). *Democracy against capitalism*. Cambridge: Cambridge University Press.

——. (1997). Labor, the state, and class struggle. *Monthly Review*, 49(3), 1–14.

——. (2005). *Empire of capital*. London: Verso.

——. (2012). *The Ellen Meiksins wood reader* (L. Patriquin, Ed.). Leiden and Boston: Brill.

World Bank. (n.d.). Expense (% of GDP) – European Union. *World Bank*. Retrieved from: https://data.worldbank.org/indicator/GC.XPN.TOTL.GD.ZS?locations=EU

World Economic Forum. (2020). Productivity vs wages: How wages in America have stagnated. *World Economic Forum*. Retrieved from: www.weforum.org/agenda/2020/11/productivity-workforce-america-united-states-wages-stagnate

Wright, E. (1978). *Class, crisis and the state*. London: New Left Books.

——. (1985). *Classes*. London: Verso.

——. (1989). *The debate on classes*. London: Verso.

——. (1993). Class analysis, history and emancipation. *New Left Review*, 1(202).

——. (2005). Foundations of a neo-Marxist class analysis. In E. O. Wright (Ed.), *Approaches to class analysis* (pp. 4–30). Cambridge: Cambridge University Press.

Zaifer, A. (2018). Variegated privatisation: Class, capital accumulation and state in Turkey's privatisation process in the 1980s and 1990s. *Critical Sociology*, *46*(1), 141–156.

Ziemann, W. and Lanzendorfer, M. (1977). The state in peripheral societies. *Socialist Register*, *14*, 141–177.

Index

Note: Terms such as class, capitalism, capital, capitalist/s, bourgeois/bourgeoisie, labour/labourers, workers, Marx, Marxism and Marxists, do not appear as *independent* entries because of their regular occurrence throughout the book. The term 'state' also does not appear as an *independent* entry, but almost all the keywords below are related to the state.

abolition of class relations 4, 12, 17, 45, 48, 69, 82–85, 94, 119, 125, 135–136, 164, 225–229, 291–293, 299
aboriginal *see* indigenous communities
abstract analysis *see* abstraction, theory
abstraction 39, 44, 52, 56, 188
academia 23, 44, 50, 148, 180, 192, 221, 274
accumulation *see* capitalist accumulation
accumulation by class differentiation 263; *see also* class differentiation
accumulation by dispossession of small-scale producers 263, 268; *see also* primitive accumulation
accumulation by exploitation 155, 263; *see also* exploitation; subsumption
accumulation strategies 27, 95, 176–177, 186, 271, 274
administration (of affairs of the state) 68, 85, 116, 178, 250, 273, 289
administrative districts *see* geographical form of the state
administrative machinery *see* state institutions
administrators *see* state actors
advanced capitalism 1, 4–7, 13, 18, 28, 36, 39–40, 83, 90, 109, 112, 119, 123, 196–197, 203–204, 254–260, 263–267, 270, 273, 281, 288, 291–292, 294, 298
advanced countries *see* advanced capitalism
Africa 115, 255, 295, 297
African American 255; *see also* racism
agency 3, 18, 22, 28, 30, 37, 44, 173–175
agency of state actors *see* state actors
agribusiness 121, 152, 177, 288
agriculture *see* farming

Alavi, H. 27, 32–33, 273, 294, 297
Albo, G. 254
alienating or alienation 59, 65, 129–130, 252, 287
Althusser, L. 23, 61, 86, 217, 225
Altvater, E. 26
America or American *see* United States
Amin, S. 74, 257–259
Analytical Marxism 28, 35, 134
anarchism 33, 164, 237; *see also* Bakunin
ancient society 49, 60, 63–64, 76–77
Anderson, K. 262, 294
antagonism 9, 13, 39, 42, 61, 64, 69, 72, 86, 92, 98, 182, 213, 217, 229, 232
Anti-begging Act 130, 137
anti-capitalism 11, 94, 117, 155, 168, 176, 273, 293; *see also* revolution
anti-feudalism 263, 290–291
anti-imperialism 269, 275, 278, 283, 287, 290; *see also* imperialism
anti-Marxism 44
anti-oppression 83, 277; *see also* oppression
anti-theft laws 132
anti-value 153; *see also* value
apparatuses *see* state apparatuses
aristocracy 76, 78; *see also* landowners
army or arms 7, 9, 53, 74, 77, 113, 151, 169, 175–178, 221, 232, 241, 252, 261, 284
Aronowitz, S. 2, 19, 55, 177
Arrighi, G. 31
Asia 74, 271, 287
austerity *see* neoliberal(ism)
Australia 104, 203
autonomy fetishism or 'autonomism' 5, 38, 41

autonomy of the state *see* relative autonomy
average rate of profit 153, 157–158, 160, 211, 213, 215, 222

Bagchi, A. 262
bailout package 2, 141, 159, 208
Bakunin, M. 164
balance of power 3, 32, 44, 51, 129, 208, 217, 244, 259, 261, 279, 284, 296, 298; *see also* equilibrium; parallelogram of forces
Banaji, J. 86, 294
Bangladesh 290
banks 26, 28, 32, 48, 55, 98, 103, 121, 127, 129, 135–136, 159, 246, 255, 294, 296; state-owned 121, 127, 135, 192, 269
Barbara-Harriss, W. 297
Bardhan, P. 28, 274
bargaining power of workers 114, 145–146, 186, 206, 210–211, 213, 223–224, 262
Barker, C. 50, 243
Barrow, C. 3, 19, 52, 170, 179–180, 191–192, 231, 250–151, 254
Bayart, J. 294
Bentham, J. 17, 100–101, 111, 125
Biden, J. 205, 249, 255
Bidet, J. 6
Bidwai, P. 257
Bin, D. 270
Bismarck 86, 122
BJP, the 93, 192, 288
Blinken, A. 255
Bloch, M. 85
Block, F. 28, 31, 55, 134
Bonapartism 29, 86–87, 282; *see also* autonomy
Bonefeld, W. 113, 251
border or boundary 25, 31, 48, 51, 53, 71, 86, 89–90, 120–121, 161, 185, 241, 243, 245, 254–255
bourgeois discourse/scholarship 115, 237, 239; *see also* ideology
Brass, T. 111
Bratsis 2, 19, 44, 54–55, 177
Brazil 130, 270, 272, 277–278, 283, 288
breakdown tendency 159, 265; *see also* economic crisis; Grossman, H.
Breckenridge, K. 294
Brenner, N. 241
Brenner, R. 25, 53, 75–76
Bretton Woods institutions 207, 289; *see also* IMF; imperialism; World Bank
bribe 121, 184, 208, 219, 273
Bridges, A. 98

Britain 19, 54, 104, 112, 122, 169, 178, 189, 199, 203, 231, 233, 235
British colonial state 104, 178
built environment 26, 101, 141–142, 144, 146; *see also* space
Bukharin, N. 175
bureaucracy or bureaucrats *see* state bureaucracy
bureaucratism 84–85, 240, 247–248, 250–251, 285; *see also* state bureaucracy
Burkett, P. 39, 296
business confidence 28, 192–193, 245
Business Council 179; *see also* organizations of capital
Business Roundtable 179; *see also* organizations of capital
business schools 143, 168; *see also* academia; organizations of capital; universities

Callinicos, A. 26, 30, 32, 41, 103, 263
Canada 112, 137–138, 169, 197, 203, 240, 254
Canadian criminal code 137
capital/capitalist accumulation 8, 15, 17–18, 25–27, 30–32, 40, 51, 54, 88–90, 94–95, 117, 122, 135, 140, 143, 151–156, 160–161, 173, 177, 184–187, 195, 203, 211, 215, 224–225, 239–248, 251, 264, 266–268, 288, 291, 296
capital circuit 17, 128, 140–153, 160–162, 181, 274
capitalist class agency 3, 22–23, 175–181; *see also* organizations of capital; state institutions
capitalist crisis *see* economic crisis
capitalist decay 264, 265, 268, 273; *see also* imperialism
capitalist development 33, 39, 151, 156, 161, 185, 187, 191, 215, 243, 261, 275, 288–291; *see also* development
capitalist exploitation 25, 27, 41, 81, 83, 86, 134, 146–149, 165, 167, 185, 221–222, 243, 273
capitalist form of private property 6, 13–17, 53, 88, 92–97, 125–128, 130–136, 139–140, 147, 160, 164, 173, 191, 199, 221–223, 229; guardian of the 96, 191; two sources of the 135–136
capitalist fractions 43, 92–93, 151, 178, 183, 186, 196, 204–205, 207, 213, 217, 273; hegemonic 5, 17, 23, 27, 34, 133, 140, 153–154, 176, 182–183, 186; *see also* capitalist fractions
capitalist ideology *see* ideology

capitalist production 15, 17, 20, 24, 26, 51–52, 81, 88, 90, 103–105, 117, 127, 130–131, 133, 139–166, 148, 168–172, 199, 201–202, 209, 213, 235–236, 258–259, 267, 284–285, 288

capitalist relations *see* capitalist structure

capitalists' interests 3, 11, 18, 20, 25, 27, 30, 34, 38, 42, 50, 95–96, 131–133, 140, 151, 154–155, 173, 176–179, 183–187, 190–195, 200–207, 210–213, 216–217, 220–222, 241, 245, 273, 275, 278

capitalist structure 14–18, 23–28, 42, 57, 91–92, 96–97, 134, 137, 213, 222, 261–264, 290–293

capital mobility *see* mobility of capital

Capital volume 1 1, 3, 6, 17, 19, 22, 51–52, 57, 59, 88, 95, 99, 109, 117, 135, 139–140, 158, 171, 195, 210, 229

Capital volume 3 17, 63, 74, 95, 158, 171

Carchedi, G. 156; *see also* crisis

Carter, A. 33, 41; *see also* anarchism

caste 68, 73, 77, 116, 197, 211, 255, 262, 268, 274, 280, 283, 290; *see also* ethnicity; identity; racism

Catholicism 60; *see also* religion

Central Asians 255

centralization of capital 144, 153–154, 160, 165, 248, 254, 267, 269; *see also* concentration of capital

Chamber of Commerce 72, 179, 183, 192, 197–198, 236; *see also* organizations of capital

Chartist movement 232; *see also* struggle; trade union

Chatterjee, P. 286, 287, 298

Chibber, V. 294

child/children 64, 98, 109, 111, 115, 123, 145, 155, 158, 165, 169, 171–172, 196–197, 203–207, 210–211, 214, 230–237, 273, 276, 294

child care 104, 122, 196, 218

child labour *see* child

Children Employment Commission 232

China 2, 60, 75, 112–113, 267

Choonara, J. 170

CIA 255; *see also* coercion; military

cities *see* city-regions; geography; scale; urban

citizens 23, 57, 64, 66, 116, 123, 131, 151–152, 241, 246–247, 282, 284, 292, 295; *see also* sovereignty

city-regions 128, 244–246, 263, 271, 276, 290, 298; *see also* rural; urban

civil servants *see* bureaucracy

civil society 9, 46, 63, 80, 92, 247, 255

Clarke, S. 40, 43–44, 217, 219–220, 241

class alliance 257, 267, 271

class antagonism 41, 44, 61, 66, 81, 92, 97, 284–285; *see also* antagonism

class basis of the peripheral state 267–276; *see also* peripheral state

class consciousness 44, 56, 179, 189, 209, 221, 227

class differentiation 17, 102, 126–128, 133, 135–136, 139, 263, 293

class exploitation 61, 64–67, 75, 81, 94, 191, 294

class fractions 9–10, 34, 73, 167, 187, 217

class relations or class society 4–5, 10, 13–16, 19–21, 28–29, 32–33, 40–44, 54, 57–92, 97, 131, 146, 162–164, 190–191, 217, 239–241, 244, 250–252, 256–259, 263, 272, 277, 281, 290–291

class rule *see* class relations

class-state *see* state in class-societies

class struggle 3–4, 6–7, 11–12, 19, 43–45, 51–52, 58, 65, 67, 69, 75, 94–96, 109, 112, 154, 178–179, 188, 198–202, 208–209, 213, 216–221, 245, 248–249, 259–260, 276–278, 281, 285, 291–292

class theory 5, 16, 20, 57, 85, 97

class unity 37, 200

Cleaver, H. 6–7, 127, 295

C-M-C, or C-M-C'-R-C *see* labour circuit

coercion 8, 12, 16, 26, 33, 38, 50, 55, 58, 65, 67, 74, 78, 81, 87, 90–91, 94, 96, 101–102, 113, 116, 120–121, 129–133, 147, 153, 156, 184, 222, 242, 251, 257, 262, 268, 275, 281–285, 295, 298

coercive powers *see* coercion

collective consumption 246, 274

Colletti, L. 20

colonial-era Land Acquisition Act 296

colonial(ism) 116, 129, 137, 144, 230–231, 246, 260, 262, 266, 281–282, 284–288, 291, 298; *see also* imperialism

colonized or colonies 27–28, 33, 104, 153, 262, 288; *see also* colonial

combined development 84, 119, 240, 246, 260–263; *see also* law of uneven development; Trotsky, L.

commerce *see* trade

commodification 7, 26–27, 34, 104, 108, 145, 161, 197–198, 271, 276

commodity 6–7, 16–18, 26, 99–120, 122, 125, 127–128, 130–131, 133, 139–147, 150–152, 154, 160, 163–164, 181, 210, 213, 218, 239, 267, 288 commodity circulation 13, 16–18, 24–26, 34, 40, 51, 60, 80, 83, 88, 94–95, 99–111, 114–118, 121, 125–128, 133–135, 139–142, 145–147, 150, 160, 167, 172, 195, 199, 210, 237, 239, 266, 269, 278, 295; guardian of 40, 100–101, 104, 114, 119, 119 (*see also* imperialism); simple (C-M-C′) 109

commodity exchange or commodity relations *see* commodity circulation

commodity fetishism 8, 60, 110–111, 116, 123; geographical form of 111

commodity labour power *see* labour power

commodity owners or commodity producers 10, 35, 100–105, 108–109, 113–116, 127, 131, 135, 142, 145–146, 153, 163, 259; *see also* small-scale producers

commodity production 7, 17, 102–103, 116, 127, 135, 145–146, 165, 259

common people *see* masses; small-scale producers

commons or common property 69, 73, 131, 143–145, 200, 235, 252, 268, 277

communication 119, 142, 200, 226, 241; *see also* geography; space

communism or communist *see* socialism

competition (in capitalist economy) 8, 13, 16, 25, 27, 33, 39, 75, 95–97, 112, 118–119, 130, 134, 151–155, 158–159, 164, 176–179, 183, 200–203, 233, 242–245, 251, 255, 258, 260, 262, 265, 278, 280, 295

comprador bourgeoisie 274, 295

concentration of capital 65, 144, 149, 153–155, 160, 164–165, 242, 245, 248, 254, 269; *see also* centralization of capital; monopoly

concessions (granted by the state) 4–6, 11, 25, 29, 43, 51–52, 94, 145, 163, 178, 182, 198–200, 203–204, 211–230, 233, 236, 251, 277–287, 293, 297; limited character of 28, 51, 111, 118, 167, 203–204, 207, 224, 228, 234, 237, 254, 278, 285–286

concrete 4,15–16, 50, 65, 79, 89–91, 100,116, 120, 175, 179–181, 185, 188, 215, 240, 252, 254

concrete forms of more general processes *see* abstraction; concrete; theory

conjuncture 2, 24–25, 28, 32, 34, 42, 56, 79, 139, 156, 158, 185, 254; *see also* concrete

conquest of state power 8, 12, 20, 97, 226, 228, 293; *see also* revolution

consciousness 44, 47, 87, 174, 179, 217, 228

consent 38, 58, 94, 101, 129, 137, 198, 217, 221, 224, 241, 298

constant capital 123, 143, 155–160, 165

constituencies, electoral 251, 255

constitution 61, 85, 116, 123, 169, 220, 229–230, 249, 269–270, 290

consumption or consumer 65, 68–69, 83–84, 113, 121, 182, 186, 208, 237, 256–258, 263, 268, 280, 283, 293, 295, 297

Corn Laws 232

corporate social responsibility 181, 192

corruption 270, 273, 277; *see also* bribe

cost of reproduction of labour power *see* reproduction of labour power; value of labour power

courts 9, 51, 67–68, 70, 145, 173, 205, 220, 229, 231, 284; *see also* judiciary; law

Covid-19 pandemic *see* health; illness; pandemic

Cox, K. 176, 202, 245–246, 254, 294

Creaven, S. 41, 53, 72, 86, 96, 181–182, 193

credit *see* loans

crime or criminalization 80, 104, 129, 137, 182, 237

crisis *see* economic crisis; legitimacy, crisis of

culture 60, 65, 71, 83, 152, 216, 226, 244, 252, 261, 292; *see also* academia; media; racism; religion

Davidson, N. 98, 123, 168, 171, 189, 193, 243, 264

debt *see* loans

deception or lies 267, 284–285

de-colonization 289

de-commodification 116, 161, 197–198

defence contracts *see* military

deindustrialization 262, 273

Deleuze, G. 19

democracy, or democratic state form 3–5, 19, 31, 35, 40, 45, 48, 50, 66, 78–79, 93–94, 97, 179, 208, 237, 248, 251, 253, 267, 277, 280–286, 290–293, 298

Democratic party of the US 45

democratic rights 4–5, 14, 79, 217, 226–227, 278, 284, 287, 292–293

de-monetization 103

despotic control of capital over labour 146, 149, 155–156, 205, 216, 247

development 9–10, 28, 33, 39, 48–49, 53, 61–63, 68, 79, 82–84, 88, 93, 95, 98, 117–119, 142–143, 162, 180, 185, 225, 229–230, 240, 242, 244, 256, 258–261, 263, 267–268, 270, 274–275, 281, 286–287, 291, 293, 296–297

developmentalist state *see* developmental
role of the state
development of productive forces *see*
development, capitalist development
dialectics or dialectical approach 8–14, 50,
72, 80, 146, 174, 220, 239, 246, 259, 284
diaspora *see* emigration, immigration
Dimoulis, D. 123
direct producers 14, 16, 61, 63, 65–66, 69,
72, 74, 79, 81, 83, 126–131, 133, 135,
160, 282–283
dirigisme 267, 269, 288–289, 293, 298; *see
also* neoliberal
disarticulated development 257–258; *see
also* global periphery
disciplining of labour 90, 129, 138, 238,
267, 270–271
discourse 6, 148, 274–275, 284, 287
dispossession 8, 17, 39, 90, 94, 129, 135,
145, 160, 262–263, 268, 282, 288, 291,
293, 297–299
division of labour 58–59, 80, 100, 120, 182,
252; *see also* combined development; law
of uneven development
Domhoff, G. 191–192
Draper, H. 182
Dreze, J. 280

Eagleton, T. 72–73, 96, 98
East Asia 39–40, 270, 296
East India Company 122; *see also* colonial;
imperialism
eco-capitalism 152
ecological 11, 55, 83, 152, 237, 277,
288, 293
ecological crisis 14, 201
economic crisis 2–3, 13, 17, 19, 60, 79, 83,
96, 140, 150, 156–160, 167, 171–172,
186–188, 195, 201, 208, 210–215, 224,
269, 273, 286, 296
economic determination of the state in
class societies 58–61; *see also* state in class
societies
economic development *see* development
economic exploitation *see* exploitation
economic power 15, 49, 71, 90, 97, 140,
179, 183, 242; political power *vs* 97; *see
also* state power
education 11, 50, 53, 106–110, 130, 133,
145, 149, 152, 169, 197, 204, 207, 214,
216–217, 227–230, 232–235, 237,
247–248, 250, 252, 270, 281; *see also*
culture; schools
education clauses 206, 235
Egypt 75, 298

Eighteenth Brumaire 19
election 36, 85, 181, 184, 281, 284–286,
297; secretive funding for 181, 192; *see
also* democracy; vote
Ellner, S. 2, 45–46
embedded particularism *see* state autonomy
emergence of class society 64
emigration 123, 235, 274, 295
eminent domain 144, 295–296; *see also*
land; property
employment 53–54, 90, 95, 145, 168,
193, 196–197, 207, 222, 228, 230, 236,
251–253, 276–281
Engels, F. 1, 4, 6, 22, 58–61, 64–66,
69–70, 79–80, 83, 85–86, 92–94, 97,
119, 130–131, 164, 169, 174–175, 226,
240–241, 249
England 75, 104, 113, 123, 169–170,
199–200, 231–236, 254
England's Factory Act 204, 206, 229–231,
233, 236
environment 26, 73, 101, 106, 108,
141–142, 144, 146, 152, 176, 201–202,
237, 241, 255; *see also* ecological; water
environmental change 34, 71, 83, 86, 88,
105–106, 152, 201, 207, 216, 237,
269, 277
equal exchange 24, 109, 114, 116, 127,
146, 150, 153, 201, 210
equality 17, 100–102, 108–109, 111, 125,
128–129, 133, 163, 203, 250, 281
equilibrium 30, 34, 44, 52, 79; *see also*
parallelogram of forces
Esping-Anderson, G. 34
ethnicity or ethnic 149, 246, 262, 278,
280, 287, 290
ethnic supremacism 285; *see also* racism
Euro-centricism 14
euro-communism *see* communism; socialism
Europe 75, 112, 168, 193
European Economic Community 254
Evans, P. 294
exchange value 16, 91, 99–101, 105,
110–111, 116–117, 190, 269
exploitation 6–8, 12, 24–25,
63, 66, 69–74, 81, 83, 86–87,
92–93, 123, 127–129, 134–136,
146–149, 151, 154–160,
164–165, 169, 171–172,
200–205, 210–211, 215, 219, 248,
250, 263–264, 272–273, 276, 287,
291–294; primary vs secondary 135
exploited classes 13–14, 58, 62–63, 66, 69,
71, 80–81, 86, 276–277, 280–281, 286,
292; *see also* masses

exports 120, 153, 159, 243, 258, 262, 267, 270, 272, 279–280, 288, 296

export subsidies from the state 152–153

expropriation of small-scale producers *see* primitive accumulation

extra-economic 7, 10, 32, 50, 59, 96, 101, 104, 107, 116, 128, 130–132, 149, 151, 153, 184, 201, 262, 282

factories 62, 136, 141, 147, 172, 177, 179, 191, 204, 228, 230–237, 273

Factory Acts 154–155, 170–172, 196, 199, 201, 228, 230–232, 234–236; *see also* state policies

factory inspectors 7, 132, 178, 205, 233–234, 236; *see also* state policies

falling profitability *see* economic crisis

family 1, 59, 64, 71, 77, 122, 125, 158, 165, 169, 196, 200, 213–214, 222, 271

family labour 127, 299

farmers 90, 114–115, 121, 136–137, 152, 197–198, 202, 222, 235, 291, 299; *see also* small-scale producers

farming 76–77, 107, 136, 141, 177–179, 198, 231–233, 244, 256, 262, 271–272, 277, 281, 292, 295, 298

farm laws 121, 272; *see also* state policies

fascist/fascistic 20, 60, 78, 96, 187, 236, 253, 255, 278, 284, 287–288, 293

fetishism *see* commodity fetishism

fettering of productive forces 79, 242, 271–272

feudal/feudalism 41, 49, 53, 62, 66, 71, 73–74, 77–78, 82, 93, 96, 111, 122, 193, 217, 239, 263, 278–279, 291

finance or financial capital 32–33, 55, 95, 135, 137, 141, 144, 153, 171, 204, 207, 266–267, 270, 273, 277, 280, 289, 292, 294, 295, 297; *see also* insurance industry; loans

financial institutions 55, 90, 98, 295

floating population *see* reserve army of labour

Foley, D. 171

Folley, A. 180

food 64–65, 76, 105, 109, 113–115, 117, 122, 125, 130, 132, 195–198, 208, 230, 237, 271–272, 277, 279, 292, 288; subsidized 90, 123, 152, 159, 196–197, 218

food riots 130

foreign capital 28, 30, 141, 145, 177, 258, 270, 275, 282–283, 287, 296; *see also* global; international

forests 64, 83, 141; *see also* ecological; environment

Foucault, M. 19

fractions of capital 40, 193, 296

France 1–2,19, 23, 75–76, 86, 92, 170, 199, 231–232, 252–253

freedom and equality 100–102, 111, 128, 133, 163

freedom of capitalists 133, 134

free labour 107–108, 111–112, 149

free press 280

Gates, B. 257

GDP 122, 168, 183, 204, 233

gender 61, 64, 73, 110, 117, 149, 187, 208–209, 244, 255, 262, 268, 283, 295

general formula for capital *see* capital circuit

geo-economics 168

geographical form of the state 13, 18, 64, 75, 96, 104, 111, 197, 239–241, 243, 251; *see also* scale

geography or geographical 48–49, 64, 101, 104, 106, 111–112, 118, 120, 123, 151–152, 174, 200, 215, 240–246, 252, 261, 293; *see also* global; rural; scale; urban

geo-politics 29, 33, 41, 73, 260, 270

German ideology 22, 59, 70, 122

Germany 25, 64, 86, 122, 203, 232–233

gerrymandering 251

Gerstenberger, H. 55, 246

Gindin, S. 32, 47–48, 179, 188, 193

Glassman, J. 294

global or global character of capitalism 2–3, 5, 18, 33, 40, 90, 103–106, 110, 112, 118–121, 133, 137, 161, 177, 240–244, 251, 254, 256, 258, 262–264, 266–268, 282, 287, 293–296

global periphery 1, 5, 7, 18–19, 27, 39, 79, 85–86, 96, 99, 112, 119–120, 151, 155, 181, 183, 204, 243, 248, 256–283, 286–288, 290–298; absence of auto-centric accumulation in 257–259; *see also* peripheral state

Global South *see* global periphery

global state, impossibility of 243

global working class 251

God 68; *see also* religion

Godelier, M. 294

Goldman Sachs 159

Google 168

Google's censorship tools 255

Gordon, T. 116–117

government 11, 19, 25, 30, 35, 46, 53–54, 85, 121, 123–124, 133, 137–138, 143, 159, 161, 168, 170, 180–181, 192, 194, 198, 202, 207, 221–222, 227, 230–234,

236–237, 241, 253–254, 265, 270, 273, 282, 284, 289, 295–296, 298–299; *see also* state institutions
Gramsci, A. 12, 34, 45, 58, 162
Greece 45, 50, 75
Green Revolution policy 271, 278–279
Grossman, H. 17, 26, 159, 186, 265–266
ground rent *see* rent
Grundrisse 64, 142, 161
Guattari, F. 19
Guha, R. 298
Gulalp, H. 294, 296

Habib, I. 76–78
Hahnel, R. 237
Harman, C. 25, 30, 41, 89, 122, 168, 177, 184–185, 189
Harris, J. 29, 40–41, 295
Hart-Landsberg, M. 39, 296
Hartley Act 209
Harvey, D. 7, 25, 31, 49–50, 53–54, 89, 117, 142, 168, 178, 186, 193, 241–244, 246, 261, 266
Hay, C. 20, 53
health 19, 26, 28, 88, 107, 114, 123, 150, 155, 165, 169–170, 176, 195, 198, 201–203, 214, 216, 229, 232, 234; *see also* illness
healthcare 7, 11, 35, 105, 108, 110, 113, 115, 122–123, 130, 132, 145, 152, 170 195, 202, 214, 229, 234, 237, 252, 270, 281, 292; *see also* illness
hegemonic fractions *see* capitalist fractions
hegemony 24, 151, 179, 298
Heinrich, M. 25, 46, 131, 137, 213
Heritage Foundation 133
Herring, R. 270
hidden abode (of production) *see* workplace
Hinduism, or Hindus 60, 115, 235
Hirsch, J. 24–26, 157, 243
history or historical change 5, 9–10, 15, 19, 48, 52, 60–61, 64, 66–67, 73, 79, 81, 89, 103, 109, 112, 156, 174, 193, 198–199, 227, 229, 239, 241, 244, 249, 253, 256, 287
Hoffman, J. 85
Holloway, J. 20, 25, 43
home market 272, 298
human needs 105, 108, 110, 227
Human Rights Watch 123

identity 40, 94, 145, 179, 192, 217, 228, 255, 268, 285–287
ideology or ideological 11–12, 21–23, 32, 34, 36, 44, 50–54, 60, 70, 74, 82, 89,

94, 129, 155, 171,182, 189, 216, 224, 242–243, 249, 254, 269, 273–275, 280, 283–290, 296–299
illness 134, 150, 169–170, 201–202, 214, 237, 254, 256, 277
illusions/illusory 8, 35, 131, 163–164, 173, 211, 220, 284–285, 293
ILO 111–112, 123–124, 169, 230
IMF (International Monetary Fund) 47, 90, 177, 254, 270, 287, 296
immigration or immigrants 29, 41, 145, 210, 212; state control over 29
imperialism 5, 8, 13, 20, 26, 28, 39–40, 86, 95–96, 101, 104, 119, 135, 177, 224–228, 238, 241, 243, 256–299, 283; new 262, 287, 295
imperialist capital 86, 264, 266–272, 276, 281
imperialist state *see* state of imperialist countries
imperialized countries/states *see* global periphery; imperialism
income 2, 34–35, 47, 55, 65, 68, 77, 82–83, 113–115, 123, 150, 168, 171, 186, 189, 191, 197, 204, 236, 249, 271, 280, 291, 293
income inequality *see* inequality
independent producers *see* small-scale producers
India 60, 76–78, 103, 121–124, 136–137, 168–170, 172, 179, 192, 230, 233, 254–255, 257, 271–272, 277–278, 287, 290, 298; colonial 137, 144, 230–231; the Congress party of 93; constitution of 123, 169, 230; government of 121, 137, 230, 233; the Hindu-fascistic organization of 60, 236, 255; Penal Code of 137, 230; Vedic age of 77–78
Indian Institute of Management 168; *see also* Business schools; organizations of capital
Indian Parliament 60
Indian Supreme Court 229
India's Companies Act 192
indigenous communities 183, 255, 260, 268, 284, 292
Indonesia 272, 296
industrialization 53, 41, 62, 92–93, 112, 130, 143–145, 151–156, 165, 168, 171–172, 176–179, 182–183, 188, 191–194, 202, 230, 232, 244, 257–258, 260, 269, 271, 274, 284, 294, 296–297
Indus valley state 76
inequality 11, 14, 35, 68–69, 83–84, 88, 102, 116, 128, 134, 163–164, 170, 248, 263, 281–283, 289

inflation 110, 196, 220, 234, 266, 296
injustice 147, 163–164, 179, 232
in-migration 112
institutions *see* state institutions
insurance industry 159, 171, 177
intellectuals 60, 192, 274, 289, 292–293; *see also* academia; culture
interest rate policy 113, 187, 211; *see also* inflation; unemployment
internal relation 14–15, 58, 88–98, 134, 145, 160, 174, 222; *see also* dialectical approach
international or foreign 28–29, 90, 120, 123, 159, 183, 208, 243, 246, 256, 262, 264, 267, 274, 295; *see also* global character of capitalism
investment 27–28, 35, 53, 89–90, 116, 123, 142–144, 148, 152–156, 159–160, 168, 170–171, 176–177, 180, 183, 187, 215, 246, 265, 267, 269, 296
investment strike 51, 89–90
Iraq 298
isolated country 84–85, 119, 121; *see also* law of value; socialism in one country
Israeli intelligence 255
Italy 122

Janvry, A. 258, 271, 294
Japan 82, 190, 193–194, 250
Jessop, B. 19, 25, 27, 32, 36–38, 40, 42–43, 54, 56, 186
Jewish question 70
judiciary or judicial 53, 60–61, 101, 129, 279, 285; *see also* state institutions
jurisdiction 26, 71, 95, 106, 118, 167, 185, 197, 241, 245–246, 251, 254; *see also* territory
justice 55, 164, 169, 173, 233

Kalecki, M. 236
Kautsky, K. 36, 50
Kaviraj, S. 274
Keynesianism 31, 35; *see also* social democracy, reformism
knowledge 136, 146, 151, 174, 179–180
Kohli, A. 274
Kollontai, A. 213–214
Kotz, D. 19
Krugman, P. 123

laboring body 105, 113–114, 124, 149, 165, 201–202, 216, 256, 282, 288; *see also* health
labour circuit 18, 99, 107, 109, 128, 195–197; *see also* capital circuit

labour freedom 107, 111–112, 196, 232; *see also* labour unfreedom
labour laws 124, 215, 235, 272, 296
labour market 91, 108–111, 116, 130, 137, 146, 196, 201, 209, 236, 244
labour market policies *see* labour laws
labour merchants or labour contractors *see* labour market; unfree labour
labour struggle *see* labour strike
labour power 16–17, 26, 99–128, 130–133, 136, 143–150, 158–160, 163, 169, 195–196, 201–202, 213, 216, 223, 229, 231, 245–246, 271–272, 276, 278; *see also* value of labour power
labour process 7, 16–17, 91, 139, 146–147, 149, 155–156, 206
labour productivity 118, 149, 151, 167, 256, 259, 261, 272
labour strike 114–115, 146, 158, 173, 199–200, 209, 210, 212, 217–220, 222, 226, 231, 245–246, 276, 283–84, 297
labour value *see* value
laissez-faire 31, 162; *see also* neoliberalism
land 74–75, 77, 125, 128–132, 135–136, 141–142, 253, 263, 265, 270–281, 288, 292–295, 297–298
land acquisition *see* primitive accumulation
land bank *see* primitive accumulation
landless 130, 136, 298; *see also* propertyless
landlords or landowners 13, 28, 33, 41, 53–54, 57, 70, 74, 76, 97, 127, 132, 164, 169, 173, 183–184, 187, 191, 197–198, 202–203, 216, 231–232, 235, 248, 258, 267, 271–272, 275, 278–281, 283–285, 287, 292–293, 296–298
land reforms policy 197, 253, 271–272, 278–280, 292–293, 297; *see also* state policies
land revenue 77
landscape 52, 152, 241, 245; *see also* built environment
Lasslett, K. 2, 54
latent state of wage-labour 7, 35; *see also* Lebowitz, M.
Latin America 50, 271, 283, 296
law of capitalist production 201
law of commodity exchange *see* commodity circulation/exchange
law of commodity fetishism 110
law of competition 259
law of eminent domain 295
law of capitalist exploitation 146
law of motion of capitalism 25, 229, 139
law of supply and demand 210, 218
law of supply and demand of labour 210

law of uneven development 120, 151–152, 104, 118, 197, 244, 246, 261

law of value 8, 40, 106, 118–121, 132, 135, 185, 188, 242, 258–260, 266–267

laws of the state 7, 35–36, 59, 66, 103–104, 108, 110, 113–114, 121, 123, 130–133, 137, 139, 145, 146, 150, 156, 158–159, 163–165, 168, 170, 172, 178, 185, 187, 196, 199, 201, 204–207, 223, 229–233, 236, 242, 246, 249, 254–255, 272, 278, 280

LDCs (less developed countries) *see* global periphery

Lebowitz, M. 6, 35, 44, 55

left-Eurocommunist position *see* Eurocommunism

leftist governments 46

Left parties 180, 298

Leftwich, A. 294, 297

legislations *see* laws of the state

legislators or legislature 36, 53, 192, 213, 235, 245; *see also* democracy

legitimacy or legitimation 19, 27, 98, 184–185, 257, 284–291, 298; crisis of 27, 185, 289, 290, 298

Lenin 6, 8–14, 16–17, 20–21, 39, 44–48, 52, 55, 58–59, 62–63, 66–69, 78–79, 83–86, 126–128, 175, 218–219, 226–227, 247–249, 264–266; critique of 21, 83

less developed countries *see* LDCs

level of analysis of class relations *see* class relations

Levien, M. 298

Leys, C. 294

liberal bourgeois democracies *see* democracy

liberalization *see* neoliberalism

liberals 3, 55, 179, 205

Libya 255

limits to/on the state *see* state, limits to/on

livelihood 60, 127, 299

living standards 55, 210, 222, 249, 260

living wage *see* wage

loans 3, 15–16, 19, 63, 88–90, 103, 115, 121, 127, 131, 135, 137, 141, 144, 153, 185, 262, 269–271, 276, 280, 292, 296, 298; payday 115, 131, 141, 197, 278, 292; *see also* finance

loan sharks *see* loans

loan waivers *see* loans

lobbyists 23, 179–180; *see also* Peet

localities *see* local-ness

local-ness (of economy and the state) 2, 26, 46, 49, 74, 61, 142, 200, 233, 236, 240–246, 242–246, 254, 258, 275, 292, 297; *see also* geography

location 113, 129, 167, 174, 176, 208, 264, 283

long hours of work *see* working day

long-term interests of capital *see* capitalists' interests

lower classes 63, 77, 248, 257, 276, 280, 286–287, 289–291, 297–298

low-wage platform 268, 272

low wages 151, 155, 163, 178, 196, 201, 204, 259–260, 262, 273, 277, 284

Lukacs, G. 20, 221, 227

lumpen-proletariat 191

Luxemburg, R. 11, 45, 55, 186, 215–216, 226

machinery or machines 34, 67, 79, 113, 118, 123, 140–141, 143, 148, 154–155, 158, 160, 171, 206, 210, 230–231, 237, 261–262, 268; *see also* productive forces, technological change

Maher, S. 48–49

Mandel, E. 68, 142–143, 179, 185, 248–250

Maniatis, T. 204

Mann, M. 247

Maoist 286

market 4–5, 19, 26–27, 63, 74, 101, 105–111, 117–122, 128–129, 134–138, 141–144, 151–153, 160, 168, 171, 177, 187, 196–197, 202, 211, 220–222, 243, 246, 258, 261–267, 274, 279, 284, 290, 295–97

masses 4–6, 11–15, 18–20, 22–23, 25, 38–39, 51, 59, 63, 67–68, 72, 77, 85–86, 89, 90–97, 103–105, 110–111, 132, 136, 148–149, 173, 177–180, 183–185, 187–189, 198–200, 205, 208, 213, 217, 220–227, 240, 244–245, 247–253, 274, 280–285, 287–288, 292–293

materialist method 5, 25, 174, 105, 239; *see also* theory

Mayer, T. 35

McCartney 297

McDonough 19

McLennan, D. 86

M-C-M′, 17, 140–141, 181, 184–185

McNally, D. 2, 252–253

Meckstroth, T. 22, 30

means of production *see* productive forces

mechanisms 5, 9–11, 13, 22, 28, 34, 38, 51, 53, 68, 71, 92–93, 95–96, 108, 128–129, 144, 158, 173–174, 185, 193,

205, 207, 211, 239, 264, 278–279, 287, 293, 295
medieval or middle ages 60, 82, 191–193
media 23, 180–181, 221, 242, 244, 274
mental degradation *see* illness
merchants or mercantile capital 49, 76, 104, 115, 122, 127, 258–259, 271, 292
Mexico 257, 269
micro-enterprises 131, 137, 197, 297
Mieville, C. 102–103, 121
Migdal, J. 9
migrants 245; *see also* emigration, immigration
Migrant Workers Center 169
Miliband, R. 21, 23, 29–31, 46, 49–50, 52–53, 55, 85–86, 183
Milios, J. 123
military or militarism 26, 28, 31, 33, 41, 67, 71, 77–78, 85, 90, 96, 119, 151, 143, 168, 186, 208, 211, 218, 232, 237, 241–247, 253, 255, 264–265, 267, 283, 294–298
Miller, R. 231
mines or minerals 106, 122, 136, 141, 143, 230, 232, 235, 255, 266, 281, 288; *see also* ecological; environment
minimum support price policy for farmers 121, 197–198; *see also* state policies
minimum wage policy 34, 145, 148, 196, 202–207, 212, 222, 229, 233–234, 245–246; *see also* state
minorities 16, 66–67, 73, 81, 84, 90, 94, 146, 218, 249, 252, 278, 280, 282, 287, 292–293
MNCs 28, 267, 272, 287
mobility of capital 29, 40, 90, 142, 168, 215, 224, 237, 241, 246; *see also* geography
mobility of labour 112, 123, 142, 168; *see also* geography
mode of production 21, 37, 59–60, 62, 71, 73–74, 86, 104–105, 108, 119, 153, 155, 165, 193, 201, 216, 268, 289–290
monarchy 76, 78–79
money 4, 25, 31, 54, 88, 90, 95, 103–104, 107–108, 110–111, 114–117, 121–123, 127–128, 136, 140–141, 143, 153, 160, 163, 171, 181, 184, 186–188, 196, 207–208, 220, 241, 253, 269, 272, 279, 284–285, 297–298
money capital 41, 176, 184, 241
moneylending 26, 103, 127, 135, 137, 143, 171, 218, 259; *see also* finance; loans
monopolies/monopoly 14, 24, 41, 57, 61, 66, 90, 92, 97, 120, 122, 146, 161, 179, 236, 264–266, 292, 299

movement, political *see* struggle
Mughul emperor 77–78
multiple states system 29, 38, 42, 53, 159, 243, 261, 263
municipalities 201, 236, 282
myths 284, 291

NAFTA 295; *see also* trade
nation 5, 26, 35, 68, 72, 92, 95, 104, 109, 113, 118–119, 121, 123, 135, 156, 176, 182, 191, 199, 200–201, 204–205, 208, 215, 240–242, 244–245, 251, 253, 262, 264, 275, 282, 286–288, 290–291
national scale *see* nation; scale
National Association of Manufacturers 192; *see also* organizations of capital
national borders or national boundaries *see* borders or boundaries
national bourgeoisie 28, 33, 142, 282; *see also* MNCs; TNCs; world bourgeoisie
nationalism 242–243, 287; anti-imperialist 287; ethnic 285
nationalist chauvinism 260
nationalization 48, 134–135, 143–144, 153, 172, 269, 274; *see also* socialism
National Labor Relations Board 231
national question, new 287
national character of the state 18, 49, 71, 104–106, 119–122, 161, 197, 242–245, 247, 251, 296
National Stock Exchange in India 170
nation of workers and small-scale producers 287; *see also* nation
NATO 90; *see also* military
natural resources 26, 143, 146, 264, 266, 274; state-owned 144
necessaries 68, 109, 114, 132, 145, 147–148, 197, 248, 253, 288, 294
Nehru, J. 205, 289
neoliberal-capitalist *see* neoliberal
neoliberal or neoliberalism 1–2, 7, 11, 20, 23, 28, 31, 54, 60, 140–141, 144–145, 159–162, 186, 207, 209, 215, 218, 230, 237, 269, 272, 275, 279–280, 285–291, 293, 296–298
neoliberal state *see* neoliberal
New Deal legislation 231
nobility 66, 70, 86; hereditary military 82, 193; *see also* feudal
no compete agreements 112; *see also* unfree labour; United States
non-bourgeois or non-capitalist 10, 17, 38, 75, 135, 139, 268, 299
non-commodities 104, 109, 126, 130, 179
non-correspondence approach 28

Nordic countries 104
North America 104, 168, 228, 298; *see also* Canada; United States

Obama administrations 205, 255
Obama administration's drone assassination program 255
objective conditions 10, 53, 65, 167, 217, 238, 259, 267; *see also* materialist method
obstacles 11–12, 15, 36, 79, 89, 107, 110, 120, 142, 221, 260–261, 268, 284, 291
Offe, C. 25–27, 40, 168, 186, 193, 237
O'Kane, C. 2, 20
Ollman, B. 7, 9, 20, 46, 82, 98, 190, 193–194, 203
opportunity zone fund 152, 170, 197, 246, 170–171; *see also* United States
opposition parties 184, 280; *see also* democracy; election
opposition to alienation/dispossession 129
oppression 4, 14, 55, 67, 69, 79, 81, 217, 228, 244, 250, 277–278, 294; *see also* gender; racism
ordinary people *see* masses
organic composition of capital 154, 187; *see also* value ratios
Organization of Economic Cooperation and Development 254
organizations of capital 28, 96, 179, 188, 191–192, 245, 254, 270, 284
organizations of masses/labour 36, 46, 48, 55, 72, 124, 145, 148, 155, 161, 169, 180, 199, 209, 218, 225, 227, 245, 280, 283, 286, 299; *see also* trade union
organizations of the state, state's organizations 28
Ougaard, M. 28, 257–258, 270, 273, 294, 296
out-migration 112, 154
outsourcing 144, 151, 267–268; *see also* exploitation; MNCs
overaccumulation of capital 157, 171; *see also* economic crisis
over-developed state 27–28, 33, 273–274; *see also* global periphery
overproduction 157, 171–172
overseas 41, 184
overthrow of class relations *see* abolition of class relations
overwork 150–151, 201, 229
owners of private property *see* private property

Pakistan 278, 283, 297
pandemic 2, 83, 86, 117, 170, 172, 182, 187, 198, 201, 230, 236–237, 252, 254

Panitch, L. 21, 32, 46–48, 50, 54–55, 179, 188, 193
parallelogram of forces 34, 174; *see also* balance of power
parents or parental authority 64, 110, 165, 172, 214, 232, 236; *see also* children
parliament 7, 22, 50, 179, 195, 199, 201, 204, 232–236, 248, 255; *see also* state institutions
parliamentarism 68; *see also* ideology
Parliamentary Acts 198
Parliamentary fancy 198
partnership 28–30, 273, 290; public private 144
partnership of state and capital 29–30, 86
part-time wage-earners 276
Pashukanis, E. 102, 121
Patnaik, P. 23, 207, 266, 288–289, 294
Patnaik, U. 266, 280, 294
patriotic billionaires 202
pawnshop 74; *see also* loans; moneylending
PCP (Petty commodity production) *see* small-scale producers
peasants 5, 19, 63, 66, 75–78, 126–127, 136, 173, 206, 249, 253, 260, 262, 269, 271–272, 278–279, 282, 287–288, 295, 297–298; middle 63, 276; poor 63, 136, 272, 276, 292; well-to-do 63, 136; *see also* small-scale producers
peculiar commodity 107; *see also* labour power
Peet, R. 180
pension benefits 159, 213, 276
peripheral state 13, 19, 256–200; *see also* imperialism; over-developed state
periphery or peripheral countries *see* global periphery
personification 55, 114, 163, 211, 217
personification of capital 55
personification of labour-time 163
personnel of the state 23, 32, 46, 53, 70, 74, 175, 207, 288–290; *see also* bureaucracy
Petras, J. 261, 283, 294, 296; *see also* imperialism
petty bourgeoisie 44, 62–63, 221–222, 288, 289, 299
petty commodity production *see* PCP
physical infrastructures 33, 141–142, 153, 241, 293
Picciotto, S. 20, 25, 244
Piven, F. 200
place or place-specificity 186, 215, 240–241, 245; *see also* geography
Polanyi, K. 35, 40, 134

police 7, 9, 68, 90, 94, 129, 137, 162, 208, 217–219, 221, 241, 245, 249, 252, 284
policies *see* state policies
political capital circuit 181
political hegemony 23–24, 50
political parties or politics 3, 15, 18, 20, 22, 27, 40, 45–47, 53, 60, 71, 93–94, 116, 145, 152, 156, 173–179, 181–184, 190–192, 194–195, 205, 220–221, 247–250, 255, 260, 267–270, 273, 277, 280–284, 286, 288, 289, 292, 298–299; bourgeois 94, 179, 181, 188, 190, 221, 227–228, 251, 275, 277, 280, 285; left 21, 36, 46–47, 55, 195, 225, 247, 248, 298
political power 15–16, 19, 24–27, 31–32, 34, 40, 42, 47, 49, 53–54, 70–71, 74–75, 77, 81, 86, 90–97, 113–114, 145–146, 149, 165, 174, 179, 184, 199, 206–211, 213, 220, 223–226, 236, 243, 247, 250, 262, 274–275, 277, 279, 281, 283–284, 287, 292
political reformism *see* reformism
political reforms *see* reforms
political turnover time 177
politicians *see* political parties
politicism 5
population 2, 76, 86, 91, 102, 109, 117, 151, 154, 200, 211, 245, 274, 277–278, 282, 286, 288, 293
Portugal 45
post-capitalist 17, 83, 99; *see also* communism; socialism
post-colonial 33, 130, 161, 278, 283, 286–288, 290–291, 296, 298; *see also* global periphery
post-Marx 11–12
post-Marxist or post-modernist Marxist 12, 28, 30, 36, 41, 82, 134
post-modernism 1–2, 134
post-revolution 58, 120, 190, 293; *see also* revolution; socialism
post-revolution societies 14, 39, 84, 119
Poulantzas, N. 21, 23–25, 34, 38–40, 43–46, 48–50, 52–53, 55, 86, 157, 221–222
poverty 11, 59, 88, 95, 98, 109, 129, 141, 152, 165, 184, 196–197, 211, 223, 236–237, 247–248, 252, 255, 265, 269, 280–281, 283, 287, 294
poverty line 109, 196, 234
power bloc 23–24, 34, 43, 221, 267, 270–271
power elite 192

powerlessness 70, 91, 280
PPP (public private partnership) 144, 151, 296
pre-capitalist societies 1, 5, 14, 40, 58, 62, 73–76, 82, 96, 111, 126, 131, 133, 149, 200, 271, 276
pre-capitalist state 5, 78
precarity 88, 214, 277, 286
pre-neoliberal *see* dirigisme
primacy 6, 40, 42, 52, 64, 80
primacy of class/property relations 40, 42
primitive accumulation 24, 88, 127–132, 135–136, 139–144, 153, 165, 226, 262–263, 266–270, 277–278, 282, 295–296; reverse 131
primitive communistic 63
prisons 9, 58, 67–68, 90, 237, 241; *see also* coercion
private property 14–18, 20, 34, 36, 54–55, 57, 63–64, 75–77, 80–84, 88, 91–96, 100–102, 107, 113–114, 123–138, 141, 144–145, 160–162, 189–190, 193, 210, 262, 267, 272, 275, 297
private property in labour 128; *see also* small-scale producers
private property in labour power 136
private property changed to capitalist private property 135
private sector 142–144, 152–153, 181, 185, 220, 249, 269; *see also* primitive accumulation
privatization 131, 152, 159, 177, 236, 262, 268–269, 271, 277, 280, 284–285, 296
production 3–4, 16–27, 36, 42, 59–71, 74, 86–87, 91–92, 103–110, 125–136, 139–146, 152–166, 190, 195–198, 210, 229, 256–263, 266–268, 272, 288, 292; *see also* capitalist production
production of value and surplus value 4, 13, 62, 136, 140, 156
production process 141–144, 152, 160, 236, 259
production relations 11, 16–17, 27, 83, 103, 163, 210, 276
productive forces 3, 16–17, 24, 50, 57, 61–62, 65–70, 74, 79, 81–87, 90–92, 96–97, 106–109, 113–115, 118–122, 125–134, 139–154, 159–166, 171, 181, 185, 193, 209, 211, 213, 219, 222–227, 232, 237, 256–259, 262–263, 266, 268, 272, 275–281, 291–296; *see also* development; machines; research and development; technological change

productivity 106, 118, 119, 143, 166, 225, 257, 278, 282, 294
productivity bonuses 225
professor *see* academia
profit 36, 94–95, 117–118, 129, 141–145, 150–153, 156–161, 167–169, 171–172, 176, 184, 189, 192, 199, 210–211, 215, 220–222, 241, 261–267, 271–275, 296
profitability 53–54, 117, 156, 171, 192, 202, 241, 251, 265, 273
proletarianization 127, 135, 282, 297
proletarians, or proletariat 16, 45–46, 55, 62, 85, 91, 97, 103, 111, 129, 135, 200, 208, 217, 222, 226–228, 238, 249, 257, 263–264, 276, 282
proletarian state 4, 46, 293–294; *see also* revolution; socialism
propertied classes or property-owners 8, 13, 19, 28, 31, 57, 64–67, 73, 83, 88, 92, 96, 101, 115, 127, 136, 207, 235, 251, 260, 267, 271–273, 275–280, 286, 293, 298
property 5, 8, 14–18, 20, 34, 36, 40, 58, 62–74, 77, 81–92, 95–97, 100–103, 107–108, 125–139, 142, 146–147, 160–164, 169, 183, 186, 191, 195, 205, 219–222, 253, 262, 269, 277, 281, 284, 294–95
property circuit (P-S-C) 128–129
propertyless 82, 216; *see also* primitive accumulation
property relations *see* property
property rights *see* property
Proudhon style 164
provinces or provincial 77, 186, 215, 236, 242, 244, 246, 251–252, 254, 298; *see also* localness; scale
pro-worker policies *see* state policies
Przeworski, A. 35
public institutions *see* state institutions
public power 16, 58, 67, 75, 102, 249; *see also* political power
public sector 19, 121, 152, 192, 220, 269, 277

quantitative easing 2, 141, 153, 171, 255; *see also* money

race or racism 73, 112, 116–117, 149, 208–209, 228, 244, 249, 262, 264, 268, 285, 287, 292, 295
Radice, H. 244, 294
radio/TV stations *see* media
railways *see* transportation

rational/rationality 53, 111, 214–215, 288
raw materials 133, 141–143, 146, 148, 211, 232, 237, 258–259, 266, 272, 296; *see also* productive forces
research and development 143, 149, 168, 265; *see also* science
redistribution 13, 19, 34, 36, 75, 153, 197, 265; *see also* inequality
reformism 11, 44–50, 97, 178, 184, 193, 199, 226–227, 238, 252, 274
reforms 36, 45, 47, 49–50, 89, 134, 170, 219–222, 224, 227, 238, 271, 292–293
region/s or regional 15, 49, 63, 74–75, 89, 145, 151, 179, 215, 217, 224–225, 229, 244–247, 251, 269–272, 285
regulation *see* state policies
relative autonomy of the state *see* state autonomy
religion 14, 60–61, 73, 76, 115, 129, 191, 217, 221, 260, 268, 285, 290
rent 41, 51–53, 74–78, 127, 131–133, 168–169, 171, 184, 189, 197, 216, 258, 261, 271–276
representatives 183–184, 247, 255, 298; *see also* democracy
repression by the state *see* coercion
reprivatization 144; *see also* primitive accumulation
reproduction 35, 59, 61, 64, 96, 109–110, 112, 117, 140, 169, 196, 200–201, 213–217, 242–245, 277, 294, 296
reproduction based on unpaid labour at home 294
reproduction of labour power 109, 112, 114, 145, 148, 169, 196, 200–202, 209, 256
Republican party 93; *see also* United States
reserve army of labour 26, 145, 154, 158, 159, 169, 186, 197, 206, 210–212, 216, 218, 225, 230, 233, 243, 261–262, 267–269
resistance *see* struggle
Resnick, S. 54, 82, 134, 187
resource-based productive capital 241
resources 13, 16, 25, 28–30, 37, 55, 65, 68–70, 111, 141–144, 183, 200, 241, 255, 262, 264–265, 274, 277–281, 292, 297
revenue 25, 35, 41, 78, 89, 143, 156, 182, 185, 189, 208, 211; *see also* state revenue
revisionism 4, 19
revolutionary Marxism *see* communism; Lenin; Luxemburg, R.; revolution; socialism; transitional demand; Trotsky, L.

Revolution betrayed 83–84
revolution or revolt 1, 8–11, 16, 20,
    39–40, 43–49, 68, 78, 81, 84–87, 97,
    118–119, 134–135, 161–164, 172,
    182, 198, 205, 217–221, 225–228,
    238, 263, 290–293, 298–299; dual
    power as a strategy of 45, 47; practical
    implication of state theory presented,
    for 81–85, 97, 111–121, 134–136, 156,
    165–166, 225–229, 251–253, 291–294,
    297 (*see also* abolition of class relations;
    revolution; socialism); *see also* struggle
Richards, A. 258, 294
rights 12, 17, 20, 34, 39, 75, 100, 102,
    108, 123, 126–127, 132, 139, 146, 150,
    168–169, 236, 241, 246
right to work 168, 209
right-wing 187, 192, 205, 288
roads *see* transportation
Roberts, M. 156, 159, 171, 204, 262
Roberts, W. 30
Robinson, J. 222
Robinson, W. 264, 295
Ronge, V. 20, 40, 168, 237
Rothstein, B. 219
ruling class 36, 38, 66, 68, 70–73, 82,
    112–113, 133, 160, 181–182, 193–194,
    202, 211, 226, 279–280, 287, 290
ruling class ideology *see* ideology
rural areas 63, 76–79, 121, 128, 130, 133,
    136, 142, 151, 188, 226, 244–245, 255,
    260, 267, 269, 271–272, 275–278,
    281, 284, 287, 290, 298; *see also* cities;
    geography; urban
ruralization of capitalist production and
    exchange 142, 244; *see also* urbanization
    of capitalism
Russia 2, 33, 48, 82, 86, 119, 126, 134,
    193–194

Saad-Filho, A. 2, 54
safety 34, 148, 155, 169, 178, 181, 201,
    208, 216, 280; *see also* health; workplace
safety nets *see* concessions
Samatar, A. 294
Sartre, J. 20, 68, 72
Saul, J. 294
Sayer, A. 240
scale division of labour within the state 18,
    28, 75, 122, 170, 240, 245, 251, 254,
    259, 252, 254, 262, 286–288, 298; *see
    also* Cox, K.
scale or scalar 9, 59, 75, 96, 99, 103, 110,
    126, 130, 171, 176, 186, 215, 224,
    239–246, 251–252, 262, 298

scarcity 65, 248, 274
Schmidt, I. 220, 237
scholars 5, 15, 48–49, 58, 89, 183, 285,
    298; *see also* academia; ideology
schools 3, 35, 51, 68, 107, 109, 189, 208,
    214, 221, 228, 235, 237, 252–253, 274;
    see also education
science 2, 4, 52, 67, 106, 116, 118, 143,
    159, 168
seizure of state power *see* revolution
selectivity 32, 37–38, 42, 54
semi-proletarians 63, 127, 135, 206, 236,
    257, 263–264, 276; *see also* small-scale
    producers
Sen, A. 237, 280–281
separation of direct producers from means
    of production *see* primitive accumulation
separation of the economic from the
    political 6, 15, 32, 39, 51, 90, 96, 193,
    218–221
separation of workers from means of
    production 81, 219–220
serfdom or serfs 61–62, 66, 74–78, 126,
    261–262
servants 30, 75–76, 183, 248
services 113, 116, 151–152, 156, 171, 180,
    185, 189, 211, 218, 258, 264, 267, 272
servitude 60, 70–71, 74, 134
Shaikh, A. 233
Shandro, A. 86
shelter 64–65, 105, 108–109, 114, 117,
    130, 208, 218, 233
Sheppard, E. 123
SHGs (self-help groups) 137
short-term interests of capitalists *see*
    capitalists' interests
Skocpol, T. 28–30, 41
slave-owners *see* slavery
slaves or slavery 57, 61–67, 70, 73–79,
    123, 126, 132, 209, 213–214, 228,
    267, 277
small-scale owners/producers 5, 11, 16–17,
    62–63, 76, 93, 102, 110, 114–115, 121,
    125–136, 139, 141–144, 162, 164–165,
    178, 196–198, 200–203, 211, 215–216,
    221–222, 245–247, 249–251, 256–258,
    262, 266–278, 285–288, 292–299; *see
    also* direct producers; masses; primitive
    accumulation
Smith, M. 140, 156
Smith, N. 242, 244, 246, 261
Smith, J. 267
social democracy/democratic 35, 46, 48,
    50, 55, 48, 253
social formation 23, 44, 53, 193, 291

socialism or socialists 3, 8, 11–12, 18, 35–42, 45–49, 51, 55, 74, 82–87, 103, 117–121, 130, 134–135, 140, 165, 205, 225–229, 262–263, 269–270, 283, 287, 290–293, 299; democratic 45, 48; Polanyian 134; *see also* revolution

socialism in one country 17, 99, 118–121; *see also* isolatedness; socialism

socialist/Left fear-mongering 205

socialize means of production 26, 90, 106, 127; *see also* socialism

social relations 9–10, 12, 17, 27, 32, 42, 59, 84, 92, 239–242, 245, 256, 259, 263; *see also* structure

social statistics 129, 207

social wage *see* wage

software *see* technology

South Africa 277

South America 270, 283

South Asia 104, 277

sovereignty 74, 246, 251, 254, 282, 295; *see also* citizenship

Soviet democracy 84

space or spatial 3, 9, 17, 20, 31, 34, 39, 61, 64, 101, 103, 139, 142, 148, 174, 176, 187–188, 200–201, 206, 239, 241–242, 245, 252, 275, 284, 294–295; *see also* time-space

spaces of engagement 295; *see also* Cox, K.

spaces of dependence 245; *see also* Cox, K.

spatial fix *see* space

special economic zones 149, 156, 246, 257

Sri Lanka 278, 290

Stalinism 40

stalwarts of state theory 49

state autonomy 1, 3, 5–6, 11, 13, 19–20, 23–29, 31–36, 39–41, 45–46, 49–50, 52–55, 82, 181–184, 188–189, 219, 242, 247, 250, 270, 273–275, 277, 289

state actors 3, 6, 18–19, 22, 25, 28–41, 53–58, 70–73, 93–96, 162, 171–193, 203–204, 207, 220, 244, 247, 249–250, 273–275, 277, 280, 285, 288–289, 297, 299; agency of 181–185; non-class character of 188–191; *see also* bureaucrats; politicians

state and illusory common interests 163–164

state and tendencies/counter-tendencies to crisis 11, 156–160, 167

state as not the main cause of humanity's problems 164; *see also* anarchism; politicism

state as undemocratic 252, 263, 277, 283–285; *see also* fascist/fascistic

state as a permanent Trades' Union of the capitalists 199

state as a process 75–76

state as representing powerlessness of the masses 70, 91, 280

state in class societies 4, 13–14, 18, 57–87, 131, 172, 210, 239; forms of 73–78

state in the 'two arms' view 14, 70, 58, 69–71, 90, 92, 176, 218, 290; *see also* internal relation

state apparatuses 6, 31, 33, 45, 49, 53–58, 66–68, 71, 80, 89, 102, 130, 178, 182, 193, 209, 216–217, 221, 241, 247, 249, 254, 273–274, 296; *see also* bureaucracy; state institutions

state's basic and non-basic tasks *see* state functions

state bourgeoisie 297

state's branches 58, 120–121, 158, 192, 203, 224, 232, 245, 254, 261, 298; *see also* scale division of labour within the state

state budget *see* state spending

state bureaucracy or bureaucratic state form 3, 18, 22, 27–30, 41, 53–54, 67, 78, 85, 96, 152, 173–175, 178–185, 189–194, 207, 221, 229, 247–254, 269–270, 273–274, 278, 283–285, 289, 292–293, 297; *see also* bureaucratism

state capitalism 18, 129, 140, 159–162, 172, 269, 279, 289; state-ism as different from 162

state coercion *see* coercion

state, compromises by 24–25, 34; *see also* concessions; equilibrium; parallelogram of forces

state, constraints on 4, 15, 23–25, 28, 30, 37–38, 49, 51, 56, 89–90, 105, 117, 174, 215, 224, 237, 251–252, 291, 294; *see also* limits on/to the state

state contracts 151, 270

state derivationism 7, 20, 25

state's developmental role 2, 28, 39–40, 49, 95, 168, 258, 269–270, 286, 291, 294, 298

state elites *see* state actors

state forms 13, 18–19, 79, 96, 117, 206–207, 218, 239–255, 251, 254; bureaucratic (*see* bureaucracy); democratic (*see* democratic); developmental (*see* developmental role of the state)

state functions 4, 13, 18, 23, 27, 29, 32, 34, 40, 46, 54, 58–59, 67, 69, 71–72, 79, 82–85, 101–102, 104, 140, 152, 180, 183, 185–186, 204, 248, 252, 280

state institutions 9, 11, 15–16, 28, 32, 42–43, 45, 47–51, 64–65, 67, 76, 117,

130, 156, 165, 175–179, 185–190, 207, 215, 221, 229, 235, 244–246, 251–255, 264, 266; *see also* apparatuses; bureaucracy

state's institutional separation from economy 27, 51, 185, 193; *see also* Offe, C.; state in the 'two arms' view

state in the instrumentalist conception 13, 22–23, 38–39, 45–46, 53, 55, 173–177, 179, 181, 188, 192, 218

state's internal relation with capitalism 88–98

state laws *see* laws of the state

state, limits on/to 8, 24, 30, 94–95, 112, 117–121, 133, 150, 160, 167, 173, 184–187, 203, 208–211, 214–215, 222–225, 275; *see also* concessions

state machine *see* institution

state managers *see* state actors

state of exception 156

state of imperialist countries 95, 119, 243, 258, 261–267, 273–274, 281, 295, 298; as guarding the guardians 104, 119

state's organizations 12, 18, 28–29, 43, 47, 55, 60, 67–68,70, 103, 170, 188, 192, 237, 240, 241, 248, 254, 273, 284; *see also* apparatus; bureaucracy

state personnel *see* state actors

state policies 2–3, 11, 18, 20, 23, 27, 31, 34–35, 41–42, 54–55, 93, 95, 103, 107–110, 123, 131, 141, 145, 152, 154–156, 162, 165, 168–170, 175–180, 183–184, 186–188, 192–202, 205, 207–215, 218, 222, 231, 233, 245–250, 253–255, 269–275, 279–281, 295–298; pro-business 186, 207, 272, 297; pro-poor or pro-worker 18, 42, 55, 109, 112, 158, 188, 195–238, 253, 262, 278–280, 287, 290

state power 3, 11–13, 16, 22–25, 29–31, 34, 39–43, 49, 55, 70–71, 74, 79–82, 86, 90–94, 97–99, 164, 241–245, 249–252, 275

state property 129, 135, 162, 275; *see also* commons; socialism; state bourgeoisie

state-provided welfare 25, 27, 39, 46, 109, 111, 152, 168, 180, 187, 196, 202, 204–205, 207, 211, 213–214, 218, 220, 229, 233, 237, 251, 288

state regulation 34, 103, 154–156, 165, 168, 178, 197, 201, 208, 231, 248, 269; *see also* policies

state revenue 25, 41, 54, 88, 141, 189, 208, 253, 270; *see also* state spending; tax

state-scales 244; *see also* scale; scale division of labour within the state

state seen in terms of causal mechanisms *see* mechanisms

state-space 167, 241; *see also* geography, scale, scale division of labour within the state

state spending 122, 156, 168, 208, 237, 264, 279

state subsidies for capital 123, 161, 242

state theory, existing 1–9, 11–12, 16, 19, 22–37; reformism of 145–150 (*see also* reformism); style of writing in 52; theoretical problems with 3–6, 38–44, 50–53, 82; *see also* dialectics; theory

strategic selectivity *see* selectivity

strategies 20, 36–37, 42–49, 52, 177, 187, 266, 269, 272, 275, 287, 289, 291, 296

structure 3, 9–10, 14, 15, 22–23, 27, 31, 33, 37–38, 42–44, 46, 52, 57, 65, 69–70, 75, 79, 81, 83–84, 90, 174–175, 183–185, 188, 190, 217, 239, 247–250, 275–276, 284–285; *see also* agency

structure of relations *see* agency; structure

structured coherence 37, 180, 244, 273; *see also* city; Harvey, D.

struggle, or struggle by workers 4, 6, 10–11, 13–16, 18, 25, 36, 40–41, 43–45, 47–49, 51, 55, 65, 67, 69–70, 77, 81, 86, 93, 97, 103–104, 112, 140, 149, 156, 163, 173–174, 178, 180–184, 198–200, 205–208, 214–221, 224–228, 232, 237, 246, 259–263, 276–278, 282–283, 287, 292–293, 297

struggle for concessions *see* struggle

sub-national *see* geography; local; provinces; scale; state-scales

subsistence 57, 60, 81–82, 84, 87, 90, 104, 108–109, 113, 115, 122, 125–127, 129–134, 137–138, 143, 145, 160, 209, 213, 277

subsumption of labour by capital 19, 158, 259–261, 263, 268; formal (FSL) 158, 256, 259, 261, 262, 267, 268, 282, 293; hybrid 259, 263; real (RSL) 244, 256, 259–261, 263, 268, 277, 291

super-exploitation 169, 246, 272; *see also* exploitation

surplus 14, 24, 33, 61–67, 69–70, 73–79, 81, 94, 126, 146, 149, 153, 160, 187, 203, 211

surplus labour 14, 57, 62–65, 71, 73–75, 81, 86, 92, 125–126, 132–134, 140, 148, 150, 157–160

surplus population *see* reserve army
surplus product *see* surplus
surplus transfer 5, 266, 268
surplus value 4, 16, 41, 91–92,
    111–112, 132, 135–136, 139–140,
    143, 146–147, 151–153, 156–160,
    168, 186–193, 201, 210–211, 216,
    223–224, 230, 237, 270–271, 278;
    absolute 158, 256, 259; relative 256,
    259, 261; *see also* surplus
Sweden 203, 233
Switzerland 254
Syria 255
Syriza 50

Taft-Hartley Act 209
Tanzania 290
Tata group of businesses in India 192
tax breaks 123, 128, 152–153, 170, 191,
    197, 208
tax or taxation 3–4, 15–16, 25, 35, 51–54,
    70, 74–78, 88–90, 109, 123, 127–128,
    145, 152–153, 158–161, 170–171, 180,
    183–186, 202–204, 208, 211, 220, 233,
    249, 242, 270–201
technological change 33, 48, 79, 106, 109,
    118–120, 141, 143, 148–151, 154–159,
    167, 168, 176, 206, 210, 241, 256,
    259–262, 277, 279, 282, 296–297; *see
    also* productive forces
technology *see* technological change
temporal fix 206
temporality 9, 31, 49, 54, 114, 176, 240,
    243–244, 251–252
territories or territoriality 26–28, 31–33,
    49, 54, 77, 103–106, 122–123, 215,
    225, 240–247, 251–252, 264
Thapar, R. 77
The Communist Manifesto 20, 22, 55
The state and revolution 1, 8, 10, 16, 20, 39,
    44, 85
theft by capitalism 19, 132, 137
theory 4–5, 7, 8, 13–16, 19–20, 33, 36,
    38–39, 46–52, 84, 212, 224, 227, 294
Therborn, G. 192
Third international 119
Thomas, P. 12, 43, 45, 53
Thompson 294
time-space 101, 174
totality 13–14, 17, 44, 58, 70, 90–92, 97,
    176, 178, 187, 293
town-country dichotomy 64
towns 64, 76, 121–122, 142, 201, 260,
    267, 271, 281

trade 41, 47, 59, 64, 88, 96, 103–104, 123,
    127, 144, 156, 159, 188, 218, 266, 272,
    295; free 104, 112, 122; unequal 265, 267
trade union 12, 35, 47, 54, 72, 123–124,
    159, 168, 178, 199, 202, 208–209,
    215–218, 225–228, 231, 233, 237–238,
    246; revolutionary 227
transition or transitional 10,12, 45, 58, 84,
    129, 190, 258–261, 263, 268, 291
transitional demand 228, 292
transitional state 8, 12, 14, 39, 83, 120,
    227; *see also* socialism
Transnational Capitalist Class 254, 295; *see
    also* MNCs; Robinson, W.
transportation 60, 76, 83, 85, 122,
    141–144, 152, 161, 200, 225, 241–242,
    244, 252–253, 269, 269, 279; *see also*
    geography; space
Treasury 122
trial and error 30, 32, 186; *see also* strategic
    action
tributary stage or régimes 74, 86
tribute 74, 76–77, 109, 122, 266
Trotsky, L. 8, 11, 14, 18, 50, 52, 57,
    62, 67–69, 71, 83–86, 97, 118–120,
    161–162, 194, 222, 224–228, 260–262,
    269, 282–283
TRPF *see* economic crisis
Trump administration 54, 152
Turkish power bloc 278, 296
typology as a method of concept formation
    197–198; *see also* theory
typology of private property 17, 125

unemployment 11, 35, 88, 98, 113–114,
    131, 155–156, 158, 187, 200, 205,
    210–212, 215, 225, 230, 236
unemployment insurance policy 186, 211,
    213, 216, 245
unequal exchange 101, 116, 125, 133,
    144, 266
uneven development *see* law of even
    development
unfreedom in pre-capitalist societies and
    freedom 126
unfree labour 70, 76–77, 96, 102, 108,
    111–112, 123, 126, 128, 132, 149, 159,
    163, 169, 191, 196, 229–230, 262, 267,
    272, 296
union *see* trade union
unitary state *see* scale division of labour
    within the state
United Kingdom *see* Britain
United Nations 255

United States 2, 22, 45, 49, 54, 57, 93, 112, 122–123, 152, 168, 170, 179, 191, 197, 200, 202–206, 209, 228, 233, 236, 240, 245–246, 249, 252, 254–257, 270, 283
unreasoning trust in the state 11–12, 52; *see also* ideology
USSR 40
universities 168, 180, 189, 192, 237, 241, 252–253; *see also* academia; culture; ideology
urban capitalist class 28, 79, 267, 270–272, 275, 284
urbanization of capital 142, 244
urbanization of class relations 64
urban or urbanizing 18–19, 49, 62–64, 71, 76, 130, 133, 142, 170, 200, 215, 226, 228, 242–246, 251, 255–256, 260, 267, 271–273, 276–278, 295, 297–298
urban working class 245, 271
use-values 99–100, 102, 104–105, 107–108, 113–115, 117, 125, 139, 144, 147, 150–151, 218, 239, 246, 266, 274
Usurious Loans Act 137; *see also* loans; moneylending
utilities 55, 100, 176, 292

vaccine 104, 125, 177; *see also* health; healthcare; illness
vagabondage 130, 137
value (or value relations) 7–8, 16–17, 26, 95, 99–109, 116–121, 132–136, 139–143, 145–148, 152, 154, 159–160, 167–171, 183–186, 193, 196, 210, 215, 222–224, 258–260, 264–267, 274; of a commodity (c + v + s) 143
value of labour power 108–109, 112, 116, 143, 145, 149, 158–159, 163, 168, 196, 212, 216, 223; *see also* reproduction of labour power
value ratio: c/v 154, 157–159, 167, 210, 212, 213, 214, 266; c + v 210–214; c + v + s 143; s/v 157
variable capital 143, 154, 156, 159, 212, 253
Veltmeyer, H. 261, 283, 294, 296
Venezuela 137
villages *see* rural
violence 54, 58–59, 65, 67, 74, 78, 93–94, 97, 102–103, 127, 131, 221
Vogel, L. 294
voluntarism 55
vote or voters 184, 235, 251, 255, 284–286, 292; *see also* democracy, election

Wage Act 206
wage 90, 108–116, 123, 129–133, 145, 148–151, 154–159, 168–169, 196, 198–200, 209–216, 220, 227–228, 233–237, 246, 253, 263, 272, 276, 292; living 11, 90, 145, 229, 279, 281, 292; social 109, 196, 203–204, 213, 218, 233, 237, 262; *see also* welfare
Wallerstein, I. 35
Walmart tax 123
wars *see* military
Washington Consensus 296; *see also* neoliberalism
water or water bodies 77, 105, 130, 141–142, 152, 237, 241, 270, 273, 279; *see also* environment
wealth 13, 15, 17, 53–54, 67, 70, 83, 92–95, 99–100, 117, 132, 135, 139, 148, 170, 172, 180, 184, 188, 216, 239, 253, 291
Weber, M. 9, 28, 36
welfare or welfare state *see* state-provided welfare
Western societies 27–28, 137
Williams, R. 20, 105
Wolpe, H. 294
women 64, 70, 106, 109–110, 114, 116, 137, 165, 205–206, 214–217, 231, 233, 249, 252, 255, 276, 282, 294
women's body 124
Wood, E. 19, 28, 75, 86, 96, 265
work 6, 27–29, 52–53, 85–87, 108, 111–115, 122–123, 130–133, 146–151, 154–155, 163, 169–170, 173, 180, 195–197, 203–207, 216–218, 225, 228–237, 250, 261–262, 272–278, 292
Workers' enquiry by Marx 233
working conditions 169, 198, 150, 201, 214, 236, 277; *see also* workplace
working day 113, 132, 137, 150–151, 154–158, 163, 165, 169–170, 172, 196, 199, 201, 205–207, 210, 230, 292; long 129, 137, 150–151, 158, 163, 196, 200–201, 204, 223, 230, 259–260, 262, 277, 284–285
working class 15, 48, 55, 89, 195, 198, 200, 211, 214, 227, 228, 245, 248, 251–252, 271, 277
workplace 17, 62, 74, 139, 145–149, 154–156, 165, 169–170, 196, 203, 205, 232, 236, 280, 282
workplace committees 208
workplace safety (legislation) 148, 169, 200, 208, 229

Workshops' Regulation Act 236
World Bank 23, 168, 177, 254, 270, 287,
   289, 295–296
world bourgeoisie 295; *see also* MNCs; TNCs
World Economic Forum 294
world economy or world market 5, 28,
   49, 93, 96, 106, 110, 112, 118–120,
   167–168, 176, 240, 242, 244, 251, 264,
   261, 264, 266, 291
world geography 103; *see also* geography;
   scale
world-historical existence of individuals
   103, 111; *see also* global; international
world history 103

world labour supply 295
world monopolies 225
World Wars 39, 230
Wright, E. 20, 34–36, 43, 50, 134, 193,
   197–198, 253

Yankee capitalists 122
Yellen, J. 255; *see also* United States
Yemen 255
Yorkshire mine-owner 235

Zapatista movement 277
Ziemann, W. 294
Zimbabwe 265, 295, 297

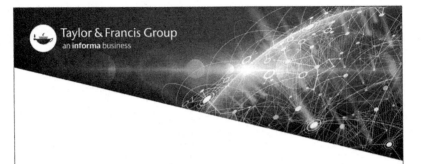

Printed in the United States
by Baker & Taylor Publisher Services